Guidelines for Writers

RHETORIC, READER, HANDBOOK

GUIDELINES FOR WRITERS

RHETORIC, READER, HANDBOOK

Judith Stanford
Rivier College

McGraw-Hill, Inc.
New York ▪ St. Louis ▪ San Francisco ▪ Auckland ▪ Bogotá ▪ Caracas
Lisbon ▪ London ▪ Madrid ▪ Mexico ▪ Milan ▪ Montreal
New Delhi ▪ Paris ▪ San Juan ▪ Singapore ▪ Sydney ▪ Tokyo ▪ Toronto

GUIDELINES FOR WRITERS
Rhetoric, Reader, Handbook

Acknowledgments appear on pages 429-431 and on this page by reference.

1 2 3 4 5 6 7 8 9 0 DOC DOC 9 0 9 8 7 6 5 4 3 2

ISBN 0-07-060778-8

This book was set in Cheltenham Light by
Arcata Graphics/Kingsport.
The editors were Lesley Denton and Scott Amerman;
the text design was done by Keithley Associates, Inc.;
the cover was designed by Wanda Lubelska;
the production supervisor was Janelle S. Travers.
R. R. Donnelley & Sons Company was printer and binder.

Library of Congress Cataloging-in-Publication Data

Stanford, Judith Dupras, (date).
Guidelines for writers: rhetoric, reader, handbook/Judith Stanford.
p. cm.
Includes index.
ISBN 0-07-060778-8
1. English language—Rhetoric. 2. English language—Grammar—Handbooks, manuals, etc. 3. College readers. I. Title.
PE1408.S675 1993
808'.042—dc20 92-37917

ABOUT THE AUTHOR

Judith Stanford teaches literature, writing, and study skills at Rivier College in Nashua, New Hampshire, where she is Coordinator of Advanced Tutorials and Study Skills. She is the co-author, with Rebecca Burnett, of *The Writing Connection;* a contributing author, with Robert DiYanni, Eric Gould, and William Smith, of *The Art of Reading;* and author of *Responding to Literature.* She has consulted extensively and written instructional material for many other writing, literature, and study skills texts.

For Rebecca,
An Extraordinary Teacher
and an Even Better Friend

CONTENTS

PREFACE

During the past ten years, research in composition studies has noted a disturbing discrepancy between the approaches offered to students by many basic English textbooks and the reading and writing they are asked to do in their other courses. This book aims to bridge that gap by introducing thinking patterns students need to lead them clearly and directly into—and through—the complex mazes of reading and writing they will face during their college years and afterward in their professional lives.

Guidelines sees reading and writing as interconnected skills and makes the following assumptions:

All writers compose with greater understanding and sensitivity if they are also confident readers.

All readers understand and enjoy what they read more fully if they learn to become engaged with what they are reading.

Students—especially those who arrive at college not entirely comfortable with their reading and writing skills—need to learn that they have a right to have opinions. In fact, they have not only the right, but also the obligation, to think about what they read and to explain their responses both orally and in writing. Often students arrive in basic English classes convinced that their primary task is to parrot what the "authority" who wrote a text said. To move students from this view of learning, *Guidelines* offers the following possibilities:

Section One: Reading and Writing to Respond works to dispel the passive learner role and to engage students actively in their own education through reading thoughtfully and writing responses to what they read.

Section Two: Reading and Writing to Evaluate shows students how to move from response to establishing and applying criteria that allow them to make informed judgments about what they read and to discuss those judgments in writing.

Section Three: Reading and Writing to Compare moves to a more complex pattern of thinking—reading and writing to identify, evaluate, and write about similarities and differences.

Section Four: Reading and Writing to Argue explains how to read writing that seeks to persuade and how to write persuasively.

Section Five is a thematic anthology. Part I provides selections related to the family; Part II to learning and teaching; Part III to television and the movies; and Part IV to working. These readings have been carefully selected to interest students yet also to challenge them to think beyond easy responses and comfortable observations. Each section provides six selections, which vary in length and difficulty, beginning with less difficult pieces and moving to those that are more complex.

Each selection is introduced with a brief overview, a set of predicting questions, and a list of words students may not know. Following the selections are topics for reading, writing, and discussion, which are carefully planned to emphasize response, evaluation, comparison, and argument.

Finally, to address concerns often voiced by developing writers, *Guidelines* offers a series of Appendixes:

A Revision Guidelines and Proofreading/Editing Guidelines
B Guide to Editing: A handbook that offers an overview of essential principles of grammar and mechanics and provides exercises for practice (answer keys are provided for some of the exercises so that students can use this section for self-teaching)
C Preparing for and Taking Essay Exams
D Guide to Research: A detailed guide through the processes of library research and of writing a researched argument
E Documenting Sources (MLA and APA Formats)

SPECIAL FEATURE—BOXED GUIDELINES *Throughout the text, frequent boxed guidelines sum up the writing and reading skills provided within each chapter and within the appendixes. A summary of these guidelines appears on the inside front cover and affords both instructors and students easy access to them.*

ACKNOWLEDGMENTS

My husband, Don, and my sons, Aaron and David, deserve my greatest thanks for the encouragement, wit, and intelligence they willingly shared while I worked on this project. Special thanks go to Arline Dupras for the research and word processing she provided and especially for being a teacher who has always believed in the abilities of her students and for showing me the way to keep hope alive in the classroom.

Joan O'Brien of the Sylvan Learning Center in Chelmsford, Massachusetts, provides me with an ideal role model of the innovative, caring teacher and offers unflagging and deeply appreciated personal and professional support.

I would also like to thank my colleagues in the Writing/Learning Center and in the English Department at Rivier College for the ideas and approaches they willingly share, particularly their optimism and energy as they work with students. I particularly want to thank Leslie Van Wagner for her useful and creative contributions to the Instructor's Guide that accompanies *Guidelines for Writers.*

I greatly appreciate and applaud the students in my Study Skills for Adults classes at Rivier College who, over the past five years, have given me fine advice on many of the exercises and selections included in this book.

The following reviewers of this text offered wise, helpful suggestions for which I am sincerely thankful: Cathy Bernard, New York Technical College of CUNY; Elizabeth Buckley, East Texas State University; Marian Calabrese, Sacred Heart University; Marlene Clarke, University of California–Davis; Will Davis, University of Texas; Patricia Eney, Goucher College; Jan Gerzema, Indiana University–Northwest; Paula Gibson, Cardinal Stritch College; Diane Gould, Shoreline Community College; Mark Harris, Jackson Community College; Chris Hayes, University of Georgia; Barbara Henning, Long Island University–Brooklyn Campus; Kate Kiefer, Colorado State College; Virginia Kirk, Howard Community College; Marla Knudson, California State University–Los Angeles; Vladen Madsen, Brooklyn College; Audrey Roth, Miami–Dade Community College–South; Christie Rubio, American River College; Ed Sams, Gavilan College; Bill Smith, Virginia Commonwealth University; Charlotte Smith, New York University; J.T. Stewart, Seattle Central Community College; Katherine Williams, New York Institute of Technology; and Gary Zacharias, Palomar College.

At McGraw-Hill, Scott Amerman and Janelle Travers guided the process of production with great skill while Elsa Peterson ably faced the challenging task of obtaining permissions. My editor, Lesley Denton, deserves special thanks for believing in this project from the beginning and for overseeing the detailed, careful development of the book with patience and determination.

Judith Stanford

Guidelines for Writers

RHETORIC, READER, HANDBOOK

SECTION ONE

READING AND WRITING TO RESPOND

This chapter suggests that every day we respond to hundreds of written messages and focuses attention on the following issues related to reading, responding, and writing.

- *Purposes for reading*
- *Patterns readers use for various purposes*
- *Strategies for effective reading*
- *Writing in response to reading*

IF YOU ARE DRIVING INTO A BUSY intersection and read the word "STOP" on a familiar red and white sign, you react by stepping on the brakes. This is a simple example of responding to reading. Every day we are bombarded by written messages—in newspapers, on billboards, on the packages of food we eat, and in hundreds of other places. Because we see so much printed material every day of our lives, most of us have trained ourselves to respond actively to only a tiny fraction of the information and ideas we read. The stop sign relates directly to our safety, so we consciously respond to it. On the other hand, an advertising message on a billboard may be something we read only casually and react to subconsciously, if at all.

DAILY READING Learning to read for college classes, and for the professional world, requires paying attention to the reading you do every day. Watch carefully for your responses to what you read and notice why you choose to read some things carefully, some more casually, and some not at all. Considering your responses to reading will help you to become more aware of how and why you read. This survey can be put to use as you work on developing strategies for reading more effectively and efficiently, in both academic and professional situations.

EXERCISE 1 *Make a list of all the reading you can remember doing for the past several days. Include signs, advertising, newspapers, magazines, printed information given on television, and, of course, any books you read either as class assignments or for pleasure. In addition, make a list of printed matter to which you were exposed but that, for one reason or another, you decided not to read (for example, junk mail, notices posted on bulletin boards, certain sections of your daily newspaper).*

READING FOR A PURPOSE

As you made notes on your reading for the past several days, you almost certainly noticed that you read for different purposes. For instance, if you read the directions for putting together a new appliance, you were reading for practical information. You probably read very carefully so that you would not leave out an important step. If you read an editorial in your local paper, you were probably looking for ideas—for ways of considering a specific issue. You may have read the editorial quickly, just looking for the editor's main points. If your sociology professor assigned a chapter in the textbook, you may have skimmed through it rapidly to get a general impression of the topics covered. Then you may have gone back to find specific details you needed to know for the quiz that was promised. Your reading survey, then, most likely showed you that you read for a variety of purposes and that you read differently for those different purposes.

EXERCISE 2 *Using the notes that you made for Exercise 1, jot down the purpose for which you read each item in your first list. Note also the way purpose may have influenced how you chose to read. For instance, did you read some things more quickly than others? Did you return to read some things more than once?*

Reading Patterns

As you consider your notes on the way you read, you may find the following explanation of reading patterns helpful. While each of these strategies may be used differently by different readers, the explanations that follow the terms suggest the purposes for which many readers use these approaches.

SCANNING: Looking over a large body of written material very quickly to see what might be of interest or significance. This is the way many people approach a newspaper. They read the headlines, looking for something that may attract their attention. Scanning is also a useful technique for getting an overview of a textbook. You use the same process you do with a newspaper. At the beginning of the semester, you read the Table of Contents (which is like reading the headlines in a newspaper) and then you move rapidly through the book, just glancing at major chapter headings (which is like reading the titles of newspaper articles). This process makes you familiar with the book's organization and with its major topics.

SKIMMING: Skimming is similar to scanning, but requires somewhat closer attention. You do this kind of reading when you find a newspaper article that sounds interesting and look through it quickly, maybe reading the first and last paragraphs to see whether you really want to spend time reading the whole article carefully. In reading for classes, skimming helps you gain an overview of a chapter or an article your professor has assigned. Just as you do with the newspaper, you look through it quickly, paying particular attention to the first and last paragraphs and noting any headings in boldfaced type. These strategies give you some idea of the topics you'll be working with when you go back to read the chapter closely.

CASUAL READING: You read casually when you read for pleasure. Your favorite mystery, science-fiction adventure, romance, or popular magazine article provides the chance to relax. Your eyes move rapidly and you rush from one page to the next, intent on discovering what is happening (in fact, critics often describe best-selling novels as "page-turners"). Two or three days later, you probably do not remember much of what you read, but it doesn't matter because you were reading for enjoyment, not to retain specific information. Although casual reading may not seem like a process you would use in school, in fact it can be very valuable. For example, make it a habit to pick up copies of books or magazines. The latest editions of magazines and journals are often placed on an easily accessible rack in the main reference room of the library. Just read them casually (out of curiosity and interest, but without worrying about understanding every word). You'll find them a great source of new ideas that may spark a direction for a paper or project you've been assigned.

INFORMATIONAL READING: When you read an insurance policy for the first time, looking for its main provisions, but not pondering or trying to remember every detail, you are doing informational reading. You are informing yourself, formulating questions for your insurance agent, and noting sections you want to go back and read more carefully. Obviously, this reading strategy translates easily and usefully into the academic or professional context. For example, when you read a chapter in a textbook for the first time, you watch for the author's primary points and note questions about those points.

CLOSE READING: You read closely when specific details become important to you. Before you finally decide whether to purchase that insurance policy, or when you are filling out a job application, or when you are facing your income tax form, you read closely. You are careful and thorough no matter how difficult or tedious you may find the reading because you know that your understanding is essential. When you are reading for classes, some of your assignments require this close attention. If you are studying material that has been specifically assigned for an exam, for example, you read carefully and intensely. You are trying to connect major ideas and to recognize important examples and details that support those main ideas. For most people, close reading is a somewhat slow process. Although your reading speed will increase as you practice the strategies described in this book, you should not worry if you cannot race through difficult material at the same rate you can skim, scan, read casually, or read for information.

REREADING: People go back to a book, an article, or a poem for many different reasons and at many different times. Sometimes, for instance, you reread immediately after finishing an initial reading, perhaps because you didn't understand something or perhaps because you want to verify a fact or statistic. Sometimes you reread several weeks or even months after the first reading because you are studying for an exam or preparing to write a paper. And sometimes you return to a book years after your first reading because you remember it with pleasure and want to enjoy it again. Whenever you reread, you can be assured that you will see things you did not see the first (or second or third) time you read the same material. Sometimes that is because you simply skipped over or didn't pay attention to certain details during your previous reading. But at other times you will discover new things because you have changed since the last time you read that work. For instance, you may have studied other aspects of the subject or you may have had experiences that make you a more perceptive reader. Think, for example, of books children often read—the Dr. Seuss books, for instance. A child enjoys the rhyme, the rhythm, the humor, but when that same child matures and reads Dr. Seuss to a younger brother or sister, she or he often recognizes clever criticisms of certain types of people or certain kinds of actions. The words on the page have not changed, but they take on new meaning because the reader has changed and now brings adult knowledge and adult sensibility to the rereading.

GUIDELINES: READING PATTERNS

Scanning: Looking over a large body of written material very quickly to see what might be of interest or significance.

Skimming: Reading to get an overview. Skimming is similar to scanning, but requires somewhat closer attention.

Casual reading: Reading rapidly for entertainment or to gain nonessential information.

Informational reading: Reading to note essential points and to raise important questions without pondering or trying to remember every detail.

Close reading: Reading carefully, paying attention to specific details as well as to main ideas.

Rereading: Reading material you have already read, perhaps to gain clearer understanding or new insights.

RESPONDING TO READING

Obviously, there are many ways to react to what you read. In the example that opened this chapter, the reader acts physically by stepping on the car brakes in response to reading a stop sign. Often people discuss what they have read with someone else. Or readers may think silently about what they've read. In school and in professional reading, any of these responses may occur. But the response that is most often expected in school and in the professional world—and the response with which many people have the least experience—is the written response.

Exercises 1 and 2 asked you to keep track of your reading and to consider your process. You did this by taking notes; you responded to what you read by writing about it. Developing skill in writing about what you read begins most logically with training yourself to notice how you react as you read. As the opening paragraph of this chapter suggests, modern society bombards us with so many written messages that most of us have—in understandable self-defense—shut off our minds to much of what we see in print. Effective academic reading requires resisting that impulse to shut off the energy of your intelligence whenever you encounter something that at first glance seems difficult, boring, or even incorrect.

A second defense mechanism that keeps people from reacting to academic reading relates to what are perhaps best called "old voices." Nearly all of us have a supply of old voices that we hear over and over again, echoing in our minds. These old voices may belong to a carping relative, an unfairly critical teacher, or perhaps an overbearing friend. The message is couched in different words but the meaning is always the same: "What gives *you* the right to have an opinion?"

Of course, we all have opinions in spite of hearing old voices, but many people have decided that the safest response in school is to sit passively and wait for the teacher to deliver information or to read a book and accept as truth whatever the author ("the authority") has written. Now is the time to work to change that pattern. Learn to value your own response to what you read. Certainly, you may later change your mind about an initial thought or feeling, but for true learning to take place, it's essential to drop the passive learning/reading pattern and, instead, to take charge of your own education by becoming actively involved.

Active Reading—Notetaking

The first step toward active reading is to remember that writing in response to what you read assures that you will become engaged in what the writer is saying. (If you look back at the list of reading approaches, you'll see that informational reading, close reading, and rereading lead most naturally to written responses because these processes require more time and attention than do the others.)

It's easy to read a whole chapter in a book—even to read a chapter and leave it colorfully marked with yellow highlighter—and still not have any clear idea what the author means. However, if you make it a strict rule to read with a pen or pencil always in hand and to use that pen or pencil to write comments in the margin or take notes on a separate sheet of paper, you will be carrying on a "conversation" with the author. You may still, of course, find parts of what you have read puzzling or difficult to understand, but you will not be playing the role of passive receiver. Instead you will be recording your own feelings, thoughts, questions, and ideas, creating a kind of dialogue with the book.

NOTE: PLEASE WRITE IN THE BOOK! If you are like many students, you'll find this request shocking because in most elementary and high schools students are forbidden to write in books. *Please write in the book!* I repeat this advice because books thoughtfully marked up with margin-filling notes are almost always the sign of an engaged, careful reader. Many students have told me they don't want to write in their books because they want to sell them back to the bookstore at the end of the semester. Please know that once you have bought a book, it is considered "used" (unless it is returned, unmarked, within a very few days). Writing in the text does not further diminish its value as a used book. You now own your books, and you can *and should* write in them.

I would be particularly interested to see pages of this text on which you have written comments, questions, or observations. As you read and write in this book during the coming weeks, please consider photocopying a well-marked page or two and sending it to me at McGraw-Hill publishers, College Division (English editor), 1221 Avenue of the Americas, New York, NY 10020, so that I may consider including your "conversation" in the next edition of this text.

Response Notes

When you read for information or read closely—and when you keep your mind fully alert and open—you will find yourself responding to what you read. Remember that your initial response does not have to be (and usually is not) a neatly formulated understanding or evaluation of every point the writer is making. Read the following paragraph, along with the marginal notes, to see how one student, April Byrne, reacted to a paragraph from Kirkpatrick Sale's essay, "The Miracle of Technofix," which first appeared in *Newsweek*. April's philosophy professor had asked students to read something relating to the impact of technology on our society and to use what they read to find an idea for writing.

what about other nations?

Somehow this nation has become caught up in what I call the mire of "technofix." This is the belief, reinforced in us by the highest corporate and political forces, that all our current crises can be solved, or at least significantly eased, by the application of modern high technology. In the words of former

? meaning?

How does "technofix" come into my life?

But technology does help solve problems.

What are these forces?

When did Sale write this? What crises were happening then? Now?

Does Sale agree with this expert? He doesn't seem to. Why?

Atomic Energy Commission chairman Glenn Seaborg: "We must pursue the idea that it is more science, better science, more wisely applied that is going to free us from our predicaments."

check definitions same as "crises"?

Science is not always right!

April's notes suggest several important ways of responding to reading.

1 *She asks questions about words she does not fully understand.*

("Meaning?" April wants to understand the word "mire," which is unfamiliar to her. "Check definition—same as 'crisis'?" Here April knows what the word "predicaments" means but she wants to see how its definition relates to the word "crisis" that Sale used earlier.)

2 *She looks for connections and relationships, similarities and differences.*

("What about other nations?" Sale talks about the overdependence of the United States on technology, and April wonders whether he—or she herself—would say the same about other nations.)

3 *She asks questions about general statements that need clarification.*

("What are these forces?" Sale claims that "the highest corporate and political forces" are responsible for making us believe technology is a cure-all. April very wisely wonders exactly what those forces are.)

4 *She asks questions about the background of the article.*

("When did Sale write this? What crises were happening?" April looked at the date of the article and saw that it was written in 1980. If she wanted to, she could then check to find out what problems were most important in that year.)

5 *She asks questions about the author's use of quotations.*

("Does Sale agree with this expert? He doesn't seem to—Why?" April sees that Sale is using a quotation from an expert, but she also notices that Sale doesn't seem to agree. So she notes the dilemma: The author [one authority] and the Atomic Energy Commission chairman [another authority] disagree.)

6 *She asks questions that make connections between the article and her own experience.*

("How does 'technofix' come into my life?")

7 *She makes statements that may disagree with what the author or a quoted authority says.*

("But technology does help solve problems." "Science is not always right!")

These seven ways of responding represent only a fraction of the possibilities. They are meant to suggest options, not to prescribe limits. Note that of the seven ways April responded to this paragraph, five take the form of questions. When you are considering possibilities as you read, it's often helpful to phrase your observations as questions rather than statements. Questions help keep options open and encourage exploration. Flat statements sometimes seem like endings; questions are more likely to provide beginnings.

GUIDELINES: RESPONSE NOTES

Try the following strategies as you make notes in response to what you read.

1. Ask questions about words you do not fully understand.
2. Look for connections and relationships, similarities and differences.
3. Ask questions about general statements that need clarification.
4. Ask questions about the background of the material you are reading.
5. Ask questions about the author's use of quotations.
6. Ask questions that make connections between the article and your own experience.
7. Make observations that may disagree with what the author or a quoted authority says.

EXERCISE 3 *Keeping in mind some of the ways April responded and remaining open to other ways of responding, write marginal notes for the following paragraph or for a paragraph in any of your textbooks. If you choose a paragraph from another text, your instructor may ask you to submit a photocopy of both the paragraph and your annotations (the questions, comments, and observations you write as marginal notes).*

Drs. David and Myra Sadker of American University in Washington, D.C., sent observers to 100 classrooms in five states to sit in on teaching sessions. The Sadkers' researchers cited instances of boys being taught differently from girls in elementary schools (where women teachers far outnumber men) and in secondary schools (where more than half the teachers are male). The bias generally is unintentional and unconscious, says Myra Sadker, dean of the School of Education at American University. She notes: "We've met teachers who call themselves feminists. They show me their nonsexist textbooks and nonsexist bulletin boards. They insist there is equity in their classrooms. Then," she continues, "I videotape them as they're teaching—and they're amazed. If they hadn't seen themselves at work on film, they'd never have believed that they were treating boys and girls so differently."

from Claire Safran, "Hidden Lessons: Do Little Boys Get a Better Education Than Little Girls?" *Parade,* 1983.

WRITING IN RESPONSE TO READING

Making response notes can be an initial step to writing a fully developed paragraph or essay. Writing notes often leads you to discover possibilities you may not have seen at first.

Response Notes as Sources for New Ideas

Many times, writing response notes helps you to find a topic that leads to more extensive and complex writing. For instance, April's assignment called for her to read an article relating to technology and to write on a topic discussing the impact of technology on some aspect of modern life. April remembered an article she had seen in *Newsweek* and decided to reread it. She found the article, photocopied it, and as she read the article (one paragraph of which is reprinted on pages 8–9), she was careful to write in the margin any question, observation, or comment that came to mind. She knew she might be able to use at least some of those marginal annotations later when she began to work on finding a specific topic for her paper.

DISCOVERY STRATEGIES Making marginal notes, then, is one way of responding to what you read. Those notes lead easily to other types of responses that can help you discover new ideas and possibilities. As you plan to write papers, try several of the following discovery strategies to see which works best for you.

BRAINSTORMING When you brainstorm, you simply let your thoughts flow onto paper. You let images and ideas come in whatever order they choose, without worrying about formalities like sentence structure, spelling, or punctuation. You can brainstorm about anything, of course, but when you use this strategy in connection with something you are reading, it's helpful to begin with one of your marginal notes. When you begin a brainstorming session with a particular statement or question, you are doing what is called "focused brainstorming"; that is, you start with a particular focus in mind. For example, April's question "What about other nations?" led to this session of brainstorming.

> U.S. caught by technology—what about other countries?—technology essential for underdeveloped nations—what about countries like Japan?—maybe further ahead than U.S.—are they trapped?—what are the traps in the U.S.? Different from Japan? Developing nations? maybe technology a luxury—or worrying about technology a luxury.

April takes her question about technology in many different directions here. She opens up the possibility of several writing topics that she may want to pursue more formally later. For instance, she could write about the dangers of technology to developing countries; she could compare the use of technology in developing countries to the use of technology in the United States; or she could look at the possible traps technology has set for the Japanese culture.

LISTING Another useful strategy for discovering ideas is listing. April might have taken her statement "But technology does help solve problems" and developed a list to expand and develop that response.

Mammograms
Laser treatment
Fax
Remote control telephones for elderly
Car theft detection systems
Microsurgery
Airport traffic control
Computerized reservation service
Beepers for emergency calls
Airbags for cars
Microwave ovens

MAPPING Mapping is another way to find writing topics. Mapping may use a marginal annotation or perhaps an idea, question, or observation that resulted from brainstorming as a focal point. Consider, for instance, the following example of mapping, showing how April could have used the idea of technology in developing nations as a starting point.

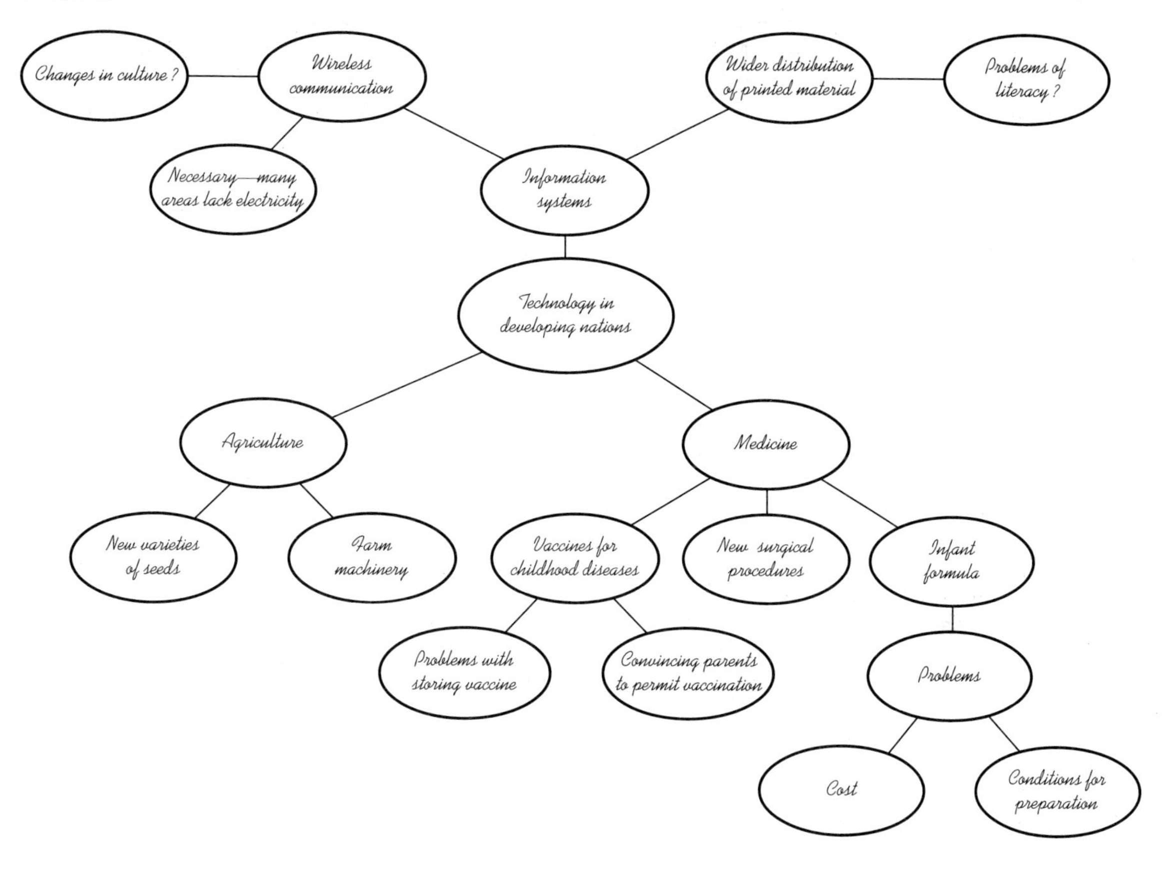

GROUPING After you have made a list (like the one on page 12), it's often helpful to stop and see whether the items in a list might usefully be grouped into categories. For instance, April could put her items in categories like this:

COMMUNICATIONS:

Fax
Remote control telephones for elderly
Airport traffic control
Beepers for emergency calls

MEDICAL:

Mammograms
Laser treatment
Microsurgery
Beepers for emergency calls

TRAVEL:

Airport traffic control
Airbags for cars
Computerized reservation service

By grouping the listed items, April creates possible topics for writing, for instance, "technology and medicine" or "communications advances through technology." (Note that some of the items in the list fit into more than one category and some do not fit into these categories. Don't worry about "rough edges" like these. Writing responses includes lots of exploration, some of which you might use for a current writing project, much of which you'll discard or store in your memory rather than using immediately.)

ASKING THE JOURNALIST'S QUESTIONS Asking certain standard questions—like the ones reporters regularly ask—can help you take a concept and discover how you might use it as a writing topic. For example, April might have looked at her marginal annotation "But technology does help solve problems" and considered these questions: Who? What? Where? When? Why? How? Here are specific inquiries she might have made:

1. Whose problems is technology most likely to solve?
   Who develops technological solutions to problems?
   Who pays for these solutions?
2. What exactly is meant by the term "technology"?
   What problems can technology solve?
   What different kinds of technology are used to solve problems?
3. Where is technology most apt to be used to solve problems?
   Where is technology useless or unhelpful?
4. When was technology first used to solve problems?
5. Why do so many people expect technology to solve their problems?
   Why do some people fear technology?
6. How is a technological solution different from any other solution to a problem?

Using any of these questions, April could explore further and find a topic for writing.

KEEPING AN IDEA JOURNAL Keeping an idea journal is one of the most valuable ways to discover topics for writing. If you keep an idea journal, you may write about many things you observe in your day-to-day life. In addition, journal writing can help develop the way you respond to what you read. Writing in an idea journal has many advantages. First, you have a place where you keep all your writing inspirations together. Second, the audience for an idea journal is usually yourself, so you can write freely without worrying about structure and—more important—without worrying whether your responses are "right" or "wrong" in someone else's eyes. The idea journal offers a chance to try out as many thoughts and observations as you have time to jot down and provides the opportunity to take risks. Later, you can sort out your responses, evaluate them, and decide which you might want to develop for a wider audience (for a class presentation or paper, for example).

An entry in an idea journal can be personal or impersonal, as you choose. This example develops one of April's personal responses to Kirkpatrick Sale's "The Miracle of Technofix."

> When I read this article, I just had to stop and think about what Sale was saying. Particularly in the paragraph about "technofix." I really thought this new word was great—technofix, because that's what a lot of people today seem to think. That technology can fix anything. Everyone has to have microwave ovens, hair dryers, power tools—any new way to save time. I'm always looking for saving time, too. I'd hate to have to live without what seems really necessary now, like refrigerators. But how about hair dryers and CD players? Now I'm beginning to think about stuff like how some of these things affect the environment. Like I keep hearing about problems with all the plastic. Maybe Sale is getting around to that in the rest of the article.

April's entry in her idea journal is personal and honest. She plays with Sale's new word "technofix" and applies it to her own life. Toward the end of the entry, she moves toward a complication: the conflict of what technology gives with what it might take away. This journal entry, then, opens many possibilities for further writing. April might, for instance, work further on her own definition of technofix and its applications to her life. Or she might consider the environmental problems surrounding one particular technological advance.

(*Note:* The idea journal described here is one that a writer chooses to keep for himself or herself. You may also find that instructors—for this class as well as others—ask you to keep journals for various purposes, using various formats. For instance, in some courses the instructor collects and reads journals. In some courses journals are graded. In others, the instructor writes comments responding to what has been written but does not give a grade. Still other instructors simply check the journal as complete or incomplete. Whatever the format, a class journal can almost always serve as a fine source for topics for papers.)

GUIDELINES: STRATEGIES FOR DISCOVERING NEW IDEAS AND TOPICS FOR WRITING

1. *Brainstorming:* Write without stopping for a set period of time (ten minutes, perhaps); then read what you have written to see what ideas you have discovered. For *focused brainstorming,* write down a thought, observation, or quotation that interests you. Then follow the brainstorming process just described.
2. *Mapping:* Use a thought, observation, or quotation that interests you as a focus. Draw a diagram going in as many different directions as possible. Consider what you have drawn to find potential topics for writing.
3. *Listing:* Use a thought, observation, or quotation that interests you as the guiding item. Under that item, list everything that comes to mind. Consider what you have listed as potential topics.
4. *Grouping:* Using a list created by the process just described, find similar items and group them to create possible topics for writing.
5. *Asking the journalist's questions:* Using a thought, observation, or quotation that interests you as the focus, ask the following questions: Who? What? When? Where? Why? How? Explore the questions you discover to see how they might lead to new ideas and possibly to topics for writing.
6. *Keeping an idea journal:* In a notebook or on notecards, write about your thoughts, observations, or reactions to something you have read. Write freely, without concern for organization or punctuation. The point of the idea journal is to find new ideas and, in some cases, to turn those ideas into topics for writing.

EXERCISE 4 *Using the notes you made in Exercise 3, try brainstorming, mapping, listing, grouping, asking the journalist's questions, and writing a journal entry. After you have finished, make a list of topics you have discovered that might be useful for future writing projects.*

EXERCISE 5 *Find a paragraph that interests you in a newspaper, magazine, book, or in the anthology section of this text (pages*

151–288). Make a photocopy of the paragraph. Read and respond to the paragraph by making marginal notes, then by brainstorming, mapping, listing, grouping, using the journalist's questions, and writing an entry in an idea journal. After you have finished, make a list of topics you have discovered that might be useful for future writing projects.

NARROWING THE TOPIC After reading, making marginal notes, and then using discovery strategies, most writers find they have plenty of ideas. The question then changes from "What can I possibly say about this article, chapter, or essay?" to "How can I possibly write about so many ideas?" Obviously, you need to choose from among the options you have discovered, and even after you make a choice, you may find that you need to think about it further, to refine it, to make it clearer in your mind before you start writing.

For instance, April knew that she would be writing in response to Kirkpatrick Sale's comments on "technofix," and she used several of the discovery strategies described on pages 11–16 as initial steps to explore some of the marginal comments she wrote when she first read Sale's essay. April found that some of the ideas that interested her most were very broad, general topics. For example, one idea was raised by a political science course April was taking called Developing Nations. Some of the points her professor had made in class lectures led her to see the idea of technology in developing countries as intriguing. She knew, however, that she could not do justice to such a broad topic in a short paper, so she decided to work at finding a more specific topic.

April started with this general topic:

Technology in developing countries

Then she made a list. (For a fuller explanation of listing as a discovery strategy, see page 12.) You'll notice as you read the list that April thought about her topic by *describing*, by *considering cause and effect*, and by *comparing*. Of course there are many other ways to narrow a topic, but these ways of thinking helped April to look at her broad topic in several different ways. Here's her list:

Describe one kind of technology that has become available to developing nations.

Explain what effects a technological development has had on developing nations (or maybe on one developing nation).

Discuss what caused a technological development to be made or why it was introduced to a particular developing country at a particular time.

Compare the way developing countries (or one country) were before they got one specific technological development to the way they were after.

GUIDELINES: NARROWING A TOPIC

1 Think about ways to *describe* the topic.
2 Think about ways to *discuss causes* relating to the topic.
3 Think about ways to *discuss effects* relating to the topic.
4 Think about ways to *compare* the topic to something.
5 Think about ways to *contrast* the topic with something.

EXERCISE 6 *Using the list of topics you discovered in Exercise 5, select four topics to narrow and refine. Although there are many ways to narrow a topic, you might use April's strategy of thinking about ways to describe, compare, or discover cause-and-effect relationships related to your broad topic.*

Even after this refining session, April saw that she still had work to do. Each of her topics mentioned "a technological development." But, of course, there are hundreds of technological developments. April decided to make a list of various technological developments she knew about, including some her political science professor had mentioned in class discussions. She came up with these possibilities:

Vaccines for childhood diseases
New varieties of seeds
Farm machinery
Automatic weapons
Infant formula

April looked over this list and decided on the following specific topic for her paper:

The effects of sending infant formula to developing nations

EXERCISE 7 *Using the topics you generated for Exercise 6, find one or more that needs to be made more specific. Use listing (see explanation of listing, page 12) as a strategy to find possibilities. Finally, decide on a topic that could be used as the basis for a short paper (250–500 words).*

FOCUSING A THESIS STATEMENT To write her response, April knew she needed more than a topic. She knew she wanted to talk about infant formula and developing nations, but now she needed to decide what she wanted to say about that topic. April had included "infant formula" on her list of specific technologies because her political science professor had mentioned the problems experienced in some developing countries where new mothers were being given free formula during the early days of their babies' lives.

She then decided to use the following statement as the preliminary *thesis* (central idea) on which to base her response:

> *Preliminary thesis statement:* Infant formula causes problems in developing nations.

This was a useful place for April to begin planning her essay. She now had not only a topic (infant formula in developing nations), but also something to say about that topic (that infant formula causes problems). April knew that this statement was *preliminary.* She might change it after she began to write, but it provided a way to start planning the essay.

When you are focusing a thesis statement, it's essential to remember these points:

1 A thesis statement makes an assertion about the topic.

YES: Infant formula causes problems in developing nations.

2 A thesis statement is *not* a broadly general statement that gives no idea of the topic.

NO: There are many problems with technology.

NO: Infant formula can be a problem.

3 A thesis statement is *not* merely a flat announcement of topic.

NO: In this paper I will talk about sending infant formula to developing nations.

NO: Infant formula is being sent to developing nations.

GUIDELINES: FOCUSING A THESIS STATEMENT

1 The thesis statement includes the topic.
2 The thesis statement tells what the writer will say about the topic.
3 The thesis statement focuses specifically on the topic, not on broad generalities.
4 The thesis statement makes an assertion about the topic rather than simply announcing the topic.

EXERCISE 8 *Using the topic you identified in Exercise 7, write a statement focusing a preliminary thesis statement. Again, consider that this thesis statement would lead to a paper approximately 250–500 words long.*

Alternative Exercise *Suggest preliminary central ideas for the following narrowed topics. Remember that a thesis statement does not simply identify a topic. A thesis statement should focus on the point the writer wants to make about a topic.*

EXAMPLES:

NARROWED TOPIC:	*PRELIMINARY THESIS STATEMENT:*
1 Ways of training staff for nursing homes	More effective ways of training staff members for nursing homes need to be developed.
2 Effects of corporate day-care centers	Corporate day-care centers raise employee morale and decrease absenteeism.

Following the above examples, write preliminary thesis statements for these narrowed topics.

NARROWED TOPIC:	*PRELIMINARY THESIS STATEMENT:*
1 Effects of students' employment on their study patterns	
2 Differences between required courses and elective courses	
3 Ways of reducing wastefulness on college campuses	
4 Main cause(s) of anxiety for college students	
5 Similarities between learning a physical skill and learning a mental (intellectual) skill	

Planning: *Audience*

When April first began thinking about her paper, she kept in mind her primary audience: her professor. April listened to the instructions the professor gave, and she also noted topics that seemed to interest her. April realized that to write an effective paper she needed to find a topic that both she and her audience would find meaningful. As she began to work on the paper, April discovered that she needed to do more specific thinking about her audience. Her new concern came in response to the professor's announcement that the papers would be read aloud in class. Now the audience had expanded to include April's fellow students. She realized that she would have to consider them as well as her instructor when she chose her topic, narrowed it, and decided on a central focus. While there are many ways to think about audience, April considered the following concerns:

1 Interest: What approach to the topic would capture the readers' attention?
2 Level of knowledge: What background information must be given and what terms must be explained or defined to enable readers to understand the topic?
3 Opinions: What opinions might readers already have about the topic? How can those opinions best be considered and acknowledged even if the writer does not agree with them?

April believed that most class members would be interested in her topic and her central focus. She thought about class discussions and about conversations she'd had with her fellow students. They seemed to be especially sympathetic to people they saw as having very little power to control—or even to understand—the impact of technology on their lives. Newborns in developing nations certainly fit this category. Also, she believed that most people relate strongly to circumstances that affect children in any way. Several class members were returning students who had children of their own. Many others had mentioned younger brothers and sisters. These people, April reasoned, would be able to identify with the plight of new mothers in developing nations who were faced with gifts of infant formula and encouraged to continue with this method of feeding their babies.

April also realized, however, that several people in the class planned to be business majors and at least two students were public relations majors. She knew she would need to be careful not to present unfairly the companies that were sending (and selling) the formula or to present them simply as greedy monsters. She wanted to at least acknowledge their point of view in a reasonable, calm way.

GUIDELINES: EVALUATING AUDIENCE

1 Consider what will *interest* your audience.
2 Consider what *level of knowledge* your audience has

about your topic so you can decide what facts, definitions, and explanations you need to give them.

3 Consider what *opinions* readers already have about the topic. Decide how those opinions may best be considered and acknowledged even if you do not agree with them.

EXERCISE 9 *Choose one of the preliminary central ideas you developed for either of the options in Exercise 8. Consider how you would think about writing a paper on that thesis statement for a specific audience.*

To do this exercise, first briefly describe your audience (for instance, "a group of elementary school students"; "a committee of faculty members"; "members of a labor union"). Next, evaluate your audience (using the guidelines on pages 21–22) and explain how your evaluation would affect your approach to your paper.

Planning: *Organization*

After deciding on a preliminary thesis statement and after evaluating her audience, April was anxious to get started. She really wasn't sure where to begin, but she knew that she should have some idea of where she was going. She read over the notes she had made from discussions and lectures in her political science class. Then she jotted down the main points she wanted to make. (Notice that April is using the strategy of listing. This strategy is described on pages 12 and 18 as a way to find a topic and also as a way to narrow a topic. It's important to note that the process of writing is not simply a list of steps to be followed and checked off. For instance, strategies that help at the beginning of a writing task also often help at many other stages.) April's list looked like this:

Companies looking for new markets give gift packs including formula to new mothers in developing countries.
This technology may be good for a country like U.S.—provides choices for parents.
Advertising in developing nations shows mothers in rich countries like the U.S. using this formula.
Mothers in developing nations try the formula.
They don't have enough money to buy enough formula so they water it down—water often polluted.

They don't have sanitary conditions to prepare formula so babies often get sick—many die.

April looked over her list carefully. As she read, she remembered that the assignment asked her to respond to some aspect of modern technology. She then decided that she needed to add something to show that infant formula was developed through new technologies. April also rearranged several of her points so that they emphasized the effects of the gift and sale of formula in developing nations. She also added a final point because she saw that her response would need an ending that tied her points together.

Here's what her revised guide looked like:

1 New technology includes infant formula—scientifically developed and packaged.
2 May be good for country like U.S.—gives choices for parents.
3 Formula causes problems in developing nations.
4 Companies looking for new markets give gift packs—including formula—to new mothers in developing nations.
5 Advertising shows mothers in rich countries like U.S. using this formula.
6 Mothers in developing nations try the formula.
7 They don't have enough money to buy enough formula so they water it down—water often polluted.
8 They don't have sanitary conditions to prepare formula so babies often get sick—many die.
9 Shows example of complications of new technologies—may be good in some situations but not in others.

April has organized her thoughts very simply and clearly. She starts her guide with a few observations that explain her topic and her thesis (statements 1, 2, 3). She then moves to statements that develop her point that a problem exists (statements 4, 5, 6). Next she has two statements that explain the effects of the problem (statements 7, 8). Her final statement (statement 9) sums up what she has said.

EXERCISE 10 *Using one of the topics and central ideas you defined in Exercise 8, make a list of the main points you would make to develop this topic. Next, think about those points and arrange them into a sentence guide that you could use as a basis for writing an essay responding to your chosen topic.*

Drafting

April thought getting started on the actual writing would be the most difficult part of her assignment. However, with her guideline of statements, she had an easy place to begin. She simply took her first observation and used that to write the initial sentence of her draft. Then she continued, working in the ideas from her guide as she progressed. Here's a copy of her first draft.

---

1 New technology includes infant formula that is scientifically developed and packaged. This technology may be good for a country like the United States. Because it provides choices for parents.

2 Formula causes problems in developing nations.

3 There are companies that sell formula that are looking for new markets and so they look in places like developing nations because in other nations that are wealthier like the U.S. or European countries many parents already use formula to feed their babies, and so these companies do things like give free packages with stuff like formula in it to mothers in developing countries who have just had babies.

4 There's also advertising that shows pictures of mothers in wealthy nations and these mothers have healthy babies and they are feeding the babies with formula. So this makes the mothers who get the gift packs want to feed their babies formula.

5 But there's two problems with this.

6 One, they don't have enough money to buy enough formula after the free formula is gone. So they buy what they can afford.

7 And there's two problems with this which starts when these mothers add too much water to the formula. To make it last longer.

8 One, the watered-down formula is not nutritious enough for the baby, two the water may be polluted. And another problem is that they often don't have sanitary conditions to prepare or store the formula. Because of these problems, babies often get sick and many of them die.

9 So you can see that even though some technology is good, it is not always good and can be bad.

REVISING After April finished her draft, she put it away for a day before she looked at it again. When she read it over, she thought she had good ideas but she was not really happy with the paper. Using guidelines similar to those on pages 290–291, she decided to revise.

Revising writing means looking at it again—literally "re" seeing—and trying to discover why and how certain things need to be changed. When you revise, you are looking for more than just punctuation mistakes, misspellings, and typographical errors. In fact, you should try to forget these fine points of editing until you have looked at the larger issues; for example, the way you've organized your material or how you've explained and developed your main idea.

EXERCISE 11 *Read Appendix A, pages 289–292. Then use those guidelines to evaluate April's draft. Make a list of your observations about her paper. Include both statements and questions. After making your list, compare it (if possible) with the lists of two or three other students and decide what advice you might give for revising this response. Finally, read the description of April's revision process that follows and compare your way of "re-seeing" her paper with hers.*

APRIL'S REVISION PROCESS April knew what her thesis was supposed to be, but as she read her draft, it didn't seem clear. She started to take notes so she would remember what she believed she needed to do. Her notes included both observations and questions:

Thesis? Maybe mention in first paragraph?
No connection between first and second paragraph.
Paragraphs look funny. How to change? Can one sentence be a paragraph?
Final paragraph—final sentence—seems too obvious.
Some sentences are too long and confusing.
I say "there's two problems" twice—but it's not clear what two problems. They aren't the same. Make clear.
Title?

As April read over her list for revision, she saw that she needed to make several changes. Some changes she believed she knew how to make, but she wasn't sure why her paragraphs didn't seem right to her. She made an appointment with her English professor and took both the draft and the list of revision issues to her office for a conference.

Her professor read April's drafts and comments. Then she asked April what she thought most needed to be changed. April answered that the thesis statement had to be clearer but that what worried her most were the paragraphs. April's professor agreed that the central focus was the most important point to be addressed; she also gave April advice on working with her paragraphs by providing the suggestions in the guidelines below.

GUIDELINES: REVISING PARAGRAPHS

1 Make sure the paragraph deals with only one main idea.
2 Check to be sure there is a *topic sentence* if the main idea

of the paragraph seems unclear. Most paragraphs have a topic sentence that states the main idea (usually the first or last sentence).

3. Make sure that other sentences provide sufficient details, reasons, or examples to support the idea expressed in the guiding sentence.
4. Make sure that each sentence is written clearly and makes sense.
5. Make sure the paragraph is neither too long nor too short to convey one main idea effectively. Most well-developed paragraphs have from four to ten sentences.

After considering these guidelines, April realized that many of her paragraphs did not have clear main ideas and that most of them only had one or two sentences. She saw that she needed to rethink the way her paragraphs were developed, considering what she wanted each paragraph to contribute to the essay.

Before April left the office, her professor suggested that focusing and developing the thesis statement was related to revising the problems with her paragraphs. Once she defined her thesis more specifically, she could then see how each paragraph should contribute to and support that idea. Keeping these points in mind, April wrote the following revision.

REVISION: The High Cost of Infant Formula

1 New technology has allowed scientists to develop infant formula that can feed babies, in a country like the United States, this development may be good. Providing hope for abandoned babies or for babies whose mothers are sick. Also, many new mothers in the United States leave the hospital with gift packs that include formula. This gift gives them a choice about how to feed their babies. However, gifts of infant formula to new mothers in developing nations have caused serious problems.

2 Companies that sell infant formula are always looking for new markets. Most women in somewhat wealthy countries like the United States or European countries already know about formula, so these companies look for other countries. These companies have discovered that mothers in developing nations provide a new market. During the past several years. Companies that make

formula have begun to give gift packs that include formula to new mothers in developing nations.

3 These gift packs include samples of the formula, sample bottles, and instructions on how to prepare the formula. The packs also include advertising that shows pictures of women from rich countries like the United States feeding their babies with formula. The mothers in developing countries then often decide that the formula will be best for their babies. Unfortunately, there are two serious problems with this decision.

4 The first problem is that most of these mothers do not have the money to buy enough formula for their babies. These mothers often add too much water to the formula. To try to make it last longer. This watered down formula is not nutritious enough for the baby, also, the water is often polluted. If the water is polluted, the baby will very likely get sick. Even if it is not, the baby will not grow and develop normally. Because the formula has been weakened.

5 The second problem is that many homes in developing nations do not have modern plumbing or refrigerators. In these homes, it's very hard or impossible for the infant formula to be prepared in a sanitary way. Also, the prepared formula can spoil easily. Because there's no way to keep it refrigerated. Both these situations can make the formula unsafe. Babies who drink formula under these conditions often become sick and many die.

6 Infant formula is like many other products of new technology, it seems to be something that is good or at least convenient and not harmful. In some circumstances, however, formula can be very harmful. People should think very carefully about possible good and bad effects of new technology. I think we should do everything legally possible to keep companies from marketing formula in third world countries.

COMMENTARY ON THE REVISION In this revision, April has concentrated on two key points:

1. Making her thesis statement clear
2. Restructuring and developing her paragraphs

Here's how she accomplished her goals:

1. In the first paragraph she describes the new technology and acknowledges its benefits. She has explained these benefits more clearly and fully than in her first draft. The final sentence in the paragraph moves to explain the thesis: In contrast to the possible benefits of formula in nations like the United States, this modern de-

velopment causes problems in developing nations. Note that the ideas in the first two paragraphs of the original draft have been combined and developed. In addition, the thesis statement is more specific. Instead of saying "formula causes problems," April has revised her tentative thesis to this new, more precise assertion: "Gifts of infant formula to new mothers in developing nations have caused serious problems."

2 In her second paragraph, April provides information necessary to explain who gives gifts of formula to new mothers and why these gifts are given. Notice that instead of one long, rather confusing sentence (original paragraph 3), April now uses several clearly written sentences to develop her idea. In addition, April made some minor changes; for example, she eliminated the word "stuff," which is too general and informal for a paper she will read to a class and pass in to a professor.

3 The third paragraph tells exactly what is in the gift packs and describes the advertising that accompanies the formula. Again, this paragraph definitely relates to the thesis as it is stated in the final sentence of the opening paragraph. Note that April combined information from the original paragraphs 3 and 4 to create one well-developed paragraph. Then she took the original paragraph 5 (a single sentence) and revised it to lead into her next paragraph.

4 Paragraph 4 develops one of the two problems mentioned in the final sentence of paragraph 3. The content of this paragraph obviously relates to the thesis stated in the opening paragraph.

5 Paragraph 5 develops the second of the two problems mentioned in the final sentence of paragraph 3. By organizing the discussion of the effects of gifts of infant formula into two broad categories, April straightened out the confusion of paragraphs 6–8 in her original draft and made clear how this information relates to her thesis.

6 April's original final paragraph was one sentence that made a very general statement not clearly connected to her specific central idea. Her revised final paragraph follows more precisely from what she has written in earlier paragraphs. In addition, she suggests a possible way of approaching the problem she describes rather than simply stating that a problem exists.

EXERCISE 12 *Using the same paragraph checklist April used (pages 25–26), and using her revision as an example, rewrite the following response so that it has clearly organized, well-developed paragraphs. Be prepared to explain your revisions by making a paragraph-by-paragraph analysis similar to the analysis of April's revision on pages 27–28.*

Note: You will not need to add extra sentences or to change sen-

tence structure. This exercise simply asks you to rearrange the sentences into logical paragraphs.

After you have finished the revision, suggest a title for the response.

RESPONSE TO "HIDDEN LESSONS"

(*The following response was written by Aaron Arthur after he read the paragraph from "Hidden Lessons" [pages 10–11]. He used many of the same steps described in April's process as he worked toward this draft.*)

Children learn hidden lessons in many places besides classrooms.

They learn hidden lessons on the playground and on school buses. Perhaps the most important hidden lessons they learn are taught at home.

All of these lessons can give stereotyped messages about the ways boys and girls are supposed to behave. On the playground, boys still are more likely to be active than girls are.

Even in grade schools, you can see girls flocking around the playground supervisors, just talking and standing there. The boys are usually running around either playing sports or else wrestling with each other.

When a girl does get involved in an active or rough game and she gets hurt, the playground supervisor acts very concerned and may send the girl inside to "rest up."

If boys get hurt they are either ignored or told that they "asked for it" because they were "fooling around." On school buses, the drivers are looking for boys to be the troublemakers. If something gets thrown on a bus, the driver assumes that a boy threw it.

A girl might open a window without permission and the most that will happen is that the driver will tell her to close it. If a boy does something like that, he will get yelled at or maybe reported to the principal.

When one school bus driver was asked why she yelled at boys and not at girls, she said, "Because girls have tenderer feelings than boys!"

In many homes, boys are expected to help out with all the heavy chores, like shoveling snow or carrying out trash. Many parents also expect them to do work like washing dishes and folding clothes.

These are jobs that used to be considered "women's work."

Girls may have to help with these jobs, but not very many of them have to shovel snow or carry out trash.

The message I see being given on the playground, on school buses, and in many homes is that boys still have to play male roles.

Girls can do things that boys do, like playing rough games, but they get sympathy if they get hurt. Girls get special attention and they don't have to live up to the same rules boys do.

I think the hidden message is that today it's easier to be a girl than to be a boy.

Proofreading

After April finished the revision (pages 26–27), she read it over and decided that she had done a good job of focusing her main idea and reworking her paragraph structure. She noticed, however, that some of her sentences did not sound right as she read her paper aloud. After asking her professor's advice, April saw that she needed to pay special attention to problems with sentence fragments and comma splices. Using explanations and guidelines similar to those on pages 291–292, April proofread her essay and made the necessary changes before bringing her paper to class.

EXERCISE 13 *Read Editor's Focus 1 and 2, pages 300–305 and pages 305–312. Then use those explanations and strategies to proofread and edit April's draft (pages 26–27). When you see changes that are needed, make them. Then compare your changes (if possible) with those made by two or three other students. Finally, compare your editing of April's paper with the changes she made for her final draft.*

FINAL DRAFT: The High Cost of Infant Formula

1 New technology has allowed scientists to develop infant formula that can feed babies. In a country like the United States, this development may be good. Formula provides hope for abandoned babies or for babies whose mothers are sick. Also, many new mothers in the United States leave the hospital with gift packs that include formula. This gift gives them a choice about how to feed their babies. However, gifts of infant formula to new mothers in developing nations have caused serious problems.

2 Companies that sell infant formula are always looking for new markets. Most women in somewhat wealthy countries like the United States or European countries already know about formula, so these companies look for other countries. These companies have discovered that mothers in developing nations provide a new market. During the past several years, companies that make formula have begun to give gift packs that include formula to new mothers in developing nations.

3 These gift packs include samples of the formula, sample bottles, and instructions on how to prepare the formula. The packs also include advertising that shows pictures of women from rich countries like the United States feeding their babies with formula. The mothers in developing countries then often decide that the formula will be best for their babies. Unfortunately, there are two serious problems with this decision.

4 The first problem is that most of these mothers do not have the money to buy enough formula for their babies. These mothers often add too much water to the formula to try to make it last longer. This watered-down formula is not nutritious enough for the baby. Also, the water is often polluted. If the water is polluted, the baby will very likely get sick. Even if it is not, the baby will not grow and develop normally because the formula has been weakened.

5 The second problem is that many homes in developing nations do not have modern plumbing or refrigerators. In these homes, it's very hard or impossible for the infant formula to be prepared in a sanitary way. Also, the prepared formula can spoil easily because there's no way to keep it refrigerated. Both these situations can make the formula unsafe. Babies who drink formula under these conditions often become sick and many die.

6 Infant formula is like many other products of new technology. It seems to be something that is good or at least convenient and not harmful. In some circumstances, however, formula can be very harmful. People should think very carefully about possible good and bad effects of new technology. I think we should do everything legally possible to keep companies from marketing formula in third world countries.

EXERCISE 14 *Some of the following paragraphs come from magazines or newspapers, others come from college textbooks like the ones you will be reading in introductory courses. These paragraphs provide the opportunity to practice the skills of close reading, rereading, and notetaking.*

After carefully considering the notes you write, choose one question, observation, or reaction as the starting point for a written response.

You might discover a focus for your response by brainstorming, mapping, listing, grouping, asking the journalist's questions, or writing an entry in an idea journal. Then follow the steps described above for April's paper: Narrow the topic, develop a preliminary main idea, consider your audience and organization, draft carefully, revise thoughtfully, and proofread accurately.

PARAGRAPHS FOR PRACTICE: READING, RESPONDING, THINKING, WRITING

1 As you can imagine, especially in a prison where there was heavy emphasis on rehabilitation, an inmate was smiled upon if he demonstrated an unusually intense interest in books. There was a sizable number of well-read inmates, especially the popular debaters. Some were said by many to be practically walking encyclopedias. They were almost celebrities. No university would ask any student to devour literature as I did when this new world opened to me, of being able to read and *understand.*

from Malcolm X, *The Autobiography of Malcolm X.*

2 Who are we kidding? The problem with drinking isn't so much "alcoholism." The problem is death and destruction—of lives, property, relationships. Warped personalities and blunted perceptions may be annoying, but that is inconsequential when weighed against the protection of life. Yet there is a parking lot next to every cocktail lounge.

from John S. Hoppock, "The Costs of Drinking," *New York Times,* July 1, 1981.

3 How can scientists and physicians treat people with Alzheimer's disease before it destroys their mental abilities? Although it may sound like science fiction, researchers are now exploring the possibility of transplanting brain tissue. Experiments on rats suggest that cells transplanted from a normal brain into a diseased one may blunt the effects of brain disease. When a researcher injects a toxin into the brain stem region that secretes acetylcholine in the cerebral cortex, some of the nerves are destroyed. The amount of acetylcholine decreases in the cerebrum, and the nerve-damaged animal behaves much like an Alzheimer's sufferer. But when the researcher then removes neurons from the equivalent brain stem region of an embryonic rat and injects those brain cells into the cerebrum of the rat with damaged nerves, the animal's memories return to normal.

from John H. Postlethwait and Janet L. Hopson, *The Nature of Life.*

4 Little girls tend to play in small groups or, even more common, in pairs. Their social life usually centers around a best friend, and friendships are made, maintained, and broken by talk, especially "secrets." The secrets themselves may or may not be important, but the fact of telling them is all-important. It's hard for newcomers to get into these tight groups, but anyone who is admitted is treated as an equal. Girls like to play cooperatively; if they can't cooperate, the group breaks up.

Little boys tend to play in larger groups, often outdoors, and they spend more time doing than talking. It's easy for boys to get into a group, but once in they must jockey for status. One of the ways they do so is through talk—telling stories and jokes, arguing about who is best at what, challenging and sidetracking the talk of other boys and withstanding the others' challenges in order to maintain their own story and, consequently, their status.

from Deborah Tannen, *That's Not What I Meant! How Conversational Style Makes or Breaks Your Relations with Others.*

5 The extent to which society relies upon **specialization** is astounding. The vast majority of consumers produce virtually none of the goods and services they consume and, conversely, consume little or nothing of what they produce. The hammer-shop laborer who spends a lifetime stamping out parts for jet engines may never "consume" an airplane trip. The assembly-line worker who devotes eight hours a day to the installation of windows in Camaros may own a Honda. Few households seriously consider any extensive production of their own food, shelter, and clothing. Many farmers sell their milk to the local dairy and then buy margarine at the Podunk general store. Society learned long ago that self-sufficiency breeds inefficiency. The jack-of-all-trades may be a very colorful individual, but is certainly lacking in efficiency.

from Campbell R. McConnell and Stanley L. Brue, *Macroeconomics.*

6 "Stress and the Secretary" has become the hottest new syndrome on the heart circuit. It seems that it isn't those Daring Young Women in their Dress-for-Success Suits who are following men down the cardiovascular trail to ruin. Nor is it the female professionals who are winning their equal place in intensive care units. It is powerlessness and not power that corrupts women's hearts. And clerical workers are the number one victims. In the prestigious Framingham study, Dr. Suzanne Haynes, an epidemiologist with the National Heart, Lung, and Blood Institute, found that working women as a whole have no higher rate of heart disease than housewives. But women employed in clerical and sales occupations do. Their coronary disease rates are twice that of other women.

from Ellen Goodman, "Being a Secretary Can Be Hazardous to Your Health," *The Boston Globe,* 1987.

GUIDELINES: WRITING A RESPONSE

1 Use the reading and notetaking strategies described in this chapter.
2 Follow the process of writing demonstrated on pages 11–31.
3 Make clear in the introduction the point you are making. (In the sample on pages 30–31, the last sentence of paragraph 1 indicates that the essay will discuss problems related to distribution of infant formula in developing nations.)
4 Make sure to have a logical organization planned. (In the sample on pages 30–31, the last sentence in paragraph 3 shows that the author will discuss two possible solutions.)
5 Use a separate paragraph for each new idea.
6 Make sure each paragraph follows the guidelines for revising paragraphs (pages 25–26).
7 Make sure the concluding paragraph does more than summarize what you have said. Your concluding paragraph should offer a comment or evaluation based on what you have said in your paper.

SECTION TWO

READING AND WRITING TO EVALUATE

This chapter suggests that in our daily lives, as well as in our academic lives, we make and observe evaluations. Attention is focused on the following issues related to reading and writing to evaluate.

- *Defining the process of evaluation*
- *Understanding what you read*
- *Discovering the meanings of words from context*
- *Reading and writing to find the main idea*
- *Reading and writing to identify supporting points*
- *Identifying aspects to evaluate and considering criteria for evaluating*
- *Planning an evaluation*
- *Writing an evaluation*

WHEN YOU WATCH A FILM REviewer on television, read reviews of a book in a newspaper or magazine, or listen to a friend's opinion of the latest video release, you are observing the process of evaluation. To evaluate means to make a judgment about something.

Reviews of films, books, or videos provide a clear demonstration of the way evaluation works. Consider, for example, two film reviewers, Siskel and Ebert, who, on their weekly television program, offer their judgments on recently released movies. Whoever speaks first gives an overview of the film, letting viewers know its main idea. Then one reviewer, let's say Siskel, picks out relevant aspects of the film (perhaps camera angles, plot, and dialogue) and gives his opinion, using criteria he has developed to judge each aspect. To back up his opinion, he gives specific examples from the film. Then the other reviewer, Ebert, gives his judgment. Sometimes he discusses the same aspects; sometimes different aspects. The criteria he uses are his own; they may or may not be similar to the standards Siskel used. Sometimes Ebert agrees with Siskel; often he does not. If Siskel agrees, he gives additional evidence to support the points that Ebert has made. If he disagrees, he provides examples from the film to show why his evaluation differs from Siskel's.

EVALUATION: DEFINING THE PROCESS

From the description of these two film reviewers at work, you learn a great deal about the process of evaluation. To evaluate:

- First you need an *overview* of what you are considering (in the case of Siskel and Ebert, understanding the main idea of the film).
- Second, you need to decide on *specific points* or *aspects* you will evaluate. (Siskel and Ebert would decide to consider certain elements of the film, for example, camera angles, plot, and dialogue.)
- Third, you need to consider the *standards* (also called *criteria*) by which you will judge these points or aspects. (Both Siskel and Ebert have thought about what qualities they must find in a film in order to give it the "thumbs up" rating of approval. Their standards may differ. Siskel, for instance, may admire the use of many unusual camera angles, while Ebert may believe that varied camera angles confuse the viewer and obscure the film's action.)
- Fourth, you need to determine exactly what *judgments* your standards lead you to make about the points or aspects you have decided to discuss. (For instance, if Siskel values a variety of unusual camera angles, and if the film provides this variety, he would make a positive judgment about that aspect of the film.)

- Fifth, you need to offer *reasons, examples,* and *details* to support what you have said. (Siskel would mention specific scenes where the camera angles were varied. He would also give reasons for valuing the unusual camera angles, explaining, for example, that they added emphasis to the action of the scene or mirrored the emotions of a particular character.)

(*Note:* As you consider these five steps that define the process of evaluation, be aware that *different, perhaps equally valid, judgments may be made of the aspects being evaluated.* For example, although Siskel and Ebert are both considered expert reviewers, they often disagree about a film's strengths and weaknesses. Ebert, for instance, might argue that the scenes Siskel praised for their innovative camera angles were, in fact, confusing and pretentious.)

As part of your academic and future professional life, you can expect to be asked to make evaluations frequently. Sometimes these evaluations will be brief and informal—done in your head or as part of a discussion or conversation. At other times, you'll be expected to write a formal evaluation. A professor, or perhaps a supervisor at work, may call an evaluation by a different name. For instance, you may be asked to write a *critique* or a *review* of a book, an article, or a proposed course of action. Whatever term is used, the process is basically the same: You are being asked to make a judgment, following the five steps described above.

Remember that the point in making an evaluation is not to find the one correct response, but rather to think through your reaction carefully to be sure it makes sense and to be sure you can support your ideas in the most convincing way possible.

EXERCISE 1 *We all make evaluations in our work, in school, and in our personal lives. When you consider an idea, object, proposal, or even a person, and make a judgment, you are evaluating. For instance, before each semester begins, you look at the college catalogue and get an overview of all the courses available to you. You read the descriptions, talk with faculty advisers and with fellow students. Perhaps you also go to the bookstore and browse through the books that various courses require. Then you make a choice, deciding which classes you will take.*

Or consider the way you make plans for a weekend. Perhaps you think about chores that have to be done as well as activities you would enjoy. You may evaluate each chore, considering how important it is to get that task done during the weekend. Then you choose to do some chores and set others aside to be done at another time. For pleasure, you may want to go to a movie. You call local theaters to see what's playing, and then you make a choice based, perhaps, on what you've heard about these films or what you like and dislike about the actors playing the main roles. To make these decisions, you go through the process of evaluation.

For the next several days, note carefully the evaluations you make. Make a list of these evaluations and write a brief description of the process you go through and the decisions you reach. Discuss each of the five steps described above:

1. Provide an overview showing that you understand clearly what you are evaluating.
2. List the specific points or aspects you evaluate.
3. List and explain the standards (criteria) you are using to make the evaluation.
4. Describe the judgments you make by applying these standards to the aspects you identify.
5. Provide reasons, examples, and details to explain and support the judgments you make.

Alternative Exercise *Think back on important evaluations you have made in the past. Make a list of these evaluations and write a brief description of the process you followed. (Include the five steps described above.) As a conclusion, make a brief reevaluation explaining why you do or do not think the evaluation you made in the past was wise.*

EVALUATION: UNDERSTANDING WHAT YOU READ

Both academic and professional evaluations often require writing a judgment about something you have read. To understand what you read—and to get an overview of the author's main idea and supporting points—you must often deal with unfamiliar words.

Dealing with Unfamiliar Words

Many readers spend a lot of time worrying about unfamiliar words. In elementary and high school, you may have been told to look up all unfamiliar words in the dictionary. While a dictionary is an absolutely essential tool for every literate person, most readers have neither the time nor the need to look up every unfamiliar word they encounter. Stop for a moment to think of how you learned all the words you now know. At age five or six, you went off to school comfortably using thousands of words, yet you'd never studied vocabulary lists or looked words up in a dictionary. How did you learn these words?

Obviously you acquired your vocabulary from hearing other people use the words; you came to know their meaning from the context in which they were used. When you learned to read, you developed another method to build your vocabulary. As you read, you encounter new words and, just as you learn the meaning of the words you hear by their context, so, too, do you understand the meaning of most new words you read by their context.

Because using a dictionary takes time and distracts you from what you are reading, you should use it mainly in two circumstances:

1 When you cannot discover the meaning of a word from the context in which it appears *and* the word seems essential to understanding what you are reading
2 When you can discover the meaning of the word from its context but you are interested in knowing more than just the meaning (perhaps you want to know the pronunciation, the word's origin, or its alternative meanings)

Of course, sometimes when you are reading you may not recognize a word or be able to discover its meaning from the context, but it may be a word that you can see you don't have to know to comprehend the author's idea. In that case, your *curiosity* may lead you to the dictionary. However, if you are pressured by *time constraints,* you may just read over the word without worrying about its precise meaning.

The following examples taken from *Cultural Anthropology,* a textbook by Daniel G. Bates and Fred Plog, demonstrate the ways you can discover the meanings of words from their context:

1 *Internal definition:* The author may provide the definition for the word within the sentence or paragraph where the word is first used.

   EXAMPLE:
   "Out of this habit of thought emerged the idea of *evolution,* the process by which small but cumulative changes in a species can, over time, lead to its transformation."

   EXPLANATION:
   You might not know the word *evolution,* but Professors Bates and Plog built in a definition for you, "the process by which small but cumulative changes in a species can, over time, lead to its transformation." Sometimes an internal definition will come just before a term, or it might come in the next sentence.

2 *Example definition:* The author may provide an example or a series of examples to define a new term.

EXAMPLE:
"Our basic *physiological* requirements—such as the need for food, water, shelter, sleep, and sexual activity—underlie a good deal of our behavior."

EXPLANATION:
When anthropology students read this sentence, they can discover the meaning of *physiological* by paying attention to the examples. Obviously, *physiological* needs, as defined by Bates and Plog, are the needs of the body rather than emotional, spiritual needs.

3 *Contrast definition:* The author may provide a clue to the meaning of a word by providing a contrast or opposite to the word.

EXAMPLE:
"No field as complex as anthropology is *monolithic;* the variety of views among its practitioners is reflected in their research."

EXPLANATION:
Even though you may not be able to state the dictionary definition of *monolithic* (representing massive uniformity or sameness), you can certainly tell that it is the opposite of *varied* by reading the phrase that immediately follows it. "Variety of views" tells you that *monolithic* would represent a single view.

4 *Synonym definition:* The author may use a synonym (a word that means the same thing as another word) to help explain an unfamiliar term.

EXAMPLE:
"Another approach or *school* of cultural anthropology that became prominent in the United States is often referred to as the 'culture area' approach."

EXPLANATION:
If you did not know the use of the word *school* to mean *approach,* you would understand that meaning here because Bates and Plog twice provide the synonym *approach* while they are describing the "culture area" school of cultural anthropology.

EXERCISE 2 *Using the strategies described above, use context clues to define the italicized words in the following excerpts from* Cultural Anthropology *by Daniel G. Bates and Fred Plog. In addition to explaining the italicized words, state which strategy you used.*

1 "*Mechanization*—the replacement of human and animal labor by mechanical devices—began long before the industrial age."

2 "One activity, unfortunately, involves the production of *illegal substances*—opium, cocaine, marijuana."

3 "The *exodus* from the countryside began. Family after family packed up, most of them headed directly for San Juan, Puerto Rico's major city."

4 "These families bore no resemblance to the stereotypical isolated and *autonomous* urban household. On the contrary, each household was enmeshed in a tight network of reciprocal-aid relationships with kin, friends, and neighbors, perhaps even more so than they had been in their villages."

5 "And since people preferred to marry within the neighborhood and generally named their neighbors as *compadres,* that is godparents, the neighborhood kinship network was constantly growing."

GUIDELINES: DISCOVERING MEANING FROM CONTEXT

1. *Internal definition:* The author may provide the definition for the word within the sentence or paragraph where the word is first used.
2. *Example definition:* The author may provide an example or a series of examples to define a new term.
3. *Contrast definition:* The author may provide a clue to the meaning of a word by providing a contrast or opposite to the word.
4. *Synonym definition:* The author may use a synonym (a word that means the same thing as another word) to help explain an unfamiliar term.

Reading and Writing to Find the Main Idea

Understanding how to deal with unfamiliar words enables you to read with confidence as you work toward the first step of evaluation: getting an overview. You want to find the author's main idea. The main idea includes both the author's subject and what the author says about that subject. To understand the process of finding the main idea, read the following article and the explanation that follows it.

NEVER GET SICK IN JULY

MARILYN MACHLOWITZ

Marilyn Machlowitz is a management psychologist as well as an author. Since receiving her Ph.D. in psychology from Yale, she has been widely published in both professional journals and popular magazines. In addition, she is the author of *Workaholics* (1980), a book that details the problems in the lives of those who value their work over all else. The following article, which first appeared in *Esquire* magazine (July 1978), raises some troubling questions about hospital care.

---

1 One Harvard medical school professor warns his students to stay home—as he does—on the Fourth of July. He fears he will become one of the holiday's highway casualties and wind up in an emergency room with an inexperienced intern "practicing" medicine on *him.* Just the mention of July makes medical students, nurses, interns, residents, and "real doctors" roll their eyes. While hospital administrators maintain that nothing is amiss that month, members of the medical profession know what happens when the house staff turns over and the interns take over each July 1.

2 This July 1, more than 13,000 new doctors will invade over 600 hospitals across the country. Within minutes they will be overwhelmed. Last July 1, less than a month after finishing medical school, Dr. John Baumann, then twenty-five, walked into Washington, D.C.'s, Walter Reed Army Medical Center. He was immediately faced with caring for "eighteen of the sickest people I had ever seen."

3 Pity the patient who serves as guinea pig at ten A.M.—or three A.M.—that first day. Indeed according to Dr. Russell K. Laros, Jr., professor and vice-chairman of obstetrics, gynecology, and reproductive sciences at the University of California, San Francisco, "There is no question that patients throughout the country are mismanaged during July. Without the most meticulous supervision," he adds, "serious errors can be made."

4 And they are. Internship provides the first chance to practice one's illegible scrawl on prescription blanks, a golden opportunity to make lots of mistakes. Interns—who are still known to most people by that name, even though they are now officially called first-year residents—have ordered the wrong drug in the wrong dosage to be administered the wrong way at the wrong times to the wrong patient. While minor mistakes are most common, serious errors are the sources of hospital horror stories. One intern prescribed an anti-depressant without knowing that it would inactivate the patient's previously prescribed antihypertensive medication (a medicine used to lower high blood pressure). The patient then experienced a rapid increase in blood pressure and suffered a stroke.

5 When interns do not know what to do, when they cannot

covertly consult *The Washington Manual* (a handbook of medical therapeutics), they can always order tests. The first time one intern attempted to perform a pleural biopsy—a fairly difficult procedure—he punctured the patient's lung. When an acquaintance of mine entered an emergency room one Friday she wound up having a spinal tap. While negative findings are often necessary to rule out alternative diagnoses, some of the tests are really unwarranted. Interns admit that the results are required only so they can cover themselves in case a resident or attending physician decides to give them the third degree.

6 Interns' hours only increase their inadequacy. Dr. Jay Dobkin, president of the Physicians National Housestaff Association, a Washington-based organization representing 12,000 interns and residents, says that "working conditions . . . directly impact and influence the quality of patient care. After thirty-six hours 'on,' most interns find their abilities compromised." Indeed, their schedules (they average 110 hours a week) and their salaries (last year, they averaged $13,145.00) make interns the chief source of cheap labor. No other hospital personnel will do as much "scut" work—drawing blood, for instance—or dirty work, such as manually disimpacting severely constipated patients.

7 Even private patients fall prey to interns, because many physicians prefer being affiliated with hospitals that have interns to perform these routine duties around the clock. One way to reduce the likelihood of falling into the hands of an intern is to rely upon a physician in group practice whose partners can provide substitute coverage. Then, too, it probably pays to select a physician who has hospital privileges at the best teaching institution in town. There at least, you are unlikely to encounter any interns who slept through school, as some medical students admit they do: only the most able students survive the computer-matching process to win the prestigious positions at university hospitals. It may be reassuring to remember that while veteran nurses joke about scheduling their vacations to start July 1, they monitor interns most carefully and manage to catch many mistakes. Residents bear much more responsibility for supervision and surveillance, and Dr. Lawrence Boxt, president of the 5,000-member, Manhattan-based Committee of Interns and Residents and a resident himself, emphasizes that residents are especially vigilant during July. One of the interns he represents agreed: "You're watched like a hawk. You have so much support and backup. They're not going to let you kill anybody." So no one who requires emergency medical attention should hesitate to be hospitalized in July.

8 I asked Dr. Boxt whether he also had any advice for someone about to enter a hospital for elective surgery.

9 "Yes," he said. "Stay away."

After reading Machlowitz's article, you can see that her subject is the influx of new interns to hospital staffs in July. To state the main idea, however, you have to go further. You have to discover what Machlowitz is saying about that staff change.

Main Idea = Subject + What Author Says About Subject

READING INTRODUCTIONS AND CONCLUSIONS TO DETERMINE MAIN IDEA Whether you are reading an article, a chapter in a book, or even a whole book, two places that often give an overview of the main idea are the introduction and the conclusion. Frequently authors state their main ideas in one or two sentences somewhere in the first few paragraphs. For example, in "Never Get Sick in July" the last sentence in paragraph 1 announces the topic and suggests the writer's approach, "While hospital administrators maintain that nothing is amiss that month, members of the medical profession know what happens when the house staff turns over and the interns take over each July 1."

From this sentence, the reader can tell that Machlowitz is going to discuss the July staff change. The first part of the sentence indicates that hospital administrators see no problems, while the last part of the sentence suggests that medical professionals who "know what happens" do see problems. The last three paragraphs of "Never Get Sick in July" also suggest the main idea. Note particularly the final four sentences, which indicate that, while emergency care in July will probably be given competently, anyone who faces elective surgery should postpone it. Those sentences underline Machlowitz's primary point and indicate that her main purpose will be to give information about what happens when medical staffs change over in July.

Of course, it is important to realize that introductions and conclusions vary widely. Not every introduction makes the main idea obvious. For instance, many writers begin an article or a book with a series of examples or a list of statistics or a brief story that leads into a statement of the main idea. So you may have to read several paragraphs before you find out how the writer is using those illustrations and how they relate to the central idea. Similarly, not every conclusion offers a neat summary of what has gone before. Instead, a writer may propose possible solutions to a problem or ask a series of questions about the main idea or offer a quotation intended to make the reader think further about the topic.

EXERCISE 3 *Read the following opening paragraphs and predict what the main idea of the whole essay or article will be. Remember that the main idea includes both the subject and what the author will say about that subject. If you encounter unfamiliar words, try to determine their meaning from context clues.*

> The evil of athletic violence touches nearly everyone. It tarnishes what may be our only religion. Brutality in games blasphemes play, perhaps our purest form of free expression. It blurs the clarity of open competition, obscuring our joy in victory as well as our dignity in defeat. It robs us of innocence, surprise, and self-respect. It spoils our fun.
>
> *from* Robert Yeager, "Violence in Sports," in *Seasons of Shame: The New Violence in Sports.*

> You ask me what is poverty? Listen to me. Here I am, dirty, smelly, and with no "proper" underwear on and with the stench of my rotting teeth near you. I will tell you. Listen to me. Listen without pity. I cannot use your pity. Listen with understanding. Put yourself in my dirty, worn-out ill-fitting shoes, and hear me.
>
> *from* Jo Goodwin Parker, "What Is Poverty?" in *America's Other Children: Public Schools Outside Suburbia.*

> The first thing people remember about failing at math is that it felt like sudden death. Whether the incident occurred while learning "word problems" in sixth grade, coping with equations in high school, or first confronting calculus and statistics in college, failure came suddenly and in a very frightening way. An idea or new operation was not just difficult, it was impossible! And, instead of asking questions or taking the lesson slowly, most people remember having had the feeling that they would never go any further in mathematics. If we assume that the curriculum was reasonable, and that the new idea was but the next in a series of learnable concepts, the feeling of utter defeat was simply not rational; yet "math anxious" college students and adults have revealed that no matter how much the teacher reassured them, they could not overcome that feeling.
>
> *from* Sheila Tobias, "Who's Afraid of Math, and Why?" in *Overcoming Math Anxiety.*

EXERCISE 4 *Read the following concluding paragraphs and speculate what the main idea of the whole essay or article might have been. Remember that the main idea includes both the subject and what the author will say about that subject. If you encounter unfamiliar words, try to discover their meaning from context clues.*

When is a place too empty or too crowded? That's a judgment everyone has to make for himself. In Manhattan people press together in subways and on street corners without batting an eye. But in America a hundred years ago the sound of an axe in the next clearing signalled that it was time to move on.

from Blythe Hamer, "The Thick and Thin of It," in *Science.*

What, then, can we conclude about mathematics and sex? If math anxiety is in part the result of math avoidance, why not require girls to take as much math as they can possibly master? If being the only girl in "trig" is the reason so many women drop math at the end of high school, why not provide psychological counseling and support for those young women who wish to go on? Since ability in mathematics is considered by many to be unfeminine, perhaps fear of success, more than any bodily or mental dysfunction, may interfere with girls' ability to learn math.

from Sheila Tobias, "Who's Afraid of Math, and Why?" in *Overcoming Math Anxiety.*

The high-tech repair problems we already face are testimony to the need for mechanically skilled engineers, technicians, and repair people. All of these are good occupational bets for the next twenty years. But better incentives will have to be created to attract and develop the skills needed to keep our technology viable.

from John Naisbitt, "Needed: High Tech Skills," in *Megatrends.*

READING TO IDENTIFY PURPOSE AND DETERMINE MAIN IDEA

In addition to considering introductions and conclusions, often you can determine what the author is saying about the subject—the main idea—by considering his or her purpose for writing the essay. As you read to discover an author's purpose, you ask questions like these: Is the writer primarily concerned with providing new information? With explaining how to do something? With entertaining the reader? With making a comparison? With making an evaluation? With arguing for a particular point of view or course of action?

For instance, to get at the main idea of "Never Get Sick in July," you might ask: Is Marilyn Machlowitz simply describing the staff change? Or is she praising it? Or criticizing it? Or making suggestions for change? In other words, you have to ask yourself exactly what Machlowitz is doing with her subject. In this case, the author's purpose is to explain the problems that come from the sudden changeover of interns. She is not merely describing the changes; she is taking a definite point of view (claiming that the changes cause problems). So if you were to state the main idea of Machlowitz's article, you might say something like this:

> In her article, "Never Get Sick in July," Marilyn Machlowitz reveals the dangers arising from the changeover of hospital staff interns each year on July 1 and urges the public to be aware of these dangers.

GUIDELINES: IDENTIFYING PURPOSE

To identify a writer's purpose, ask yourself these questions:

1. Is this writer primarily concerned with providing new information?
2. Is this writer primarily concerned with explaining how to do something?
3. Is this writer primarily concerned with entertaining the reader?
4. Is this writer primarily concerned with making a comparison?
5. Is this writer primarily concerned with making a judgment?
6. Is this writer primarily concerned with arguing for a particular point of view or course of action?

EXERCISE 5 *Choose a selection from the anthology section of this book (pages 151–288) or an article from a magazine. Following the guidelines for identifying purpose, and paying special attention to opening and closing paragraphs, write a sentence or two stating the main idea of the selection. Remember that the main idea includes both the author's subject and what the author says about that subject. (If you choose a selection from a source other than the text, your instructor may ask you to make a photocopy of the article to accompany your statement of main idea.)*

WRITING TO DEFINE THE MAIN IDEA: SUMMARIZING When you summarize, you write, in your own words, a short version of something you have read. This shortened version, as you would expect, provides an overview rather than recounting every detail, reason, and example an author uses. Therefore, writing a summary is an extremely helpful way to define an author's main idea, as well as the key points that support that idea.

When you are asked to evaluate, writing a summary is often a useful part of the initial discovery process. Writing the summary ensures that you clearly understand the author's main idea. In addition to helping you define the author's main idea and key supporting points, a summary may sometimes be used later as part of the opening paragraph of the evaluation.

> (*Note:* In addition to summarizing as part of the process of evaluating, you may also be asked to summarize as part of many other writing assignments both in school and in professional life.)

When you summarize, remember that a summary is always briefer than the material summarized. You are describing the author's main idea and the key points that support that idea. Do not include less important details, reasons, and examples. Generally, you follow the organization of the material being summarized (beginning, for example, with the author's main idea, then moving to the first major supporting point, the second major supporting point, and so on). Keep in mind that you use primarily your *own* words, not the words of the author. *If you do use a phrase or sentence taken directly from the work you are summarizing, enclose it in quotation marks.* It's important, also, to remember that a summary should be objective. That is, a summary should include only what the author says, not your judgments, observations, or opinions.

SAMPLE SUMMARY The following is a useful summary of Marilyn Machlowitz's article (pages 42–44).

> In her essay "Never Get Sick in July," Marilyn Machlowitz describes the problems that occur when new interns join the staffs of U.S. hospitals on July first. These brand-new doctors are faced with caring for emergency room patients who are seriously sick or badly injured. Often the interns prescribe the wrong medicine or order unnecessary tests that make the patients even sicker. Some patients have even died. Machlowitz explains how interns are supervised, and she also describes how to avoid encountering problems with interns. Her advice is summed up by her title: "Never Get Sick in July."

COMMENTARY ON SAMPLE SUMMARY Notice that the summary is much shorter than the original article, using only six sentences to provide an overview of the article's nine paragraphs. The first sentence provides the main idea of the article—to describe the problems that occur when new interns join the staffs of U.S. hospitals on July first. The second, third, and fourth sentences give three of the main points Machlowitz provides to support her main idea. These points are given in the order in which they appear in "Never Get Sick in July." The fifth sentence indicates advice provided in the article's conclusion, and the sixth sentence sums up Machlowitz's main idea. This summary does not include any minor details. It uses primarily original words; where the author's words are quoted (in the final sentence), they are enclosed in quotation marks. The summary is objective. It includes only Machlowitz's ideas and opinions. If you were planning to write an evaluation of Machlowitz's article, making a summary like this one would assure you that you understood her main idea and would lead you to the next step in evaluating—identifying supporting points.

GUIDELINES: WRITING A SUMMARY

1. A summary is briefer than the material summarized.
2. A summary often begins with a sentence that gives the title, the author's name, and the main idea.
3. A summary usually follows the structure of the material being summarized. (It begins with the author's first point, progresses to the second, then the third, and so forth.)
4. A summary includes only major points, not minor details.
5. A summary uses primarily your own words, not the words of the author.
6. Any phrases or sentences taken directly from the work being summarized must be enclosed in quotation marks.
7. A summary is objective and, therefore, includes only what the author says, not your opinion, observations, or judgments.

EXERCISE 6 *Choose a selection from the anthology section of this book (pages 151–288) or an article from a magazine. Write a summary following the guidelines and using the example (page 48) as a model. (If you choose an article that is not in this book, your instructor may ask you to make a photocopy to accompany your summary.)*

Reading and Writing to Consider Supporting Points

After you have summarized to identify what you believe to be the author's main idea and major supporting points, it's important to reread the whole work carefully to be certain that the supporting points really do develop what you believe to be the main idea.

READING TO IDENTIFY THE PURPOSE OF SUPPORTING POINTS

In a brief essay like "Never Get Sick in July" each paragraph in the main body often introduces and develops one supporting point. Consider, for instance, paragraphs 4–7 in Machlowitz's essay.

Paragraph 4: Provides examples (and discusses causes and effects) of mistakes interns make in prescribing medications.
Paragraph 5: Provides illustrations of mistakes (and discusses causes and effects) interns make in diagnosing.
Paragraph 6: Provides reasons why interns are prone to make mistakes.
Paragraph 7: Explains that problems with interns can affect private patients as well as those who come to emergency rooms, yet also offers possible ways for potential patients to protect themselves.

In addition to

Providing examples and illustrations (Machlowitz, paragraphs 4 and 5)
Discussing causes and effects (Machlowitz, paragraphs 4 and 5)
Giving reasons (Machlowitz, paragraph 6)
Suggesting solutions (Machlowitz, paragraph 7)

paragraphs that provide supporting points may, among other things, do any of the following:

Tell a brief story
Give a description
Make comparisons
Provide a definition
Show how something (or things) may be divided into useful categories

As you read any work—essay, article, chapter in a book, or whole book—be aware of the importance of supporting information. If you believe you have identified an author's main idea but, as you read, none of the details—or few of the details—support that idea, then you are faced with a dilemma. Either you have misread, in which case you need to adjust what you see as the main idea, or the author has done a poor job of developing the main idea. If, after careful rereading, you decide that the latter is the case, you need to decide why the details do not support the main idea or why more details are needed to support the main idea adequately.

The process of evaluation begins when you take the following steps:

1. Read to determine the main idea
2. Reread to identify the supporting points
3. Think about why or whether those points do, in fact, clearly relate to and develop the main idea

EXERCISE 7 *Using the same article or essay you used for Exercise 6, identify the supporting points. As you consider each paragraph, identify its purpose. For example, does it provide examples or illustrations? Discuss causes and effects? Give reasons? Suggest solutions? Tell a brief story? Give a description? Make comparisons? Provide a definition? Or show how something (or things) may be divided into useful categories? After you have identified the purpose of the paragraph, explain whether you think the information provided in the paragraph clearly relates to the main idea you have identified. Explain why or why not.*

WRITING AN OUTLINE TO IDENTIFY SUPPORTING POINTS To discover supporting points, try outlining what you have read. Making an outline helps you to see how the author has developed the main idea and gives you a chance to begin evaluating how well those supporting points work.

Outlines may be written in either sentences or phrases. Outlines use a series of numbered and lettered headings to organize information. The following sample outline provides an overview of the supporting details in "Never Get Sick in July."

I. New interns begin work July 1
II. Mistakes often made by interns
    A. Errors in medications
    B. Errors in diagnosis
    C. Unnecessary tests ordered
III. Reasons for errors
    A. Interns overworked
    B. Interns not experienced

IV. Ways for patients to protect themselves
  A. Choose physician with a group practice
  B. Choose good teaching hospital
    1. Experienced nurses to supervise interns
    2. Experienced residents to supervise interns
    3. High-ability interns
  C. Avoid elective procedures in July

GUIDELINES: WRITING AN OUTLINE

1 An outline may use sentences or phrases.
2 An outline uses a series of numbered and lettered headings to organize information.
3 The headings look like this:
I First important idea
  A First point relating to I
    1 First point relating to A
    2 Second point relating to A
  B Second point relating to I
    1 First point relating to B
    2 Second point relating to B
II Second important idea
  A First point relating to II
    1 First point relating to A
    2 Second point relating to A
    3 Third point relating to A
4 The outline may have as many headings and subheadings as necessary.

EXERCISE 8 *Choose a selection from the anthology section of this book (pages 151–288) or an article from a magazine. Read the article and write a sentence or two explaining what you believe to be the author's main idea. Then, to identify supporting details, make an outline following the guidelines and using the example (page 50) as a model. Be prepared to explain whether you believe each supporting detail you have noted supports the main idea you have stated. (If you choose an article that is not in this book, your instructor may ask you to make a photocopy to accompany your summary.)*

IDENTIFYING ASPECTS TO EVALUATE AND CONSIDERING CRITERIA FOR EVALUATING

After finding the main idea and noting supporting points, you are ready to evaluate what you have read. Once you understand clearly what the writer has said, you can make judgments about his or her ideas and the way he or she presents those ideas. To make those judgments, you follow a process that has two interconnected parts. You must decide what aspects of the article, essay, or book you will judge, and you must consider the criteria you will use for making those judgments.

Evaluating the Use of Quotations

Sometimes when you think about what you have read, you find yourself responding strongly to certain points the author has made. For instance, as you considered Marilyn Machlowitz's "Never Get Sick in July," you might have wondered about the accuracy of the quotation in paragraph 3. By thinking about the quotation, you note an aspect to evaluate. To actually make the evaluation, you have to do one of two things: either you call on criteria you already have established or you develop criteria.

When a writer uses a quotation to support a point, you have every reason to expect that writer to cite his or her source and to show why the source should be considered an authority on the subject. "Citing the source" and "establishing the authority of the source," then, are two criteria that may be used to evaluate an author's use of quotations.

Another point to consider when evaluating a source is whether an author *argues for or against the point made by the source.* An author should make clear whether he or she agrees or disagrees with the source. If the author agrees with the source, the quotation should support the author's point. If the author disagrees with the source, the reasons for the disagreement should be clearly explained.

If you look back at Machlowitz's third paragraph, you will note that she does cite her source—Dr. Russell K. Laros, Jr.—and she lists credentials that indicate his expertise on medical matters. He is "professor and vice-chairman of obstetrics, gynecology, and reproductive sciences at the University of California, San Francisco." She definitely agrees with Laros and the quotation works effectively to support her own ideas.

GUIDELINES: EVALUATING THE USE OF QUOTATIONS

1. Read the quotation carefully to be certain you understand what it means.
2. Note the source of the quotation and evaluate whether that source is reliable and up-to-date.
3. Recognize that words and ideas in quotation marks come from the quoted source and not from the author who is using the quotation. The author may either agree or disagree with the quotation.
4. Note whether the author is using the quotation to *support* a point or to argue *against* the idea suggested by the quotation.
5. Note whether a quotation used as support does, in fact, provide positive evidence, as the author claims.
6. Note whether a quotation that the author argues against has been convincingly refuted.

Identifying Aspects to Evaluate and Establishing Criteria

Evaluating the use of quotations is one part of making judgments about what you have read. There are many other aspects to consider.

The following guidelines will help you both to identify aspects of an essay, article, or book to evaluate and to establish criteria by which to judge those aspects.

GUIDELINES: IDENTIFYING ASPECTS TO EVALUATE/ESTABLISHING CRITERIA FOR EVALUATING

1. Do the writer's reasons, details, examples, and illustrations adequately support and develop the main idea? If not, why not? Should some of the reasons, details, examples, or illustrations be omitted? Why? Can you think of additional reasons, details, examples, or illustrations that should have been included? Why?

2. Has the writer provided new ways of looking at an idea, individual, or circumstance or has the writer simply rehashed already-familiar points?
3. Does the writer offer solutions to a problem? If so, does the writer convince you that those solutions are workable? That they are the best possible solutions? Why or why not?
4. Does the writer analyze causes of an action, circumstance, or problem? If so, do the causes seem convincing? Are there other causes that are ignored or unfairly dismissed? Explain.
5. Does the writer provide definitions for important terms? If not, which terms need to be defined more clearly? Why?
6. Does the writer quote authorities as supporting evidence? If so, are the authorities and their qualifications clearly identified? Do their qualifications convince you that the evidence they give is reliable? Why or why not?
7. Does the writer use statistics as supporting evidence? If so, are there any reasons why those statistics should be challenged?
8. Does the writer use recent evidence or are sources outdated and, therefore, unconvincing?

Of course, when you evaluate, you will not answer every one of the questions suggested in these guidelines. The questions simply suggest ways of developing criteria for looking critically at what you read. To see how evaluation works, do the following exercise.

EXERCISE 9 *Read the following essay. Using approaches from Chapter 1 or from this chapter, predict the main idea and discover the supporting details. (When possible, use context clues to understand the meanings of unfamiliar words.) Write down the main idea; then write a brief (one-paragraph) summary. Next make an outline showing the primary supporting details. Then, using the guidelines, note what aspects of the following essay you might choose to evaluate; consider, also, the criteria you might use to evaluate those aspects.*

STUDENTS IN SHOCK

JOHN KELLMAYER

1 If you feel overwhelmed by your college experiences, you are not alone—many of today's college students are suffering from a form of shock. Going to college has always had its ups and downs, but today the "downs" of the college experience are more numerous and difficult, a fact that the schools are responding to with increased support services.

2 Lisa is a good example of a student in shock. She is an attractive, intelligent twenty-year-old college junior at a state university. Having been a straight-A student in high school and a member of the basketball and softball teams there, she remembers her high school days with fondness. Lisa was popular then and had a steady boyfriend for the last two years of school.

3 Now, only three years later, Lisa is miserable. She has changed her major four times already and is forced to hold down two part-time jobs in order to pay her tuition. She suffers from sleeping and eating disorders and believes she has no close friends. Sometimes she bursts out crying for no apparent reason. On more than one occasion, she has considered taking her own life.

4 Dan, too, suffers from student shock. He is nineteen and a freshman at a local community college. He began college as an accounting major but hated that field. So he switched to computer programming because he heard the job prospects were excellent in that area. Unfortunately, he discovered that he had little aptitude for programming and changed majors again, this time to psychology. He likes psychology but has heard horror stories about the difficulty of finding a job in that field without a graduate degree. Now he's considering switching majors again. To help pay for school, Dan works nights and weekends as a sales clerk at K-Mart. He doesn't get along with his boss, but since he needs the money, Dan feels he has no choice except to stay on the job. A few months ago, his girlfriend of a year and a half broke up with him.

5 Not surprisingly, Dan has started to suffer from depression and migraine headaches. He believes that in spite of all his hard work, he just isn't getting anywhere. He can't remember ever being this unhappy. A few times he considered talking to somebody in the college psychological counseling center. He rejected that idea, though, because he doesn't want people to think there's something wrong with him.

6 What is happening to Lisa and Dan happens to millions of college students each year. As a result, roughly one-quarter of the student population at any time will suffer from symptoms of depression. Of that group, almost half will experience depression intense enough to warrant professional help. At schools across the country, psychological counselors are booked up months in advance. Stress-related problems such as anxiety, migraine headaches, insomnia, anorexia, and bulimia are epidemic on college campuses.

7 Suicide rates and self-inflicted injuries among college students are higher now than at any other time in history. The suicide rate among college youth is fifty percent higher than among nonstudents of the same age. It is estimated that each year more than five hundred college students take their own lives.

8 College health officials believe that these reported problems represent only the tip of the iceberg. They fear that most students, like Lisa and Dan, suffer in silence.

9 There are three reasons today's college students are suffering more than in earlier generations. First is a weakening family support structure. The transition from high school to college has always been difficult, but in the past there was more family support to help get through it. Today, with divorce rates at a historical high and many parents experiencing their own psychological difficulties, the traditional family is not always available for guidance and support. And when students who do not find stability at home are bombarded with numerous new and stressful experiences, the results can be devastating.

10 Another problem college students face is financial pressure. In the last decade tuition costs have skyrocketed—up about sixty-six percent at public colleges and ninety percent at private schools. For students living away from home, costs range from five thousand dollars to as much as twelve thousand a year and more. And at the same time that tuition costs have been rising dramatically, there has been a cutback in federal aid to students. College loans are now much harder to obtain and are available only at near-market interest rates. Consequently, most college students must work at least part-time. And for some students, the pressure to do well in school while holding down a job is too much to handle.

11 A final cause of student shock is the large selection of majors available. Because of the magnitude and difficulty of choosing a major, college can prove a time of great indecision. Many students switch majors, some a number of times. As a result, it is becoming commonplace to take five or six years to get a degree. It can be

depressing to students not only to have taken courses that don't count towards a degree but also to be faced with the added tuition costs. In some cases these costs become so high that they force students to drop out of college.

12 While there is no magic cure-all for student shock, colleges have begun to recognize the problem and are trying in a number of ways to help students cope with the pressures they face. First of all, many colleges are upgrading their psychological counseling centers to handle the greater demand for services. Additional staff is being hired, and experts are doing research to learn more about the psychological problems of college students. Some schools even advertise these services in student newspapers and on campus radio stations. Also, upperclassmen are being trained as peer counselors. These peer counselors may be able to act as a first line of defense in the battle for students' well-being by spotting and helping to solve problems before they become too big for students to handle.

13 In addition, stress-management workshops have become common on college campuses. At these workshops, instructors teach students various techniques for dealing with stress, including biofeedback, meditation, and exercise.

14 Finally, many schools are improving their vocational counseling services. By giving students more relevant information about possible majors and career choices, colleges can lessen the anxiety and indecision often associated with choosing a major.

15 If you ever feel that you're "in shock," remember that your experience is not unique. Try to put things in perspective. Certainly, the end of a romance or failing an exam is not an event to look forward to. But realize that rejection and failure happen to everyone sooner or later. And don't be reluctant to talk to somebody about your problems. The useful services available on campus won't help you if you don't take advantage of them.

EXERCISE 10 *Compare your evaluation of "Students in Shock" as described in Exercise 9 to the sample evaluation that follows. Note that these observations are not the only possibilities. Your responses may be different. For instance, you may have written an outline using phrases rather than complete sentences or you may have expressed the main idea in a different way. The point here is not to find one perfect way to read and think about "Students in Shock," but rather to understand a process for reading, writing, and thinking to evaluate.*

SAMPLE: THE PROCESS OF READING TO EVALUATE

Finding the Main Idea

The second sentence in the first paragraph gives Kellmayer's main idea: Going to college causes more problems and difficulties for students today than it did in the past, and colleges are trying to take care of those problems by offering support services.

Summarizing

According to John Kellmayer, author of "Students in Shock," going to college causes more problems and difficulties for students today than it did in the past. As a result, many students become depressed or suffer from physical illnesses caused by stress. Today's students have to face three main difficulties not faced by earlier generations. One is weakening family ties, another is financial difficulty, and a third is the wide choice of majors. To help students with these problems, many colleges offer various forms of counseling and workshops to lessen stress.

Outlining Supporting Details

I. College students today encounter many stressful situations.
   A. Example: Lisa has to work two jobs to pay tuition and misses her high school life.
   B. Example: Dan has to work at a difficult job, just broke up with his girlfriend, and has trouble deciding on a major.
   C. Statistics show problem of student depression.
   D. Statistics show rising student suicide rate.

II. Today's students face situations not found years ago.
   A. Today, a weakening family structure provides less moral support.
   B. Today, financial pressures have increased.
   C. Today, number of choices for majors has increased.

III. Colleges provide new services to help students cope with stress.
   A. Colleges upgrade psychological counseling centers.
   B. Colleges train upperclassmen as peer counselors.
   C. Colleges offer stress management seminars.
   D. Colleges improve vocational counseling services.

Evaluating Supporting Details and Developing Criteria

When you want to evaluate supporting details, it's helpful to be able to sort them out into some kind of order.

GROUPING DETAILS Notice that in this sample outline, there are three groups of supporting details. Each group supports a separate part of the author's main idea. Look back at the main idea. Kellmayer's subject is college stress and he says three things about it. He claims (1) that college students today experience stress, (2) that their stress is worse than that experienced by students in the past, and (3) that colleges are addressing this problem.

Making the outline leads logically to sorting the supporting details into three groups that relate to the three parts of Kellmayer's main idea.

1 Evidence that today's college students have problems
2 Three reasons today's students suffer more than earlier generations
3 Ways colleges respond to these problems

ASKING QUESTIONS ABOUT SUPPORTING DETAILS This grouping process allows you to focus more clearly and to think about questions you might have. Imagine questions you would ask Kellmayer if you could talk to him in person. Starting with the first part of his essay, you might ask questions like this:

1 Lisa and Dan both seem to be young students. Are stress and depression also part of the lives of older students?
2 The situations described in Lisa's and Dan's lives don't really seem so terrible. Why are they reacting so strongly?
3 Where do the statistics come from? What is the source?
4 If the statistics are right about the suicide rate, what makes Kellmayer think the college pressures alone are what cause the suicides? Have other factors been considered?

As you move to the second part of the essay, questions like these might come to mind:

1 Have tests been done to show that students with "weakened family structure" react more negatively to stress than students with family support?

2 Do students really face more stress now concerning college costs than they did, for instance, during the Depression?
3 Have students in the past who had to hold part-time jobs generally reacted negatively? If not, why do those who have to hold part-time jobs today react this way?
4 Does a wide choice of majors really cause stress? More stress than when people's choices were severely limited?
5 How are today's students' future options shakier and more frightening than those of students who graduated or attended college during wartime and thus faced required military service or the required military service of those they loved immediately upon leaving?

As you read and thought about the final section, you may have wondered:

1 Are all these new services colleges provide really addressing students' problems?
2 Has anybody taken a survey of students to ask them what they need?
3 Has anybody considered alternatives? For example, instead of offering new services, might colleges look at what factors contribute stress to students' lives?
4 Have colleges asked students how administrators and faculty could help students deal with stress?

As you can see, these questions suggest both points to evaluate and criteria for making judgments to writing an evaluation.

MAKING INFERENCES Often a writer provides facts and observations and then expects the reader to make *inferences*, that is, to draw certain conclusions or arrive at certain points without having them actually stated. For instance, the questions (pages 60–61) about the supporting details in the essay "Students in Shock" suggest that Kellmayer implies more than he actually states. He never comes right out and says that going to college in the past was much less stressful than it is today, but when he says, "There are three reasons today's college students are suffering more than in earlier generations," you can *infer* that campus life was easier and more comfortable in some bygone golden era.

It's important to understand that inference provides a possible point for evaluation and for developing criteria to evaluate. For example, while it may be easy to accept Kellmayer's three reasons if you look only at today's world, it's hard to find them completely valid when you really think about the circumstances of college students during times like the Depression and World War II or the Vietnam era. (The *points to be evaluated* are Kellmayer's three reasons; the *criterion* used to evaluate them would be considering them in a broad, rather than a narrow, historical context.)

Thoughtful readers, then, look at the implications of what a writer says as well as what he or she actually states.

GUIDELINES: MAKING INFERENCES

1. First, identify the main idea and supporting details.
2. Next, look for what is suggested, although not actually stated, in these details.
3. Identify the author's tone (attitude toward the subject). Understanding the author's attitude often helps the reader to discover points that are implied rather than overtly stated.
4. Watch for hints or suggestions that might lead to a fuller understanding of an idea or point that is mentioned only briefly.

PLANNING AN EVALUATION

If you were to continue with Exercise 10, you might use the statement of main idea, the outline of supporting details, the points you identified for evaluation, and the criteria you developed to determine a focus for an evaluation.

Certainly you could not address all of the questions raised; you would have to decide what you considered most important and plan your evaluation to discuss that point or points. It's helpful to remember that an evaluation generally takes a clear stand. On the one hand, you might see problems with some of the writer's ideas or the presentation of those ideas, and to write an evaluation you would explain those problems. On the other hand, you might agree with most of the author's points. If you agree, you must expand upon the ideas, or explain why you agree in a way that does more than simply restate what the author has said.

Two pitfalls to consider when making an evaluation:

1. *Avoid taking the stance that you both agree and disagree with the author without clearly developing your viewpoint.*

(Of course most authors *will* present some points you disagree with and some that you agree with. But the focus of an evaluation should be firm and should not waver cautiously from one side to the other. A paper that jumps back and forth really does not make judgments; it sits on the fence of caution. Real evaluation requires taking some risks.)

2 *Avoid merely summarizing.*

(Of course, you'll need to sum up the author's main idea and mention the points you are critiquing, but beware of just repeating what has already been said. This is another evasive, fence-sitting strategy. Unfortunately, taking this approach avoids the whole purpose of evaluation, which is for you to explore and examine *your own ideas* in relationship to those you have read.)

WRITING TO EVALUATE

Keeping in mind the process, as well as the pitfalls, just described, Ron Lieberman, a forty-six-year-old Vietnam veteran who had retired from the army and returned to college, thought about the critique of "Students in Shock" he was planning to write for his English composition class.

Discovering a Focus for Evaluating

Ron looked at the list of questions he had made and decided that what he really wanted to challenge was Kellmayer's contention that today's college students face more difficult circumstances than did students in the past. Ron wrote the following journal entry, exploring his idea.

> Kellmayer says students today face more stress. Well, I don't think so—for example, in the sixties we had the draft. I was in college—didn't really care or know what for. Didn't study, too many parties to go to. We did a lot of parties—didn't want to think too much about the draft but everyone was afraid to flunk out because of Vietnam and the draft. Well, all the guys—of course the girls weren't drafted, but there was a lot of tears because of brothers, boyfriends, etc. I don't think money and family problems today are anything compared to thinking about going into a war (which the government back then called a "police action"). It's hard to feel very sorry for the students he described. Like the girl who has to work two jobs and keeps

changing her major. Lots of people work hard—the "major-changing" stuff is ridiculous. Same with the guy who also works and broke up with his girlfriend. He has problems with a major, too. None of this stuff seems really bad to me. Like in the Depression people had no money (more or less) and probably would be glad to have a bunch of majors to think about.

Ron was able to respond to the article by considering his own experiences as well as by thinking about what he knew of other historical periods (for instance, the Depression). He did not believe that stress is worse today than at any other time. As he began to plan to write a response, Ron looked closely at each of Kellmayer's supporting details and decided which ones he would consider. He decided to focus on two major issues: (1) Kellmayer's examples and (2) his comparisons with past circumstances.

Considering Audience and Tone

Since Ron knew his instructor would ask students to read their essays aloud, he thought about other students in the class. All but five of the students appeared to be under twenty-five, so Ron realized his essay would not be sympathetically received if he simply dismissed today's college pressures. Ron also noted that twelve of the eighteen students in the class were women. As he reread his journal entry, he realized that he was thinking primarily from a man's point of view and decided to think also about the woman's point of view as he planned and wrote his essay. Here's a list he made to think about women as students:

Years ago many colleges didn't accept women.
Many majors were not open to women.
Other majors did not welcome women.
Professions were then limited because of lack of proper education.
Was less scholarship money available? Check.

Making this list helped Ron to consider details that might be of particular interest and concern to the women who would be part of his audience.

Determining a Tentative Main Idea and Drafting an Introduction

After deciding on the specific points he wanted to evaluate and after thinking about his audience, Ron developed the following tentative main idea:

> In the essay "Student's in Shock," John Kellmayer's examples and comparisons do not show that today's student's are under more stress than students were in the past.

Ron then decided to draft an introduction. His instructor had given the following guidelines for the introduction of an evaluation:

GUIDELINES: DRAFTING AN INTRODUCTION FOR AN EVALUATION

1. Somewhere in your introduction (usually in your first paragraph) give the name of the article, the author's name, and a brief overview of the author's main point.
2. Indicate the specific points you will discuss.
3. Explain briefly the stand you are going to take.

Here's the introduction Ron drafted:

1 According to John Kellmayer, the author of "Students in Shock," todays college students experience more stress than students did in the past. He describes modern students experiences and suggests reasons for what he see's as todays increased stress. He really gets off the track by not thinking about so many students in past times. There are a lot of examples like the Depression and Vietnam.

2 Also, Kellmayer's examples are not convincing. Why should anybody feel sorry for Lisa or Dan that he talks about? Although, its true that working two jobs and going to school is hard.

3 Also, he doesn't make a strong comparison to show that conditions today are worse than those in the past. Again, I think about the Depression, Vietnam, and also there weren't as many rights for women.

As Ron read his introduction, he wasn't entirely happy with it. He had included his main idea, but it was spread out over paragraphs 2 and 3, which made the main idea not clearly focused. Also, he noticed right away that none of the three short introductory paragraphs was very well developed. He thought of combining the three paragraphs, but then there seemed to be too many ideas in one paragraph. Finally, he decided to continue writing and return to the introduction after he was further along.

While Ron was not entirely satisfied with his introduction, he saw that he had given some sense of his main idea. And he was pleased with the way paragraphs 2 and 3 showed a way to organize his writing. First, he would talk about Kellmayer's examples. Then he would talk about Kellmayer's comparisons with past circumstances. In each case, he would identify points to evaluate and then use the criteria he established to make judgments about those points.

Here's the paragraph Ron wrote to give his evaluation of Kellmayer's examples:

> Kellmayer describes the circumstances of two college students, Lisa and Dan. Lisa thinks sadly about her good times in high school and is exhausted from working two jobs. Dan has switched majors many times. He works a lot of hours. He has just broken up with his girlfriend. These are difficult circumstances. They do not seem nearly as stressful as many that are faced by other people. Some have serious family problems like divorce, illness, or death. And some of these people who have these problems are college students. Lisa and Dan may lead difficult lives, but they have choices. They could go to school part-time, for example, if they found their work schedules too stressful. Kellmayer makes them sound as if they are trapped. In fact they have more freedom than many people. It's hard to feel much pity for Lisa and Dan. They could change their own circumstances. Many other people are worse off than they are which also makes you feel unsympathetic.

In this paragraph, Ron briefly explains Kellmayer's examples and then evaluates them by giving his own examples that suggest Lisa and Dan are not very convincing as objects of pity.

Following the plan suggested by his introduction, Ron next moves to evaluate Kellmayer's claim that things are worse now than they were in the past.

> Today there may be more divorce and more discussion of family problems. Can we assume that acting on problems is necessarily a worse or more stressful situation than ignoring them? In the past, plenty of people experienced "psychological difficulties." They didn't always run out and get help the way people do now. Kellmayer assumes that the family of the past was always, or nearly always, available to give support to the college student. This is a giant generalization. Families in the past were often larger than they are today. This is one example that could challenge Kellmayers generalization. Parent's had to think about more children than they do now.

College costs have become outrageous. Does Kellmayer seriously think, however, that people today are in as bad financial shape as they were during the Depression? It's easy to think that only rich people went to school then. Thats not true, though. There were state schools long before the Depression. Of course, their costs were lower than they are now. Still the American success story of the starving, struggling student came at least in part from students in the 1930s.

These men and women often put themselves through school because finances were at their worst due to the Depression. Most of their parents couldn't afford to put them through. So these people certainly were working outside jobs and studying, too.

Its true that having more choices can raise more concerns. In general we think having more choices gives more freedom. Years ago women had the choice of very few professions. Today they can enter nearly all professions open to men. Most people think these additional choices are positive. Many women regarded life without choice as extremely stressful. Consider the life of a slave which was entirely without choice but was also without any freedom. The slave certainly faced more difficult circumstances than the modern college student. The slaves problem was lack of choice.

After writing the three introductory paragraphs and then developing a series of paragraphs that evaluated Kellmayer's examples and reasons, Ron ran out of time and put his draft away. He knew the paper still needed a conclusion as well as revision of the introduction. The next evening he took it out and read it over. In addition to the weak spots he'd already identified, Ron felt that his paper did not flow smoothly. As he read it aloud, he could hear that something was not quite right, but he couldn't identify the problem. Ron decided to take his paper to his campus Writing Center to get some help.

EXERCISE 11 *Before reading the section below on revising, reread and annotate Ron's essay with the suggestions you would make to him as he revises his paper. To help with this process, reread Guidelines: Identifying Aspects to Evaluate, pages 54–55.*

EXERCISE 12 *To develop possible revision strategies that Ron might use, try rewriting his introduction and drafting a conclusion to his paper.*

Planning to Revise

Ron arrived at the Writing Center with his draft-in-progress and the following list of questions:

1 Introduction—paragraphs too short? Combine? How?
2 Introduction—focus main idea more clearly? How? Where?
3 Paragraphs in main body of paper—don't sound right—don't flow together.
4 Some sentences sound funny. Can't seem to say what I mean.

The tutor at the Writing Center, Eleanor, quickly read Ron's draft and his questions. Here's a section of the transcript of the tape recording she and Ron made of their discussion:

ELEANOR You seem to think the opening paragraphs are too short.
RON Right—not developed—not enough . . . I don't know.
ELEANOR And you thought about combining them?
RON Yeah—I tried that, but . . . it's too long and complicated . . . and anyway . . . the main idea problem . . .
ELEANOR I think you have the right idea. Try combining, but also see if you can cut out some things that make the paragraph too long. Also, maybe try putting the main idea in one sentence . . . maybe . . . I think that might work.
RON Okay. So combining but also cutting . . . I see . . . okay.
ELEANOR And with the business about the sentences not sounding right . . . I'm jumping ahead here . . . but I think it's the same basic thing. Try combining and cutting. Put the sentences together where you can. Get rid of things you repeat.
RON I don't know how, though . . . if I did, I would have done it.
ELEANOR Okay, I'll show you in a few minutes . . . and we have a handout that may help . . . guidelines for combining sentences.
RON Okay. And the paragraphs in the main paper?
ELEANOR Actually, your paragraphs look okay to me . . . I think what you're seeing is a problem with connections. Maybe you could read your paper again, but look for how you get from one idea to the next. I mean from paragraph to paragraph . . . also, look . . . from sentence to sentence.
RON I see what you mean . . . especially where I talk about his examples then jump, here, to where I talk about his reasons.

Ron continued the discussion with Eleanor, then made a plan for his revision. He focused on providing better connections (sometimes called *transitions*) between sentences and between paragraphs. As part of this strategy, he worked on combining sentences to make his thoughts flow more smoothly and logically. After thinking about the introduction, Ron saw that he needed to be especially careful to focus clearly on his main idea. To work on transitions—including sentence combining—Ron used the following guidelines.

GUIDELINES: PROVIDING EFFECTIVE TRANSITIONS

1 Repeat a key word or phrase.

EXAMPLE

Three senior senators stated to the press their opposition to *tax increases.* The same *three senators* later voted to raise *taxes* on gasoline and cigarettes. Apparently, these *three senators* have an odd way of defining *"tax increases"!*

2 Use parallel structure (phrases or sentences that are organized in the same way).

EXAMPLE

On Monday morning, three senior senators stated to the press their opposition to tax increases. *On Monday afternoon,* the same three senators voted to raise taxes on gasoline and cigarettes. *On the following Tuesday,* constituents voted to defeat these three senators in their bids for reelection.

3 Use transitional expressions.

EXAMPLES

To show time relationships: next, after, before, following, first, second, during, in the past

To show cause or effect: therefore, because, thus, consequently, resulting in, causing, due to, as a result, hence

To show similarity or difference: in comparison, similarly, in like manner, on the contrary, on the other hand, nevertheless, but, yet, still

To add a point: and, also, in addition, further, besides, then

To conclude: thus, therefore, in short, in summary, in conclusion

4 Combine sentences (see strategies and examples in the guidelines immediately following).

GUIDELINES: COMBINING SENTENCES EFFECTIVELY

1 Sentences are combined for three primary reasons:

A To show the relationship between the sentences

EXAMPLE

Relationship unclear: The Black Death killed millions of people. Infected rats swarmed through Europe.

Relationship clear: Because infected rats swarmed through Europe, the Black Death killed millions of people.

or

The Black Death killed millions of people, and then infected rats swarmed through Europe.

B To eliminate unnecessary words

EXAMPLE

Wordy: Angola was first colonized by the Portuguese. They started the first colony there in the fifteenth century.

Concise: Angola was first colonized by the Portuguese in the fifteenth century.

C To eliminate a series of short, choppy sentences

EXAMPLE

Choppy: Octavio Paz is a writer. He is from Mexico. He won the Nobel Prize for Literature. That was in 1990.

Smooth: Octavio Paz, a Mexican writer, won the Nobel Prize for Literature in 1990.

2 There are many ways to combine sentences. Here are two possibilities:

A Combine two sentences by using a conjunction (a word like *and, but, or, nor,* or *so*).

EXAMPLE

Original sentences: The market continued to rise. Interest rates fell.

Combined sentence: The market continued to rise, but interest rates fell.

(*Note:* When you combine two complete sentences by using a conjunction [a word like *and, but, so, or, nor*] a comma is needed before the conjunction.)

B Combine two sentences by keeping one a complete sentence and using only a word or group of words from the other sentence.

EXAMPLE

Original sentences: The first Queen Elizabeth never married. She was known as the Virgin Queen.
Combined sentence: Known as the Virgin Queen, the first Queen Elizabeth never married.
Combined sentence: The first Queen Elizabeth, who was known as the Virgin Queen, never married.
(*Note:* Sentences can often be combined in several different ways.)

EXERCISE 13 *Using the guidelines for transitions (page 69) and for sentence combining (page 70), revise Ron's original paper. As you revise, consider the introduction you rewrote and the conclusion you drafted for Exercise 12. After you have completed your revision, make brief notes explaining the major changes you made. Then, if possible, compare your changes with those made by one or more of your classmates. Finally, compare your revisions with the revision below and with the evaluation of the revision that follows each paragraph.*

RON LIEBERMAN'S REVISED EVALUATION

According to John Kellmayer, the author of "Students in Shock," todays college students experience more stress than students did in the past. He describes modern students experiences and suggests reasons for what he see's as todays increased stress. His examples, however, are not always convincing, and he doesn't make a strong comparison to demonstrate that present conditions are worse than those in the past.

Comment *After a great deal of work, Ron cut most of paragraphs 2 and 3. He decided that he was giving too much detail for an introduction. By eliminating repetition and by keeping on track, he wrote a focused introduction. The final sentence in this paragraph makes his main idea clear and also indicates that, in the rest of the paper, he will be evaluating Kellmayer's examples and his comparison of present conditions with past conditions.*

Kellmayer describes the circumstances of two college students, Lisa and Dan. Lisa thinks sadly about her good times in high school and is exhausted from working two jobs. Dan has switched majors many times, works long hours, and has just broken up with his girlfriend. These are difficult circumstances; however, they do not seem nearly as stressful as many that are faced by other people. Some people, including many college students, have serious family problems like divorce, illness, or death. Lisa and Dan may lead difficult lives, but they have choices. For example, they could go to school part-time if they found their work schedules too stressful. Kellmayer makes them sound as if they are trapped, but, in fact, they have more freedom than many people. It's hard to feel much pity for Lisa and Dan when they could change their own circumstances and when many other people are worse off than they are.

Comment *In this paragraph, Ron saw many sentences that could be combined. As he combined sentences, he kept in mind that he needed to make clear the relationships between his ideas. He also worked at eliminating useless repetition.*

After Kellmayer finishes explaining the examples of Lisa and Dan, he discusses what he sees as three reasons why college is more stressful today than it was in the past. The three reasons he gives are these: (1) today's "weakening family support structure"; (2) rising college costs; (3) the large selection of majors. While all three of these circumstances do exist, it's difficult to see why they should make college life far more stressful than in the past.

Comment *Ron realized that his paper made a big jump from discussing examples to discussing the contrasts Kellmayer mentioned. Ron tried writing a transitional sentence, but it didn't work very well because he was leading into three paragraphs rather than into one single paragraph. Finally, he wrote this separate transitional paragraph. In this transitional paragraph, he made clear the three points he would be discussing in the rest of the paper.*

Note: The words that are taken directly from Kellmayer's article ("weakening family support structure") are enclosed in quotation marks. When you use someone else's words, be sure to put them in quotation marks.

Today there may be more divorce and more discussion of family problems, but can we assume that acting on problems is necessarily a worse or more stressful situation than ignoring them?

In the past, plenty of people experienced "psychological difficulties," but they were less apt to get help the way people do now. Kellmayer makes a giant generalization when he assumes that the family of the past was always, or nearly always, available to give support to the college student. For example, families in the past were often larger than they are today, so parent's had to think about more children than they do now.

Comment *In addition to combining sentences, Ron also made some changes in word choice. For example, he changed "run out and get help," which he thought sounded too informal, to "less apt to get help."*

Kellmayer believes that in addition to lacking family support, today's students are faced with more serious financial problems than ever before. No one can deny that college costs have become outrageous. Does Kellmayer seriously believe, however, that people today are in as bad financial shape as they were during the Depression? It's easy to think that only rich people went to school then, but thats not true. The American success story of the starving, struggling student came at least in part from students in the 1930s, who put themselves through school when finances were at their worst for most United States citizens.

Comment *Ron adds a transitional sentence at the beginning of the paragraph to make it connect more logically with the previous paragraph. In addition, he eliminates the sentence about state schools because it isn't really relevant to the point of the paragraph (poor students also worked their way through private colleges and universities). Finally, he deleted many repetitious words and phrases.*

Kellmayer's final reason for stress being greater today is that there are more majors today. Its true that having more choices can raise more concerns, but in general we think having more choices gives more freedom. For example, years ago women had the choice of very few professions. Today they can enter nearly all professions open to men. Most people think these additional choices are positive. Many women regarded life without choice as extremely stressful. To make an extreme comparison, consider the life of a slave which was entirely without choice but was also without any freedom. The slave certainly faced more difficult circumstances because of lack of choice than the modern college student does because of having a great deal of choice.

Comment *Again Ron adds an introductory transitional sentence as well as other transitional elements like "for example" (sentence 3), which make the ideas in the paragraph flow together more logically and smoothly.*

> Yes, todays students face stress, but Kellmayer does not provide a convincing case that they face more stress than students in the past. He seems to think that the good old days on campus were happy and carefree but he doesn't consider era's like the Depression or the periods when this country was at war and students knew they (or people they loved) were faced with military service. Perhaps what Kellmayer really needs to do is to study carefully college students of the past to find out what pressures they faced and what strategies they developed for coping with the stress. Those strategies, rather than more and more services, may be the answer for todays' college students.

Comment *Ron added this conclusion, which sums up the focus of his evaluation. In this paragraph, Ron briefly reviews Kellmayer's ideas as well as his own main objections to those ideas. In addition, Ron suggests an action Kellmayer might have taken to address the problem described.*

Proofreading and Editing

After completing his revision, Ron read through what he believed was his final draft. He noticed two problems:

1. He had no title.
2. He wasn't sure that he had used apostrophes correctly.

EXERCISE 14 *Suggest a title for Ron's evaluation. Your title should not simply repeat Kellmayer's but should instead reflect what Ron's essay says about Kellmayer's ideas. Remember that, in general, a title is a carefully thought-out phrase and not a complete sentence.*

EXERCISE 15 *After reading Editor's Focus 9 (Appendix B, Guide to Editing, pages 293–382), proofread Ron's evaluation and insert any apostrophes that have been omitted. In addition, delete any apostrophes that have been used incorrectly.*

EXERCISE 16 *Read the following article and use the strategies described in Section One and this section to identify and evaluate main and supporting ideas. Then write a short (250–500 words) evaluation. Remember to focus on only two or three points; you cannot effectively address all of Landers's ideas in a short evaluation.*

As you work, consider the guidelines on page 84.

EXERCISE 17 *After writing your evaluation, reread Landers's article and plan another evaluation. This time take an approach that is entirely different from the one you took in your essay. In other words, if you found points of agreement, you should now look for points of disagreement. The purpose of this exercise is twofold: (1) to emphasize that there is seldom only one "correct" way to evaluate any piece of writing and (2) to encourage thinking in many different directions as you read and plan writing.*

WHAT DO CHILDREN OWE THEIR PARENTS?

ANN LANDERS

1 "What is your mother doing these days?" I asked a friend who recently returned from a visit with her family in New York. "Mother is very busy doing what she does best," was the reply. "She's the East Coast distributor for guilt."

2 I often hear this sentiment expressed by young marrieds, who are irritated and resent their invisible burden. There's a tremendous amount of guilt around these days, and many of the victims don't know if it is being laid on them by self-centered, punitive parents—or if they really *are* rotten kids.

3 What *do* children owe their parents, anyway? Not just married children, but *all* children—from six years of age to 66. No one can speak for everyone, but since this question has been raised by many people groping for answers, I shall try to respond.

4 First, let's start with teenagers. Here are the basics: You owe your parents consideration, loyalty, and respect. The Biblical injunction "Honor thy father and thy mother" is simple and clear. "But what if they are drunks and abusive and failures, not only as parents but as human beings? Are we still supposed to 'honor' them? Do we still owe them consideration, loyalty, and respect?" This question is often put to me. "Yes," is my answer. Honor them because they gave you life. Give them consideration and loyalty for the same reason.

5 *Consideration* is a word that needs no definition, but loyalty as it relates to the family is sometimes vague. What does it mean? It means hanging in there when things go wrong. It means keeping

family matters inside the family. The child who speaks ill of his parents and runs them down to outsiders says more about himself than he says about them.

6 Respect is difficult to bestow when it hasn't been earned—and sad to say, some parents have not earned it. If you feel your parents have not earned your respect, try to find it in your heart to substitute understanding and compassion. Granted, this is a great deal to ask of a teenager, but if you can do it, it will help you grow as a person. Look beyond the brittle façade and you'll see people who are bitterly ashamed of their inability to measure up. They're insecure and shaky—struggling with unresolved problems stemming from their childhood. To fail as a parent is extremely painful. They suffer a lot. But most parents are not drunks; nor are they abusive. They are plain, ordinary people with good intentions and feet of clay—trying desperately to survive in a dangerous, untidy world. They are out there every day, on the front lines, battling inflation, obesity, chronic fatigue, obsolescence, and crabgrass.

7 Nearly 48% of the work force in America today is female. This means great numbers of mothers are wearing two hats, or three. They're working at part-time (or full-time) jobs, trying to run a house, raise children, and participate in community activities. What do children owe parents who fit this description? Here are the fundamentals. They owe them prompt and honest answers to the following questions:

- Where are you going?
- Who are your companions?
- How do you plan to get there?
- When will you be home?

8 Teenagers frequently write to complain that their parents want to pick their friends. Do they have a right to do this? The answer is, "No." I never fail to point out, however, that when parents are critical of a teenager's friends, they usually have a good reason. Bad company can be bad news. But in the final analysis, the choice of friends should be up to the individual. If he or she makes poor selections, he or she will have to pay for it.

9 Parents have the right to expect their children to pick up after themselves and perform simple household chores. For example, every member of the family over six years of age should clean the bathtub and the sink so it will be in respectable condition for the next person. He or she should also run errands and help in the

kitchen if asked—in other words, carry a share of the load without feeling persecuted. The days of "hired help" are, for the most part, gone. And this is good. Boys as well as girls should be taught to cook and clean, do laundry, and sew on buttons. This is not "sissy stuff." It makes for independence and self-reliance.

10 What do teenagers and college students owe their parents in terms of time and attention? There's no pat answer. Some parents are extremely demanding; others are loose hangers. Some children can't wait to move out of the house; others must be pushed out. A college student shouldn't be expected to write home every day, but certainly a postcard once a week isn't asking too much if parents wish this. A phone call (collect, of course) on Sunday should not be impossible to manage if parents want it. What about vacations? Do children owe it to their parents to come home, rather than go to Fort Lauderdale or to a ski resort? Yes, they do, if the parents want them home and are footing the bills for education and transportation.

11 What do working children who live at home owe their parents in terms of financial compensation? The following letter is typical of what I read at least two dozen times a week:

> DEAR ANN LANDERS:
> Our daughter is 26 years old. She chose business school over college and is now number-one secretary to the president of a large firm. We are pleased that Terry still lives with us and doesn't want an apartment of her own, but I feel we are being taken advantage of.
>
> Terry has no savings account. She buys expensive clothes, has her own car, vacations in Europe, and doesn't give us one cent for room and board. She pays the telephone bill, because the long-distance calls are hers. I do her laundry, clean her room, fix her breakfast every morning, and dinner whenever she wants it.
>
> Our home is paid for and Terry knows we are not hard up for money, but it would be awfully nice to have a little extra coming in. My husband says not to 'rock the boat' or she might move. What do you say? If you believe she should pay—how much? Thanks for your help, Ann.
>
> *A Pittsburgh Mom*

I replied,

> DEAR MOM:
> Terry should give you 20% of her paycheck. If she thinks she can get lodging, breakfast, laundry, and maid-service elsewhere for less—let her try it.

> The fact that you are not hard up for money is no excuse for your daughter's selfishness. Share this letter with your husband; and I hope together you will muster up the courage to talk to Terry promptly.

12 When sons and daughters marry, things change considerably. Even though parents have a tendency to forever think of their children as "children," they should be granted a totally different status when they establish a family unit of their own. Should Mom be forever and always the No. 1 woman in Sonny's life? Not at all. A loving mother willingly relinquishes that place to her daughter-in-law. She remembers how *she* felt about *her* husband's mother when *she* married. By the same token, a kind and thoughtful daughter-in-law will be considerate of her husband's mother so she will not feel displaced. Life's cycles have an ironic way of evening up the score. The woman who finds herself with a mother-in-law problem might do well to think ahead a few years when *her* son will marry and *she* will become the mother-in-law.

13 Getting down to specifics, what do married children owe their parents in terms of time and attention? According to my readers, this is a major problem among marrieds in their 30's and 40's. Here are some questions from this week's mailing:

From Lubbock, Tex.:

> My mother telephones me at least four times a day. She wants to know if the children ate a good breakfast, who wore what at a party last night, what am I fixing for supper, has my husband's boss said anything about a raise . . . ?

From Nashville, Tenn.:

> My husband's mother asks me every two weeks if I am pregnant yet. She keeps reminding me that I'm not getting any younger and she would give anything to have a grandchild. The woman is getting on my nerves.

From Richmond, Va.:

> My husband's parents are in their mid-70's. He spends at least five hours every Saturday driving them to the supermarket, the dentist, the doctor, the pharmacy, the optometrist, the greenhouse, the dry cleaners, and so on. My in-laws have two daughters who live in town, but they never bother them—my husband is the one they run ragged. Does he owe them this kind of service?

From San Diego, Calif.:

> My mother is 64, a widow, attractive, and well-read. When we have guests for an evening, she's hurt if she isn't included. I love her dearly, but Mom has strong opinions and I have the feeling our friends resent her. Am I obligated to include her because she is my mother?

14 There are no rules to cover every situation, but here are suggestions that can be tailored to fit a great many:

- Countless people are also victims of friends who have black-cord fever—also known as telephonitis. The best protection against these types is to develop a technique for getting off the phone after a reasonable period of time. The victim should have prepared sentences handy and read them when the need arises. Sample: "Sorry, dear. I have a million things to do this morning and I must hang up now. We'll talk again soon."
- People have no right to complain about being trapped or taken advantage of if they don't have the gumption to assert themselves. I tell them repeatedly, "No one can exploit you without your permission." This includes refusing to answer "nun-uvyer-bizniz" type questions. Sample comeback: "Now why in the world would *you* be interested in *that?*"
- No woman owes her in-laws grandchildren. Any person who pressures a woman to "give us a grandchild" should be put in her place.
- Running errands and chauffeuring aged parents can be time- and energy-consuming, but it may be essential when no alternatives exist. If there are other children (or nieces and nephews) who might help out, they certainly should be asked to do so. Where time is more valuable than money, a paid driver may relieve a lot of tension.
- Including parents in social activities is not essential, and parents should not expect it. No excuses are necessary.

15 Perhaps the most anxiety-producing problem is one that hits in the late 40's or early 50's—about the same time some adults are going through the mid-life crisis: what to do with Mama when Papa dies. Or, if Mama goes first, what should be done with Papa? Circumstances alter cases. Some mamas wouldn't live with their children on a bet. The same goes for some papas. Many factors

should be considered at the outset first—how would Grandma or Grandpa fit in with the family? Is she or he too bossy? Would there be trouble in the kitchen? Would the children feel that too many people are telling them what to do? Finances are another major consideration. Does the surviving parent have sufficient money to maintain his or her own place? The issue of health is also important. Is Mama or Papa well enough to live alone? The answers to these questions should be carefully reviewed before a decision.

16 Strictly from a standpoint of morality and decency, do you owe your parents a place in your home if he or she would like to move in? I say, "No." If they need housing or care, it goes without saying you should provide it, but you do not owe them a place under your roof if it would create dissension and conflict in your family. The ideal solution is to keep the surviving parent in his or her own home if it is economically feasible. When money is a problem, all the children should ante up and share the cost. (Often this is easier said than done.) Endless family fights have resulted because brother George or sister Mabel say they can't help out with the old folks because they have kids in college. Yet they go to Florida or Arizona every winter, belong to the country club, and drive new cars.

17 The most serious crisis arises when Mama or Papa becomes ill or too old to take care of themselves. Nursing homes are expensive, and many old people don't want to go there. What then? Some heroic women have taken in a parent or an in-law (or both) at tremendous personal sacrifice. This can be the most physically exhausting and emotionally draining job in the world, since old folks tend to be senile, incontinent, ill-tempered, and in need of constant watching. I implore daughters and daughters-in-law not to feel guilty if they are unable to do it. The woman who does make this sacrifice, in my opinion, deserves a place at God's right hand, come reckoning time.

18 In the final analysis, none of us goes through life debt-free. We all owe something to somebody. But the most noble motivation for giving is not prompted by a sense of duty—it flows freely from unselfish love.

from Ann Landers, "What Do Children Owe Their Parents?" *Family Circle*, 1978.

EXERCISE 18 *Read the following two essays that evaluate Landers's article. Note that one agrees with Landers and one disagrees. As you read, annotate each essay. Which essay do you find most convincing? Most similar to your own views? How would you respond to the points made by the students who wrote these evaluations?*

SAMPLE EVALUATIONS

ESSAY I

CONSIDERATION, LOYALTY, AND RESPECT: EARNED OR DESERVED?

PAULINE BUDNI

1 In her article "What Do Children Owe Their Parents?" Ann Landers says to teenagers, "Here are the basics: You owe your parents consideration, loyalty, and respect." She goes on to claim that even if parents are "drunks and abusive" they still deserve these three responses from their children. While I understand the honorable principles behind this advice, I question whether Landers has thought out all the implications.

2 Landers says that "*consideration* is a word that needs no definition." I think it does. To me, *consideration* doesn't mean just politely listening to what another person says or does. It also means thinking carefully about the person's words or actions and then acting on the conclusions you have drawn.

3 I would agree that teenagers should listen to their parents and should really try to understand what their mothers or fathers are saying. After listening in this way, the child must then make at least some decisions on his or her own. For example, if a parent expresses violently prejudiced views and refuses to allow a child to be friends with a person of another race, the child must listen. Then, however, after careful *consideration,* the child should make a decision based on his or her own standards. This decision may be different from what the parents want.

4 Next, think about Landers's claim that teenagers must respect their parents. She does admit that if teenagers cannot respect a behavior, they may instead substitute "understanding and compassion." This asks a great deal from a teenager, and, in some cases, the understanding and compassion can actually be harmful to the parent. For example, look at Landers's own example of the alcoholic. Many alcohol programs say that families of alcoholics should stop giving unlimited "understanding and compassion" and

instead let alcoholics experience the effects of their disease. Many alcoholics cannot admit they need help until they are no longer being supported by "understanding" families.

5 Finally, I wonder whether Landers really thinks a child who is being physically, sexually, or severely verbally abused should stay loyal to the abusing parent. This is a point I feel very strongly about. Abused teenagers who continue to remain loyal can put their lives (both physical and emotional) in jeopardy.

6 As a parent of teenagers, I am sympathetic with much of what Landers has to say. I do think my daughters "owe me" polite responses to questions about where they are going and who they are going with. I do think they "owe me" cooperation in keeping our household running. But I do not think they—or any children—automatically owe consideration, respect, and loyalty no matter what their circumstances. Young people should be encouraged to be open to their parents but also to love and value themselves. Teenagers must be helped to discover the difference between normal family conflict and hurtful or dangerous situations that they have every right to rebel against.

ESSAY II

WHAT ABOUT LOVE?

JOSEPH WYNN

1 In her article, "What Do Children Owe Their Parents?" Ann Landers states that teenagers owe their parents consideration, loyalty, and respect. I agree with Landers, but she does not carry her ideas far enough or explain them fully. Instead of explaining her points on teenagers, she goes on quickly to talk about what adult children owe their parents. This article should be revised to make more specific recommendations.

2 For instance, Landers suggests that consideration and loyalty mean being there even when times are difficult. In addition, she stresses the importance of "keeping family matters inside the family." This seems a negative approach. It is an approach that looks only at the unhappy times that might make family members unhappy or even ashamed.

3 Consideration is also important when times are good. Teenagers should not think they can just rally around when there's a disaster.

They should also be an active part, for example, of family celebrations. Mom shouldn't have to plan every birthday (especially her own), and Dad shouldn't always be the one to make the arrangements for family outings. Teens should be willing to participate in these ways.

4 In addition to consideration and loyalty, Landers says that teens owe their parents respect. Again she stresses mostly negative examples. She points out the problems parents face and the pain of failing as parents. She seems more concerned with what family members are doing wrong than with what they are doing right.

5 Instead of focusing almost entirely on the problems of being a parent, she should point out that nearly every parent has many successes and makes many positive contributions. I believe this is true even of many alcoholic parents. Landers should point out to teens how much time, money, and physical and emotional energy nearly all parents spend on their children.

6 Teens should keep a list of "things my parents did for me this week." The list might include such things as "cooking my meals," "doing my laundry," "giving me my lunch money" in addition to the more obvious things like "driving me to soccer practice" or "helping me with my algebra homework." A list like this would really surprise most teenagers, and they would probably be willing to give the respect Landers asks for.

7 What Landers leaves out of her essay entirely is a fourth emotion teens owe their parents. They owe their parents love. This is a serious omission because love is absolutely essential. It may seem hard to love some of the abusive parents Landers describes, but certainly no harder than to give them consideration, loyalty, and respect. Nearly all of the world's religions teach people that they should love one another. If people should even try to love their enemies, how can they not make the effort to love their parents? And if teens love their parents, consideration, loyalty, and respect would come naturally.

EXERCISE 19 *Keeping the example of Ron Lieberman's process in mind (pages 63–74) and referring also to the two sample evaluations of "What Do Children Owe Their Parents?" choose either a selection from the anthology section of this book (pages 151–288) or an article from a newspaper or magazine. Write an evaluation of the selection you choose. You may find the guidelines on the following page helpful.*

GUIDELINES: WRITING AN EVALUATION

1 After careful reading, notetaking, thinking, and planning, begin the rough draft of your essay by writing an opening paragraph that briefly summarizes the article, emphasizing the points to which you will respond.

2 In the opening paragraph, make clear what approach you are taking. Are you focusing primarily on negative or positive aspects of what you read?

3 In the opening paragraph, be sure to mention the title and author of the work you are evaluating.

4 In the main body of your evaluation, discuss your reactions to the author's points. Remember to follow the guide you set up in your opening paragraph. You cannot discuss every single point. Concentrate on two or three.

5 Use a separate and well-developed paragraph (or set of paragraphs) to discuss each of the points you've chosen to evaluate.

6 Make sure you have provided transitions (connections) between your ideas as you move from sentence to sentence and, especially, from paragraph to paragraph. Your readers need to know how your ideas are related to one another to form a whole.

7 If you use any of the author's phrases or sentences, make sure to enclose them in quotation marks.

8 After you have explained your evaluations of the author's main points, write a concluding paragraph that follows logically from what you have said. You should do more than summarize. For example, you might offer an alternative view, provide a possible solution to a problem, or analyze the significance of what you discovered as you wrote.

9 If possible, put the draft away for several days.

10 Finally, follow the steps for revision and proofreading suggested in Section One (pages 24–26) and the revision guidelines in Appendix A.

READING AND WRITING TO COMPARE

This chapter demonstrates the importance of seeing differences and similarities, that is, making comparisons and contrasts. Attention is focused on the following issues related to reading and writing to compare.

- *Discovering comparisons and contrasts when you read*
- *Identifying purposes for comparing or contrasting*
- *Understanding the structure of comparison*
- *Writing a comparison*
- *Reading and writing to compare sources*
- *Discussing as a way to discover ideas*
- *Planning a writing conference to aid revision*
- *Revising introductions*
- *Revising organization*
- *Revising conclusions*

A FILM COMEDY, *WORKING GIRL,* tells the modern Cinderella story of a secretary, Tess, who outwits her ruthless boss—a wealthy, Harvard-educated woman—and wins herself a place on the corporate ladder to success. While the film's plot unrolls a standard Hollywood cliché, Tess's method deserves consideration. She has earned a degree in business by going to evening school, and she wisely applies the theory she learned to what she observes in everyday life. While Tess's boss sticks strictly to procedures taught in her courses, Tess makes connections between what her textbooks and professors said and what she reads in the newspaper and sees in the outside world. In the end, her ability to compare—to see similarities and differences—makes her the winner.

While Tess's fairy-tale success story is light-years away from the real world, one part of it is true. Educators agree that those who gain the most from their schooling learn to see relationships and to understand their significance. Education, then, is not a series of separately boxed courses or unrelated disciplines. And, of course, education is not strictly confined to the classroom. Each course you take has elements that relate to other courses and to your professional and personal life. Conversely, the activities of your professional and personal life contribute as much to your education as do your textbooks and your professors' lectures.

Whenever you are learning something—whether it be formally in school, on the job, at home, or in a recreational setting—be alert to comparisons and contrasts. Ask yourself how what you are observing, reading, hearing, or thinking might relate to something else you already have stored in your memory.

This chapter focuses on ways to find and explore similarities and differences. Keep in mind that identifying relationships—seeing what is the same or different—is only the first step. The comparison process requires answering the question "So what?" In other words, when you see similarities and differences between, for example, the economic causes of the Revolutionary War and the economic causes of the Civil War, what insights does that give you about American military history? Just making two lists labeled "same" and "different" does not qualify as true comparison. It's important to work hard to see the significance of the relationships you have identified.

EXERCISE 1 *Consider similarities and differences between things you learn in your classes and things you observe or experience outside the academic world. For instance, if you are taking a sociology course, notice incidents in newspapers, on television, or in your daily life that reflect (or contradict) the principles of human group behavior you are studying.*

After thinking about these connections, make a list of the comparisons and contrasts you noticed. Then brainstorm or write a journal entry about one relationship that particularly interested you. Try to note what you think is intriguing or significant about the similarities and differences you have described.

DISCOVERING COMPARISONS AND CONTRASTS WHEN YOU READ

When you read an article or section of a book that makes comparisons, of course you use the same skills as when you read to respond or to evaluate. You want to identify the author's main idea and then to discover what details, reasons, and examples are provided to support that idea. In addition, however, you need to be aware of specific strategies that are useful for identifying and evaluating comparisons.

Identifying Purposes for Comparing or Contrasting

Comparisons are written for many reasons. Identifying the author's purpose will help you predict the main idea. Consider, for instance, the following possibilities:

1 *To suggest new ways of looking at objects or ideas that seem nearly identical by exploring their differences.*

(For example, read the following paragraph from John McPhee's essay "Oranges." While all oranges may seem similar, he emphasizes their distinctions by describing the contrasts between Florida and California oranges. Note that McPhee is *not* saying that *either* orange is superior; he is simply suggesting how they differ.)

An orange grown in Florida usually has a thin and tightly fitting skin, and it is also heavy with juice. Californians say that if you want to eat a Florida orange you have to get into a bathtub first. California oranges are light in weight and have thick skins that break easily and come off in hunks. The flesh inside is marvelously sweet, and the segments almost separate themselves. In Florida, it is said that you can run over a California orange with a ten-ton truck and not even wet the pavement.

from John McPhee, *Oranges.*

2 *To suggest that one idea, object, or way of thinking is superior to another by emphasizing the differences between the two.*

(Consider, for instance, the following paragraph from Suzanne Britt Jordan's essay "That Lean and Hungry Look." Using humorous images, Jordan describes the differences she sees between fat and thin people, and in addition, lets readers know which type of person she prefers.)

The main problem with thin people is they oppress. Their good intentions, bony torsos, tight ships, neat corners, cerebral machinations, and pat solutions loom like dark clouds over the loose, comfortable, spread-out, soft world of the fat. Long after fat people have removed their coats and shoes and put their feet up on the coffee table, thin people are still sitting on the edge of the sofa, looking neat as a pin, discussing rutabagas. Fat people are heavily into fits of laughter, slapping their thighs and whooping it up, while thin people are still politely waiting for the punch line.

from Suzanne Britt Jordan, "That Lean and Hungry Look," *Newsweek,* 1978.

3 *To show that a commonly accepted way of thinking about an idea, person, event, or concept should be challenged with other possibilities.*

(For instance, Edward T. Hall, a professor of anthropology, uses comparison and contrast to suggest that the way Americans think about the concepts of "social and personal space" is not as universal as we might assume. This paragraph concludes Hall's evaluation of problems between two roommates, one American and one British.)

It took some time, but finally we were able to identify most of the contrasting features of the American and British problems that were in conflict in this case. When the American wants to be alone he goes into a room and shuts the door—he depends on architectural features for screening. For an American to refuse to talk to someone else present in the room, to give them the "silent treatment," is the ultimate form of rejection and a sure sign of great displeasure. The English, on the other hand, lacking rooms of their own since childhood, never developed the practice of using space as a refuge from others. They have in effect internalized a set of barriers, which they erect and which others are supposed to recognize. Therefore the more an

Englishman shuts himself off when he is with an American the more likely the American is to break in to assure himself that all is well. Tension lasts until the two get to know each other. The important point is that the spatial and architectural needs of each are not the same at all.

from Edward T. Hall, *The Hidden Dimension,* ch. XI.

4 *To show that two objects, people, ideas, concepts, or places that seem very different do, in fact, have significant similarities. This kind of comparison is called an* ***analogy****. (In the paragraph that follows, Robert Jastrow introduces an essay that explains how computers work by comparing them to human brains.)*

Circuits, wires and computing are strange terms to use for a biological organ like the brain, made largely of water, and without electronic parts. Nonetheless, they are accurate terms because brains work in very much the same ways as computers. Brains think; computers add and subtract; but both devices seem to work on the basis of the same fundamental steps in logical reasoning.

from Robert Jastrow, *The Enchanted Loom.*

Understanding the Structure of Comparison

As you read a comparison, you also need to pay attention to how the author organizes the information.

One way to organize a comparison can be called the "subject by subject" method. In this method, the writer first discusses subject A and gives all the points concerning that subject. Then the writer discusses subject B and gives all the points concerning that subject. (Edward T. Hall's paragraph on the British and American roommates uses this pattern.)

Another way to organize a comparison can be called the "point by point" method. In this method, the writer considers one point (example, detail, reason) and talks about subject A and subject B in relation to that point. The writer then goes on to the next point and talks about subject A and subject B in relation to that point. (The last two sentences of the paragraph by Suzanne Britt Jordan demonstrate this approach.)

To see how these patterns would look for a longer piece of writing, consider this outline for an essay that compares the reasons a student chose one college rather than another. If the writer uses the "subject by subject" method, the outline for that essay might look like this:

I. Introduction
II. College A
  A. Cost
  B. Location
  C. Majors offered
III. College B
  A. Cost
  B. Location
  C. Majors offered
IV. Conclusion

If the writer were using the "point by point" approach, the outline might look like this:

I. Introduction
II. Cost
  A. College A
  B. College B
III. Location
  A. College A
  B. College B
IV. Majors offered
  A. College A
  B. College B
V. Conclusion

There are many variations of these two basic organizational strategies, but understanding these two patterns provides an approach for reading material that compares and also for planning to write your own essays evaluating similarities and differences.

GUIDELINES: READING AND RESPONDING TO MATERIAL THAT COMPARES

1 After skimming the material, write a statement predicting the author's main idea.
2 Note whether the author stresses similarities or differences.
3 Note why the author makes the comparison.
4 Make lists of details and evidence. The way you organize your lists will depend on the way the writer has or-

ganized the subject (for example, the "subject by subject" or the "point by point" method).

5 Sort your lists into groups, if possible, to make the comparisons and contrasts clearer in your mind.
6 Consider your lists, as well as any other notes you have made. Then read the author's conclusion carefully, noticing what point he or she makes. In other words, how does the author answer the question, "So what?" (Perhaps the author suggests an alternative view, offers a solution to a problem, or predicts a future effect.)
7 Consider your own response to and evaluation of the comparison and contrast described by the author. For example, do you agree with the author? If so, try listing additional reasons to support that point of view. If not, make a list of your points of disagreement.
8 Write a paragraph explaining your own answer to "So what?" based on what you have read. Use the lists described in points 4 and 7 to focus your response.

EXERCISE 2 *Read any of the comparison/contrast paragraphs on pages 87–89. Annotate and take notes as you read. Then write a journal entry or response paragraph explaining your reactions to the observations and evaluations made by the authors. For example, do you agree with what you have read? Do the authors' points make you think of any examples of your own to compare or contrast with their ideas? As you do this exercise, you may want to consult the guidelines for reading and responding to material that compares (pages 90–91).*

EXERCISE 3 *As you read (either for classes or outside of school) and as you listen to the radio or watch television for the next few days, watch for comparisons made by authors, newscasters, talk show hosts, or others. Then choose one or two comparisons that particularly intrigue you.*

First write a brief paragraph summarizing the comparison and then explain why you found the comparison interesting (or strange, maddening, puzzling, enlightening, and so forth). As you do this exercise, you may want to consult the guidelines for reading and responding to material that compares (pages 90–91).

READING TO COMPARE

The following excerpt from an economics textbook compares and contrasts the benefits and drawbacks of lotteries run by state governments. Try reading the excerpt as if you were preparing to write a take-home essay exam that asked you to discuss the two sides of the state-run lottery controversy and to explain your own evaluation of the controversy. Such an exam question would clearly require discovering and thinking about similarities and differences.

As you read the excerpt, use the approaches to reading explained in the first two sections and in the guidelines on page 90. Be sure to interact with the text in writing. For example, after you have skimmed the essay, write several predicting questions. As you read, make notes in the margins. When you finish reading, write a list of significant points, a journal entry, a summary, or an outline or try brainstorming about a point or points to which you had a strong response.

LOTTERIES: FACTS AND CONTROVERSIES

1 In 1987 some 28 states and the District of Columbia had lotteries which sold over $12 billion worth of tickets. The average lottery returns about 50 percent of its gross revenues to ticket purchasers as prizes and 40 percent goes to the state treasury. The remaining 10 percent is for designing and promoting the lottery and for commissions to retail outlets which sell tickets. Although states sponsoring lotteries currently obtain only 1 to 2 percent of their total revenues in this way, per capita sales of lottery tickets increased by 14 percent per year over the 1975–1985 period. Lotteries have been quite controversial.

2 Critics make the following arguments. First, the 40 percent of gross revenues from lotteries which goes to the state governments is, in effect, a 40 percent tax on ticket purchasers. This tax is higher than the taxes on cigarettes and liquor. Furthermore, research indicates that the "lottery tax" is highly regressive in that there is little relationship between ticket purchases and household incomes. The 5 percent of the adults who patronize lotteries most heavily account for about one-half of total ticket sales; on average, these heavy bettors spend about $1200 per year on tickets. Second,

critics argue that it is ethically wrong for the state to sponsor gambling. Gambling is generally regarded as immoral and, in other forms, is illegal in most states. It is also held that lotteries may whet the appetite for gambling and generate compulsive gamblers who will impoverish themselves and their families to the end that they become wards of the state.

3 But there are counterarguments. It is contended, in the first place, that lottery revenue should not be regarded as a tax. Tax collections are compulsory and involve coercion; the purchase of a lottery ticket is voluntary and entails free consumer choice. A second and related argument is that within wide limits it is not appropriate to make moral judgments about how people should spend their incomes. Individuals achieve the maximum satisfaction from their incomes by spending without interference. If some people derive satisfaction from participating in lotteries, they should be free to do so. Finally, lotteries are competitive with illegal gambling and thereby may be socially beneficial in curtailing the power of organized crime.

4 Two observations seem quite certain at the moment. One is that total lottery revenue will continue to increase. Why? Because more and more states are establishing lotteries and people seem to enjoy gambling, particularly when they feel their losses are being used for "good causes." The other point is that this source of revenue will remain controversial.

from Campbell R. McConnell and Stanley L. Brue, *Macroeconomics.*

Understanding Reading Through Discussion

After reading, annotating, taking notes, and writing a journal entry in response to "Lotteries: Facts and Controversies," one of the best ways to evaluate those initial responses is to discuss with others the writing and thinking you have done.

While group discussions follow many different paths, the most productive usually take place when members of the group arrive ready to begin work. Group members should understand the purpose of the discussion. The purpose may be set by an instructor, for example, to discover possible topics for a paper or to gather evidence for a debate. Or the purpose may be set by the group, for example, to prepare for an exam. Group members should arrive for discussion prepared with reading, annotating, notetaking, and writing predictions completed. If there will be time limits, set either by the professor or by the group, all members should be aware of these limits before the discussion begins. The group should plan the order and priority of discussion topics with the time limit in mind.

While group discussion can be extremely productive, it's also easy to get off track, so group members should work to keep themselves and each other on task. Of course, creative explorations should not be stifled, but irrelevant personal conversations can distract the group from its purpose.

Finally, group members should remember that discussions do not always lead to consensus. In fact, seeing multiple possibilities and learning that more than one approach to a problem exist are among the rewards of group work.

SAMPLE DISCUSSION After reading "Lotteries: Facts and Controversies" and responding in writing, one group of students compared their notes, predicting questions, summaries, and outlines. As they discussed, they kept in mind their goal: to prepare for writing a take-home essay exam. As you read the following excerpts from the taped transcript of their discussion, note how their awareness of thinking comparatively helped them to focus their discussion as they gathered additional notes and explored their responses to what they read.

KAREN So, what do you think the point is here? What's important?

JOSHUA OK . . . the main idea . . . which I put down from the first paragraph . . . "Lotteries have been quite controversial" . . . the main idea sounds like people think there's problems with the lottery . . . or some people think . . .

KAMAHL To me, there's *some* problems . . . "controversial" is not *all* problems . . . "controversial" . . . I think . . . is like both pro and con. So it goes into two sections, like lists, which I put down: "Lotteries-Bad" . . . and the other is "Lotteries-Good" . . . but here's "Lotteries-Bad":

1 Forty percent gross revenues from lotteries are really a tax.
2 Forty percent is higher than any other tax.
3 No relationship between amount of income and playing lottery.
4 Only about 5 percent of the population play the lotteries heavily.
5 Heavy bettor spends average of $1200 per year on lotteries.
6 Gambling is immoral and should not be encouraged by state.
7 Most other gambling is illegal, so why should lottery be legal?
8 Lotteries may encourage compulsive gambling.

ELENA OK, so do we agree with the list of "Gambling-Bad"?

KAREN Let me look at the list, Kamahl. (*Reads*) The first ones—number one through five—I think they all go together. Because in the book it says . . . after the thing about spending $1200 . . . it says, "Second, critics argue. . . ." So if it's "Second" there, then everything before is, like, first. Right?

KAMAHL OK. And then, there's no "third" here, so everything else—the stuff about immorality and compulsive gambling—all that goes together, too?

ELENA Right, so it's just two main things . . . I'd say maybe "excessive taxation" and "moral wrongness" . . . well, "wrongness" isn't the word, but, you know . . .

JOSHUA Maybe "excessive taxation"? . . . and "immoral action"?

OTHER THREE (*Voices together*) Good. Right. Okay.

ELENA So, two main points against states running lotteries. Then the other stuff goes under those points, like evidence . . . examples . . . whatever.

KAMAHL So now you want my other list?

JOSHUA "Lotteries-Good." Do it.

KAMAHL OK, there's probably categories . . . but I just have it all together here . . . "Lotteries-Good":

1 Lotteries not a tax.
2 You're not forced to play the lottery.
3 Morals are up to individual people.
4 The state can't decide what's moral.
5 If people enjoy playing the lottery, they should be able to.
6 Lotteries compete with illegal gambling.
7 They help fight organized crime.

KAREN So are there two categories, like with the "Lotteries-Bad" list?

ELENA No, because look. The paragraph that starts "But there are counterarguments . . ." you have "in the first place," then "a second and related argument," and . . . here . . . "finally."

KAREN But "finally" . . . why is that third? Sounds like a summary.

KAMAHL No, look at it. It's really a whole different thing. About organized crime.

ELENA So we have three main groups here. For "Lotteries-Good," what about "Voluntary purchase, not unfair tax" . . . second, "Individuals, not state, determine morality" . . . then . . . "Fight organized crime."

KAREN OK. I see that the organized crime stuff is listed as a new reason. It's definitely not a summary. But I still think if we're putting this together to look at the comparisons we can get two categories to match . . . somewhat . . . the "Lotteries-Bad" categories. Because I think, really, it's two basic giant issues. One is the "unfair tax or voluntary purchase" issue. And the second is the "morality" issue. Because the organized crime thing seems to me to fit under "morality."

KAMAHL OK. I see that. It's not exactly . . . what you would say . . . equal to the first list, but you could have the categories made up that way so that you would have two main areas to compare under "Lotteries-Good" and "Lotteries-Bad." You would have one section—which Karen says—"unfair tax vs. voluntary purchase" and the second section "immoral vs. moral."

KAREN OK, good, so we're running out of time here so maybe we better get to the big "So what?" question. After we have the lists—the two categories and then the reasons, details . . . whatever . . . that go with the categories—what does that mean?

ELENA Well, in the book, to me it ends with no decision. I mean, basically the conclusion is just: one, the states will get more and more money from the lottery, and two, some people will argue against lotteries and some for lotteries. So it seems to me like the book just says what we already have—which is "lotteries-bad vs. lotteries-good."

JOSHUA Absolutely, I agree with Elena. I was waiting for something about whether it's moral or what. I mean I have an uncle who spends, say, probably, $50 a month on lottery tickets. One time he won $400. So big deal because he's spent about . . . who knows . . . like more than $4000 buying tickets.

KAREN OK, so maybe we want to think about something more than the conclusion here. I mean, to me, the important "so what" in the book . . . and it's like a conclusion . . . you can see they get it from some of the numbers in the first paragraph . . . is that total lottery revenue will rise.

JOSHUA OK. I agree. I can see that. It's important . . . more and more people are spending more and more money. Because, basically, a lottery ticket stays the same price.

KAMAHL But even if more people are playing the lottery, is that wrong? I think a lot of people have a little fun. Not spending a lot like Josh's uncle. People abuse everything—like drinking too much. But some people—a lot of people—just like to drink a little, and a lot of people just like to buy a lottery ticket to have a little dream—"What if I won . . . ? What if I had a million?" Hey, so nobody here ever bought a ticket?

KAREN OK, so we all have our experiences. And Josh looks at the whole morality thing one way and, Kamahl, you look at it another way. But what does that have to do with planning this essay for the economics exam? Do your own personal experiences come into it? For me, I don't think the professor wants to hear "My aunt (or my uncle) this or that. . . ."

KAMAHL Right. Anyway, for me the "unfair taxation" is much more important. It's really a tax on the poor—the lottery. You can tell from the statistics.

KAREN OK, so, we don't all really agree on the "So what." But we have the lists and the groups we made. Which seems like a good start.

EVALUATING THE SAMPLE DISCUSSION The sample discussion is provided to demonstrate a way of carefully reading and thinking about an essay or a section of a book that explores similarities and differences. Of course, you may not always have the chance to discuss what you read with others, but evaluating what happened as Kamahl, Elena, Josh, and Karen worked together suggests strategies that can be helpful even when you are reading alone. (Note: Most of the strategies can be used with any reading assignment, whether or not the authors are making a comparison.)

1 *The group kept in mind their purpose for reading.*

They were gathering information for writing an essay exam so they took notes that would best enable them to plan an answer to the professor's possible question regarding the contrasts in opinions on state-operated lotteries.

2 *The group followed a chronological plan.*

First, they identified the authors' main idea, then they moved through the essay section by section, and finally they evaluated the conclusion.

3 *Group members were not afraid to question one another's ideas or to take a suggestion that was made by one person and modify it.*

Whether you evaluate your reading on your own or with others, you should always remain alert to questions. It's tempting to accept the first response that comes to your mind as being "good enough," but creating a critical voice or a number of critical voices that challenge that first response will help you think more perceptively.

4 *Group members sometimes got off the track and discussed issues that did not become part of the information they later agreed was important.*

Note, for example, Josh's observations about his uncle. Being able to make personal connections with what you read usually makes it more meaningful and interesting. You should not hesitate to explore all possible paths in your early responses to something you've read. Who knows which direction may prove to be most useful? On the other hand, you should be willing, as the group here demonstrates, to discard or put aside information that doesn't fit with your goal.

5 *Group members worked to organize the information they discovered using what they knew about comparison and contrast to formulate the structure.*

Notice the lists, the groupings of items on the lists, and—especially—the way these students regroup the arguments for state-run lotteries so that those categories will compare more effectively with the arguments against state-run lotteries.

6 *Group members spent time trying to discover the authors' answer to "So what?" as well as their own answer to that question.*

They recognized the importance of going beyond listing and sorting evidence; they saw the need to make connections.

7 *Group members often referred to their own notes to clarify a point or make a connection clear.*

Note, for instance, Kamahl's references to his lists.

8 *When a point was unclear, someone in the group often looked back at the text.*

Rereading is an extremely important learning strategy. It's easy to forget what you've read or to remember an idea only vaguely. Going back to check the information, and perhaps to reinterpret it in the light of new evidence you may have found in the meantime, helps you to think clearly about what the text says.

9 *When group members read the text, they looked for "verbal markers" to help them understand and organize the comparisons in their minds.*

For instance, Elena calls attention to the paragraph that starts "But there are counterarguments . . ." and notes that the authors suggest three distinct points by their use of the transitional phrases "in the first place," "a second and related argument," and "finally."

GUIDELINES: GROUP DISCUSSIONS

1 Group members should understand the purpose of the discussion.
2 Group members should arrive for discussion prepared.
3 Group members should be aware of the time limits within which they must work.

4 Group members should work to keep one another on task.
5 Group members should remember that group discussions do not always lead to consensus. Seeing multiple possibilities and learning that more than one approach to a problem exist are among the rewards of group work.

FROM READING, THINKING, AND DISCUSSING TO WRITING

After finishing the discussion, Elena, Josh, Kamahl, and Karen felt reasonably well prepared to write the take-home exam. Their professor's question told them to look for significant connections, for similarities and differences, as they were reading. In addition, everyone in the group knew that the professor's topic asked them to explain the points of the controversy and then to answer the question "So what?"

Kamahl and Elena planned and wrote the following answers. Note that Kamahl used the "whole subject" method of organizing his essay while Elena used the "point by point" approach. Both students also kept in mind guidelines for writing a comparison/contrast essay (pages 121–122).

Sample Essays: Comparison and Contrast

KAMAHL'S EXAM ESSAY

1 Government officials as well as common citizens hold different opinions about whether or not states should run lotteries. Both those who think states should run lotteries and those who think states should not run lotteries look at the issue from two points of view. One view sees the lottery as a tax issue; the other as a moral issue.

2 Those who think the states should not run a lottery have two main arguments. The first is that the lottery is really an unfair form of taxation. Since 40% of the gross revenues from lotteries go to the state which is much more than from any other tax and since only a small percentage of people play the lottery, opponents argue that the lottery is really an excessive tax. The second main argument has to do with morality. Some opponents object to the state encouraging an activity which, in most of its other forms, is illegal. These people point out that gambling can be an illness, just like alcoholism is an illness. They say the state should not support an activity which can lead to families living in poverty because the main wage-earner gambles all the income away.

3 On the other hand, there are also government officials and citizens who think that state-run lotteries are perfectly fine. They answer the charge of "unfair" taxation with the response that lotteries cannot be compared to taxes because they are voluntary. A person doesn't have to buy a lottery ticket, although that same person would be forced, for example, to pay a state income tax or sales tax. Concerning the charge of immorality, the supporters of state-run lotteries say that it's not up to the state to decide what's moral; the individual should decide on morality. Supporters also point out that lotteries may, in fact, help fight organized crime because they fight illegal gambling.

4 Those who argue against state-run lotteries seem to have the approach that the state should be acting as some sort of parent to the citizen. They seem to think that the state should protect the people against their own desire. Most people know that they have very little chance to win the lottery, but they buy tickets just to have the pleasure of imagining what might happen. Why should the state protect them against their dreams? People need to accept responsibility for their own actions. Since the state can profit and lottery players are not forced to buy their tickets, the arguments for state-run lotteries seem strongest to me.

ELENA'S EXAM ESSAY

1 State-run lotteries bring up two important questions: (1) Are state-run lotteries an excessive form of taxation? (2) Are state-run lotteries immoral? The answers to these questions divide people

into two groups, those who support state-run lotteries and those who oppose them.

2 First is the question of taxation. The lottery's purpose is to generate income for the state so, although it is not called a tax, it really acts like taxes do. If it is considered a tax, it is certainly excessive since 40% of the gross revenue from lotteries goes to the state. This is a much higher percentage than any other tax. Furthermore only a very small percentage of the population are heavy bettors (spending more than $1,000 a year on lotteries). Most important, according to those who oppose state-run lotteries, there is no relationship between the amount of income of an individual and the amount that person spends on the lottery (and therefore gives a percentage to the state). A relatively poor person who spends a great deal on the lottery is therefore, in a way, "taxed" far more heavily in terms of percentage of income than a wealthy person who spends the same amount on the lottery. On the other hand, as those who support state-run lotteries point out, there is a good argument for not considering the lottery a tax. Lottery playing is voluntary whereas tax paying is required by law. If the lottery is looked at as an act of choice, then the arguments concerning unfair taxation do not apply.

3 The question of unfair taxation vs. voluntary act is certainly significant, but the moral issues raised by state-run lotteries are equally important. Those who oppose state-run lotteries point out that gambling is an immoral act and therefore should not be encouraged by the state. They point out that most other gambling is illegal so it is inconsistent for the state to support this one particular form of betting. Further, opponents believe that legal lottery playing may encourage compulsive bettors who cannot control their desire to gamble. On the other hand, those who support state-run lotteries argue that morality should (within reasonable limits) be determined by the individual, not by the state. Supporters believe that as long as people enjoy buying megabucks tickets the state may as well profit. They see this kind of betting as a form of entertainment, not an action that should be viewed as immoral. In addition, supporters point out that since lotteries compete with illegal gambling they may even help fight organized crime.

4 Supporters of state-supported gambling seem overly optimistic. The argument that playing the lottery is voluntary and that lottery profits are therefore not taxes fails to take into consideration those who are forced to bear the cost of someone else's gambling. The spouse and children of compulsive gamblers are often the biggest losers. This leads to the question of morality. Should the state

control the morals of its citizens? The answer is obvious: The state already does. For instance, in many states a person cannot buy liquor on Sunday. Those laws have to do with the state's determination that it is "not right" to buy alcohol on a day traditionally set aside for religious worship. If the state can make decisions about when someone can buy alcohol, it can certainly make decisions about whether or not someone should gamble. And, in fact, in the cases of most gambling activities the state does say "No." Since the state forbids most gambling because of its moral implications, it seems highly inconsistent for the same state to run its own lottery—not to mention the advertising campaigns designed to encourage more and more people to become bettors.

EXERCISE 4 *Using the guidelines in Appendix C, pages 384–385 (Writing the Essay Exam) and the guidelines for writing a comparison/contrast essay (pages 121–122), evaluate the exam responses written by Kamahl and Elena. In what ways are they the same? How do they differ? Does one response seem stronger than the other? Do they both seem equally strong? Why? What changes, if any, would you suggest?*

EXERCISE 5 *Read the following selection, "Clothing and Fashion," from* Nation of Nations, *an American history textbook, as though you were reading it for a course in American history. Follow the reading strategies described in Sections One and Two, as well as the specific strategies described in this section for reading to compare. Be sure to write in response to what you read (marginal notes, lists, journal entries, brainstorming).*

CLOTHING AND FASHION

"BARBARIC" DRESS—INDIAN AND EUROPEAN

1 It was remarkable to sixteenth-century Europeans how many things seemed to be missing from Indian culture. Even more remarkable, the Indians themselves did not seem to notice. Michel de Montaigne, a French philosopher who had never been to America but liked to talk with explorers and read their accounts, managed to compile quite a list. According to Montaigne, Indians had "no kind of traffic [trade], no knowledge of letters, no intelligence of numbers, no name of magistrate, nor of politics, no use of service [servants], of riches, or of poverty, no contracts, no successions, no partitions, no occupation but idle, no apparel but natural. . . ." When other Europeans, with and without experience in America, made similar lists, they never failed to mention that last crucial item missing in Indian culture—clothing. Even European men and women who could not read and who never traveled beyond their villages associated America's inhabitants with nakedness, for woodcuts, engravings, and paintings showed native peoples either entirely nude or clad in the skimpiest of loincloths or grass skirts.

2 Europeans interpreted the simplicity of Indian dress in two different ways. Some saw the lack of clothing—like their supposed lack of commerce, law, government, and religion—as evidence of "barbarism." Andre Thevet, a shocked French visitor to Brazil in 1557, voiced this point of view when he attributed nakedness to native lasciviousness. If the Indians could weave hammocks, he sniffed, why not shirts? But other Europeans esteemed unashamed nakedness as the Indians' badge of innocence. As remnants of a bygone "golden age," they believed, Indians needed clothing no more than government, laws, regular employment, or other corruptions of civilization. Jean de Lery, another French traveler to Brazil, remarked that the elaborate clothes and jewels worn by Parisian women were "without comparison a source of greater evils than the ordinary nudity of the savage women who in their natural state are not a whit less beautiful."

3 In fact, Indians were no more "naked" than they were without trade, politics, employment, or religion. While the simplest tribes of the Caribbean and Brazil wore little, the members of more advanced Indian cultures in Central and North America covered themselves with animal pelts sewn into mantles and robes, breechclouts, leggings, and moccasins. They wrought bird feathers into headdresses and ear decorations and fashioned reptile skins into belts and pouches. Even more formidably clad were the Eskimos of the far North, who dressed head to foot in sealskin suits with waterproofed seams, turning the furry side inward for warmth in the winter and outward in the summer.

4 By the late sixteenth century, Europeans, and especially the English, were paying more heed to what the Indians wore, hoping to assure prospective colonists that the natives would not affront European standards of modesty. Captain John Smith, for example, left detailed descriptions of the attire of Virginia's tribes, noting in a telling comparison that "the better sort use large mantels of deare skins not much differing in fashion from the Irish mantels." Even more reassuringly, Smith added, "The women are alwaies covered about their midles with a skin and very shamefust [modest] to be seen bare." Later accounts of Indian dress also advertised the riches of America. In a narrative of his voyage to

Roanoke in 1584, Arthur Barlowe remarked that the wife of a local Indian leader sported a fur-lined cloak, a band of white coral about her forehead, and long pendant pearl earrings "of the bigness of good pease."

5 If natives struck whites as starkly underdressed, Europeans seemed, by the Indians' standards, grotesquely overdressed. Indeed, European fashion was ill-suited to the environment between the Chesapeake and the Caribbean. Elizabethan gentlemen strutted in silk stockings attached with garters to padded, puffed knee breeches, topped by long-sleeved shirts and tight quilted jackets called "doublets." Men of lesser status wore coarse woolen hose, canvas breeches, shirts, and fitted vests known as "jerkins"; when at work, they donned aprons of dressed leather. Women wore gowns with long, full skirts, low-cut bodices, aprons, and hosiery held up by garters. Ladies went in silk and wore hoods and mantles to ward off the sun, while the rest dressed in flannels or canvas and covered their heads with linen caps or coifs. Both sexes favored long hair, and men sported mustaches and beards. Such fashions complicated life in the American environment, especially since heavy clothing and even shoes rotted rapidly from sweat and humidity. The pungent aroma of Europeans also compounded the discomfort of natives who came in contact with them. For despite sweltering heat, the whites who swaddled themselves in woolens and brocades also disdained regular bathing and regarded Indian devotion to daily washing as another uncivilized oddity.

6 It would have been natural for Indians to wonder why the barbaric newcomers did not adapt their dress to a new setting. The answer may be that for Europeans—entering an alien environment inhabited by peoples whom they identified as "naked savages"—the psychological risk of shedding familiar apparel was simply too great. However inappropriate or even unhealthy, heavy, elaborate dress afforded the comfort of familiarity and distinguished "civilized" newcomer from "savage" native in America.

from James West Davidson et al., *Nation of Nations.*

EXERCISE 6 *After reading "Clothing and Fashion," discuss your notes and observations with a small group of classmates. Assume that you are preparing the material for an essay exam in an American history course. Before you begin this exercise, reread the sample discussion on pages 94–97 as well as Guidelines: Group Discussions (page 98). During the discussion, make notes that you think would be helpful in preparing to write an essay exam.*

EXERCISE 7 *Using the notes gathered in Exercise 6, write a brief essay in response to the following exam topic.*

Compare and contrast the attitudes of Native Americans (Indians) and European settlers toward each other as suggested by their responses to each other's clothing. As part of your conclusion, consider why understanding these differences might be important today.

READING AND WRITING ABOUT TWO OR MORE WORKS ON THE SAME TOPIC

Sometimes when you read one essay or one section in a textbook, you discover that the writer's purpose is to point out similarities and differences between two topics he or she is discussing. More often, however, both in the academic and professional worlds, you will read various authors writing on a single topic that interests you (or that you must explore for a class or work assignment). In that case, you apply the strategies suggested for reading for comparison (pages 90–91), but you recognize that you are looking for significant contrasts or similarities *among different sources* rather than *within one source.*

Reading to Compare Sources

When you are reading different sources, the points discussed do not always match as neatly as they do when you are reading a single source that compares (for instance, the discussion of state lotteries, pages 92–93, or the commentary on Native American and European dress customs in the American colonial period, pages 102–104).

If your purpose in reading different sources is to make a comparison, you have to establish the points you want to examine based on the information you gain from the works you read. Sometimes one work will entirely ignore a particular point that is stressed by another work in which the author takes a different approach to the topic. You'll have to decide whether, in your paper, you also want to ignore that point or whether, instead, you want to note its omission and comment on the discrepancy. You may want to ask, for instance, why one writer chose to include that point and the other writer chose to ignore it.

For many students, reading different writers' views on the same subject presents a dilemma. Often one "expert" on a subject will hold entirely different views from another "expert" on the same subject. When this happens, you might ask, "Well, who is right?" The answer *may* be that one expert is right and the other wrong, but it's more likely that there is no single easy answer.

Becoming educated requires learning to tolerate ambiguity, that is, learning that there are few absolute "answers"—and no easy "answers"—to the complex questions we face in today's rapidly changing world. Even scientific principles and math theorems thought to be "truth" as recently as the late nineteenth century and the earlier twentieth century are constantly being challenged and modified today. For instance, if you went to school twenty years ago, you learned that Pluto was the farthest planet from the sun. Now, because of the elliptical orbits of Neptune and Pluto, Neptune enjoys that distinction. So right now, it is no longer a "fact" that Pluto is the farthest planet from our sun—although in a few years it will once again occupy that position.

So, as you make comparisons among the opinions of many experts, remember that you will find discrepancies. These contrasts make the topics addressed thought-provoking and should lead you to ask probing questions about what you are reading. Sometimes you will read two contrasting views and then seek the opinions of others (in reading, in conversations, in class discussions, in lectures) to evaluate the differences you have discovered. Sometimes you will simply note the differences and, in that case, the "So what?" toward which you progress may simply be an elaboration of the questions raised by—yet not satisfactorily answered by—the two opposing views you have read. Yet another possibility would be noting a surprising similarity. For instance, you might read articles by two writers whose politics are known to be opposed. Yet on one particular issue, these two writers might agree. Their unexpected agreement constitutes a comparison worthy of exploration.

GUIDELINES: READING AND COMPARING MORE THAN ONE SOURCE ON THE SAME TOPIC

1. Read each source, noting the main idea, supporting details, and conclusion.
2. Be aware that the points discussed by each source may not match exactly. (For example, one source may omit entirely a point discussed at length by another source.)
3. Note which points of similarity (comparison) you find significant.
4. Note which points of difference (contrast) you find significant.
5. Be aware that experts often disagree; part of your task

in making a comparison is to evaluate the reasons for such disagreement.

6 Consider your own conclusion, based on consideration of your sources' ideas and your evaluation of those ideas.

EXERCISE 8 *To develop your skill at reading two views of the same subject, read the following two essays on gun control that first appeared in* Time *magazine in January 1990. First read one essay, using the strategies described in the first two chapters; then read the second essay, using the same strategies. As you read the second essay, you will find that you are beginning to make comparisons.*

Next, reread the first essay, this time working consciously to develop categories and lists of similarities and differences.

After considering these comparisons, plan a paper explaining what you have discovered. Consider questions such as these: Will you emphasize the similarities or the differences between these two articles? Why? What categories can you develop to organize the points you plan to discuss in your comparison? How will you introduce the comparison so that the reader understands what your focus will be? How will you conclude your essay? (What is your answer to the reader's "So what?" What significance do you find in comparing Sarah Brady's views with J. Warren Cassidy's views?) As you read, use the guidelines on pages 106–107.

THE CASE FOR FIREARMS . . .

THE N.R.A.'S EXECUTIVE VICE PRESIDENT SAYS GUNS WILL KEEP AMERICA FREE

J. WARREN CASSIDY

1 The American people have a right "to keep and bear arms." This right is protected by the Second Amendment to the Constitution, just as the right to publish editorial comment in this magazine is protected by the First Amendment. Americans remain committed to the constitutional right to free speech even when their most

powerful oracles have, at times, abused the First Amendment's inherent powers. Obviously the American people believe no democracy can survive without a free voice.

2 In the same light, the authors of the Bill of Rights knew that a democratic republic has a right—indeed, a need—to keep and bear arms. Millions of American citizens just as adamantly believe the Second Amendment is crucial to the maintenance of the democratic process. Many express this belief through membership in the National Rifle Association of America.

3 Our cause is neither trendy nor fashionable, but a basic American belief that spans generations. The N.R.A.'s strength has never originated in Washington but instead has reached outward and upward from Biloxi, Albuquerque, Concord, Tampa, Topeka—from every point on the compass and from communities large and small. Those who fail to grasp this widespread commitment will never understand the depth of political and philosophical dedication symbolized by the letters N.R.A.

4 Scholars who have devoted careers to the study of the Second Amendment agree in principle that the right to keep and bear arms is fundamental to our concept of democracy. No high-court decision has yet found grounds to challenge this basic freedom. Yet some who oppose this freedom want to waive the constitutionality of the "gun control" question for the sake of their particular—and sometimes peculiar—brand of social reform.

5 In doing so they seem ready, even eager, to disregard a constitutional right exercised by at least 70 million Americans who own firearms. Contrary to current antigun evangelism, these gun owners are not bad people. They are hardworking, law abiding, tax paying. They are safe, sane and courteous in their use of guns. They have never been, nor will they ever be, a threat to law-and-order.

6 History repeatedly warns us that human character cannot be scrubbed free of its defects through vain attempts to regulate inanimate objects such as guns. What has worked in the past, and what we see working now, are tough, N.R.A.-supported measures that punish the incorrigible minority who place themselves outside the law.

7 As a result of such measures, violent crimes with firearms, like assault and robbery, have stabilized or are actually declining. We see proof that levels of firearm ownership cannot be associated with levels of criminal violence, except for their deterrent value. On the other hand, tough laws designed to incarcerate violent offenders offer something gun control cannot: swift, sure justice meted out with no accompanying erosion of individual liberty.

8 Violent crime continues to rise in cities like New York and Washington even after severe firearm-control statutes were rushed into place. Criminals, understandably, have illegal ways of obtaining guns. Antigun laws—the waiting periods, background checks, handgun bans, et al.—only harass those who obey them. Why should an honest citizen be deprived of a firearm for sport or self-defense when, for a gangster, obtaining a gun is just a matter of showing up on the right street corner with enough money?

9 Antigun opinion steadfastly ignores these realities known to rank-and-file police officers—men and women who face crime firsthand, not police administrators who face mayors and editors. These law-enforcement professionals tell us that expecting firearm restrictions to act as crime-prevention measures is wishful thinking. They point out that proposed gun laws would not have stopped heinous crimes committed by the likes of John Hinckley Jr., Patrick Purdy, Laurie Dann or mentally disturbed, usually addicted killers. How can such crimes be used as examples of what gun control could prevent?

10 There are better ways to advance our society than to excuse criminal behavior. The N.R.A. initiated the first hunter-safety program, which has trained millions of young hunters. We are the shooting sports' leading safety organization, with more than 26,000 certified instructors training 750,000 students and trainees last year alone. Through 1989 there were 9,818 N.R.A.-certified law-enforcement instructors teaching marksmanship to thousands of peace officers.

11 Frankly, we would rather keep investing N.R.A. resources in such worthwhile efforts instead of spending our time and members' money debunking the failed and flawed promises of gun prohibitionists.

12 If you agree, I invite you to join the N.R.A.

. . . AND THE CASE AGAINST THEM

THE HEAD OF HANDGUN CONTROL SAYS WEAPONS ARE KILLING THE FUTURE

SARAH BRADY

1 As America enters the next decade, it does so with an appalling legacy of gun violence. The 1980s were tragic years that saw nearly

a quarter of a million Americans die from handguns—four times as many as were killed in the Viet Nam War. We began the decade by witnessing yet another President, Ronald Reagan, become a victim of a would-be assassin's bullet. That day my husband Jim, his press secretary, also became a statistic in America's handgun war.

2 Gun violence is an epidemic in this country. In too many cities, the news each night reports another death by a gun. As dealers push out in search of new addicts, Smalltown, U.S.A., is introduced to the mindless gun violence fostered by the drug trade.

3 And we are killing our future. Every day a child in this country loses his or her life to a handgun. Hundreds more are permanently injured, often because a careless adult left within easy reach a loaded handgun purchased for self-defense.

4 Despite the carnage, America stands poised to face an even greater escalation of bloodshed. The growing popularity of military-style assault weapons could turn our streets into combat zones. Assault weapons, designed solely to mow down human beings, are turning up at an alarming rate in the hands of those most prone to violence—drug dealers, gang members, hate groups and the mentally ill.

5 The Stockton, Calif., massacre of little children was a warning to our policymakers. But Congress lacked the courage to do anything. During the year of inaction on Capitol Hill, we have seen too many other tragedies brought about by assault weapons. In Louisville an ex-employee of a printing plant went on a shooting spree with a Chinese-made semiautomatic version of the AK-47, gunning down 21 people, killing eight and himself. Two Colorado women were murdered and several others injured by a junkie using a stolen MAC-11 semiautomatic pistol. And Congress votes itself a pay raise.

6 The National Rifle Association, meanwhile, breathes a sigh of relief, gratified that your attention is now elsewhere. The only cooling-off period the N.R.A. favors is a postponement of legislative action. It counts on public anger to fade before such outrage can be directed at legislators. The N.R.A. runs feel-good ads saying guns are not the problem and there is nothing we can do to prevent criminals from getting guns. In fact, it has said that guns in the wrong hands are the "price we pay for freedom." I guess I'm just not willing to hand the next John Hinckley a deadly handgun. Neither is the nation's law-enforcement community, the men and women who put their lives on the line for the rest of us every day.

7 Two pieces of federal legislation can make a difference right now. First, we must require a national waiting period before the

purchase of a handgun, to allow for a criminal-records check. Police know that waiting periods work. In the 20 years that New Jersey has required a background check, authorities have stopped more than 10,000 convicted felons from purchasing handguns.

8 We must also stop the sale and domestic production of semiautomatic assault weapons. These killing machines clearly have no legitimate sporting purpose, as President Bush recognized when he permanently banned their importation.

9 These public-safety measures are supported by the vast majority of Americans—including gun owners. In fact, these measures are so sensible that I never realized the campaign to pass them into law would be such an uphill battle. But it can be done.

10 Jim Brady knows the importance of a waiting period. He knows the living hell of a gunshot wound. Jim and I are not afraid to take on the N.R.A. leaders, and we will fight them everywhere we can. As Jim said in his congressional testimony, "I don't question the rights of responsible gun owners. That's not the issue. The issue is whether the John Hinckleys of the world should be able to walk into gun stores and purchase handguns instantly. Are you willing and ready to cast a vote for a commonsense public-safety bill endorsed by experts—law enforcement?"

11 Are we as a nation going to accept America's bloodshed, or are we ready to stand up and do what is right? When are we going to say "Enough"? We can change the direction in which America is headed. We can prevent the 1990s from being bloodier than the past ten years. If each of you picks up a pen and writes to your Senators and Representatives tonight, you would be surprised at how quickly we could collect the votes we need to win the war for a safer America.

12 Let us enter a new decade committed to finding solutions to the problem of gun violence. Let your legislators know that voting with the gun lobby—and against public safety—is no longer acceptable. Let us send a signal to lawmakers that we demand action, not excuses.

Writing to Compare Sources

George Atamian read these two articles on gun control as preparation for a paper he was writing for his English class. After reading and making marginal notes on Cassidy's and Brady's ideas, George discussed the two articles on gun control with a group of classmates. He came away understanding that people had very definite ideas on the issues. Strong words and emotional phrases from the discussion echoed in his mind, but he still had no clear sense of what he might want to write about. He realized he needed to focus his thoughts and to sort out the impressions he had gained both from his reading and from his discussion.

DISCOVERING SIMILARITIES AND DIFFERENCES Because George was working with two articles that expressed very different viewpoints, he decided to make a chart that would help him to see clearly where Cassidy and Brady disagreed and also to discover whether or not they agreed on anything. He experimented with different formats for the chart and finally came up with this one:

BRADY:	*CASSIDY:*
Wants controls on sales and ownership of handguns and automatic weapons	Wants no gun control for any reason
Does not discuss constitutional issues	Defends Second Amendment rights—compares Second Amendment to First Amendment
Says "nation's law-enforcement community is against legal sale of handguns and automatic weapons"	Says "rank-and-file police officers" do not favor gun control
Gives personal example of husband, Jim Brady	Does not give personal example
Uses strong words like "epidemic," "carnage," "escalation of bloodshed"	Uses strong words like "evangelists," "gun prohibitionists"

NARROWING THE TOPIC AND DETERMINING A TENTATIVE MAIN IDEA After making a chart, George thought about narrowing the topic so that he could find a main idea. He saw that the two writers had very little in common, yet he had real difficulty figuring out what to say about the differences he saw. Finally he decided to write two statements, one describing what Cassidy thought and one describing what Brady thought. Here's what he wrote:

> Cassidy believes that no laws should be passed to control any purchase of guns or any right to own guns.
>
> Brady believes that the sale of certain types of guns should be either banned or strictly controlled.

George knew that he still had not found what he wanted to say about these two different views, but he decided to continue, hoping that he would find his own main idea as he worked.

CONSIDERING ORGANIZATION, AUDIENCE, AND VOICE George thought organizing his paper would be the easiest part. He looked at his chart and decided to talk first about Cassidy and then about Brady. He planned to discuss the points he had listed in the same order he had used in the chart.

The audience for this paper was George's instructor. Since the instructor had made the assignment, George knew that he could expect a well-informed reader who was familiar with the two articles. Because of the reader's knowledge, George would not need to summarize the articles in detail nor would he need to provide such information as an expanded explanation of the First and Second amendments. He could reasonably expect his instructor to know these things.

Although George felt that he was more sympathetic with Brady's viewpoint than with Cassidy's, he wanted his writing voice to reflect the unbiased, balanced approach he planned to take. He decided to compare various aspects of the two articles without exaggerating or ridiculing either writer's viewpoint. On the other hand, he wanted his instructor to know that he had thought carefully about his own responses to Cassidy's and Brady's views. He decided to convey his ideas on the subject firmly, without apologizing, and to keep his writing free of expressions like "although this could be wrong—" or "this may be off track, but—."

DRAFTING Keeping in mind his chart, his two statements about the authors' main ideas, his plan for organizing his ideas, and his evaluation of audience and voice, George wrote the following draft.

EXERCISE 9 *As you read the draft, keep in mind the guidelines for writing a comparison (pages 121–122), the comments on revision strategies in Sections One and Two, and Revision Guidelines (Appendix A, pages 290–291). Write marginal comments and make notes indicating where you think the draft is strong as well as where you would recommend revision.*

Be sure to consider major revision strategies, such as reorganizing the paper's ideas. Then write a paragraph summarizing the suggestions you would make to George Atamian as he reworks this draft into a final copy. (Note: The paragraphs are numbered to make discussion of the draft easier.)

THE NRA VS. GUN CONTROL

1 J. Warren Cassidy, the N.R.A's (National Rifle Association) executive vice president argues that no laws should be passed to control any purchase of guns or any right to own guns (Time, Jan. 29, 1990, p. 22). Sarah Brady, whose husband was seriously injured by a handgun wound, takes a very different stand. She believes that the sale of certain types of guns should be either banned or strictly controlled (Time, Jan. 29, 1990, p. 23).

2 Cassidy opens his argument with a comparison of the first and second amendments. Pointing out the guarantee by the second amendment for a citizen's right to bear arms is just as important as the first amendment that guarantees freedom of speech and a free press. What he doesn't say anything about is that free speech and free press are controlled by some laws, like libel for example and pornography for another.

3 Cassidy also seems to base a lot of his argument on the idea that the common, ordinary person favors total freedom of owning guns. He says that the movement for this freedom began in places like "Biloxi, Albuquerque, Concord, Tampa, Topeka—from every point on the compass and from communities large and small." He makes it sound like the only people who favor gun control are those who are powerful and live in Washington and he implies that these people and their ideas are "fashionable" and "trendy," but the anti-gun control people are like a silent majority of little people. He also brings in the "rank-and-file police officers." He claims these lower level police who are out on the streets do not favor gun control. It is only the "police administrators who face mayors and editors" who want gun control.

4 Cassidy claims in one paragraph that because of tough laws that punish people who commit crimes with guns "violent crimes with firearms, like assault and robbery have stabilized or are actually declining." But it's confusing because in the next paragraph he says that violent crime is rising in New York and Washington.

5 The language Cassidy uses is also interesting. For instance, he accuses those who are for gun control of "evangelism." He also talks about the "failed and flawed promises of gun prohibitionists."

6 The N.R.A., according to Cassidy trains thousands of hunters and law-enforcement officers in gun safety. Which he sees as better than gun control laws. If you agree with his views, the action you should take is "to join the N.R.A."

7 Sarah Brady doesn't mention the second amendment. She begins with a personal example. Her husband, Jim Brady, who was the press secretary to President Reagan, was injured by a handgun wound during an attack on Reagan's life. She goes back to that personal example at the end of the article.

8 Throughout the article she makes many references to people who were killed by hand guns or semi-automatic weapons. For instance, "Every day a child in this country loses his or her life to a handgun." This stresses the need for safety in the home and not just on the streets. So it seems like Brady mentions plenty of "common people" who are against handguns. In fact she claims that "neither is the nation's law-enforcement community, the men and women who put their lives on the line for the rest of us everyday." So who is right? Cassidy who says the "rank-and-file" police officers oppose gun control or Brady who says they are for it?

9 Brady says that gun control can work because in 20 years in New Jersey, police have stopped more than 10,000 convicted felons from buying handguns. But what I noticed was that she didn't say whether these felons might have then got guns illegally. Which Cassidy claims is easy for them.

10 The language in Brady's essay is interesting, too, she uses words like "epidemic" and "carnage" to talk about gun violence in this country. She also says "greater escalation of bloodshed" which makes it sound like a war. In fact later she says, "We could collect the votes we need to win the war for a safer America."

11 If you agree with Brady, her suggestion is that you write to your Senators and Representatives to pass laws against handguns and automatic weapons.

12 In conclusion, Cassidy is against any kind of gun control for any reason. Brady wants controls on sales and ownership of handguns and automatic weapons. Both of them make a good argument and you can see both points of view.

REVISING THE DRAFT After writing the draft you just read, George Atamian put it away for several days (to give himself a little "distance" from what he had written). Then he started the task of actively revising (remember that revising comes, literally, from the concept of re-vision: to see again). As George read his draft, he decided that he had plenty of information, and he also saw that he had followed one of the standard patterns used to examine similarities and differences. He had discussed first the points of one stand on the issue of gun control and then the points of a different stand. In addition, George noted some mechanical errors (misspellings, punctuation problems, and so forth), but he knew he could fix those. What concerned him was that he didn't think he had communicated the information he had gathered as well as he wanted to. George made an appointment with his professor to see if she could help him come up with strategies for reworking his paper.

Before he kept this appointment, George made a list of questions, following the guidelines below, which his professor had given the class.

(Note: These guidelines are also helpful for preparing for a peer editing session or for a visit to a Writing Center tutor or consultant.)

GUIDELINES: PREPARING FOR A WRITING CONFERENCE

1. Do as much preliminary work as you can on your own.
2. Write down any questions you have.
3. Make your questions as specific as possible. (*Not* "How can I make this paper better?" *but* "Do you think I have too much information in my opening paragraph?")
4. List the strengths of your paper.
5. List the weaknesses of your paper. (Focus first on large issues—like organization or use of examples—rather than finer points, like word choice or punctuation.)
6. List strategies you think might work to remedy the weaknesses you see.
7. Use the Revision Guidelines (Appendix A, pages 290–291) to help you focus the questions and lists mentioned in points 2 to 6.

THE WRITING CONFERENCE George arrived at his professor's office with prepared questions and lists of observations about his paper. The following transcript and summary of their discussion suggests ways of talking and thinking about revising.

INSTRUCTOR So, how's the paper going? . . . I'd like to begin by hearing what you consider the greatest strength of your paper and also what you think still needs work.

GEORGE What I think is best about my paper . . . that would be the information I have. I think I have plenty of details and plenty of examples.

INSTRUCTOR Okay, good . . . and how about something that needs work?

GEORGE I don't know. The way I'm saying things doesn't seem as clear as I want. I used the, you know, the "subject-by-subject" structure but I just feel as though the organization is a problem.

DRAFTING AND REVISING AN INTRODUCTION At this point, the instructor quickly read through George's paper and suggested that he decide on a central idea. In his draft, the main idea is not really clear.

So rewriting would include planning and drafting a new opening paragraph to focus more clearly on what he planned to say about Brady's and Cassidy's viewpoints. The current opening simply announces each writer's view.

To help with revising the introduction, the instructor suggested that George consider the following guidelines:

GUIDELINES: DRAFTING AND REVISING AN INTRODUCTION

1 As you write, be aware that the introduction is often the most difficult part of the paper to plan, draft, and revise.

2 As you write, if you can't think of a perfect way to begin, don't worry. Just start with a simple sentence that relates in some way to your topic. Understand that you will then revise your introduction after you have worked on the rest of your paper.

3 As you revise, make sure your introduction lets your reader know not only what your topic is but also what you are going to say about your topic.

4 As you revise, remember that your introduction should capture your reader's attention and interest. Consider starting in one of the following ways:

- ***A*** Give a brief example to lead to your statement of main idea.
- ***B*** Use an intriguing quotation to lead to your statement of main idea.
- ***C*** Describe an incident (a very brief story) that leads to your main idea.
- ***D*** Define an important term that is part of or clearly related to your main idea.
- ***E*** Use statistics that will underline and support your statement of main idea.
- ***F*** Ask a question or series of questions; your statement of main idea may then suggest an answer.
- ***G*** Give relevant background information leading to your main idea.

The conference continued, and the instructor asked George to talk about the essay's main idea.

George I want to show how they're different—their approaches—like Brady, she doesn't mention the Second Amendment, but Cassidy harps on it. And Cassidy keeps talking about the ordinary person favoring his view but Brady says . . . more or less . . . that the common person favors her view. They both even claim that the cop-on-the-beat-type police favor their ideas . . . well . . . to my mind . . . that can't be true for both.

Instructor When you explain what you are doing, I really think you're interested in the approaches Brady and Cassidy take to making their arguments. Also, you're pointing out exactly how they are similar or different. But I don't see that clearly in your paper. Paragraph 3 and paragraph 8 do talk about the "common person," but the contrast doesn't seem very important the way you put it here. It seems like you just have lists of Cassidy's points and then Brady's points.

REORGANIZING INFORMATION The instructor's comment about lists helped George to see that his structure didn't really work very well to focus on the different approaches Brady and Cassidy took toward their topic. He realized that he had simply transferred the details he had discovered from his lists to his paper without really considering their significance and without thinking how those points might fit together to support a central idea.

George I see what you mean. Like in paragraph 5 and paragraph 10 I talk about the language they use but I don't really show the "So what?" you talked about in class.

Instructor I like the analysis you make of Brady's language—when you say she makes it sound like a war. But with Cassidy you just say the language is "interesting"—I don't really see why.

George I don't know. Maybe if I put the paragraphs on language together? But that would screw up the whole arrangement of the "whole subject" idea.

Instructor Maybe you need to consider changing that arrangement?

REVISING FOR A STRONG CONCLUSION After making a note to reconsider the organization of the paper, George went on to explain that he was concerned about his conclusion. He realized that he had simply given a summary, rather than providing an answer to the question "So what?" but he felt unsure how to do anything else. He believed that both writers made several important points, and he also felt that they had a lot more knowledge about gun control than he did.

George I just don't know about a conclusion. I mean . . . I'm not an expert in gun control . . . or a lawyer or something. I don't even know about the Supreme Court ruling stuff that Cassidy talks about.

Instructor I agree . . . it's important to talk about something you're really interested in—and something you know about. And we've talked about something that fits those criteria . . . the approach these two writers take. See . . . here in paragraphs 7 and 8 . . . about the personal references and stories Sarah Brady tells. Maybe you could do more thinking about that and then—from what you've said—I think you'd have a better conclusion. I mean a conclusion that said more than "Cassidy says this" and "Brady says that."

As George gathered up his materials to leave, the instructor offered him a copy of the following guidelines.

GUIDELINES: DRAFTING AND REVISING A CONCLUSION

1 Understand that, like introductions, conclusions are often difficult to write; conclusions often require a great deal of rethinking, refocusing, and rewriting.

2 Remember that a conclusion must follow logically from the details, reasons, and examples that have been provided in the paper.

3 Remember that a strong conclusion should do more than simply summarize the paper's main points.

4 Consider the following strategies when you are planning a conclusion:

- ***A*** Propose a solution to a problem you have discussed.
- ***B*** Suggest future possibilities (good or bad) related to your topic.
- ***C*** Resolve a contradiction you have described.
- ***D*** Explain an effect that will result from the causes you have discussed.
- ***E*** Use an apt quotation to encourage your readers to think further about your main idea.
- ***F*** Describe an incident (a brief story) that emphasizes and reinforces the concluding statement you are making.

G Provide statistics that underline and support your conclusion.

5 Avoid using a strategy in the conclusion (for example, statistics or a quotation) if you have already used it in the introduction.

DECIDING ON A PLAN FOR REVISING As soon as he could after leaving his professor's office, George sat down to make a quick list of the points he'd work on for revision.

1. Opening—focus main idea—do more than state what articles said—what am I going to say about the differences/similarities?
2. Organization? Change? Group information differently?
3. Conclusion—not summary—maybe something about approaches taken by Cassidy/Brady?

Contrasting the way Cassidy and Brady approached the topic made sense to George and he tried out some of his ideas by brainstorming:

> Both very heavy on the emotions. Like Cassidy's trying to make you think if you're a "regular guy" and not a snob you'd be in favor of the NRA position—Sarah Brady wants you to think that if we don't have gun control, a lot of kids are going to die—not to mention other people. But maybe one of them is right? So is that emotional? If they're right? Maybe not about right/wrong?

(*Note:* Even though George is revising, he's using strategies that are often considered part of the early stages of writing. For example, he used listing to organize his thoughts about his writing conference and brainstorming to explore his ideas about the different ways Cassidy and Brady approached the topic of gun control.)

The brainstorming led George to think about how he might organize a discussion of the approaches taken by Cassidy and Brady. He made some notes to help clarify his ideas.

> Main Idea: Sarah Brady and J. Warren Cassidy hold opposing views on gun control, but they use similar approaches to explain their ideas.

1 The language Brady and Cassidy use—dramatic and emotional.
2 How they picture the person who favors their position. The common, ordinary person/The law-abiding person/The law-officer.
3 How each one uses statistics.

After looking at these notes, George realized that he would be better off using the "point-by-point" method of organization rather than the "subject-by-subject" method. Coming up with this new approach to organization also led George to see that his conclusion would be in some way related to the similarities between the two authors' approaches.

EXERCISE 10 *Write a revision of George's original paper (or of one part of the original paper—for instance, the introduction or the conclusion). Keep in mind the following:*

1 The evaluation you made as part of Exercise 9
2 The conversation between George and his instructor (pages 116–119)
3 The guidelines for introductions and conclusions (pages 117 and 119–120)
4 Notes George made relating to revision (pages 120–121)
5 The revision strategies suggested in Sections One and Two
6 The Revision Guidelines in Appendix A, pages 290–291

EXERCISE 11 *Read the draft on pages 113–115 and circle any mechanical or grammatical errors you found. Use the Proofreading/Editing Guidelines in Appendix A, pages 290–291. Based on your evaluation, make a list of the particular concerns George Atamian should keep in mind as he proofreads his final paper. Be prepared to point out examples of the problems you noted.*

EXERCISE 12 *Following the strategies described in this chapter and keeping in mind the following guidelines, plan and write an essay that makes a comparison.*

GUIDELINES: WRITING A COMPARISON/CONTRAST ESSAY

1 Follow the guidelines for reading for comparison (pages 90–91).
2 Determine the purpose for making your comparison. (Sometimes the purpose will be dictated by an assignment or exam question.)
3 Consider your audience and the voice you will use.
4 Plan the essay by doing preliminary writing. Remember

that list making is a particularly useful strategy for planning a comparison essay.

5 Note whether similarities or differences seem most significant.

6 Decide how you will structure your essay. (For example, the "whole subject" approach, the "point-by-point" approach, or a combination.)

7 Open with a paragraph that focuses on the purpose and point of the comparison. For example:

DO NOT SAY:

In this paper, Baskerville College will be compared with Union University.

DO SAY:

Baskerville College offers small classes and a low ratio of students to professors, but has a small library. Union University, on the other hand, has many large classes and a high ratio of students to professors, but offers a large, well-equipped library. Prospective students must decide whether they prefer the personal attention of Baskerville or the superior facilities of Union.

8 Develop each subject (or each point) in a separate paragraph (or a series of carefully related and logically linked paragraphs).

9 Avoid slighting one side of the comparison just because you do not agree with it.

10 Provide a conclusion that offers an analysis, suggests a solution to a problem, evaluates the evidence the body of your essay provides, or in some other way shows the significance of the comparison you have made.

SECTION FOUR

READING AND WRITING TO ARGUE

This chapter explains ways to read and evaluate arguments and, in addition, demonstrates ways to develop and write arguments. The following topics are addressed:

- *Defining argument*
- *Reading an argument*
- *Identifying and evaluating rational and emotional appeals*
- *Writing an argument*
- *Observing, conversing, and interviewing to discover ideas*
- *Considering voice*

DEFINING ARGUMENT

Consider the following conversations, overheard in an airport restaurant:

CONVERSATION I:
"I can't believe you ordered raw fish!"
"Sushi."
"Whatever. Raw fish. How can you stand to even look at it?"
"It's great. You should try it."
"I did. The rubbery texture is disgusting."
"That's part of what I like—chewing, tasting."

"No way I'll ever eat that stuff again. Once was more than enough!"

CONVERSATION II:

"Listen, I've *been* to England. I lived there. They use money that you count out in twelves, not in tens."

"I've been there, too. Last year. They definitely count the money the same as we do. In tens."

"You must be thinking of some other country. Not England. I remember that weird money. Took me months to do it right."

"It was England. I was only in England. I know they count the money in tens."

CONVERSATION III:

"Why don't you give up those cancer sticks? Look at the warning right on the pack!"

"Oh, yeah? Well, you sit there with a drink. Alcohol can kill you, too. I hear alcohol's going to have a warning label, too!"

"Alcohol's not as bad as tobacco. We don't need labeling. Just on products that are really dangerous. Like *your* cigarettes."

"Come on. Think about the birth defects that are caused by alcohol. And how about drunk drivers? Alcohol should definitely have a government warning label."

Topics for Arguments

Of these three conversations, which one focuses on a legitimate topic for argument? The first conversation shows a difference in taste. Neither person is going to be convinced by the other to change. Matters of taste, then, are not topics for formal arguments.

The second conversation focuses on a fact—whether British currency is based on the decimal system. This is a fact that can be easily checked by looking in any travel guide (probably available in the very airport where the discussion took place). If the two people involved did turn to a guide book, they would find that today British currency is based on the decimal system although it used to be based on the system described by one speaker as counting by twelves. Any matter of fact that can be easily checked is not worthy of an argument. Only one person can be correct, and no amount of discussion can change that.

So, if matters of taste and matters of fact are not worthy of argument, what is left? Given the amount of controversy in the world, it should be obvious that there are thousands of possible topics. Often these topics relate to questions of values—that is, questions that require considering evidence, making evaluations, and only then coming to a conclusion. The third conversation, with its disagreement about the labeling of alcoholic beverages as potentially dangerous, provides an example of a legitimate topic for argument.

EXERCISE 1 *Keep track of any disagreements you are involved in or that you overhear. Record the substance of the disagreements briefly—perhaps in conversational form as they are written at the beginning of this section. Then evaluate your findings, explaining which disagreements would be legitimate topics for developing a formal argument.*

Example of an Argument

Read the following example, representing one side of the controversy raised by the third conversation, government warning labels for alcoholic beverages. The explanation that follows this article suggests helpful strategies for reading arguments and provides exercises for practicing those strategies.

ALCOHOL WARNING LABELS ARE LONG OVERDUE

CHRISTINE LUBINSKI

1 Culminating decades of effort by Sen. Strom Thurmond and more than 100 consumer and health organizations, on Saturday all new alcoholic beverage containers will finally be required to bear a federal warning label:

2 GOVERNMENT WARNING: (1) According to the Surgeon General, women should not drink alcoholic beverages during pregnancy because of the risk of birth defects. (2) Consumption of alcoholic beverages impairs your ability to drive a car or operate machinery, and may cause health problems.

3 Fundamental health and safety information about the nation's largest drug problem and favorite legal drug will finally extend beyond "great taste, less filling" and "reach for the silver bullet."

4 Alcohol-related birth defects are a leading known cause of mental retardation, and the only preventable one—preventable by not drinking during pregnancy. Alcohol-related traffic crashes are the leading cause of death for Americans between ages 5 and 34.

These are only two of the many types of deaths, illnesses and injuries associated with alcohol use—human suffering that exacts a national toll of nearly 100,000 lives and social and economic costs topping $116 billion every year.

5 Thurmond and Rep. John Conyers led a bipartisan effort to enact the compromise, a basic consumer-education measure opposed only by the alcoholic beverage industry. The labeling brings long-overdue attention to the status of alcohol as a drug, one that should be used with caution and left alone entirely in high-risk situations such as when driving or pregnant.

6 Unfortunately, the new label has only increased the determination of the vintners, brewers and distillers to keep alcohol out of the nation's war on drugs. With newer products such as wine coolers and traditional "party time" TV ads, they hope instead to link alcohol with fruit juices and good times.

7 The new warning will help provide some balance. The label does not convey all the information it should, the result of legislative compromise; neither is it clear and prominent on all containers—manufacturers were given free license on how and where to label by the Bureau of Alcohol, Tobacco and Firearms. Nonetheless, the new label provides a valuable public-health message of the same type long found on drugs as harmless as aspirin. It's about time. Read the warning; heed the warning.

READING AN ARGUMENT

Determine the Writer's Main Point

As you read an argument, the first question you want to ask is this: What position does the writer support? In "Alcohol Warning Labels Are Long Overdue" the title immediately indicates Christine Lubinski's stance. Both her opening paragraph, which stresses the effort devoted to making such labeling mandatory, and her conclusion, which urges consumers to heed the new labels, show that she supports the new law.

EXERCISE 2 *Find an argument in a magazine or newspaper. Using strategies explained in this text, determine the writer's main argument. In other words, what is the topic and what attitude does the writer take regarding that topic? Your instructor may ask you to bring a copy of the argument (photocopy if you do not own the magazine* *or newspaper) for class discussion. (Note: Save this article for use in other exercises in this section.)*

Determine the Writer's Voice

One of the most important steps taken by writers of arguments is determining and considering their audience. After all, the goal of most arguments is to convince the audience that the writer's position is right—or at least worthy of consideration. To persuade, a writer must think about the readers' current knowledge of the subject, their probable beliefs and feelings about the subject, and their values (social, religious, economic, political).

Voice, then, means the attitude the writer takes both toward the topic and toward the audience. In paragraph 3, for example, Lubinski refers to alcohol as America's "favorite legal drug." By using the word "drug" she indicates a strong negative view of drinking alcoholic beverages and underlines her support for warning labels. That word choice indicates her attitude toward her subject.

Notice, on the other hand, that she does not condemn all drinking or all drinkers. Instead, she urges caution, only suggesting abstinence in "high-risk situations such as when driving or pregnant." Her restraint creates a sense of balance. Readers do not immediately have the reaction that they are listening to the views of an extremist who considers an occasional glass of wine as cause for alarm or of a grim reformer who wants to do away with any pleasure. This approach indicates her attitude toward her audience.

Creating a balanced tone is particularly important when a writer is genuinely interested in convincing the neutral reader. The person who is already converted does not need to be convinced. The person who is violently opposed to a particular view often cannot be convinced by any means. But if the writer can establish him- or herself as reasonable and knowledgeable, the reader who comes with a relatively open, but often uninformed, mind can usually be persuaded.

EXERCISE 3 *Reread and annotate J. Warren Cassidy's "The Case for Firearms" (pages 107–109) and Sarah Brady's "And the Case Against Them" (pages 109–111). (Refer to Section One, page 8, for sample annotations.) How do you think Cassidy and Brady each pictured the audience to which he or she hoped to appeal? Do you think each hoped to appeal to exactly the same audience? To which readers do you think each will be most persuasive? Why? Remember to consider both the attitude the writer takes toward the subject and the attitude the writer takes toward the audience.*

Determine and Evaluate the Writer's Development Strategies

Writers of argument usually combine two approaches to develop and support their main point: rational and emotional. *Rational appeals* include evidence intended to convince readers' minds. *Emotional appeals* try to convince readers' hearts and spirits. While rational appeals have long been considered superior to emotional appeals—and some experts claim that emotion has no place in a true argument—the fact is that humans are not creatures composed entirely of mind. We also have emotions, and there are very few arguments that do not in one way or another appeal to both aspects of our humanity.

EXERCISE 4 *Reread and annotate the paragraphs in Section One, Exercise 14 (pages 32–34). While not all of these paragraphs were parts of arguments, some lean more heavily toward an emotional approach than do others. After rereading and annotating, evaluate which paragraphs you think came from essays that emphasized emotions, which came from essays that emphasized facts, and which seem to balance emotions and facts.*

RATIONAL AND EMOTIONAL APPEALS

One thing to keep in mind while reading (or writing) an essay is that allowing emotional appeals to entirely overbalance an argument tends to make a thoughtful, intelligent audience suspicious and wary. On the other hand, an argument that gives no consideration to emotion often comes across as harsh, uncaring, and therefore unconvincing.

Identifying and Evaluating Rational Appeals

Writers appeal to their readers' minds in many ways. Consider the following possibilities.

USE OF STATISTICS Numbers give a concrete picture and most readers find statistics convincing. Note, for example, Lubinski's use of statistics in paragraph 4. She specifically describes the cost of alcohol abuse in both human lives and dollars. These costs help to build her case that alcohol is a substance worth warning the public against.

CAUTION Statistics can be manipulated and misused. For instance, consider the claim that Ivory Soap is 99 and 44/100ths percent pure.

Pure what? Pure soap? That statistic means very little. Or, suppose you are told that four out of five doctors prefer a certain brand of aspirin. Your reaction to that statistic might be quite cynical if you knew that only five doctors altogether were interviewed. Also, you want to know where statistics come from. Who made these discoveries? Lubinski falls down on this point. She does not say where she found out that alcohol use costs $116 billion every year. A skeptic might ask who carried out this survey and how it was conducted. Who determined what constituted a cost that was "social and economic"? Is she including the money people pay for their drinks at bars? If so, would that make a difference in your response to this statistic?

REFERENCE TO AUTHORITY An argument can be developed by citing a recognized expert to support a point or give an important definition. For instance, Lubinski mentions Senator Strom Thurmond and Representative John Conyers as supporting the bill that eventually made alcohol warning labels mandatory. She notes that the two come from different political parties (they are "bipartisan"; paragraph 5) and thereby attempts to establish their actions as sincere rather than as simply politically motivated.

CAUTION The audience must be convinced that the expert really has knowledge in the field being discussed. For instance, Lubinski says in the opening paragraph that Senator Thurmond has given "decades of effort" to the passage of this bill. She assumes—and hopes readers will assume—that during these "decades," Thurmond had plenty of time to weigh both sides of the question and to educate himself about the topic. Since we readily make this assumption, we find Thurmond's views on the mandatory labeling of alcohol convincing.

We might find the senator less convincing, however, if he retired from Congress and then started appearing on television urging us to use this brand of luggage or that brand of mouthwash. What makes him an expert on either of those products?

ESTABLISHING CAUSE AND EFFECT A writer making an argument may try to show cause and effect. Lubinski, for instance, argues that misuse of alcohol causes "deaths, illnesses, and injuries" (paragraph 4). If the reader is willing to accept that cause-and-effect relationship, then Lubinski assumes the reader will also be willing to accept the reasonableness of labeling alcoholic beverages with warnings.

CAUTION Whether the main point of the argument is to convince the reader of a cause-and-effect relationship or the cause-and-effect relationship is used, as it is here, to develop the argument, the writer must take care. For example, the writer must convince the reader that the relationship between the cause and the effect is not coincidental. If Lubinski were challenged, she would have to show that alcohol was the only, or at least the main, cause of the deaths she cites.

In addition, a writer must be careful not to claim that because one event happened after another, the first event caused the second. For instance, if an observer were to note that 99.9 percent of marijuana users in the United States drank milk when they were babies, that observer would not be justified in claiming that drinking milk in infancy caused marijuana use later in life. Obviously, nearly everyone in the United States (with the exception of those who are allergic) drinks milk during infancy. Some grow up to use marijuana; others do not. No cause-and-effect relationship can be proven.

PROVIDING REASONS The writer of an argument often establishes a viewpoint and then offers reasons why the reader should accept that view. As a reader, it's important to identify just what those reasons are and to ask yourself whether (and why) you find them convincing. For instance, Lubinski argues that "health and safety information about the nation's largest drug problem and favorite legal drug will finally extend beyond 'great taste, less filling' and 'reach for the silver bullet' " (paragraph 3). Another reason she gives is that "the labeling brings long-overdue attention to the status of alcohol as a drug" (paragraph 5). As a careful reader, you need to decide whether you find those reasons convincing evidence for Lubinski's argument that passage of the labeling bill should be looked on as a positive step.

CAUTION It's often easy to challenge another person's main argument. But when that person offers a reason, it's far too simple to sit back and say, "Oh, well, then, *that's* the explanation." Or, on the other hand, if you agree with an argument, it's easy to look at reasons given by supporters and passively agree without really evaluating.

Remember that if the reasons underlying an argument cannot stand up to critical evaluation, then the whole argument needs to be challenged. Perhaps the idea of the argument *is* correct, but the reasons may need to be strengthened. For instance, Lubinski's reason that information about alcoholic beverages will say more than "great taste, less filling" might be challenged by an opponent of the labeling law. Such an opponent might point out that public education programs have certainly spread the word about the dangers of alcohol, arguing that a small label will not attract as much attention as a large billboard or a television commercial. As you read the reasons supporting an argument, always keep in mind how an opponent might question or attack those reasons.

EXERCISE 5 *Reread the article you found for Exercise 2. Make a list of the reasons the writer provides to support the main argument. For each reason, try to identify the rational appeal (pages 128–131) the writer uses. Then go through the list and think of as many ways as you can to challenge those reasons. (Considering the "cautions" identified on pages 128–131 will help you to discover ways to challenge.) After making this evaluation, decide which reasons you would advise the writer to keep if he or she were revising the argument. Which would you advise the writer to omit? Which would you advise changing? Explain the changes you suggest.*

PROVIDING AN ESSENTIAL DEFINITION Writers often work at convincing an audience by trying to persuade them to agree on a key definition. For example, if a writer wants readers to believe that alcoholism is a disease, that writer must define both the word "alcoholism" and the word "disease," since not everyone assigns the same meaning to these words. Frequently, moving an audience to agree on a definition, in fact, convinces them to agree with the writer's main argument.

CAUTION While it would be absurd to expect writers to define every word they use, looking carefully for important terms that seem vague or "fuzzy" to you is important. For example, if you were to challenge Lubinski, you might ask her to define "alcohol-related." What exactly does that term mean? Why does she not say "alcohol-caused"? Is there, in fact, some question about whether the birth defects and accidents she mentions are actually *caused* by alcohol? She might be able to explain the term "alcohol-related" to your satisfaction, but you have a right to expect a clear definition.

Remember, also, that you have a right to question a definition. Some writers offer a definition as though it were an accepted truth, yet you may find yourself disagreeing. For instance, a writer might begin an argument for making flag burning illegal because it is unpatriotic by saying, "We can all agree that 'patriotic' means defending your country, whether it's right or wrong." You are not obliged to accept this definition—and if you do not, you are then likely to question the writer's main argument.

EXERCISE 6 *Reread "The Case for Firearms [pages 107–109] . . . and the Case Against Them [pages 109–111]." Find any key terms that Cassidy and Brady define. Do those definitions agree with your own definitions of those terms? Explain. Do you find any key terms that are not defined? Explain why you think Cassidy or Brady should define those terms. (In other words, explain why they are important to the development of the main argument.)*

Emotional Appeals: An Example

Legitimate emotional appeals are more difficult to explain than are legitimate rational appeals. To a great extent, whether an emotional appeal is legitimate depends on your interpretation. Consider, for instance, the following transcript of the most famous speech of Martin Luther King, Jr. As you read, make a check in the margin next to sentences that you believe appeal strongly to the reader's emotion.

I HAVE A DREAM

MARTIN LUTHER KING, JR.

1 Five score years ago, a great American, in whose symbolic shadow we stand, signed the Emancipation Proclamation. This momentous decree came as a great beacon light of hope to millions of Negro slaves who had been seared in the flames of withering injustice. It came as a joyous daybreak to end the long night of captivity.

2 But one hundred years later, we must face the tragic fact that the Negro is still not free. One hundred years later, the life of the Negro is still sadly crippled by the manacles of segregation and the chains of discrimination. One hundred years later, the Negro lives on a lonely island of poverty in the midst of a vast ocean of material prosperity. One hundred years later, the Negro is still languishing in the corners of American society and finds himself an exile in his own land. So we have come here today to dramatize an appalling condition.

3 In a sense we have come to our nation's capital to cash a check. When the architects of our republic wrote the magnificent words of the Constitution and the Declaration of Independence, they were signing a promissory note to which every American was to fall heir. This note was a promise that all men would be guaranteed the unalienable rights of life, liberty, and the pursuit of happiness.

4 It is obvious today that America has defaulted on this promissory note insofar as her citizens of color are concerned. Instead of honoring this sacred obligation, America has given the Negro people a bad check; a check which has come back marked "insufficient funds." But we refuse to believe that the bank of justice is bankrupt. We refuse to believe that there are insufficient funds in the great vaults of opportunity of this nation. So we have

come to cash this check—a check that will give us upon demand the riches of freedom and the security of justice. We have also come to this hallowed spot to remind America of the fierce urgency of *now.* This is no time to engage in the luxury of cooling off or to take the tranquilizing drugs of gradualism. *Now* is the time to make real the promises of Democracy. *Now* is the time to rise from the dark and desolate valley of segregation to the sunlit path of racial justice. *Now* is the time to open the doors of opportunity to all of God's children. *Now* is the time to lift our nation from the quicksands of racial injustice to the solid rock of brotherhood.

5 It would be fatal for the nation to overlook the urgency of the moment and to underestimate the determination of the Negro. This sweltering summer of the Negro's legitimate discontent will not pass until there is an invigorating autumn of freedom and equality. 1963 is not an end, but a beginning. Those who hope that the Negro needed to blow off steam and will now be content will have a rude awakening if the nation returns to business as usual. There will be neither rest nor tranquillity in America until the Negro is granted his citizenship rights. The whirlwinds of revolt will continue to shake the foundations of our nation until the bright day of justice emerges.

6 But there is something that I must say to my people who stand on the warm threshold which leads into the palace of justice. In the process of gaining our rightful place we must not be guilty of wrongful deeds. Let us not seek to satisfy our thirst for freedom by drinking from the cup of bitterness and hatred. We must forever conduct our struggle on the high plane of dignity and discipline. We must not allow our creative protest to degenerate into physical violence. Again and again we must rise to the majestic heights of meeting physical force with soul force. The marvelous new militancy which has engulfed the Negro community must not lead us to a distrust of all white people, for many of our white brothers, as evidenced by their presence here today, have come to realize that their destiny is tied up with our destiny and their freedom is inextricably bound to our freedom. We cannot walk alone.

7 And as we walk, we must make the pledge that we shall march ahead. We cannot turn back. There are those who are asking the devotees of civil rights, "When will you be satisfied?" We can never be satisfied as long as the Negro is the victim of the unspeakable horrors of police brutality. We can never be satisfied as long as our bodies, heavy with the fatigue of travel, cannot gain lodging in the motels of the highways and the hotels of the cities. We cannot be satisfied as long as the Negro's basic mobility is from a smaller ghetto to a larger one. We can never be satisfied as long as a Negro

in Mississippi cannot vote and a Negro in New York believes he has nothing for which to vote. No, no, we are not satisfied, and we will not be satisfied until justice rolls down like waters and righteousness like a mighty stream.

8 I am not unmindful that some of you have come here out of great trials and tribulations. Some of you have come fresh from narrow jail cells. Some of you have come from areas where your quest for freedom left you battered by the storms of persecution and staggered by the winds of police brutality. You have been the veterans of creative suffering. Continue to work with the faith that unearned suffering is redemptive.

9 Go back to Mississippi, go back to Alabama, go back to South Carolina, go back to Georgia, go back to Louisiana, go back to the slums and ghettos of our northern cities, knowing that somehow this situation can and will be changed. Let us not wallow in the valley of despair.

10 I say to you today, my friends, that in spite of the difficulties and frustrations of the moment I still have a dream. It is a dream deeply rooted in the American dream.

11 I have a dream that one day this nation will rise up and live out the true meaning of its creed: "We hold these truths to be self-evident, that all men are created equal."

12 I have a dream that one day on the red hills of Georgia the sons of former slaves and the sons of former slaveowners will be able to sit down together at the table of brotherhood.

13 I have a dream that one day even the state of Mississippi, a desert state sweltering with the heat of injustice and oppression, will be transformed into an oasis of freedom and justice.

14 I have a dream that my four little children will one day live in a nation where they will not be judged by the color of their skin but by the content of their character.

15 I have a dream today.

16 I have a dream that one day the state of Alabama, whose governor's lips are presently dripping with the words of interposition and nullification, will be transformed into a situation where little black boys and black girls will be able to join hands with little white boys and white girls and walk together as sisters and brothers.

17 I have a dream today.

18 I have a dream that one day every valley shall be exalted, every hill and mountain shall be made low, the rough places will be made plain, and the crooked places will be made straight, and the glory of the Lord shall be revealed, and all flesh shall see it together.

19 This is our hope. This is the faith with which I return to the South. With this faith we will be able to hew out of the mountain of despair a stone of hope. With this faith we will be able to transform the jangling discords of our nation into a beautiful symphony of brotherhood. With this faith we will be able to work together, to pray together, to struggle together, to go to jail together, to stand up for freedom together, knowing that we will be free one day.

20 This will be the day when all of God's children will be able to sing with new meaning

My country, 'tis of thee,
Sweet land of liberty,
Of thee I sing:
Land where my fathers died,
Land of the pilgrims' pride,
From every mountain-side
Let freedom ring.

21 And if America is to be a great nation this must become true. So let freedom ring from the prodigious hilltops of New Hampshire. Let freedom ring from the mighty mountains of New York. Let freedom ring from the heightening Alleghenies of Pennsylvania!

22 Let freedom ring from the snowcapped Rockies of Colorado!

23 Let freedom ring from the curvaceous peaks of California!

24 But not only that; let freedom ring from Stone Mountain of Georgia!

25 Let freedom ring from Lookout Mountain of Tennessee!

26 Let freedom ring from every hill and molehill of Mississippi. From every mountainside, let freedom ring.

27 When we let freedom ring, when we let it ring from every village and every hamlet, from every state and every city, we will be able to speed up that day when all of God's children, black men and white men, Jews and Gentiles, Protestants and Catholics, will be able to join hands and sing in the words of the old Negro spiritual, "Free at last! free at last! thank God almighty, we are free at last!"

In this 1963 speech, King offers rational appeals such as citing the number of years that have passed since the signing of the Emancipation Proclamation and listing the rights and privileges that were still denied to black Americans at that time. In addition, however, he appeals to the emotions of his audience, through the powerful pictures and personal examples he gives of oppressive racism. He speaks of the "heat of injustice," "storms of persecution," and "winds of police brutality," and he projects a future where his "four children will one day live in a nation where they will not be judged by the color of their skin but by the content of their character."

These emotional appeals help King's audience to visualize—as well as think about—the injustices he describes. Many people would agree that these emotional appeals provide essential—and fair—support for his rational appeals. On the other hand, those who oppose King's dream might not agree.

Identifying and Evaluating Emotional Appeals

To evaluate emotional appeals, you should watch closely for manipulation. Ask yourself whether the writer is using your feelings to convince you of something that your rational mind would otherwise reject. Is the writer trying to trick you rather than legitimately convince you?

Beware of emotional tricks like these:

BANDWAGON APPEAL A writer may pronounce that "everybody's doing it—so it must be right!" You see examples of this approach all the time in advertising when the camera pulls back and pans a crowd of beautiful, lively people all drinking Lucky Cola or smoking Instapuffs or wearing Marvin Marvelous jeans. This appeal attempts to work on the insecurities that nearly all humans have. Most of us, except the most rugged individualists, do not want to be thought of as entirely separate from others. We want to belong, not to be lonely. A bandwagon appeal suggests that if you agree to some point or buy some product you will become part of a desirable group (beautiful, smart, or active people, for example). Sometimes that group is depicted as down-to-earth "real" people (called "appeal to the people"), sometimes as extremely wealthy, influential people (snob appeal).

EXERCISE 7 *For the next several days note any examples of "bandwagon appeals" that you see or hear. Make a list and then evaluate them to identify their specific target audience (snob appeal, "just plain folks" appeal, or an appeal involving some other group). Be prepared to discuss your own response to these appeals. Do some seem more convincing to you than others?*

USING LOADED WORDS OR PHRASES Sometimes writers will use words because they know that these words will evoke a strong negative or a strong positive emotion. For instance, in the 1988 presidential campaign, many people had a negative reaction to the word "liberal." Although *Webster's New World Dictionary* notes that "*liberal* implies tolerance of others' views as well as openmindedness to ideas that challenge tradition," many voters in 1988 regarded the term as meaning someone who wanted to give away the taxpayers' money or someone who was "soft" on crime. In this climate, a political writer had only to call a candidate "liberal" to ensure that a large portion of the electorate would turn against him or her.

A loaded word or phrase is often embedded in a sentence to trick the reader into instant agreement with a point of view that should require careful thought. Consider this question: "How can anyone agree with liberal Senator Block's new tax proposal?" By inserting the word "liberal" before Senator Block's name, the writer hopes to influence those who assume that anything liberal is bad, to oppose the tax proposal without really thinking about its implications.

When you see a word or phrase to which you have a strong negative or positive reaction used as part of an argument, you need to stop and ask yourself questions like these:

- What does this word or phrase *really* mean?
- Where did I get my ideas and feelings about this word or phrase?
- Is the word or phrase used correctly, according to the definition I have arrived at after careful thought and consideration? (For instance, *is* Senator Block really a liberal?)
- Is the use of this word or phrase in any way truly relevant to the point being made?" (For instance, *if* Senator Block *is* a liberal, does that have anything to do with how I should evaluate his tax proposal?)

EXERCISE 8 *Make a list of loaded words and phrases, for instance,* communism, democracy, feminist, patriotism, chauvinist *(in other words, terms to which people generally react strongly, often without thinking). Jot down your own immediate response to the loaded term. Then look it up in a dictionary or other resource. Does your reaction change at all after reading someone else's definition? Explain.*

ATTACKING THE PERSON INSTEAD OF THE ARGUMENT Sometimes an individual's personal life is relevant to an argument. For example, if someone is arguing that he or she should be awarded a contract as a drug counselor, yet investigation reveals that this person is currently a drug abuser, that fact certainly undermines the argument.

Often, however, personal life has no real connection with an argument. Yet opponents of a particular idea will try to discredit it by attacking the individual who proposed or supports that idea. For instance, if a school committee member proposes a cut in the budget for the music program, an opponent might point out that this member had failed in her attempt to become a professional saxophone player and that the budget proposal reflects her disappointment. A concerned community parent may be tempted to listen to that point of view, but in fact, it has nothing whatsoever to do with the validity of the school committee member's argument. You need to look at the causes and projected effects of the proposed budget cuts—not at the musical ambitions of the school committee member—to reach a fair, carefully reasoned opinion.

EXERCISE 9 *Interview several people of different ages to see how many examples of personal attacks they can remember becoming part of political campaigns. Ask, for instance, if they remember any cases in which an individual's religion, marital status, or spouse's activities were called into question. Ask also how the person you are interviewing viewed the attack and what effect he or she believes the attack had on the candidate's campaign. How relevant do you think these attacks were to the campaign issues? Why do people respond so strongly when they hear such attacks?*

APPEAL TO PITY Often the appeal to pity is completely legitimate. For instance, if a writer describes starving children in a third world nation in order to support an argument for donations of food and supplies, most of us would consider that appeal legitimate and directly connected to the main point of the argument.

Sometimes, however, writers will describe a pitiful situation hoping to convince you of something that really has nothing to do with that circumstance. Consider an investigative reporter, for example, who opens an argument for better inner-city schools by describing three twelve-year-old school dropouts, one a drug addict, one an unwed mother, another a runaway living on the streets. While each of these children deserves pity, knowing about their sad situations does not immediately connect with the need for better schools. Unless the reporter can show that dropping out of school (or enduring a poor school situation) caused the problems these twelve-year-olds are facing, their stories do not contribute legitimate support to the main argument.

EXERCISE 10 *Find an example of an appeal to pity used to support an argument (in a newspaper, a magazine, or a television investigative news program). First, describe the main argument. Then explain the appeal to pity. Finally, evaluate whether you think this appeal to pity was legitimate. Remember, the sad example must relate directly to the argument for it to be legitimate.*

This assignment calls for a brief comment rather than a long analysis. You might use the following format if you were discussing Sarah Brady's argument for gun-control legislation (pages 109–111).

Main argument: Congress should pass a bill controlling the sale and domestic production of handguns and semiautomatic weapons.

Appeal to pity: Brady describes her husband's injury in terms like these: "Jim Brady knows . . . the living hell of a gunshot wound."

Legitimacy of appeal: Jim Brady was hurt by a handgun, but I wonder whether his injury should be considered as any more significant than the other injuries Sarah Brady briefly refers to. She really emphasizes her husband's case, but I think she would be more convincing if she emphasized all cases equally or maybe developed one example that was outside her own family.

(*Note:* The example shows one person's opinion. It does not represent a single, "correct" evaluation. Thinking about appeals to pity will almost certainly produce a wide range of responses.)

EXERCI3SE 11 *To review strategies for reading an argument, read and annotate the following article, "Alcohol Warning Labels Aren't Needed," which appeared as a companion piece to Lubinski's "Alcohol Warning Labels Are Long Overdue." Before reading the article, consider the following guidelines.*

GUIDELINES: EVALUATING AN ARGUMENT

1. Determine the writer's main point.
2. Determine the writer's voice.
3. Determine and evaluate the writer's development strategies.
   - *A* Rational appeals
     - Using statistics
     - Referring to authority
     - Establishing cause and effect
     - Providing reasons
     - Providing essential definitions
   - *B* Emotional appeals
     - Taking bandwagon approach
     - Using loaded words and phrases
     - Attacking the person instead of the argument
     - Appealing to pity

ALCOHOL WARNING LABELS AREN'T NEEDED

DAN WARRENSFORD

1 Is there anyone over the age of 5 who doesn't know that booze harms fetuses, embalms livers, causes esophageal cancer, is intoxicating and causes hundreds of thousands of deaths annually?

2 Well, then, why plaster warning placards on every container of hooch in the land? The only people who'll benefit are citizens under 5. Most of them aren't incipient lushes. Even if they were, they can't read.

3 Why indeed? Because Carry Nation's intemperate heirs crusaded to save us from Demon Rum by adding government warnings on every jug of firewater and can or bottle of brew. Look for the Temperance Union's label in liquor stores Saturday.

4 The messages will be:

- Pregnant women shouldn't drink.
- Alcohol can make one drunk or sick or both.

5 No kidding.

6 But are the caution notes necessary? Hardly.

7 Pregnant women who don't already realize the dangers probably don't care. Overindulgers know they'll become drunk or sick or both. These missives from government nannies are superfluous.

8 But we'll probably humor the message-mongers rather than behead them. We're used to pests, worrywarts and meddlers demanding to salvage us. This intrusion's just a minor insult added to a long list of injuries.

9 Daily, we're admonished, cajoled, cautioned, warned and wheedled not to do this or that because it's "hazardous to your health." "WARNING" is stamped, printed, painted and otherwise affixed to just about everything we can see, touch, hear, taste or smell.

10 This is theater of the absurd. Americans have become so inured to being treated as dunces that they don't even think it odd when manufacturers cast danger messages in gun barrels.

11 Consumers want booze labels informing them of brands, proofs and quantities. That's all. We need to repeal this asinine law right now.

12 If we don't, what will these public nuisances want next? Little skulls and crossbones etched on our kitchen knives? "Do not drop" tattooed on newborns?

13 Consumers must rise up and smite these nags! Defacing nanny-knows-best stickers ought to become a national sport. And harassed shoppers should send this brief note to elected overseers: "Warning. Let us alone. Ignoring this advisory can be hazardous to political health."

Strategies for Writing an Argument

As you become increasingly skilled in reading arguments critically, you can use those skills to develop your ability to write thoughtful, convincing arguments. Many course assignments—and many career-related writing projects—call for writing arguments. For instance, a history professor may ask you to investigate a controversial figure like England's King Henry VIII, then argue whether his reign could be considered positive for his country. Or at work, your supervisor might ask you to head a committee that would investigate and then argue for or against a proposal to give employees the option of a twelve-week paid maternity or paternity leave.

There are many ways to write a strong argument. The following example shows you how one student, Becky Maciejczyk, worked on an assignment for a course called "Critical Issues in Our Society."

FINDING A TOPIC Something you hear, see, or read might inspire you to write an argument (perhaps in the form of a letter to the editor). For example, you might learn that the trustees of your college plan to raise tuition, and that information might prompt you to write an article for your campus newspaper arguing against the raise. In a case like this, the topic initiates the argument. Often, however, the job of writing an argument is assigned by an instructor or by a supervisor at work. Sometimes the assignment is specific and sometimes it is not.

Becky's instructor said only that members of the class were to write a paper focusing on an issue that they considered important in our society. The assignment also required that students take a stand concerning the issue and write an argument defending that point of view. As part of the assignment, the instructor asked that students send their completed argument to a local newspaper in the form of a letter to the editor.

CONSIDERING AUDIENCE Becky was somewhat surprised and also concerned about the instructor's requiring the finished argument to be sent to a source outside the university for possible publication. To get the letter considered for publication, she realized that she would have to find a topic that would appeal to an audience made up of people from a wide variety of educational, social, ethnic, and economic backgrounds.

MAPPING Like many students, Becky liked to think visually. As she thought about the assignment, she made the diagram that appears on the next page.

After working on the diagram and looking at it for a while, Becky decided that most people in her intended audience would at least be aware of the growing problems surrounding the creation and disposal of trash. As she considered the ideas she had generated, she also recognized that nearly everyone had some connection to the problem of the trash created by the proliferation of printed material in our society. Almost everyone, for example, receives unsolicited mail.

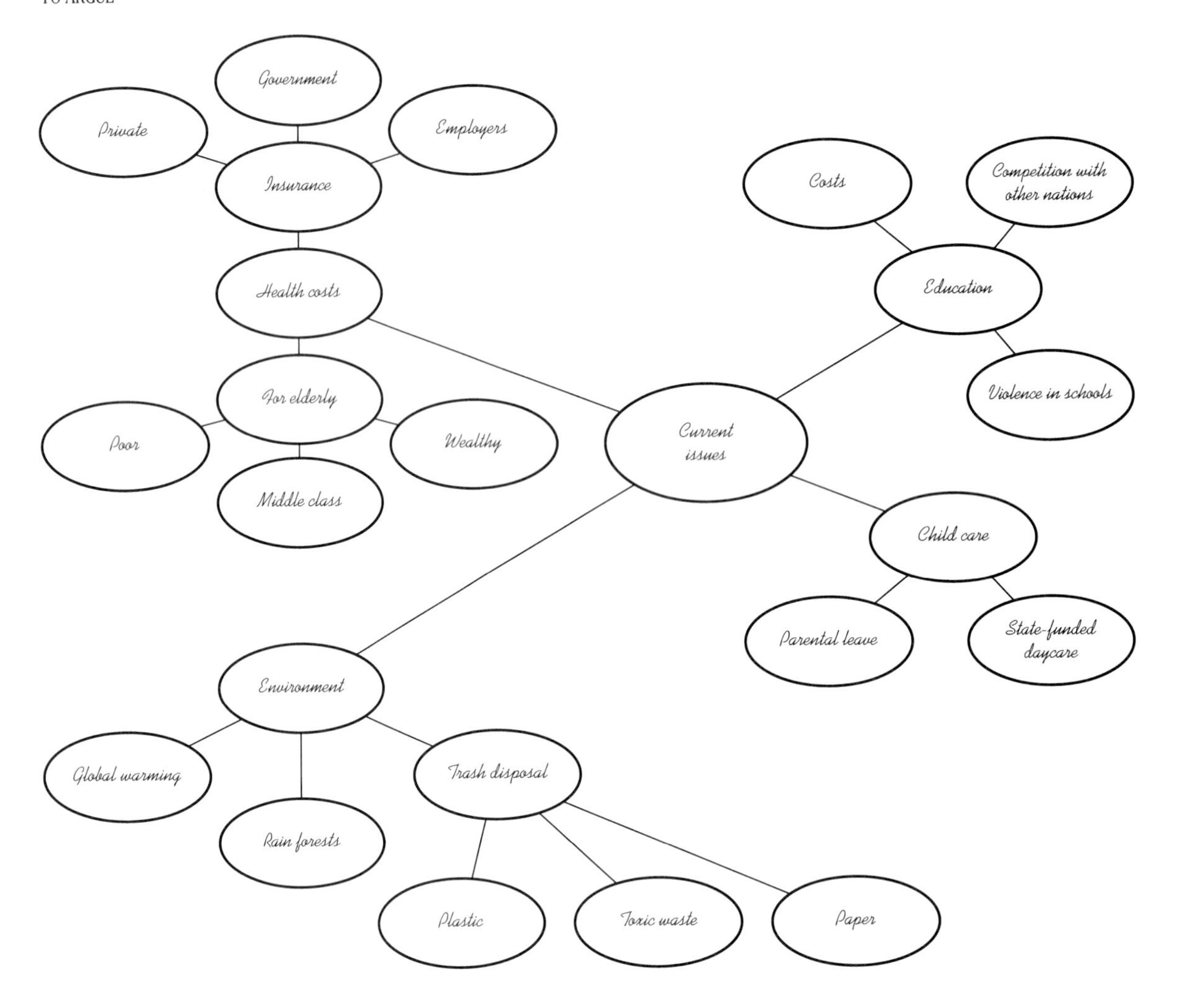

OBSERVATION AND CONVERSATIONS During the next few days, Becky watched for examples of the problem she wanted to discuss. For instance, she noticed that her campus mailbox was frequently stuffed with notices, many of which she and other students simply threw in the nearby wastebasket without even reading.

Becky also talked about her paper assignment with friends, and in a journal entry, she recorded the following conversation, which gave her an idea for further defining her topic:

> I was standing by student mailboxes, getting my mail and complaining that all I got was junk! No letters, just trash! Then my friend Tom said that this school needs a serious recycling program. And we were both sort of surprised when Tami said to us, "There *is* a recycling program . . . as I can prove by these notices I just pulled out of my box."

At that point, Becky started to look at the flyers she had taken from her mailbox. She was surprised to note that of the eight notices, two were pleas for environmental awareness. For the next week, Becky kept careful track of all the notices she found in her box. Nearly 20 percent were connected in some way to environmental concerns.

LISTING After observing the number of notices she received concerning the environment, Becky decided to make a list of other places she noticed environmental organizations using paper to communicate their concerns. She came up with these ideas:

Newsletters
Letters asking for contributions
Magazines
Informational pamphlets
Application forms for joining organizations
Posters and other signs

Making this list helped Becky to see examples of environmental groups using paper in various ways. Becky wasn't sure exactly what she wanted to say about her observations. She knew it would be foolish to argue that environmental groups should never use paper, yet she did wonder if these groups were aware of how much paper they were using.

NARROWING THE TOPIC AND PROPOSING A TENTATIVE MAIN IDEA Becky decided to talk to someone who worked for an environmental agency. She asked her professor to suggest someone; he recommended that she call Sheila Crowse, a local volunteer for a national environmental organization.

INTERVIEWING Becky called and made an appointment with Sheila Crowse. She knew that before the interview, she should make a list of her concerns. She included these questions:

1 Does your organization do mass mailings?
2 Does your organization publish a newsletter or magazine?
3 Does your organization use posters or signs?
4 How do you feel about the amount of paper you use?
5 What efforts are being made to reduce the amount of trash coming from the paper you use?
6 Are there any other organizations in our area that are working for the same issues as your organization?
7 Do you coordinate with them concerning activities and distribution of information?

Sheila was very cordial and welcomed Becky's questions. She gave Becky permission to tape their conversation. Sheila acknowledged that the organization she worked for did, indeed, do mass mailings, publish both a newsletter and a magazine, and use posters and signs. She explained that, whenever possible, they used recycled paper. Becky then asked question 5 from her list: What efforts are being made to reduce the amount of trash coming from the paper you use? Here's a transcript of Sheila's response and Becky's follow-up to that response:

SHEILA Well, of course we hope people will keep the magazines and newsletters as a resource . . . or maybe pass them on to libraries or schools.

BECKY Yes, but what exactly are you doing to encourage that? Also, everyone doesn't have storage space to keep all those magazines. And most schools and libraries would only want one copy, wouldn't they?

SHEILA True . . . but it's important to get this information into the hands . . . and minds . . . of the public.

BECKY I agree, but I still think there's a problem . . . or maybe a contradiction here . . . one of the things your group talks about is landfills being stuffed with paper . . . but you make more of it.

SHEILA Becky, I really don't have all the answers. But I see it is a concern.

This part of the interview is particularly interesting because when Sheila made her comment about the importance of getting information to the public, she (probably inadvertently) took Becky away from her question: What is the group doing to address the problem of trash generated by their use of paper? Note that Becky acknowledged what Sheila said, but then she returned to focus on the issue. She did not allow herself to get sidetracked.

When Becky asked her final two questions, she discovered that, in fact, there were several other environmental groups in the area, but Sheila did not know the exact focus of their activities. Sheila was also not aware of how those other groups distributed information.

WRITING A TENTATIVE MAIN IDEA After returning from this interview and after thinking about the list she had made. Becky knew that her argument would relate to environment groups and their use of paper to raise support for their concerns. She decided on this statement as a possible central focus:

> Environmental groups who oppose the creation and careless disposal of trash should become more aware of their own use of paper.

Planning a Draft

With a central focus in mind, Becky began the process of planning to draft her argument.

RECONSIDERING AUDIENCE While she was working to find a topic, Becky thought about her potential readers: her instructor, her fellow students, and (possibly) readers of one of the city's newspapers. Now that she was ready to write, she spent more time thinking about her audience. Her argument would, to a certain extent, be aimed at environmental groups. She would be urging them to be more aware of the way they used paper, asking them to set an example for conservation. In some ways, however, her argument would also be aimed at a more general audience. She hoped her paper would inform others of her concern and make them aware of the problem she saw.

CONSIDERING VOICE Using a voice that appeals to readers is always important. To write a convincing argument, careful consideration of voice is essential; so after evaluating her audience, Becky thought carefully about the writing voice she would use to deliver her argument.

Any discussion of choosing voice always raises the question of ethics. Is it right to make a conscious decision about the voice you will use based on what you know about your audience? Becky's English instructor addressed this issue in class, asking each student to consider his or her everyday speaking voice. The instructor noted that most of us regulate our daily speaking voices to relate to the person and to the situation we are addressing. For instance, a person talking to a child who is afraid might use a soothing, kindly voice. The same person scolding that same child would almost certainly use a harsher tone. Explaining to grandparents why one can't be at family Thanksgiving dinner calls for different words and a different way of speaking than does delivering the same news to the friends with whom the holiday will be spent. Do these changes in tone and in word choice indicate hypocrisy or dishonesty? Most people would say no. The differences simply reflect different parts of an individual. We all have many aspects that make up our whole personality. Thus, a writer composing an argument thinks about readers and brings out the "self" that is most likely to reach those readers.

Becky knew that her credibility would be greatly affected by the voice she used in her argument. Most people respond positively to a calm, thoughtful voice. Angry or sarcastic comments often alienate even a reader who is somewhat sympathetic to the writer's view. Becky knew also that a confident approach was important. She would need to explain the observations she had made clearly, logically, and without apology. Finally, she would need to explain her ideas fully enough yet simply enough so that all her readers could understand, but she would need to be careful not to overexplain because then she would sound condescending—as if she were talking down to her readers.

As you consider voice in your own writing, keep in mind the following guidelines.

GUIDELINES: CONSIDERING VOICE

1. Evaluate the audience and explain what that audience needs to know, but do not overexplain.
2. Avoid sarcasm.
3. Avoid angry expressions or inflammatory words.
4. Avoid exaggeration.
5. Choose words that indicate a calm, considered approach.
6. Present facts and observations logically and clearly to establish your authority and expertise.
7. Avoid apologizing or making excuses.

CONSIDERING ORGANIZATION Before beginning to write, Becky decided to focus on three main ways she had observed environmental groups using paper. She would discuss these uses of paper to convince her audience that there was a problem. Then, in her conclusion, she would suggest possible ways to address this problem. She wrote a very rough outline to keep herself focused on the organization she planned to follow.

Introduction—explanation of problem and statement of main idea

Evidence:

1. Letters/magazines in mailboxes
2. Flyers/pamphlets distributed door-to-door
3. Posters and signs

Conclusion—ways to cut down on using so much paper

DRAFTING As she began writing her draft, Becky composed the following opening paragraph.

In order to educate humanity concerning the effect of trash on our environment, the media has produced a large portion of what constitutes trash in our society. Thoughtless people who call themselves environmentalists can really make you mad when they are supposedly educating others. Some environmentalists don't think of anyone but themselves when they use excess paper to clutter mailboxes, survey households, and post signs on America's scenery. These environmentalists and organizations should educate themselves before they get all hot and bothered about the rest of us. Environmental groups who oppose the creation and careless disposal of trash should become more aware of their own use of paper.

Revising and Rewriting

When Becky wrote papers, she usually completed a full draft before she thought about revision. In this case, however, she was not comfortable with her first paragraph and she decided to look at it critically before she continued drafting.

Because she felt strongly about environmental groups' setting an example, Becky used several words and phrases that reflect harshly on these groups. She realized that she needed to remember her evaluation of audience and her determination to think about and present her argument in a calm, unbiased way.

Also, as she looked at this opening, Becky saw words that did not explain precisely what she meant as well as words that were not appropriate for a formal paper. After thinking about the words she had chosen, Becky rewrote her opening paragraph. As she wrote, she kept in mind the following guidelines.

GUIDELINES: EVALUATING WORD CHOICE

1. Choose words that have the correct meaning. Check the dictionary if you are not certain of a word's meaning.
2. Choose words that convey the tone you have decided to use. For example, do not use words that sound angry or sarcastic when you intend to present a calm, reasonable point of view.
3. Choose a variety of words to avoid unintentional repetition.
4. Choose words that are appropriate. For instance, do not use slang or extremely informal expressions in a paper assigned for a course.
5. Eliminate words that are not needed to express a point clearly.

EXERCISE 12 *Read and annotate Becky's original first paragraph (pages146–147), keeping in mind suggestions you would make for revision. Consult Guidelines: Evaluating Word Choice as you do this exercise.*

After reading and annotating the paragraph, suggest revisions. Then compare your suggestions with the actual changes Becky made in the revised paragraph below.

REVISED OPENING PARAGRAPH

In order to educate people concerning the problem of trash, environmentalists have sometimes produced excess trash themselves. Conservation activists cause concern when they use paper for mailings, for household surveys, and for posters. These individuals and groups certainly have admirable goals, but they should look more carefully at the potential problems they, themselves, create, and they should seek solutions. Environmental groups who oppose the creation and careless disposal of trash should become more aware of their own use of paper.

EXERCISE 13 *After reading Becky's revised opening paragraph, compare it with her original paragraph. What has she changed? What has been eliminated? What has been added? What do you think was her purpose in making these changes? What is the main idea suggested by the original paragraph? By the revision? What is the tone of the original paragraph? The revision?*

EXERCISE 14 *After evaluating the revised first paragraph, read the rest of Becky's draft. What suggestions would you make to her as she revises this draft? Refer to the Revision Guidelines (Appendix A, page 290–291). In addition, keep in mind the Guidelines for Writing an Argument (page 150).*

After making revision suggestions, reread the draft and note problems with mechanics and grammar. Refer to the Proofreading-Editing Guidelines (Appendix A, pages 291–292). Make a list of any problems, noting the paragraph where you found these errors. (Note: The continuation of Becky's draft begins with her second paragraph. The first paragraph would be the "opening paragraph" on pages 146–147.)

---

1 An informal survey showed that many flyers and advertizing letters in campus mailboxes and in home mailboxes in the Manchester area came from groups or individuals, concerned in some way, with the environment. The flyers addressed various issues. Some were invitations to attend lectures. Some asked people to go too films. Others concerned conservation strategies.

Some were pleas for a specific action. Some were requests for funds. Whatever their purpose, these flyers all did one thing, they used paper.

2 In addition to recieving "junk mail" from environmental group's, homeowners are also often visited by environmentalists who are taking surveys for one organization or another. These people, take up your time with alot of questions. Which they write down the answers to on guess what? Right! Forms that are made of paper. Then they put them in envelopes made of paper. And carry them back to their offices where they record the information and analyze the results. Using still more paper. And what about all the gas used by people who drive their cars around to carry out these surveys? Also, we should feel sorry for busy people who have to listen to these survey-takers.

3 Posting signs or notices addressing environmental issues can create more problems than they solve. For instance, one local beach is now "decorated" with large blue and white signs, posted five-hundred feet apart, and advising people not to litter.

4 I saw one person look at the signs and then throw an empty drink can on the ground. So the signs really cause litter instead of stopping it.

5 Also is the environmentalist who posted the signs thinking about how they are littering the view? Also, why do they need so many signs? This uses extra paper.

6 Of course environmental groups are needed and of course they sometimes have to use paper to educate the public. They should; however, try to conserve where it is possible. They could do the following things: (1) Each group should have a person who communicates with other groups to be sure their efforts are not duplicated. (2) Groups should try to use recycled paper and their mailings should have a notice stating that the paper is recycled. (3) Groups should avoid "overkill" and should not post an excessive number of signs or send out an excessive number of mailings regarding any one event or issue. (4) Groups should investigate alternative ways of educating the public. For instance, having events announced on public service radio or paying for one television ad rather than several mailings. (5) Groups should print a notice on all their mailings urging people to recycle the letter, pamphlet, or flyer. By following these steps, environmental groups would set an example and would make a convincing case for their own cause.

EXERCISE 15 *Choose a subject that is related to a current issue in which you've taken an interest. (Consider the following, for example:*

problems with education; rise in violent crime; poverty and the homeless; unemployment; scandals in organized sports; sex education.) Using the steps described in this chapter, think about this issue and develop a stand on a topic related to the issue. Then plan and write a paper arguing for the stand you have chosen. The following guidelines should help as you plan, write, and revise your argument.

GUIDELINES: WRITING AN ARGUMENT

1. If you are writing in response to a argument you have read, follow the strategies for reading an argument (page 126ff).
2. Determine the purpose for writing your argument. For example, will you argue against someone else's idea? Will you argue for a proposal suggested by someone else but not sufficiently well supported by the original writer? Will you argue for a new solution to an old problem? Will you argue against a law that is now in effect?
3. Consider your audience and the voice you will use.
4. Formulate a tentative thesis.
5. Gather evidence and make notes to support your argument.
6. Anticipate points that might be made against your argument and consider ways to address these points.
7. Organize and draft your argument.
8. Evaluate your use of rational and emotional appeals and revise if necessary.
9. Evaluate your word choice to make certain you have conveyed your argument accurately and have established a convincing voice.
10. Make certain your conclusion does more than summarize what you have already said. You might offer a solution, for example, or suggest broader implications of a problem you have addressed.

SECTION FIVE

AN ANTHOLOGY OF READINGS

PART ONE

THE FAMILY

GET REAL, MEN OF STEEL!

JEANNIE MacDONALD

Jeannie MacDonald, a freelance writer, lives in California. "Get Real, Men of Steel" first appeared in *Newsweek* magazine, March 25, 1991.

Predicting Questions

As you read, keep in mind the following questions, derived from this selection's title:

1 Who are the "men of steel"?
2 What does Jeannie MacDonald mean when she tells these "men of steel" to "get real"?
3 Why are the "men of steel" important to MacDonald?

Vocabulary Alert

As you read, watch for the following words: "genetic," "chromosome," "ultimatums" (paragraph 2); "personification" (paragraph 3); "boutonniere" (paragraph 4); "commiserating," "cellulite" (paragraph 5); "hyperventilating" (paragraph 6); "reticence" (paragraph 11).

If you are unfamiliar with these words, try to determine their meaning from context clues. Which unfamiliar words do you need to look up in a dictionary? (In other words, which have meanings that cannot be determined from context yet are essential to understanding the meaning of the sentence or paragraph?)

1 Recently, the editors of the "Superman" comic-book series made a startling announcement: after a whirlwind, 50-year courtship, Clark Kent has proposed to longtime love Lois Lane. Yeah, yeah, we all know marriage is serious business, but is Superman a wimp, or what? I mean, he doesn't flinch when crooks fire 147 rounds of live ammo at his chest, but he needs 50 years to work up the courage to pop the question? Get real, Man of Steel.

2 Let's face it, Superman's not the only guy who's afraid of being pinned to the matrimonial mat. In fact, I'd bet most women have, at one time or another, toyed with the idea of performing genetic tests on their boyfriends to see if they lack the Commitment Chromosome. The trouble is, talking about marriage only seems to make matters worse. So, rather than having rational conversations about the future, couples can find themselves locked in protracted wedlock wars, in which threats, tears and ultimatums are used by both sides to get their way.

3 Here's a perfect case in point. My boyfriend and I have been dating each other for almost three years now. Andy (not his real name) tells me he's never been happier. I tell Andy he's the man of my dreams. We're the personification of every goopy, soft-focus Hallmark card until I mention the dreaded M word.

4 With that, Andy's face pales. Beads of Nixonian sweat break out on his upper lip, and a slight tick takes hold in the skin beneath his left eye. Suddenly, benign words like "boutonniere" and "function hall" have the power to bring Andy to his knees but not, unfortunately, in the proposal position. Instead, he stammers something about not being "ready" and races from me, as a doomed man flees his executioner. What's going on here? Beats me. I blame all those MGM musicals I watched as a kid. They made love look so simple: boy meets girl, boy gets girl, boy buys girl a "rock" the size of New Jersey. To me, marriage is the natural next step in a solid, mutually satisfying relationship. To Andy, it's the Terror of Terrors; the black hole of baby puke, mortgages and station wagons; the ball and chain from Ward Cleaver Hell.

5 As a result, we have the "So just when *will* you be ready?" fight on a quarterly basis. Afterward, I console myself by mainlining chocolate products, playing Patsy Cline records and commiserating with my unmarried friends, who are having the same arguments with their men. "So it's not that I'm a controlling shrew or have too much cellulite?" I sniffle. "Heck, no," they assure me. "It's a 'boy thing.' They're allergic to marriage."

6 According to a private research study (mine), the average man rarely shares his beloved's eagerness to enter an "altared" state. The evidence is everywhere. Pick up any "women's" magazine and you'll find at least one article on "How to Get Your Man to Stop Hyperventilating When You Mention Marriage." Flip on Phil or Oprah, and you'll hear women moaning that men are incapable of committing themselves to anything except football and power tools. Check out the self-help section of your local bookstore and

you'll see row upon row of titles ranging from "Getting the Love You Want" to "Love Is Never Enough."

7 Despite feminism and the supposed equal rights between the sexes, we women still find ourselves in the prehistoric position of waiting for our men to do the proposing. Forget how assertive we are at the office; when it comes to getting engaged most of us curl up into the mental equivalent of the fetal position. "Me, propose to him? Isn't that illegal? Besides, who'd buy the ring?" And, really, can I find the vocabulary to do it and still keep my dignity?

8 Sometimes I wonder why I bother worrying about all this. Andy and I get along so effortlessly when I *don't* bring up the topic of marriage. Surely, with wonderful friends and a demanding career, I don't need a husband to be happy. What's more, applying the "if it ain't broke don't fix it" theory to our relationship, we're doing just fine, as is. Staying single also allows me to enjoy the benefits of courtship, while sparing myself the indignities of the stinky socks and unwashed dishes which threaten to overrun Andy's apartment.

9 Yet, in my heart of hearts, I still want to marry the big lug. Why? Because my life wouldn't be nearly as much fun without Andy in it. Because I think it's important to commit myself to something higher than my own self-centered needs. Because there's something very moving to me about standing before my relatives and friends and pledging to share a common home, history and family with the man I love. Because at the end of my life, I want to have something more meaningful to look back on than dinners in trendy restaurants and power calls from car phones.

10 *Bridal bouquets:* This month Andy and I will celebrate our third anniversary, which means we'll probably be having one of "those" talks again. But I'm not worried. Over the years I've found ways to cope with my anxiousness and Andy's anxiety about marriage. How? I tell my mother to stop with the novenas, already. I shamelessly tackle other single women when bridal bouquets are tossed. And I try not to throttle people (invariably named Cyndi or Kimberly) when they giggle and tell me that *their* boyfriends proposed on their first dates.

11 Actually, Andy's reticence toward marriage has taught me a couple of valuable lessons. I've learned that marriage isn't something you do to get out of the house or to make your parents happy. And, contrary to what movies and romance novels would have us believe, marriage isn't about fleets of bridesmaids or rental tuxes or bands playing "We've Only Just Begun." It's about forming a true partnership and loving each other enough to realize that the only right time to marry is when it's right for both people—as long as one of those people doesn't take 50 years to make up his mind!

Topics for Reading, Writing, and Discussion

RESPONDING

1 Jeannie MacDonald suggests that many men are afraid of the commitment required by marriage. Do you agree with her? Explain.

2 Imagine that you are Andy, Jeannie's boyfriend. How do you think he would respond to her comments?

EVALUATING

3 Evaluate the tone of this article. Identify parts of the article that are funny and parts that seem serious. What main idea do you think comes from the combination of humor and seriousness?

4 In the final paragraph, MacDonald mentions lessons she has learned about marriage. Make a list of these lessons and explain whether you agree or disagree with them.

COMPARING

5 Contrast MacDonald's attitude toward marriage with Andy's attitude. Considering the differences she describes, explain whether you think they have a future as a couple.

6 In paragraph 4, MacDonald describes the marriages she remembers from movies she watched when she was a child. Compare the image she describes with the view of marriage presented in films today. Use specific examples to explain the similarities or differences you see.

ARGUING

7 Reread paragraph 7, and then argue for or against the following proposition: Given today's changing social customs, it doesn't make any difference whether it's the man or the woman who proposes marriage.

8 Reread paragraph 8, and then argue for or against the following proposition: The benefits of being married outweigh the benefits of staying single.

MISSING: THE INFLUENCE OF BLACK MEN

WILLIAM RASPBERRY

William Raspberry is a syndicated columnist who often writes on issues related to the black community. "Missing: The Influence of Black Men" first appeared in the *Boston Globe* in July 1989.

Predicting Questions

As you read, keep in mind the following questions, derived from this selection's title:

1 What kind of influence does Raspberry believe is missing?
2 Why does he believe this influence is missing?
3 What does he see as the effects of the missing influence?

Vocabulary Alert

As you read, watch for the following words: "ethologist" (paragraph 9); "poignantly," "intergenerational" (paragraph 11); "feckless" (paragraph 14).

If you are unfamiliar with these words, try to determine their meaning from context clues. Which unfamiliar words do you need to look up in a dictionary? (In other words, which have meanings that cannot be determined from context yet are essential to understanding the meaning of the sentence or paragraph?)

---

1 If I could offer a single prescription for the survival of America, and particularly black America, it would be: Restore the family.

2 And if you asked me how to do it, my answer—doubtlessly oversimplified—would be: Save the boys.

3 So much of what has gone wrong in America, including the frightening growth of the poverty-stricken, crime-ridden and despairing black underclass, can be traced to the disintegration of the family structure.

4 Everybody knows it, but too many of us have been reluctant to talk straight about it. We know that children need intact families that include fathers. But we fear to say it lest we appear to be blaming hard-pressed single mothers for the very problems they are struggling to overcome.

5 The point, however, is not to assign blame but to encourage analysis that can lead the way to solutions.

6 Nathan and Julia Hare put it this way in their book *The Endangered Black Family*:

7 "There is nothing wrong with being a black-female single parent—and one rightfully makes the most of any situation in which she finds herself. But there is something wrong with why a black woman is so much more likely to experience the single-parent situation, why one race can freely imprison, send off to military duty, unemploy and otherwise destroy the oppressed black woman's eligible male supply.

8 "Also, there is something wrong with glorifying this problem instead of rising up to change it. People will speak here of 'options,' but forced or unintended options must be called by some other name."

9 That's from a pair of radical black social scientists. Now hear this from white ethologist Phon Hudkins:

10 "The family is the only social institution that is present in every single village, tribe or nation we know through history. It has a genetic base and is the rearing device for our species."

11 And from conservative Richard John Neuhaus, editor of the *Religion & Society Report*: "Millions of children do not know, and will never know, what it means to have a father. More poignantly, they do not know anyone who has a father or is a father . . . It takes little imagination to begin to understand the intergenerational consequences of this situation."

12 It strikes me as it strikes these writers—as it struck Daniel Patrick Moynihan a quarter century ago—that children unlucky to be born into single-parent households are, if not doomed, at least at serious disadvantage.

13 Hudkins believes the disadvantages include not just poverty and crime and hopelessness, but also poor health produced by the stress of family-lessness.

14 The question is what to do about the children of deteriorating and never-formed families. The first thing to do is to provide as much help as we can for these feckless children in their present circumstances: education, mentoring, role-modeling, job training, help toward self-sufficiency. The second is to devise policies to restore families. Hudkins, who has been ridiculed for his contention that female dominance is eroding America's strength, has it right in the prescription he offered in a recent open letter to the president:

15 "If families are to be formed and survive, young males must be prepared for skilled jobs to support these families. In order to do this, we must target our government aid and our compensatory education and training programs for disadvantaged young males."

16 We can't rescue America's families unless we make up our minds to save the boys.

Topics for Reading, Writing, and Discussion

RESPONDING

1 William Raspberry says in paragraph 2 that saving black families requires saving the boys. What is your response to this suggestion?

2 Do you think Raspberry's "save the boys" approach could be applied more broadly? For example, could it be applied as well to white families in this country? Explain your response.

EVALUATING

3 What is Raspberry's attitude toward black single mothers? Is he sympathetic or accusing? Explain your evaluation of his attitude.

4 Raspberry quotes many other writers in this brief article. Why do you think he includes so many secondary sources? Evaluate these sources and explain why you do or do not find them reliable and convincing.

COMPARING

5 What comparison does Raspberry's essay imply between black men/boys and black women/girls? What is your response to this implied comparison?

6 Compare the various quotations Raspberry uses. How are they similar? How are they different? If you were suggesting the addition of further expert opinion, what groups of people would you like to see represented? How would these experts make Raspberry's argument more convincing?

ARGUING

7 Write a letter to the editor responding to Raspberry's article. Assume the point of view of one of the following: a young black man; a white feminist; a black single mother.

8 Do you agree with Raspberry's observation (paragraph 12) that "children unlucky to be born into single-parent households are, if not doomed, at least at serious disadvantage"? Argue for or against this point of view.

A DRIVING FEAR

ELLEN GOODMAN

When she graduated from Radcliffe, Ellen Goodman went to work as a reporter for *Newsweek*. Since then, she has worked for a number of newspapers and journals and has become a nationally syndicated columnist. She received the Pulitzer Prize for distinguished commentary in 1980; her collections of essays include *Close to Home* (1979) and *At Large* (1980). Goodman's trenchant observations on the lives of American women and their families are demonstrated in "A Driving Fear," which first appeared in the *Boston Globe* in 1989.

Predicting Questions

As you read, keep in mind the following questions, derived from this selection's title:

1. What does Goodman mean by "a driving fear"? How does she use the word "driving"?
2. Why does she have the fear?
3. Is this a fear you share?

Vocabulary Alert

As you read, watch for the following words: "migration" (paragraph 1); "triathlon" (paragraph 2); "hibernation" (paragraph 6); "Reaganesque" (paragraph 12); "daunting" (paragraph 19).

If you are unfamiliar with these words, try to determine their meaning from context clues. Which unfamiliar words do you need to look up in a dictionary? (In other words, which have meanings that cannot be determined from context yet are essential to understanding the meaning of the sentence or paragraph?)

---

1 The geese are overhead, flying south in vee formations as crisp as a sharpened pencil. We watched them from the porch in a Maine light transformed by September clarity. Now we follow their lead, proceeding on our own annual migration.

2 The path we take also heads south, along parallel highway lines. We pass the exit to Kennebunkport where George Bush has spent his vacation in the presidential triathlon; fishing at 10, tennis at 11, horseshoes at noon.

3 Within an hour of home, the roads become clogged with our own species: back-to-school, back-to-work creatures.

4 With jars of wild blackberry jam wrapped carefully in T-shirts and towels, we are returning to the real world, although why we call it "real" I cannot tell you.

5 Is reality hard-edged and harried while fantasy is soft and leisurely? Is the real world one of obligations and the fantasy world one of pleasures?

6 Our migration takes only a few hours, but as we reach the city a familiar feeling comes out of its August hibernation. The rush that comes from being rushed.

7 A lick of anxiety accompanies us through the traffic to the airport where, in some adult variation of the old car pool, I leave my once-child on her way back to college.

8 And as I watch her, books, bags, guitar and all, the familiar watchword of the real world comes back into my mind: Hurry. The new year has begun. Hurry.

9 This is what I associate with September as much as clean notebooks and new shoes. We learn all over again to trade our own rhythms for those of school and work, and, in turn, we teach that to our children.

10 In millions of homes there is the same sudden nagging jump-start to the year. It is the sound of our own voices commanding ourselves and our kids: Stop dawdling.

11 On the streets today, there are kids with straight parts in their hair and lunch in their Batman boxes. Behind these kids there is a private tutor, at least one parent whose alarm bell precedes the school bell, whose workday begins with the urgent morning job of getting everyone out of the house. Someone who wages a small battle against the sleepy summer tug of leisure, or its evil twin, sloth.

12 This is what morning is like in America. Not the image of ripe Reaganesque fields and flags, but of pressed parents who may regret the sound of their own impatience sprinkling the breakfast cereal. It is the image of kids collected in buses and cars, delivered to buildings and redistributed to teachers and classrooms. Americans on schedule, on line, productive.

13 There is no mystery to why we trade our inner pace for a workaday lockstep. There is no living to be made on the sand.

14 Nor is there any mystery to why we become our children's trainers in this pattern. We are driven for the most part by what Barbara Ehrenreich calls succinctly in her new book title "The Fear of Falling."

15 Even the middle class in America, or especially the middle class in America, is insecure about its economic future and its children's future. That's more true now in an era when the middle is shrinking and many are slipping down or scrambling up.

16 The fear of falling attaches itself to another anxiety—"a fear of inner weakness," as Ehrenreich observes, "of growing soft, of failing to strive, of losing discipline and will."

17 We fight these anxieties in ourselves by making a virtue out of necessity; hard work. We fight it in our children by driving out daydreams with discipline. Our own days speed up and we teach, even compel, our children to keep up.

18 If we are very lucky, we find work we like and schools where our children are happy. But it's only when we step aside for a time, a week or a summer, that the pace becomes daunting, unnatural.

19 Pretty soon, I know, long before we have emptied the last jar of blackberry jam, it will seem routine again.

20 To the children on my street the school year that crackles with a fresh start will grow as worn and familiar as a chalkboard eraser. Workaday life will seem as normal as wearing a necktie instead of a T-shirt, heels instead of sneakers.

21 But today, having just left the ocean for the city, I am most aware of the deliberate, even dutiful, way we prepare our children to lead the exact life that we find so rushed. The pressure is on. Hurry, kids.

Topics for Reading, Writing, and Discussion

RESPONDING

1 What does Goodman see as the parents' role in the child's life? Do you agree with her? Explain your response to her view of the parents' role.

2 What is Goodman's main point? Where does she state that idea? What is your initial response to this idea?

EVALUATING

3 How does Goodman use Barbara Ehrenreich's book as an example to develop and support the essay's main point (see paragraphs 14–20)? Explain why you do or do not find this example effective.

4 In paragraphs 8 and 9, Goodman describes her images and impressions of September. Choose any other month, and make a list of your images and impressions of that month. Then write an essay that evaluates the significance of that month to your life.

COMPARING

5 Explain the comparison Goodman makes in the first paragraph. How does the comparison relate to what she says in the rest of the article?

6 In paragraph 12, what comparison is implied by the sentence "Americans on schedule, on line, productive"? Do your own experiences in school support or refute this comparison? Explain.

ARGUING

7 In paragraph 15, Goodman refers to the insecurity middle-class America feels about its economic future. She believes this insecurity drives parents to work compulsively and to push their children to do the same. Do you agree? Argue for or against this view.

8 In paragraph 4, Goodman questions her definition of the "real world." How would you define the "real world"? Write an argument explaining why you do or do not believe that what goes on in most classrooms will be useful to students in the "real world" (as you define this phrase).

WHY I WANT TO HAVE A FAMILY

LISA BROWN

This article first appeared in a special issue of *Newsweek*, October 1984, which focused on campus issues. Lisa Brown was a junior, majoring in American Studies at the University of Texas, when she wrote "Why I Want to Have a Family."

Predicting Questions

As you read, keep in mind the following questions, derived from this selection's title:

1 Why *does* Lisa Brown want to have a family?
2 Why would Brown think she has to explain this desire?
3 What do you think of Brown's reasons for wanting a family?

Vocabulary Alert

As you read, watch for the following words: "autonomy" (paragraph 2); "bravado," "egocentrism" (paragraph 3); "contingent" (paragraph 5); "doting" (paragraph 6).

If you are unfamiliar with these words, try to determine their meanings from context clues. Which unfamiliar words do you need to look up in a dictionary? (In other words, which have meanings that cannot be determined from context yet are essential to understanding the meaning of the sentence or paragraph?)

1 For years the theory of higher education operated something like this: men went to college to get rich, and women went to college to marry rich men. It was a wonderful little setup, almost mathematical in its precision. To disturb it would have been to rock an American institution.

2 During the '60s, though, this theory lost much of its luster. As the nation began to recognize the idiocy of relegating women to a secondary role, women soon joined men in what once were male-only pursuits. This rebellious decade pushed women toward independence, showed them their potential and compelled them to take charge of their lives. Many women took the opportunity and ran with it. Since then feminine autonomy has been the rule, not the exception, at least among college women.

3 That's the good news. The bad news is that the invisible push has turned into a shove. Some women are downright obsessive about success, to the point of becoming insular monuments to selfishness and fierce bravado, the condescending sort that hawks: "I don't need *anybody.* So there." These women dismiss children and marriage as unbearably outdated and potentially harmful to their up-and-coming careers. This notion of independence smacks of egocentrism. What do these women fear? Why can't they slow down long enough to remember that relationships and a family life are not inherently awful things?

4 Granted that for centuries women were on the receiving end of some shabby treatment. Now, in an attempt to liberate college women from the constraints that forced them almost exclusively into teaching or nursing as a career outside the home—always subject to the primary career of motherhood—some women have gone too far. Any notion of motherhood seems to be regarded as an unpleasant reminder of the past, when homemakers were imprisoned by husbands, tots and household chores. In short, many women consider motherhood a time-consuming obstacle to the great joy of working outside the home.

5 The rise of feminism isn't the only answer. Growing up has something to do with it, too. Most people find themselves in a bind as they hit their late 20s: they consider the ideals they grew up with and find that these don't necessarily mix with the ones they've acquired. The easiest thing to do, it sometimes seems, is to throw out the precepts their parents taught. Growing up, my friends and I were enchanted by the idea of starting new traditions. We didn't want self-worth to be contingent upon whether there was a man or child around the house to make us feel wanted.

6 I began to reconsider my values after my sister and a friend had babies. I was entertained by their pregnancies and fascinated by the births; I was also thankful that I wasn't the one who had to change the diapers every day. I was a doting aunt only when I wanted to be. As my sister's and friend's lives changed, though, my attitude changed. I saw their days flip-flop between frustration and joy. Though these two women lost the freedom to run off to the beach or to a bar, they gained something else—an abstract happiness that reveals itself when they talk about Jessica's or Amanda's latest escapade or vocabulary addition. Still in their 20s,

they shuffle work and motherhood with the skill of poker players. I admire them, and I marvel at their kids. Spending time with the Jessicas and Amandas of the world teaches us patience and sensitivity and gives us a clue into our own pasts. Children are also reminders that there is a future and that we must work to ensure its quality.

7 Now I feel challenged by the idea of becoming a parent. I want to decorate a nursery and design Halloween costumes; I want to answer my children's questions and help them learn to read. I want to be unselfish. But I've spent most of my life working in the opposite direction: toward independence, no emotional or financial strings attached. When I told a friend—one who likes kids but never, ever wants them—that I'd decided to accommodate motherhood, she accused me of undermining my career, my future, my life. "If that's all you want, then why are you even in college?" she asked.

8 The answer's simple: I want to be a smart mommy. I have solid career plans and look forward to working. I make a distinction between wanting kids and wanting nothing but kids. And I've accepted that I'll have to give up a few years of full-time work to allow time for being pregnant and buying Pampers. As for undermining my life, I'm proud of my decision because I think it's evidence that the women's movement is working. While liberating women from the traditional child-bearing role, the movement has given respectability to motherhood by recognizing that it's not a brainless task like dishwashing. At the same time, women who choose not to have children are not treated as oddities. That certainly wasn't the case even 15 years ago. While the graying, middle-aged bachelor was respected, the female equivalent—tagged a spinster—was automatically suspect.

9 Today, women have choices: about careers, their bodies, children. I am grateful that women are no longer forced into motherhood as a function of their biology; it's senseless to assume that having a uterus qualifies anyone to be a good parent. By the same token, it is ridiculous for women to abandon all maternal desire because it might jeopardize personal success. Some women make the decision to go childless without ever analyzing their true needs or desires. They forget that motherhood can add to personal fulfillment.

10 I wish those fiercely independent women wouldn't look down upon those of us who, for whatever reason, choose to forgo much of the excitement that runs in tandem with being single, liberated and educated. Excitement also fills a family life; it just comes in different ways.

11 I'm not in college because I'll learn how to make tastier pot roast. I'm a student because I want to make sense of the world and of myself. By doing so, I think I'll be better prepared to be a mother to the new lives that I might bring into the world. I'll also be a better me. It's a package deal I don't want to turn down.

Topics for Reading, Writing, and Discussion

RESPONDING

1. Lisa Brown thinks that a college education is important for a woman who wants to be a mother. Based on your own observations and experiences, do you agree with her? Explain your response with specific examples.
2. What is your response to Brown's statement: "I've accepted that I'll have to give up a few years of full-time work to allow time for being pregnant and buying Pampers" (paragraph 8)? Does this statement support her ardent defense of the joys of motherhood? Explain.

EVALUATING

3. What specific events caused Brown to reevaluate her own ideas about becoming a mother? How did those events affect her views of motherhood? What decisions have you made about parenthood? How did you make the evaluations necessary to reach these decisions?
4. Brown focuses her discussion on women. Evaluate her reasons and examples. Would they apply as well to men who do not opt for fatherhood? Why?

COMPARING

5. Brown wrote her essay in 1984. Do the issues she raises still concern today's college students? Explain any changes you see between the situation she describes and the situation on your own campus.
6. Make a list of the benefits you see of having children and the benefits you see of not having children. Then write an evaluation of the contrasts you see.

ARGUING

7. What does Brown believe are the reasons that some women today decide not to become mothers? What evidence does she offer to support her beliefs? How convincing do you find this evidence? Explain.
8. What makes Brown believe that "those fiercely independent women" (paragraph 10) look down on women who want to have children? Do you find her evidence convincing? Explain.

A COURAGE BORN OF BROKEN PROMISES

MICHAEL BLUMENTHAL

Michael Blumenthal, who teaches creative writing at Harvard, is currently completing work on a novel. "A Courage Born of Broken Promises" first appeared in *The New York Times*, July 1989.

Predicting Questions

As you read, keep in mind the following questions, derived from this selection's title:

1 What promises have been broken?
2 Why have those promises been broken?
3 How has courage resulted from those broken promises?

Vocabulary Alert

As you read, watch for the following words: "remunerative" (paragraph 3); "ambivalence," "Oedipal" (paragraph 6); "propinquity," "replete" (paragraph 8); "ennobled" (paragraph 10).

If you are unfamiliar with these words, try to determine their meaning from context clues. Which unfamiliar words do you need to look up in a dictionary? (In other words, which have meanings that cannot be determined from context yet are essential to understanding the meaning of the sentence or paragraph?)

---

1 I meet them everywhere—at parties, lectures, friends' houses, just taking a walk—and each time am astonished again by what I can only describe as the near miracle of their cheerfulness, their energy, their seemingly unflappable resilience and, in many cases, their lack of bitterness. They are single parents, mothers mostly, to be honest. And they seem to me a kind of army of survivors—not out of any kind of sameness or lack of individuality, but because they are a living testimonial to a generation. *My* generation. They have survived broken promises, abandoned commitments, half-neglected children and relentlessly pursued self-interest.

2 Each time I meet such a woman, in the relentless dance of our mutual singleness, I am made aware once again of the brutal injustice of her situation, the grave and undeserved difficulties and disadvantages she faces in what is in many ways the crass marketplace of the so-called "unattached" in our culture.

3 Mostly there is a kind of generic, though highly individualized, story: These are bright, attractive, creative women in their late 30's or early 40's. By now, many of them have at least one teenage child and a 10-year or more marriage behind them. Their former husbands, almost inevitably, have gone on to new marriages, new children or stepchildren, continuing advancement in their careers and material lives, and a not quite "joint" participation in that great euphemism "joint custody." Insofar as I can tell, this often means the mother has the child when the *child* needs someone, the father has him or her when the *father* needs someone. The women, in the meantime, are often attempting to juggle the care of their children with some sort of genuine artistic ambition and talent, part- or full-time (often not highly remunerative) work, some sort of graduate or professional school, and a social life as well.

4 Of course, there are men upon whom the burdens of divorce and the sacrifices required to raise children have fallen or been taken on with equal weight. But all too often it's another kind of story I hear. "My ex-husband was the only father on the whole team who didn't come to his son's all-star game," said a woman I recently met, echoing a theme I have heard all too often. And yet what astonishes me most about the single mothers I have known is *not* their desperation or self-pity, but rather their—how else can I say it?—their forgiveness.

5 For each time I encounter such a woman, as a friend, or as a potential mate, I feel myself once again implicated in what I cannot help but experience as a kind of collective guilt on the part of my gender, an unjust advantage that neither moral superiority nor general decency has earned for us. I feel it acutely each time I realize that I—who, by choice, come unburdened and, I might add, unenriched by children, forever told by the society that I am growing more "dignified" as I age—am, in some ways, at an advantage over these women. And I wonder, I truly wonder, how cheerful, how dignified, how capable of generosity and kindness and forgiveness *I* would be were I in their situation, had life dealt me the hand it has so often dealt them.

6 The truth is that I, too, barring the kind of uncontrollable passion to which I hope never again to be subject, hesitate before becoming involved with a woman who is a single parent. Having been an adolescent stepson—a situation which, from the vantage point of adulthood, provides me with a great deal of compassion

both for myself and the poor, unprepared woman who inherited my mourning and rage—I have certain fears about joining the other side of the ledger and becoming a stepfather, with all the grief, rage, ambivalence and Oedipal rivalry that that situation often, especially in adolescent children, entails.

7 Yet those women who find themselves cruelly and unjustly thrust into the harsh market of such weighings and measurings are the kind of women who, but for the inequities of gender and situation, a man—*many* men—could thank his lucky stars at being able to find.

8 At times a blessed propinquity hovers over such pairings, and all three (or four, or five, or six) people find more or less what they need. In a good friend of mine's case, a mostly grown, teen-age boy who needed and unambivalently wanted a new man in his life to replace a more or less absent father, and a childless man nearing 40 who didn't want to start that strenuous and self-sacrificing process of parenting from the beginning, happily found each other. In other instances, an even more blessed event—let's call it, for lack of a better word, love—may convert obstacles into opportunities, fears into challenges. But most cases are not nearly so simple: They are, rather, replete with jealousies, rivalries, fears, ambivalences, uncertainties, and, no doubt, opportunities as well. In most of those cases, it is single mothers who are left holding the short end of the material and emotional stick.

9 "Life is unfair," is one of the more familiar quotations John F. Kennedy left us with during his Presidency, though Marcus Aurelius made the same observation more than 1800 years earlier. I have never doubted the fact, but the lives of so many of the single parents I have met recently—hard-working, devoted, generous, intelligent, creative, high-spirited and, except for their children, alone—convince me, more than ever, that it is true.

10 Ennobled, perhaps, by their difficulties, as is said of all of us, they are nonetheless living reminders that neither the word nor the deed are the reliable acts they may have been in a safer, less complicated time. Or, on a subtler level, that—in the philosopher-scholar Robert Grudin's words—"the reason so many promises are not kept is the same as the reason they are made in the first place."

11 And they remind me, because I can see the pain that inevitably lurks behind the courage and cheerfulness, that a broken promise has a long and ongoing history. Which ought to be enough to make anyone look hard at his own past, and his own future, before daring to make one.

Topics for Reading, Writing, and Discussion

RESPONDING

1 Summarize Blumenthal's comments on "re-created" families (paragraph 8). Referring to your own observations or experiences, explain your response to his comments.

2 Why does Blumenthal "hesitate before becoming involved with a woman who is a single parent" (paragraph 6)? How does he relate his own response to single mothers to the main idea of the essay?

EVALUATING

3 Why does Blumenthal call the lives of single mothers "brutal injustice"? Evaluate the reasons and examples he gives to support this point.

4 What does Blumenthal mean in paragraph 3 when he calls joint custody a "euphemism"? How does he define joint custody? What is the irony in his definition?

COMPARING

5 Comment on the comparison Blumenthal makes between divorced fathers and divorced mothers. Do you agree with him about the similarities and differences he discusses?

6 In paragraph 5, Blumenthal says that he is both "unburdened" and "unenriched" by children. What does he mean by this statement? What positive and negative aspects do you see in the two ways of life his terms imply?

ARGUING

7 Does Blumenthal pity single mothers? Be specific in citing evidence to support your view.

8 Does Blumenthal imply any solutions to the problems he describes? Do you think there are any solutions? Explain.

I REMEMBER PAPA

HARRY DOLAN

Harry Dolan's essay "I Remember Papa" first appeared in an anthology of black writers, *From the Ashes: Voices of Watts*, edited by Budd Schulberg. The title refers to the racially motivated riots and the burning of Watts in southern California in the summer of 1970.

Predicting Questions

As you read, keep in mind the following questions, derived from this selection's title:

1 What does Dolan remember about his father?
2 Why does he find these memories significant?
3 Do you consider these memories primarily negative or primarily positive?

Vocabulary Alert

As you read, watch for the following words: "fabled" (paragraph 1); "etiquette" (paragraph 3); "potential" (paragraph 6); "volition" (paragraph 9); "spasmodically" (paragraph 12); "torrents" (paragraph 24); "multitudes" (paragraph 56).

If you are unfamiliar with these words, try to determine their meaning from context clues. Which unfamiliar words do you need to look up in a dictionary? (In other words, which have meanings that cannot be determined from context yet are essential to understanding the meaning of the sentence or paragraph?)

---

1 The other night after attending a gratifying function which had been initiated to help the black man, specifically to help build a nursery for children of working mothers, and after seeing and hearing white people make speeches professing their understanding and desire to go to any length to help, I found myself suddenly cornered and forced to defend the fabled laziness of the black man.

2 What was especially surprising was the fact that I assumed this white acquaintance—since he had paid thirty dollars to attend this dinner held for the purpose of helping the black man—did, at least in part, have some sympathy with what his, the white people, had tried to accomplish.

3 As I stood there watching his eyes I became suspect of my own sincerity, for I stood attentively nodding my head and smiling. I lit a cigarette, raised an eyebrow, performed all of the white man's laws of etiquette, and all the while I knew if it had been others of my black brothers, they would have cursed him for his smugness and invited him outside to test his theory of black man's courage and laziness. Of course I did none of these things. I grinned as he indicated in no uncertain terms that as soon as the black man got off his lazy butt and took advantage of all the blessings that had been offered him for the last two hundred years, then he, the white man, would indeed be willing to help.

4 I could have answered him—and was tempted to, for he was obviously sincere. Instead, I found an excuse to slip away and let a white man fight my battle, a friend, even a close friend. I went to a far corner and blindly played a game of pool by myself as the voices of this man and my friend dissected me. I stacked the pool balls, leaned over the table, and remembered a black man I had known.

5 It was said of him later in his life that he had let his family down. He'd been lazy, no-account, a troublemaker. Maybe so, maybe so, but I can't help remembering nights of his pacing the squeaking floor muttering to himself, coming back across the floor, sitting down, his legs trembling as he listened to the woman plead for him not to do anything bad.

6 "I'll go to hell first before I'll let you and the children starve." God, how many times had I heard him say that! How many other men standing bunched in helpless stagnation have I heard vow to take a gun and get some food for their children! Yes, they were planning to commit a crime; yes, they were potential criminals. Then. They are usually black too—another crime, it seems.

7 I remember that man, but more I remember his woman, my mother. Curiously though, I never remember her dancing, running, playing; always lying down, the smell of disinfectant strong, the deep continuous coughing, the brown paper bag filled with the toilet paper red with bubbly spit and blood, lying half concealed under the bed.

8 I never remember her eating food such as bread, meat, potatoes; only apples and only Delicious apples. In those days five cents apiece. She was a small woman, barely five foot.

9 "Junior," she would say softly. She never spoke above a whisper. "Go to the store and get me an apple." The thin trembling hand would reverse itself and slide up and under the covers and under the pillow and then return as though of its own volition, the weight almost too much, and as I'd start out the door, she would always smile and say, "Hurry, Junior."

10 I'd nod, and always, always there seemed to be a need to hurry. Those trips were always made with a feeling of breathless fear. I didn't know why then, only that for some reason I must always come back as soon as possible.

11 I was returning with an especially large apple, walking along, tempted to bite just a tiny piece, when I turned the corner and saw the black police ambulance standing in front of my door. Suddenly

I had to go to the bathroom so bad I couldn't move. I stood watching as two uniformed men came out with the stretcher, and then the sound of my mother's shrill voice hit me.

12 "Mama, Mama," she was screaming. I could see her twisting and swinging at the lady next door as she was held back. I stood there feeling the hot piss run down my trembling legs, feeling cold chills spatter through my body, causing frozen limbs to spasmodically begin to move. I forced myself toward the police wagon as the men opened the doors and slid the stretcher along the bare metal. I saw my mother's head bounce on the floor.

13 "Wait," I moaned, "don't hurt her." Then I was running, screaming, "Please don't hurt her."

14 I looked down at her pain-filled face, and she smiled, even then she smiled. I showed her the apple. The effort to nod seemed a terrible effort but she did, her eyes so very bright, so very shiny.

15 "You eat it, Junior, you and sis."

16 "What's wrong, Mama?" I asked softly. "You really, really sick now?"

17 She nodded.

18 "Your father will be home soon. Tell him I'm at the General Hospital. Tell him to—to hurry."

19 "I'll tell him, Mama," I promised. "I'll tell him to hurry, Mama." She nodded sadly and puckered her lips as she always did since we weren't allowed to kiss her.

20 That was the last time I saw my mother except at the grave. My father came to the funeral with two white men who stood on each side of him all the time. There were people crying all around us. My grandmother kept squeezing me and moaning. I saw my father try to cover his face but one of the men said something and he stood up stiffly after that. I didn't cry, because my mother seemed to look happier, more rested than I had ever seen her. For some reason, I was glad she was dead. I think maybe, except for us, she was too.

21 I was nine, my sister five. It was not until ten years later that I saw my father again.

22 We sat on opposite sides of a screen and talked into telephones. I had come there to tell him that in spite of my beginning, I had made it. I was nineteen, and a radioman in the U.S. Coast Guard, ready to fight and die for my country. There had been something mysterious about his smile.

23 "I'm proud of you, boy," he said. "You're a real man. You know I volunteered for the front lines too, but they turned me down."

24 We don't want you, I thought, we're not criminals, we're honest, strong. Then I looked again at this thief, this "Loaf-of-bread

gunman" as the papers had tagged him. He had taken five loaves of bread, along with twelve dollars. Suddenly I could not stay there condemning this man, my father. It seemed such a waste, this magnificently strong man sitting there, his tremendous chest barely moving, hands resting quietly, talking to me, his whole being showering torrents of words about me.

25 "Be careful, boy, there are so many ways to fail, the pitfall sometimes seems to be the easiest way out. Beware of my future, for you must continue, you must live. You must, for in you are all the dreams of my nights, all the ambitions of my days."

26 A bell rang and we stood up and a man pointed me toward a heavy door. I looked back, and saw him standing easy, hands at his side, so very calm, yet my mind filled to overflowing with the many things he had not said. It was to be ten years before he walked again as a free man, that is, as a physically free man.

27 I remember an earlier time, an earlier chapter of my growing up. I remember the first time my mother said we were taking lunch to my father's job. We had been down to the welfare line and I had stood with her, our feet burning against the hot pavement, and slowly moved forward in the sun. Years later I stood in chow lines over half of the world, but no desert, no burning deck was as hot as that day.

28 At last we reached the man sitting at the desk and my mother handed him the book of stamps. She smiled, a weak almost timid smile, as he checked her name and thumbed her to the food line.

29 As we headed home, my wagon was loaded with cans of corned beef, powdered milk, powdered eggs, and white margarine that she would later color yellow to look like butter.

30 At home we made sandwiches and off we went to my father's job, to take him his lunch. I pulled my sister along in my wagon, a Red Flyer.

31 It was to be a picnic, a celebration really, my father's new job.

32 I remember the wagon did not have a tongue or handle but only a rope with which I pulled it wobbling along. We were excited, my sister and I, as we left our district of dirt streets and unpaved sidewalks and began to make our way along roads called boulevards and malls we had never had occasion to travel. The streets themselves were fascinating, so different. They were twice as wide, and there were exotic trees along the sidewalks and lo and behold trees down the center of the street as far as I could see and then we turned the corner and before us stretched an overwhelming sight. An overhead highway was being built. Columns rose to staggering heights, bulldozers thrust what seemed

to me mountains of dirt before them, and hundreds, no thousands of men seemed to be crawling like ants hurrying from one point to another. Cranes lifted nets of steel and laid them in rows on the crushed rock.

33 I stared in awe at important-looking white men in metal hats, carrying rolls of papers which they intermittently studied, then pointing into space at what to me seemed only emptiness.

34 And then I saw my father. He sat among fifty other black men, all surrounded by great boulders marked with red paint. They all held steel chisels with which they cut along the marked lines. They would strike a certain point and the boulder would split into smaller pieces and as we approached there was a silence around them except for the pinging of the hammer against the chisel. In all the noise it was a lonely sound, futile, lost, oppressive. My father seemed to be concentrating, his tremendous arm whipping the air. He was stripped to the waist, black muscles popping sweat, goggled eyes for the metal and stone only. We stood there, the three of us, my mother, my sister, and I, and watched my father work for us, and as he conquered the huge boulder my chest filled with pride. Each stroke shouted for all the world to hear: This is my family and I love them! No one can tell me this was the act of a lazy man.

35 Suddenly a white man walked up and blew a whistle and the black men all looked up and stopped working. My father glanced over at me, grinned and winked. He was glistening with sweat, the smell strong and powerful. He dropped his big hand on my shoulder and guided me to a large boulder.

36 "Hey, boy, you see me beat that thing to bits? This one's next," he said, indicating the one that shaded us from the sun. "I'll pound it to gravel by nightfall." It was a challenge he expected, he welcomed. That was my lazy, shiftless father.

37 And then one day they brought him home, his thumb, index, and middle finger gone from his left hand. They sat him in the kitchen chair and mumbled something about carelessness. He sat there for two hours before he answered our pleadings.

38 "Chain broke, I—I was guiding boulder. I couldn't, I just couldn't get my hand out from under in time—I, goddam it, Jean, they took my fingers off. I layed right there, my hand under the rock, and they nipped them like butchering a hog. Look at my goddam hand."

39 My mother held him in her arms and talked to him. She spoke softly, so softly my sister and I, standing in the corner, couldn't hear the words, only the soothing softness of her voice.

40 "Joe, Joe, we can." And then he began to cry like—like I sometimes did when I was hurt deep inside and couldn't do anything about it.

41 After that there was a change in him. My father had been a fighter. He had feared no man white or black. I remember the time we were sitting on a streetcar and a woman had forgotten her fare—or maybe she never had any in the first place. Anyway, the driver slammed the doors on her and held her squeezed between them.

42 My father jumped up, snatched the driver out of the seat, and let the woman out. He and the driver had words that led to battle and Pop knocked the driver down just as a patrolman arrived. The patrolman didn't listen to any of the people that tried to explain what had happened. He just began to swing his night stick at my father's head. It was a mistake. My father hit him once and even today I can see all the people laughing at the funny look on the policeman's face as he staggered back all the way across the street and up against a building, slowly sagging down.

43 The police wagon arrived with four other policemen and one told him they were going to beat his brains in when they got him down town.

44 My pop had laughed then and backed against the building.

45 "I guess ain't no sense me going peaceable then."

46 They knocked out all his upper front teeth that day, but as he said later, "Them four white boys will think of me every time they shave."

47 They finally overpowered him and dragged him, still struggling, to the wagon. One of them kept muttering, "He's one fighting son of a black bitch, he's a fighting son of a bitch."

48 All the time I hadn't said a word or cried or yelled as they stomped and kicked him. I had shut my eyes and held my lips tightly pressed together and I had done just as he'd always told me.

49 "You stay out of it, boy, stay real quiet, and when that wagon leaves, you run behind and keep it in sight. If they lose you, you ask someone where the closest police station is—that's where I'll be. You go home and tell your mother."

50 That's the way he had been before losing his left hand. Afterwards, well, it took a lot from him. He told me one day, laughing and shaking the nub as he called it, "If I'd only had the thumb, just the lousy thumb, I'd have it made."

51 Gradually he lost the ability to see humor in the nub. I think the whole thing came to a head the night I killed the kitten.

52 We hadn't had meat or potatoes for over two weeks. Even the

grease drippings were gone and my mother was too sick to raise her head from the pillow. So I had gotten the skillet and put it in the open grate. We had two cups of flour so I mixed water with it and poured it into the greasy skillet. I can still recall the coldness of the room on my back and the warmth from the grate on my face as my sister and I knelt and hungrily watched the flour brown.

53 You know, today my wife marvels at how, no matter what she puts before me, I eat with relish. My children say that I eat very fast. I pray to God they never have to experience the causes of my obsession. But back to the story—the flour finally hardened and I broke a piece for my sister and a piece for my mother and left mine in the skillet on the table.

54 I took my mother's piece over to the bed and put it in her hand. She didn't move so I raised her hand to her mouth and she began to suck on it. Then I heard my sister scream, "Topsy is eating your food, Junior, Topsy's eating your food!" I turned around to see the cat tearing at my tiny piece of hard dough. I went wild. I leaped across the room and grabbed the kitten by the tail and began slamming her against the wall.

55 "That's my food," I kept yelling, "my food!" At last I heard my sister screaming, "She's bleeding, you're killing Topsy. Here, here, eat my bread. Please don't kill her."

56 I stopped, horrified, staring at the limp nothing I now held. It was two weeks later that they got me to speak and that same night my father left the house for the last time. I don't say that what he did was right. No, it most assuredly was wrong. But what I do ask is, what else could he have done? I need an answer quickly now, today, right away, for I tell you this, my children will not starve, not here, not in this time of millions to foreign countries and fountains to throw tons of water upward to the sky, and nothing to the hungry, thirsty multitudes a stone's throw away.

Topics for Reading, Writing, and Discussion

RESPONDING

1. Read the advice Dolan's father gives him in paragraph 25. Comment on that advice by relating it to your own experiences or observations.
2. List at least five details Dolan provides to describe his mother. What inferences about the mother—and about Dolan's childhood feelings for her—can you make? What is your response to Dolan's description of this relationship?

EVALUATING

3 Summarize the events in the first four paragraphs. As you summarize, notice Dolan's voice and tone. Evaluate the relationship between the first four paragraphs and the rest of the essay.

4 What is the father's initial attitude toward his job splitting boulders? Evaluate when and why that attitude changes. Evaluate also the effect this change has on Dolan.

COMPARING

5 Explain Dolan's feelings for his father when he first visits him in prison. Compare those feelings with the emotions Dolan later experiences. What reasons do you see for the change? What is the significance of the change?

6 In the opening section, Dolan describes his own response to an insulting and embarrassing situation. Comment on his response and compare it to your own experience (or the experience of someone you know) in a similar situation.

ARGUING

7 By the end of the essay, Dolan seems to justify his father's life. To what extent do you agree with him? Explain your reasons.

8 Dolan implies that poverty is a primary motivation for crime. Do you agree? Explain your reasons.

TOPICS FOR LONGER PAPERS: PART ONE

1 Read the selections in Part I and then write an evaluation of the views the authors take of the family unit. Are they primarily optimistic or pessimistic? Compare their reasons for optimism or pessimism. Do you find the views expressed contradictory? Or do they all fit together logically to make one unified, yet varied, picture?

2 Lisa Brown, Ellen Goodman, and Harry Dolan have very different views of the role parents play in their children's lives. Whose view do you find the most realistic? Support with examples from your own life or from your own observations.

3 Compare William Raspberry's and Michael Blumenthal's views of single-parent families. How are their subjects the same? Different? How do their approaches to their subjects differ? How are they the same? Evaluate the significance of the differences you identify.

4 Compare the views of marriage suggested by Lisa Brown and Jeannie MacDonald. Do your views correspond to those of either of these writers, or do you have a different view? Explain.
5 In his textbook *Sociology: The Core,* James W. Vander Zanden offers the following observation: "Indisputably, the meaning of marriage has been changing [during the past fifty years] and with it the family institution." Considering the readings in this section as well as your own experiences and observations, how do you see marriage as changing? What effects do these changes have on the family? Consider reading more extensively on this topic as well as interviewing experts in your community and on campus.

TOPICS REQUIRING RESEARCH: PART ONE

(For Research Strategies and Skills, Consult Appendixes D and E)

1 Find all the descriptions Lisa Brown (pages 163–166) gives of women who choose not to have children, then summarize her view of these women. Compare her picture with your own image of such women. To develop your picture, interview several women who have decided not to have children.
2 Find an article in a recent newspaper or magazine about whether to have children. Write an evaluation of that article. Be sure to start with a brief summary of the article. Focus on two or three specific points made by the author as you write your evaluation.
3 Design a questionnaire that will evaluate parents' attitudes toward their children's education. Then give the questionnaire to at least ten people who have children currently in school. Write an essay explaining the results of your survey.
4 William Raspberry's article, "Missing: The Influence of Black Men" (pages 156–158), implies that the breakdown of the family is particularly a black problem. Do research to evaluate that implication.
5 Using the periodical indexes in the library (the *Social Sciences Index* is a good place to start), find an article on single parents. Briefly summarize the author's main idea and primary supporting points. Then explain your response to the author's ideas.

6 Using *The New York Times Index*, find and read several reports on poverty and hunger in the United States today. Does the situation Harry Dolan (pages 170–177) describes as the lot of his family seem to have improved during the more than twenty years since he wrote his essay? Explain your evaluations.

P A R T   T W O

LEARNING AND TEACHING

STUDENTS' INDIFFERENCE ERODES THE PUBLIC SCHOOLS

BRENT COLLINS

Brent Collins has taught English and humanities for fifteen years at a suburban Minneapolis high school. This article appeared in the September/October 1990 issue of the *Utne Reader.*

Predicting Questions

As you read, keep in mind the following questions, derived from this selection's title:

1 Why does Collins believe students are indifferent?
2 What does he mean by the word "erodes"?
3 Does he suggest any solution to the problem of students' indifference?

Vocabulary Alert

As you read, watch for the following words: "deteriorating" (paragraph 1); "myriad," "apathy" (paragraph 2); "ironically" (paragraph 5); "biding" (paragraph 6); "mythology," "mentor," "cynically" (paragraph 8); "rhapsodized" (paragraph 15).

If you are unfamiliar with these words, try to determine their meaning from context clues. Which unfamiliar words do you need to look up in a dictionary? (In other words, which have meanings that cannot be determined from context yet are essential to understanding the meaning of the sentence or paragraph?)

1 There's no denying the deteriorating state of American education today. Schools are graduating kids who can't make change on a dollar or pick out Thailand on a world map. But who's to blame?

2 Although there are myriad reasons why our schools are failing, I believe one issue hasn't received enough attention: a growing population of students who don't care about learning. Their apathy and indifference is gradually eroding my function and purpose as an educator.

3 A creative writing class I taught last spring at my high school in suburban Minneapolis provides one example. In a class of fewer than 30 students, I dropped six for excessive absences. (Four of the six told me it was just "too hard to make it to a first hour class.") The remaining students, with a few exceptions, gazed at me blankly each morning. Many were exhausted from working late at their jobs. My best efforts—and my best jokes—failed to engage them in discussions, much less excite them about writing. Even when I allowed time in class to work on assignments, fewer than two-thirds of the students ever turned in schoolwork. By the end of the quarter, I felt more like a day-care provider than a teacher.

4 At times every teacher has to ask "Is it me?" But after 15 years in the profession, you know when you've failed the class, and when the class has failed you.

5 Ironically, these kids are not troublemakers or low achievers. They are, for the most part, nice kids with average ability—and zero motivation. But they reflect a trend I find disturbing. On the achievement ladder, the top and bottom rungs—the high achievers and special needs students—are encouraged and supported by our educational system. They are, literally, "programmed" for success. It's the average kids, those in the middle, the forgotten majority, who are losing interest and losing ground. They are less successful than ever before.

6 In my darker moments, I've likened my school to a giant holding tank where too many of these kids—uninterested, unmotivated—are simply biding their time, doing the minimum amount of work and attending class just often enough to get by. Today's "C" student is not necessarily a kid with average ability, but someone who may have done little more than put in seat time. The apathy that such students bring to the classroom is becoming epidemic.

7 For many kids, pressure to succeed in school—from peers and parents—is missing. One student told me, "My parents don't care as long as I'm passing. So why should I kill myself over grades? The money I earn from my paper route and my part-time job is more important." He'll get the same diploma as a National Merit Scholar.

8 There's a prevalent and disturbing attitude among many kids that teachers—or any other adults—can't teach them anything: the

"know-it-all" factor. During a discussion in mythology class, I asked students to name their mentors. One boy replied cynically, "I'm my own mentor." He's not alone in believing he has all the answers.

9 It's time to do something to improve schools. Here are a few ideas:

10 ▪ Let kids quit. Those who aren't interested in school or learning should be allowed to leave the system and pursue other interests. Let them work or attend trade school, with the provision that they can return to school when and if they're ready.

11 ▪ Offer incentives by throwing out grade levels and designing courses that require students to master the material at a specific level in order to pass. Kids would be motivated to learn if only to avoid spending their adult lives as high school students.

12 ▪ Stop hyping test scores and publishing propaganda about our schools. I find no comfort in knowing that 50 percent of my high school's students are on the honor roll. All this means is that too many teachers are boosting kids' egos with inflated grades in the hope that they'll eventually live up to our expectations. Self-esteem is built through true accomplishment, not through empty praise.

13 ▪ Limit class sizes so that teachers can provide individual attention and more closely monitor students' progress. The belief that teachers can effectively meet the needs of 30 or more kids with widely ranging abilities is a myth.

14 ▪ Convince parents that their ongoing involvement in education is critical to their children's success. Parents have a greater influence on their kids than any individual or institution. Their influence can be used to help their kids succeed in school. It's no secret that most highly motivated kids have highly motivated parents.

15 During a parent-teacher conference recently, one parent—after listening patiently as I rhapsodized about his daughter's accomplishments—stopped me and said, "I don't care about her grades or her class participation. Just tell me, is my daughter *learning* anything?"

16 The question is startling in its simplicity. If more parents asked teachers this question, I can only think we'd have more kids caring about learning. At least it would be a start.

Topics for Reading, Writing, and Discussion

RESPONDING

1. Do you agree that students' indifference is a major problem in public schools? Base your response on your own experiences or observations.
2. Imagine that you are one of the students Collins describes in this article. How would you respond to his accusations?

EVALUATING

3. Collins claims that many students have a "know-it-all" attitude. Does the evidence that he provides convince you that he is right? Explain your evaluation.
4. Evaluate the list of changes Collins suggests. Then explain which you agree with and which you disagree with.

COMPARING

5. Compare the classroom scenes Collins describes with high school classroom scenes you remember.
6. Compare the attitude of parents toward education as suggested in paragraph 8 with the attitudes of parents you know.

ARGUING

7. Argue for or against the following proposition: Student indifference is the primary problem in public schools today.
8. Choose any two suggestions on Collins's list of improvements and argue for or against their implementation. As part of your argument, explain what effects you think these suggestions would have.

PLAYING FAVORITES

PATRICIA KEEGAN

Patricia Keegan's article first appeared in a special section of *The New York Times*'s "Education Life" called "The Gender Card," August 1989. The essays in this section of the *Times* explored the differences between male and female students—and between the treatment accorded males and that accorded females in the United States school system.

Predicting Questions

As you read, keep in mind the following questions, derived from this selection's title:

1 Who is "playing favorites"?
2 Who is being favored?
3 Why is that group favored?

Vocabulary Alert

As you read, watch for the following words: "stereotypes" (paragraph 1); "genetically" (paragraph 6); "affiliated" (paragraph 10); "acumen" (paragraph 15); "disparity" (paragraph 20).

If you are unfamiliar with these words, try to determine their meaning from context clues. Which unfamiliar words do you need to look up in a dictionary? (In other words, which have meanings that cannot be determined from context yet are essential to understanding the meaning of the sentence or paragraph?)

---

1 There is strong evidence today that nurture—in the role of parents, teachers and a society still influenced by sex stereotypes—plays an important part in determining how and what boys and girls learn. There is even stronger evidence that, particularly since the advent of the computer, the American education system is geared more closely to boys' learning styles than to those of girls. It is a bias that a growing number of projects are aiming to correct.

2 Studies of school and college classrooms have helped broadly define gender differences in learning. Boys, for example, are competitive, girls cooperative. Boys often prefer individual work, girls do better in groups. Boys seek leadership roles, girls are more willing to be led. Boys believe that they earn high grades, while girls more often attribute their success to luck. "How we treat boys and girls obviously affects the way they learn and what they learn," said Dr. Myra Sadker, acting dean of the school of education at American University in Washington, D.C.

3 Dr. Sadker and her husband, Dr. David Sadker, also a professor of education at American University, have studied classroom interactions in all levels for more than a decade. In one study financed by the National Institute of Education, field researchers who observed more than 100 fourth-, sixth- and eighth-grade classrooms in four states and the District of Columbia found that male students received more attention from teachers and were given more time to talk in class.

4 While boys are more assertive than girls—they are eight times more likely to call out answers—the Sadkers found that teachers also called on boys more often and gave them more positive feedback than girls. Boys also received more precise feedback from teachers—praise, criticism or help with the answers they gave in class; girls, the Sadkers said, more often received bland and diffuse responses, such as "O.K." and "uh-huh." Most of the researchers in this and other studies found that boys got more attention whether the teachers were male or female.

5 Parents also affect how and what their children learn. According to Dr. Jacquelynne Eccles, who is both a professor of psychology at the University of Colorado and senior research scientist at the University of Michigan, parents—particularly mothers—believe in sex-stereotyped ability more strongly today than they did in the mid-1970's when she began her research.

6 "Parents, teachers and kids think boys have more ability in mathematics and sports and girls slightly more in English and music," said Dr. Eccles, who surveyed 1,000 Michigan families with school-age children. She re-interviewed 100 families after news stories appeared on research showing that boys were genetically better in math. About half the families had read the stories. Among those who had, the parents, particularly the mothers, had lowered their opinions of their daughters' math ability.

7 "Their attitudes have more of an impact on kids' confidence than grades, but certainly affect the likelihood that kids will spend more time on those subjects," Dr. Eccles said.

8 In response to the continuing low number of girls entering technical fields, some schools have begun programs to encourage them to take math and science courses. For example, in seventh- and eighth-grade science classes at the Montgomery Middle School, just outside Princeton, N.J., female students act as group leaders and teach lessons to their male and female classmates. Their teachers find that assigning girls leadership roles that most would not take on their own, and setting up small groups, builds the girls' self-confidence and interest in these fields.

9 Proponents of women's colleges take these findings a step further, arguing that their environment—in which, in the absence of men, women must assume leadership positions—encourages women to enter male-dominated fields such as science and math. A 1985 study by the Women's College Coalition, which represents most of the nation's 94 women's colleges, found that 5.4 percent of its graduates earned degrees in biology compared with 3.6 percent of women at coeducational colleges. In physics, the figures were 1.7 percent compared with 1.2 percent and in math, 2.3 percent compared with 1.5 percent.

10 The different treatment of students based on their gender has been observed at all levels. In a 1975 study of classroom

interaction in Suffolk County, New York, involving more than 200 children in nursery schools, two psychologists then affiliated with the State University of New York at Stony Brook, Lisa Serbin and K. Daniel O'Leary, found that teachers showed boys how to staple pieces of construction paper together for a crafts project, then let the boys do their own stapling. But the teachers did the stapling for the girls.

'GIRLS TAUGHT TO BE DEPENDENT'

11 Although no studies of the same children have been done over the long term, Dr. O'Leary said, "The findings would suggest that girls are taught to be more dependent and boys more independent." Dr. Serbin said that in this study and in later studies of nursery-school children, she found that girls "tend to remain close to the teacher while boys are more comfortable exploring on their own, working independently without teacher structure."

12 Similarly, in colleges and graduate schools, professors show male students how to use equipment and perform lab experiments, while they did the work for female students.

13 After looking at many of the studies on college-classroom interactions, the Association of American Colleges concluded that male students also receive more eye contact and far more of the professor's attention than do female students.

14 The classroom climate obviously affects women's learning and intellectual self-esteem. "Women students are much less likely than their male classmates to feel confident about their preparation for and their ability to do graduate work," according to the association's 1982 report.

15 Yet at least one recent study shows that things can change over time. Research among 4,500 adult learners at Empire State College of the State University of New York found that the women's perception of learning ability jumps ahead of the men's in their late 20's and continues higher through the early retirement years. In the midlife transition phase, between ages 37 and 43, men think their academic acumen is significantly below that of midlife women.

16 Follow-up interviews, explained Dr. Timothy Lehmann, associate vice president for research and evaluation, indicate that: "By re-entering college, women students more than men clearly recognize they are at a transition point. They go on to have a greater graduation rate than men."

17 One instrument that has provided researchers with a rich opportunity to study gender-related learning differences is the computer. In a 1987 survey of and interviews with 44 fifth-graders, Dr. Lise Motherwell of the Massachusetts Institute of Technology found that 75 percent of the boys thought the computer was more like a machine and 60 percent of the girls said it was more like a person. "Computers have become the erector sets and doll houses of the 80's," Dr. Motherwell writes in a paper soon to be published by the National Organization for Women.

WHAT COMPUTERS ARE TO GIRLS AND BOYS

18 A federally funded study to encourage girls' use of computers, conducted by the Women's Action Alliance, a national nonprofit organization furthering equality for women, based in New York City, yielded similar findings in its final report in 1986, titled "The Neuter Computer: Computers for Boys and Girls." It read, "While many boys seem to enjoy the computer for its own sake—playing around with it just to see what it can do—many girls seem to value the computer for how it can help them do what they want or have to do. In other words, computers are often means for girls but ends for boys."

19 A 1984 survey by the Alliance as part of the same study, which examined 700 seventh- and eighth-grade students in California, Nebraska and Vermont, found boys far more likely than girls to use the computer in school during free time and more likely to have a home computer and use it.

20 Hoping to reduce the disparity, the Women's Action Alliance, with money from the National Science Foundation, is sponsoring what it calls a computer-equity project involving six school districts in New York State. One of these, Orchard Park Middle School, in a suburb of Buffalo, started a computer club just for girls. The female students liked choosing their own computer activities, instead of the militaristic, competitive games usually chosen by the boys, according to Barbara Chmura, district computer coordinator. Once the girls developed more confidence about using computers, they were more likely to take part in joint projects with boys, she said.

21 Recent evidence indicates that gender-related differences in attitudes toward computers and technology continue through adulthood, even among those who use computers in their careers.

22 The Center for Children and Technology of the Bank Street College of Education in New York City interviewed more than 70 men and women in technological fields including architecture, engineering, computer programming and video production. "Women in technological fields want their work to be useful, helpful and empower others," said Dr. Margaret Honey, senior research scientist at the center. "Men don't talk that way."

23 When the subjects were asked to create a perfect technological

instrument, women proposed ways to humanize the computer, Dr. Honey said, while men "believed the computer has the goods and they want to be connected to it."

24 The ongoing Bank Street project, financed by the Spencer Foundation, now is interviewing adolescent boys and girls to find out how they view technology. The goal, as with the other programs, is to develop alternate learning programs so that girls will feel more comfortable choosing careers in technological fields still dominated by men.

Topics for Reading, Writing, and Discussion

RESPONDING

1 What is your response to the first paragraph? After reading this paragraph, formulate several predicting questions that you expect will be answered in the rest of the essay. When you finish reading, note which questions were answered, which were not, and what further questions were raised.

2 In paragraphs 15 and 16, Keegan cites a study showing that "the women's perception of learning ability jumps ahead of the men's in their late 20's." Why do you think this change might occur? What is your response to learning about this study?

EVALUATING

3 Evaluate how the introduction of computers to the classroom has affected the education of boys and of girls. What significance do you find in the differences Keegan describes?

4 Keegan suggests that boys are more competitive while girls are more cooperative in their learning styles. Boys prefer to work individually while girls prefer to work in groups. Evaluate the advantages and disadvantages of each learning style. Which do you prefer? Why?

COMPARING

5 Describe your own experiences with computers in the classroom (or in other parts of your life) and compare those experiences to Keegan's discussions of computers.

6 What differences does Keegan describe in the learning styles of boys and of girls? From your own experiences and observations, do you agree with her? Explain why or why not, using specific examples to illustrate your claims.

ARGUING

7 Throughout the essay, Keegan describes various proposals to make the learning environment in schools equally useful to both boys

and girls. Choose one of these proposals and write an argument explaining why you think it would or would not be effective.

8 What kinds of evidence does Keegan offer to support her contention that the American education system is more suited to the learning styles of boys than to the learning styles of girls? How convincing do you find this evidence? Explain.

I Show a Child What Is Possible

JACQUES D'AMBOISE

One of the finest classical dancers of our time, Jacques d'Amboise joined George Balanchine's New York City Ballet when he was fifteen. Because of his own background, d'Amboise felt a strong commitment to bring dance to inner-city children, and in 1976 he founded National Dance Institute, which today has programs in about thirty public schools in the New York City area. In this article, d'Amboise explains his inspiring approach to teaching dance.

Predicting Questions

As you read, keep in mind the following questions, derived from this selection's title:

1 What is the child being shown?
2 Who is the "I" of the title?
3 How does the "I" of the title show a child what is possible?

Vocabulary Alert

As you read, watch for the following words: "diabolically" (paragraph 1); "flaying" (paragraph 5); "triathletes" (paragraph 23).

If you are unfamiliar with these words, try to determine their meaning from context clues. Which unfamiliar words do you need to look up in a dictionary? (In other words, which have meanings that cannot be determined from context yet are essential to understanding the meaning of the sentence or paragraph?)

1 When I was 7 years old, I was forced to watch my sister's ballet classes. This was to keep me off the street and away from my pals, who ran with gangs like the ones in *West Side Story.* The class was taught by Madame Seda, a Georgian-Armenian who had a school at 181st Street and St. Nicholas Avenue in New York City. As she taught the little girls, I would sit, fidget and diabolically try to disrupt the class by making irritating little noises.

2 But she was very wise, Madame Seda. She let me get away with it, ignoring me until the end of the class, when everybody did the big jumps, a series of leaps in place, called *changements.*

3 At that point, Madame Seda turned and, stabbing a finger at me, said, "All right, little brother, if you've got so much energy, get up and do these jumps. See if you can jump as high as the girls." So I jumped. And loved it. I felt like I was flying. And she said, "Oh, that was wonderful! From now on, if you are quiet during the class, I'll let you join in the *changements.*"

4 After that, I'd sit quietly in the class and wait for the jumps. A few classes later, she said, "You've got to learn how to jump and not make any noise when you come down. You should learn to do the *pliés* [graceful knee bends] that come at the beginning of the class." So I would do *pliés,* then wait respectfully for the end of class to do the jumps.

5 Finally she said, "You jump high, and you are landing beautifully, but you look awful in the air, flaying your arms about. You've got to take the rest of the class and learn how to do beautiful hands and arms."

6 I was hooked.

7 An exceptional teacher got a bored little kid, me, interested in ballet. How? She challenged me to a test, complimented me on my effort and then immediately gave me a new challenge. She set up an environment for the achievement of excellence and cared enough to invite me to be part of it. And, without realizing it fully at the time, I made an important discovery.

8 Dance is the most immediate and accessible of the arts because it involves your own body. When you learn to move your body on a note of music, it's exciting. You have taken control of your body and, by learning to do that, you discover that you can take control of your life.

9 I took classes with Madame Seda for six months, once a week, but at the end of spring, in June 1942, she called over my mother, my sister and me and did an unbelievably modest and generous thing. She said, "You and your sister are very talented. You should go to a better teacher." She sent us to George Balanchine's school—the School of American Ballet.

10 Within a few years, I was performing children's roles. At 15, I became part of a classical ballet company. What an extraordinary

thing for a street boy from Washington Heights, with friends in gangs. Half grew up to become policemen and the other half gangsters—and I became a ballet dancer!

11 I had dreamed of being a doctor or an archaeologist or a priest. But by the time I was 17, I was a principal dancer performing major roles in the ballets, and by the time I was 21, I was doing movies, Broadway shows and choreography. I then married a ballerina from New York City Ballet, Carolyn George, and we were (and still are) blessed with two boys and twin daughters.

12 It was a joyful career that lasted four decades. That's a long time to be dancing and, inevitably, a time came when I realized that there were not many years left for me as a performer. I wasn't sure what to do next, but then I thought about how I had become a dancer, and the teachers who had graced my life. Perhaps I could engage young children, especially boys, in the magic of the arts—in dance in particular. Not necessarily to prepare them to be professional performers, but to create an awareness by giving them a chance to experience the arts. So I started National Dance Institute.

13 That was 13 years ago. Since then, with the help of fellow teachers and staff at NDI, I have taught dance to thousands of inner-city children. And in each class, I rediscover why teaching dance to children is so important.

14 Each time I can use dance to help a child discover that he can control the way he moves, I am filled with joy. At a class I recently taught at P.S. 59 in Brooklyn, there was one boy who couldn't get from his right foot to his left. He was terrified. Everyone was watching. And what he had to do was so simple: take a step with his left foot on a note of music. All his classmates could do it, but he couldn't.

15 He kept trying, but he kept doing it wrong until finally he was frozen, unable to move at all. I put my arm around him and said, "Let's do it together. We'll do it in slow motion." We did it. I stepped back and said, "Now do it alone, and fast." With his face twisted in concentration, he slammed his left foot down correctly on the note. He did it!

16 The whole class applauded. He was so excited. But I think I was even happier, because I knew what had taken place. He had discovered he could take control of his body, and from that he can learn to take control of his life. If I can open the door to show a child that that is possible, it is wonderful.

17 Dance is the art to express time and space. That is what our universe is about. We can hardly make a sentence without signifying some expression of distance, place or time: "See you later." "Meet you at the corner in five minutes."

18 Dance is the art that human beings have developed to express that we live, right now, in a world of movement and varying tempos.

19 Dance, as an art, has to be taught. However, when teaching, it's important to set up an environment where both the student and teacher can discover together. Never teach something you don't love and believe in. But how to set up that environment?

20 When I have a new group of young students and I'm starting a class, I use Madame Seda's technique. I say, "Can you do this test? I'm going to give all 100 of you exactly 10 seconds to get off your seats and be standing and spread out all over the stage floor. And do it silently. Go!" And I start a countdown. Naturally, they run, yelling and screaming, and somehow arrive with several seconds to spare. I say, "Freeze. You all failed. You made noise, and you got there too soon. I said 'exactly 10 seconds'—not 6 or 8 or 11. Go back to your seats, and we'll do it again. And if you don't get it, we'll go back and do it again until you do. And if, at the end of the hour, you still haven't gotten it, I'm not going to teach you."

21 They usually get it the second time. Never have I had to do it more than three.

22 Demand precision, be clear and absolutely truthful. When they respond—and they will—congratulate them on the extraordinary control they have just exhibited. Why is that important? Because it's the beginning of knowing yourself, knowing that you can manage yourself if you want. And it's the beginning of dance. Once the children see that we are having a class of precision, order and respect, they are relieved, and we have a great class.

23 I've taught dance to Russian children, Australian children, Indian children, Chinese children, fat children, skinny children, handicapped children, groups of Australian triathletes, New York City police, senior citizens and 3-year-olds. The technique is the same everywhere, although there are cultural differences.

24 For example, when I was in China, I would say to the children, "I want everybody to come close and watch what I am going to do." But in China they have had to deal with following a teacher when there are masses of them. And they discovered that the way to see what the teacher does is not to move close but to move away. So 100 people moved back to watch the one—me.

25 I realized they were right. How did they learn that? Thousands of years of masses of people having to follow one teacher.

26 There are cultural differences and there are differences among

people. In any group of dancers, there are some who are ready and excel more than others. There are many reasons—genetic, environment, the teachers they had. People blossom at different times.

27 But whatever the differences, someone admiring you, encouraging you, works so much better than the reverse. "You can do it, you are wonderful," works so much better than, "You're no good, the others are better than you, you've got to try harder." That never works.

28 I don't think there are any untalented children. But I think there are those whose talents never get the chance to flower. Perhaps they were never encouraged. Perhaps no one took the time to find out how to teach them. That is a tragedy.

29 However, the single most terrible thing we are doing to our children, I believe, is polluting them. I don't mean just with smog and crack, but by not teaching them the civilizing things we have taken millions of years to develop. But you cannot have a dance class without having good manners, without having respect. Dance can teach those things.

30 I think of each person as a trunk that's up in the attic. What are you going to put in the trunk? Are you going to put in machine guns, loud noises, foul language, dirty books and ignorance? Because, if you do, that's what is going to be left after you, that's what your children are going to have, and that will determine the world of the future. Or are you going to fill that trunk with music, dance, poetry, literature, good manners and loving friends?

31 I say, fill your trunk with the best that is available to you from the wealth of human culture. Those things will nourish you and your children. You can clean up your own environment and pass it on to the next generation. That's why I teach dance.

Topics for Reading, Writing, and Discussion

RESPONDING

1 Summarize briefly the story of Madame Seda and her initial meetings with d'Amboise. What was your response to this story?

2 What ideas does d'Amboise illustrate with the story he tells of the boy at P.S. 59 in Brooklyn (paragraphs 14–16)? What is your response to this story and to the ideas it supports?

EVALUATING

3 What does the story of Madame Seda's initial meeting with d'Amboise imply that she knew (or suspected) about him? How does her insight relate to the main idea of the essay?

4 Reread paragraphs 10 and 11. What purpose is served by these paragraphs? Why does he say that half his friends grew up to be policemen and the other half gangsters (a statement that is almost certainly not literally true)? What is added to the essay by this background information on d'Amboise's life?

COMPARING

5 The strategy d'Amboise describes in paragraph 27 is called positive reinforcement. The opposing strategy, called negative reinforcement, is favored by some educators. With this strategy, the student is scolded, reprimanded, and often punished. What experiences have you had with these two strategies? Describe and compare your responses to both positive and negative reinforcement.

6 Explain the analogy (comparison) d'Amboise uses to close his essay. If you thought of yourself (or someone you know) as a "trunk that's up in the attic" what would you choose to fill it with? Explain.

ARGUING

7 Comment on this statement from paragraph 16: "He had discovered he could take control of his body, and from that he can learn to take control of his life." Describe an incident from your own life (or from the life of someone you know) that challenges or supports d'Amboise's conviction that learning to control one's body is the first step toward controlling one's life.

8 Summarize the teaching technique d'Amboise describes in paragraph 20. What does he believe children learn from this exercise? Do you agree that those qualities are important for an effective learning environment? Write an argument defending your point of view.

THE TEACHER CALLED ME STUPID, MOMMY!

MARILYN HOLM CHRISTENSEN

Marilyn Holm Christensen, a family therapist, is the author of *Shall the Circle Be Unbroken?* (1986), a book about the emotional abuse of children. Herself the mother of three children, Christensen has done extensive research about the effects of emotional abuse, both in the home and at school. In this article, she offers alarming evidence of a problem in the nation's classrooms that has affected all too many children.

Predicting Questions

As you read, keep in mind the following questions, derived from this selection's title:

1 Why would the teacher call a child "stupid"?
2 What was the child's reaction?
3 What was the mother's reaction?

Vocabulary Alert

As you read, watch for the following words: "maltreatment" (paragraph 5); "devastating" (paragraph 12); "venomous" (paragraph 17); "tenure" (paragraph 30); "tirade" (paragraph 33).

If you are unfamiliar with these words, try to determine their meaning from context clues. Which unfamiliar words do you need to look up in a dictionary? (In other words, which have meanings that cannot be determined from context yet are essential to understanding the meaning of the sentence or paragraph?)

---

1 My ten-year-old daughter, Katie, was a model student—pleasant, hardworking and bright. So when she came home from school one day in tears, the last thing I suspected was that her grade school teacher had cruelly chastised her in front of the entire class. Yet it was true. Between sobs, Katie told me that Mrs. Owens* had scrawled a huge red F across her test paper and held it up for the other children to see, announcing, "Look everyone. Miss Smarty Pants got an F!"

2 My daughter had been so upset and humiliated that I had a very hard time persuading her to attend school the next day. When I reported the incident to the principal, his response angered me. "Mrs. Owens is tired of teaching but can't afford to retire," he said. "Sometimes she gets out of sorts with the kids, I know. But on the whole she's a pretty good teacher." Katie remained in the class—I'd decided that transferring her to another school would be too disruptive—and as far as I knew, no more abusive incidents occurred.

3 That was eight years ago; today Katie is a confident teenager about to enter college. But I still regret that I didn't handle the situation differently. If the same thing were to happen now, I'd go directly to the teacher and tell her just how badly she hurt my daughter.

* All names of school personnel, parents, and students have been changed to protect privacy.

4 I'd like to believe that incidents like the one my daughter experienced are rare, that school always has a beneficial effect on children, and that every teacher, coach and school counselor fosters the emotional health of students. Unfortunately, that isn't the case. According to many child abuse experts, teachers and school administrators, emotional maltreatment of students by school personnel is a widespread problem. Richard Krugman, M.D., director of the C. Henry Kempe National Center for Prevention and Treatment of Child Abuse and Neglect in Denver, says that emotional abuse exists at *all* levels of our educational system. "I've talked with students from kindergarten through medical school, and an appalling number have been victimized by emotionally abusive teachers. No matter what the child's age, that abuse robs him of his confidence—or worse."

5 Dr. Krugman estimates that between 1 and 2 percent of the teachers in this country are emotional abusers. Though that estimated percentage seems low, Dr. Krugman believes that parents should be concerned. Given the teacher-child ratio, just one teacher can do a lot of harm. For example, on the average, an elementary school teacher is responsible for 20 to 30 students each year (the figure is higher for junior high and high school teachers). Therefore, hundreds of children could be adversely affected over the course of an abusive teacher's career. The costs of ignoring such emotional maltreatment are high: When a child's self-esteem is damaged, he is less likely to grow into a successful, fulfilled adult.

6 The problem is magnified by the fact that emotional maltreatment is not recognized as such by many principals and teachers. James Garbarino, Ph.D., is president of the Erikson Institute, an organization specializing in child development and research on children at risk. He says: "The teacher who consistently erodes a child's feelings of self-worth will probably never be charged with child abuse and may even receive the support of school officials. So the kids who have been victimized are forced to suffer in isolation and silence. They may wonder whether there really is something wrong with them, thus reinforcing the teacher's abusive message."

WHEN TEACHERS BECOME BULLIES

7 What exactly is emotional maltreatment? How do you draw the line between normal discipline and abuse? According to Dr. Garbarino, "Anything a teacher says or does that is demeaning to a student, such as constant yelling or swearing, making physical threats or singling a child out for rejection, can be defined as

emotional maltreatment." Here are some common forms found in the classroom:

8 *Terrorizing:* Some emotionally abusive teachers use fear to intimidate their pupils and keep them under control. Mrs. Murdock marched up and down the aisles of her sixth-grade classroom in Ohio carrying a wooden ruler while students were taking exams or doing written work. The kids never knew when she would descend on one of them in a fury, screaming and threatening them with the ruler. Almost anything a student did—such as fidgeting or looking out a window—could send her into a rage. Her favorite punishment was locking a misbehaving child in a dark closet in the rear of the room. If the child screamed to get out, Mrs. Murdock would snicker to the class: "Johnny doesn't seem to be so brave now, does he?" One of Mrs. Murdock's pupils had recurrent nightmares for years—nightmares which left her screaming in terror at the prospect of being locked in that closet.

9 Another example of a teacher terrorizing his students came to light when one of Dr. Krugman's sons told his father about the behavior of his third-grade teacher, Mr. Hopkins. For several months, his son came home with a variety of reports about Mr. Hopkins: that he had seized one girl's homework, said that it was all wrong, ripped it up and then yelled at her until she cried; that he had, in anger, thrown objects in class; and that he had even physically abused some children. On one occasion he reportedly tied a string to a boy's chair and suddenly yanked it, knocking the child to the floor. As a result, most of Mr. Hopkins' students grew extremely fearful, and several of them suffered from night terrors. Under pressure from parents, the school board eventually transferred Mr. Hopkins out of the school, and within weeks of his departure, most of the children had recovered from their fears. Two students, however, were so shaken by their experience that they required professional counseling.

10 *Inconsistency:* The teacher who exhibits wild mood swings and unpredictable behavior in class fosters a sense of confusion and insecurity in his students. In many cases, the teacher is aware of the effect of the abuse and momentarily regrets it, but lacks the self-control needed to stop.

11 Miss Henderson, a high school English teacher in South Dakota, would snarl at students for some transgression that she had tolerated the day before. Sometimes after she'd degraded a student, she'd realize she had gone too far and look for a way to make it up. Once, after she had just finished screaming at a boy for using improper grammar, she said to him sweetly, "You've got beautiful eyes! I just can't stay angry with you when I see those eyes." As a

result, the children in Miss Henderson's class were unusually subdued and anxious and had difficulty concentrating on their work.

12 *Labeling:* Some teachers seek to control their students by calling them names. This has a devastating effect on a child's sense of self-worth. Eight-year-old Kurt, a third-grade student in Wyoming, was an inquisitive, enthusiastic boy with many interests and a superior reading ability. But at a parent-teacher conference, Kurt's mother, Linda Murray, was shocked to hear his teacher, Mrs. Evans, complain that Kurt often interrupted her and asked too many questions. Furthermore, she called him "unmotivated" and "a problem child." After the meeting, Linda talked to her son, who gave a different version of events. He said that Mrs. Evans called him "brainbox" and "wiseguy" whenever he asked a question. Humiliated, he had simply stopped "bothering" her and now just sat quietly in class. Mrs. Evans read his silence as sullenness and lack of interest. The further danger was that she would repeat her impressions to other teachers, typecasting Kurt as a problem. Although Linda decided not to take Kurt out of Mrs. Evans' class, she met with the principal to discuss her concerns and determined to closely monitor his new teacher the following year. If the problems continued, Linda vowed that she would transfer her son into another class.

13 *Ridicule:* Making hurtful or belittling remarks is perhaps one of the most common types of abuse, and it usually stems from a teacher's secret grudge or dissatisfaction. Mr. Bouchard, who taught an advanced science course in a Wyoming high school, was bitter over the fact that he hadn't been able to get into medical school. His resentment bubbled up whenever he dealt with a student who had a parent who was a physician. He'd make sarcastic remarks to the student, such as "Surely, Janet, you know the answer. After all, your father is a *doctor!*" and consistently give him or her lower grades than the other children. Several of these students, who had maintained a high grade point average in other classes, ended up dropping out of his class and transferring to a less demanding one as a result of the damage to their self-esteem.

14 *Neglect:* This occurs when a teacher simply ignores a student or deliberately isolates him from the rest of the class. Minority students and so-called slow learners are most often the targets of this kind of abuse.

15 Mrs. Adams, a teacher in Wyoming, had received many awards for her innovative teaching, but she didn't enjoy working with kids like Jimmy, who seemed slower than the other children. She scolded him for not completing assignments and ignored his

requests for help. Not surprisingly, Jimmy's performance didn't improve—it got worse.

16 Jimmy's parents disapproved of Mrs. Adams' methods and took their son to a learning specialist, who discovered that Jimmy simply had a learning style that was at odds with those employed by his teacher. Mrs. Adams preferred that her students read the classroom material on their own. Jimmy, the specialist explained, retained information much better when it was conveyed orally.

17 Jimmy's parents met with Mrs. Adams and persuaded her to change her techniques with him. She also agreed to stop pressuring him and picking on him. Soon after this, Jimmy was performing at grade level.

18 *Scapegoating:* Dr. Garbarino believes that scapegoating is a particularly noxious form of abuse. The scapegoated child is singled out by the teacher to serve as the object of punishment for the entire group. Which children are most at risk? In general, any child who in some way stands out from the rest of the class. This includes children from minority groups, the handicapped and kids at either end of the intellectual spectrum. (Slow children may try a teacher's patience; gifted kids may incite feelings of resentment.)

19 Sometimes the targeted child reminds the teacher of a personal acquaintance or relative whom the teacher particularly dislikes, or he associates the child with qualities he objects to in himself. That was the case with an Idaho teacher named Miss McCoy, who seemed to relish picking on Irene, a tall, unattractive girl who was the top student in her chemistry class. Irene reminded Miss McCoy of the unhappy, painfully shy teenager she had been 30 years before—a self Miss McCoy had done her best to forget. So whenever Miss McCoy felt angry or frustrated, she would unleash a venomous attack on Irene. After several weeks of this, a group of students in the class went to see the school principal. "She's so mean to Irene," one of the students told him. "She always takes her anger out on Irene, no matter who or what she's mad at." The principal responded by transferring Irene to another class. But he never took disciplinary action against Miss McCoy.

"SMILES AREN'T ALLOWED HERE"

20 Unfortunately, many parents meet with resistance when they make a charge of emotional abuse. The experience of Mary Smith and her eight-year-old son, Greg, who live in Wyoming, is a case in point. From the beginning of the school year, Mary had been wary of Greg's second-grade teacher, Miss Jones. "At a parent-teacher conference I attended in September," Mary said, "Miss Jones pointed to a chart displaying perfect cursive letters and said, 'This

is how I expect children to write.' " Clearly, Mary said, this teacher would accept nothing short of perfection from the unsure pencils of her second graders.

21 During the first few weeks of school, Greg confirmed his mother's suspicions when he reported that Miss Jones was a "screamer." What was worse, Greg said, she seemed to be much harder on the boys than the girls. Nor were her demands reasonable. She once ridiculed a boy for being left-handed, Greg said, and she encouraged her favorites to pick on the children she didn't like.

22 After a month had gone by, Greg began complaining of headaches, and he made excuses to avoid going to school. Mary took him to the pediatrician, who said that Greg's symptoms appeared to be stress-related. Mary suspected Miss Jones was the source, but to make certain she decided to visit the classroom herself.

23 Mary called Miss Jones several times to request permission to observe the class, and each time the teacher put her off. But Mary persisted and eventually she was allowed to observe from the back of the room.

24 It was an enlightening experience. "The children never smiled or showed any pleasure in what they were doing," Mary recalled. "When I caught my son's eye and smiled at him, he gave me a strained look that seemed to say, 'Don't you know smiles aren't allowed here?'

25 "At one point," Mary continued, "Miss Jones screamed at a boy who had poured too much glue on his paper during art class. 'What a dumb thing to do, Joey! How can you be so stupid?' she shouted. The entire class froze. But a girl who had a similar accident a few minutes later drew only a rueful smile."

26 Disturbed by what she had seen, Mary met with the principal. He listened to her complaints but said that the most he could do was transfer Greg to another school—an unappealing alternative because Mary didn't want to separate her son from his friends. The principal then informed Mary that she was the only parent who had complained about Miss Jones, hinting that the problem had more to do with Greg than with his teacher.

27 Disgusted with the principal's response, Mary contacted other parents. She discovered that, contrary to what the principal had told her, six other parents had registered complaints about Miss Jones. One mother had even transferred her child into another school and made a point of informing the principal that she had done so because of problems with Miss Jones. Several weeks later, the parents met with the principal, but he continued to defend the

teacher. Since the school year was almost over, however, the parents dropped their case. To this day, Mary is still furious at the principal for lying to her and failing to change a situation he *knew* was abusive.

WHY ISN'T ANYTHING DONE?

28 Why are some principals, when faced with a case of emotional abuse, reluctant to do anything about it? There are several reasons, say educators. First, many principals feel that it is their job to protect teachers rather than students. This is partly because principals have an investment in teachers, whom they have hired, and partly because teachers tend to be a more permanent fixture on the school scene than students, each of whom moves on after a few years. George Bailey, Ed.D., who recently retired as professor of educational administration at the University of Wyoming in Laramie, says this loyalty is misplaced. "Administrators have more of an obligation to the kids than to teachers," he says. "But some principals don't think of their job in this way. They *should*."

29 Second, it's often in the principal's best interest to maintain the status quo: A principal may fear that the superintendent and school board, who have the power to fire him, will question his management skills when confronted with an emotional abuse case and may even blame him for it.

30 Third, even in cases where a principal is convinced that the teacher should be fired and feels confident that he has the superintendent's and school board's backing and support, he may have difficulty dismissing a teacher who has tenure. (In most states, teachers earn tenure after they have been at a school for three years.) Many principals may also hesitate to fire a teacher—tenured or not—because of fear of a libel suit.

31 Additionally, an emotional abuse case is a particularly sticky one for a principal because it may be hard to prove. "While physical abuse leaves welts or bruises, the results of emotional maltreatment are often invisible," says a Montana principal who declined to be named. "If the teacher accused of abuse happens to be someone who is punctual, hardworking and otherwise competent, the principal may find himself in a tough spot—particularly if the teacher denies the accusation."

PROFILE OF AN ABUSIVE TEACHER

32 Of course, it's important to emphasize that most teachers are *not* abusive, and a single unpleasant episode does not necessarily mean that a teacher has a problem. Teachers are only human, after all, and even those with the best intentions may lose their temper in a stressful moment. Nick Johnson, a junior high school teacher

in California, recalls the time a gifted student of his was discovered cheating in a statewide math contest. "I was so disappointed that I just lost it with him," he says. "I had a lot invested in the kid. He represented not only our school but also *me.* On the drive back to our town after the test I called him every name I knew, some of them four-letter.

33 "A couple of days later I discovered that this kid had been under tremendous pressure from his parents to win," Johnson continues. "That doesn't excuse what he did, but it made me realize that my tirade must have added greatly to his misery. I apologized to him and tried the rest of the year to make it up to him."

34 The responsible teacher who catches himself being abusive toward a student once or twice and regrets it and apologizes will probably not inflict serious harm on a child. It's the teacher who falls into a daily pattern of maltreatment that most concerns experts. This kind of teacher may have serious emotional problems or be mentally ill. He compensates for his own feelings of inferiority and powerlessness by exerting rigid control over his pupils or mercilessly putting them down. Emotionally disturbed teachers tend to have problems relating to adults as well, which further isolates them and therefore magnifies stress that is a natural by-product of classroom teaching, increasing the likelihood of abuse. Ironically, though overly sensitive to real or imagined slights from others, many of these teachers are unaware of the pain and humiliation their own abusive words and actions cause students. These teachers need professional counseling before reentering the classroom.

Topics for Reading, Writing, and Discussion

RESPONDING

1 Write a paragraph that tells of an incident you experienced or witnessed in school. Then write a paragraph explaining why that incident had a positive or negative effect on you.

2 Skim the boldfaced headings and then write a short paragraph predicting what the essay will be about. In addition, try turning the boldfaced headings into questions for which you will try to find answers. As you read, see how accurate your predictions were and then jot down responses to the answers you discover.

EVALUATING

3 Why do you think Christensen opens this essay, which originally appeared in *Redbook Magazine,* with a personal story? How do you

4 According to Christensen, why are many principals reluctant to do anything about emotionally abusive teachers? Evaluate the suggestions for getting principals to act that are offered in the essay. How effective do you think these actions would be? What other suggestions can you offer that might help parents to get a reluctant principal to act?

COMPARING

5 In the section called "When Teachers Become Bullies," Christensen describes several forms of emotional abuse. Compare these forms. If you had to rate them according to how serious or destructive they are, how would you arrange them? Explain your choices.

6 Compare the profile of an abusive teacher as given in this essay to your own idea of an ideal teacher. Explain the importance of the contrasts you describe.

ARGUING

7 What strategies of argument does Christensen use to follow up her opening anecdote? (See especially paragraphs 4 through 6.) How convincing do you find those strategies? Explain.

8 What is the purpose of paragraph 7? How does Christensen develop the main idea of paragraph 7 and use it to support her argument?

GIRLHOOD AMONG GHOSTS

MAXINE HONG KINGSTON

The daughter of Chinese immigrants, Maxine Hong Kingston was born in Stockton, California, in 1940. This selection comes from her autobiographical memoir, *The Woman Warrior,* a book that looks at the contradictions faced by a girl with deep roots in Chinese culture growing to womanhood in the United States.

In this excerpt, Kingston refers to "ghosts." She has previously explained that the Chinese community regarded non-Chinese as spirits; like ghosts, they seem mysterious and not truly human. These non-Chinese "ghosts" may have mysterious powers, and their behavior cannot be explained by normal rules.

Predicting Questions

As you read, keep in mind the following questions, derived from this selection's title:

1. Who are the ghosts?
2. Why are the ghosts significant?
3. How do the ghosts relate to the writer's girlhood?

Vocabulary Alert

As you read, watch for the following words: "frenum" (paragraph 2); "skittering," "wince" (paragraph 17); "intricacies," "ideographs" (paragraph 22).

If you are unfamiliar with these words, try to determine their meaning from context clues. Which unfamiliar words do you need to look up in a dictionary? (In other words, which have meanings that cannot be determined from context yet are essential to understanding the meaning of the sentence or paragraph?)

---

1 Long ago in China, knot-makers tied string into buttons and frogs, and rope into bell pulls. There was one knot so complicated that it blinded the knot-maker. Finally an emperor outlawed this cruel knot, and the nobles could not order it anymore. If I had lived in China, I would have been an outlaw knot-maker.

2 Maybe that's why my mother cut my tongue. She pushed my tongue up and sliced the frenum. Or maybe she snipped it with a pair of nail scissors. I don't remember her doing it, only her telling me about it, but all during childhood I felt sorry for the baby whose mother waited with scissors or knife in hand for it to cry—and then, when its mouth was wide open like a baby bird's, cut. The Chinese say "a ready tongue is an evil."

3 I used to curl up my tongue in front of the mirror and tauten my frenum into a white line, itself as thin as a razor blade. I saw no scars in my mouth. I thought perhaps I had had two frena, and she had cut one. I made other children open their mouths so I could compare theirs to mine. I saw perfect pink membranes stretching into precise edges that looked easy enough to cut. Sometimes I felt very proud that my mother committed such a powerful act upon me. At other times I was terrified—the first thing my mother did when she saw me was to cut my tongue.

4 "Why did you do that to me, Mother?"

5 "I told you."

6 "Tell me again."

7 "I cut it so that you would not be tongue-tied. Your tongue would be able to move in any language. You'll be able to speak languages that are completely different from one another. You'll be able to pronounce anything. Your frenum looked too tight to do those things, so I cut it."

8 "But isn't 'a ready tongue an evil'?"

9 "Things are different in this ghost country."

10 "Did it hurt me? Did I cry and bleed?"

11 "I don't remember. Probably."

12 She didn't cut the other children's. When I asked cousins and other Chinese children whether their mothers had cut their tongues loose, they said, "What?"

13 "Why didn't you cut my brothers' and sisters' tongues?"

14 "They didn't need it."

15 "Why not? Were theirs longer than mine?"

16 "Why don't you quit blabbering and get to work?"

17 If my mother was not lying she should have cut more, scraped away the rest of the frenum skin, because I have a terrible time talking. Or she should not have cut at all, tampering with my speech. When I went to kindergarten and had to speak English for the first time, I became silent. A dumbness—a shame—still cracks my voice in two, even when I want to say "hello" casually, or ask an easy question in front of the check-out counter, or ask directions of a bus driver. I stand frozen, or I hold up the line with the complete, grammatical sentence that comes squeaking out at impossible length. "What did you say?" says the cab driver, or "Speak up," so I have to perform again, only weaker the second time. A telephone call makes my throat bleed and takes up that day's courage. It spoils my day with self-disgust when I hear my broken voice come skittering out into the open. It makes people wince to hear it. I'm getting better, though. Recently I asked the postman for special-issue stamps; I've waited since childhood for postmen to give me some of their own accord. I am making progress, a little every day.

18 My silence was thickest—total—during the three years that I covered my school paintings with black paint. I painted layers of black over houses and flowers and suns, and when I drew on the blackboard, I put a layer of chalk on top. I was making a stage curtain, and it was the moment before the curtain parted or rose. The teachers called my parents to school, and I saw they had been saving my pictures, curling and cracking, all alike and black. The teachers pointed to the pictures and looked serious, talked seriously too, but my parents did not understand English. ("The parents and teachers of criminals were executed," said my father.) My parents took the pictures home. I spread them out (so black and full of possibilities) and pretended the curtains were swinging open, flying up, one after another, sunlight underneath, mighty operas.

19 During the first silent year I spoke to no one at school, did not ask before going to the lavatory, and flunked kindergarten. My

sister also said nothing for three years, silent in the playground and silent at lunch. There were other quiet Chinese girls not of our family, but most of them got over it sooner than we did. I enjoyed the silence. At first it did not occur to me I was supposed to talk or to pass kindergarten. I talked at home and to one or two of the Chinese kids in class. I made motions and even made some jokes. I drank out of a toy saucer when the water spilled out of the cup, and everybody laughed, pointing at me, so I did it some more. I didn't know that Americans don't drink out of saucers.

20 I liked the Negro students (Black Ghosts) best because they laughed the loudest and talked to me as if I were a daring talker too. One of the Negro girls had her mother coil braids over her ears Shanghai-style like mine; we were Shanghai twins except that she was covered with black like my paintings. Two Negro kids enrolled in Chinese school, and the teachers gave them Chinese names. Some Negro kids walked me to school and home, protecting me from the Japanese kids, who hit me and chased me and stuck gum in my ears. The Japanese kids were noisy and tough. They appeared one day in kindergarten, released from concentration camp, which was a tic-tac-toe mark, like barbed wire, on the map.

21 It was when I found out I had to talk that school became a misery, that the silence became a misery. I did not speak and felt bad each time that I did not speak. I read aloud in first grade, though, and heard the barest whisper with little squeaks come out of my throat. "Louder," said the teacher, who scared the voice away again. The other Chinese girls did not talk either, so I knew the silence had to do with being a Chinese girl.

22 Reading out loud was easier than speaking because we did not have to make up what to say, but I stopped often, and the teacher would think I'd gone quiet again. I could not understand "I." The Chinese "I" has seven strokes, intricacies. How could the American "I," assuredly wearing a hat like the Chinese, have only three strokes, the middle so straight? Was it out of politeness that this writer left off strokes the way a Chinese has to write her own name small and crooked? No, it was not politeness; "I" is a capital and "you" is lowercase. I stared at that middle line and waited so long for its black center to resolve into tight strokes and dots that I forgot to pronounce it. The other troublesome word was "here," no strong consonant to hang on to, and so flat, when "here" is two mountainous ideographs. The teacher, who had already told me every day how to read "I" and "here," put me in the low corner under the stairs again, where the noisy boys usually sat.

23 When my second grade class did a play, the whole class went to the auditorium except the Chinese girls. The teacher, lovely and

Hawaiian, should have understood about us, but instead left us behind in the classroom. Our voices were too soft or nonexistent, and our parents never signed the permission slips anyway. They never signed anything unnecessary. We opened the door a crack and peeked out, but closed it again quickly. One of us (not me) won every spelling bee, though.

24 I remember telling the Hawaiian teacher, "We Chinese can't sing 'land where our fathers died.' " She argued with me about politics, while I meant because of curses. But how can I have that memory when I couldn't talk? My mother says that we, like the ghosts, have no memories.

25 After American school, we picked up our cigar boxes, in which we had arranged books, brushes, and an inkbox neatly, and went to Chinese school, from 5:00 to 7:30 P.M. There we chanted together, voices rising and falling, loud and soft, some boys shouting, everybody reading together, reciting together and not alone with one voice. When we had a memorization test, the teacher let each of us come to his desk and say the lesson to him privately, while the rest of the class practiced copying or tracing. Most of the teachers were men. The boys who were so well behaved in the American school played tricks on them and talked back to them. The girls were not mute. They screamed and yelled during recess, when there were no rules; they had fistfights. Nobody was afraid of children hurting themselves or of children hurting school property. The glass doors to the red and green balconies with the gold joy symbols were left wide open so that we could run out and climb the fire escapes. We played capture-the-flag in the auditorium, where Sun Yat-sen and Chiang Kai-shek's pictures hung at the back of the stage, the Chinese flag on their left and the American flag on their right. We climbed the teak ceremonial chairs and made flying leaps off the stage. One flag headquarters was behind the glass door and the other on stage right. Our feet drummed on the hollow stage. During recess the teachers locked themselves up in their office with the shelves of books, copybooks, inks from China. They drank tea and warmed their hands at a stove. There was no play supervision. At recess we had the school to ourselves, and also we could roam as far as we could go—downtown, Chinatown stores, home—as long as we returned before the bell rang.

26 At exactly 7:30 the teacher again picked up the brass bell that sat on his desk and swung it over our heads, while we charged down the stairs, our cheering magnified in the stairwell. Nobody had to line up.

27 Not all of the children who were silent at American school found voice at Chinese school. One new teacher said each of us had to get up and recite in front of the class, who was to listen. My sister and I had memorized the lesson perfectly. We said it to each other at home, one chanting, one listening. The teacher called on my sister to recite first. It was the first time a teacher had called on the second-born to go first. My sister was scared. She glanced at me and looked away; I looked down at my desk. I hoped that she could do it because if she could, then I would have to. She opened her mouth and a voice came out that wasn't a whisper, but it wasn't a proper voice either. I hoped that she would not cry, fear breaking up her voice like twigs underfoot. She sounded as if she were trying to sing though weeping and strangling. She did not pause or stop to end the embarrassment. She kept going until she said the last word, and then she sat down. When it was my turn, the same voice came out, a crippled animal running on broken legs. You could hear splinters in my voice, bones rubbing jagged against one another. I was loud, though. I was glad I didn't whisper. There was one little girl who whispered.

Topics for Reading, Writing, and Discussion

RESPONDING

1 Reread the final paragraph. What is your response? Do you see the situation described as a triumph? A defeat? Explain.

2 Consider the significance of the opening story about knot-makers. How does this story relate to Kingston's mother's decision to cut her daughter's frenum? Does the mother's explanation seem reasonable? Discuss your response to this episode.

EVALUATING

3 Kingston explains her early drawing style in school, but she does not interpret her action. Why do you think she put black paint over all her paintings and chalk over all her blackboard sketches? What clues do you have to help interpret these acts?

4 Silence—and its opposite, speech—is a central theme in this excerpt. Discuss what you see as Kingston's main points about the ability to speak and be heard. What does she see as the value of speaking?

COMPARING

5 Why do you think Kingston found the American word for "I" so surprising? What comparison does she make between the American word "I" and the American word "you"?

6 Many of the incidents described involve Kingston's experiences

with speaking publicly. Think of your own experiences with similar situations and describe the differences and similarities between your responses and Kingston's.

ARGUING

7 Kingston develops a complex comparison between the American and Chinese schools she attended. How are the two schools different? What does she see as the significance of these differences? Plan an argument for or against the approach to education offered by the Chinese school.

8 Should students be forced to do things they find extremely unpleasant? For example, should painfully shy students be forced to give speeches in front of a class? Write an argument for or against compelling such action.

FROM A MEMOIR OF A BILINGUAL CHILDHOOD

RICHARD RODRIGUEZ

Born in San Francisco to Mexican-American parents, Richard Rodriguez details the experience of growing up in a bilingual household in his book *Hunger of Memory: The Education of Richard Rodriguez.* The impact of the American education system on his Hispanic heritage is described in this selection.

Predicting Questions

As you read, keep in mind the following questions, derived from this selection's title:

1 What does Rodriguez remember about his childhood?
2 Why was it significant that his childhood was bilingual?
3 Does he see being bilingual as positive or negative?

Vocabulary Alert

As you read, watch for the following words: "bilingual" (paragraph 1); "intrinsically" (paragraph 4); "incongruity" (paragraph 5); "over-anglicizing" (paragraph 8); "gringo" (paragraph 9); "eccentrically" (paragraph 11); "menial" (paragraph 17); "assimilated," "paradoxically" (paragraph 20).

If you are unfamiliar with these words, try to determine their meaning from context clues. Which unfamiliar words do you need to look up in a dictionary? (In other words, which have meanings that cannot be determined from context yet are essential to understanding the meaning of the sentence or paragraph?)

---

1 Supporters of bilingual education imply today that students like me miss a great deal by not being taught in their family's language. What they seem not to recognize is that, as a socially disadvantaged child, I regarded Spanish as a private language. It was a ghetto language that deepened and strengthened my feeling of public separateness. What I needed to learn in school was that I had the right, and the obligation, to speak the public language. The odd truth is that my first-grade classmates could have become bilingual, in the conventional sense of the word, more easily than I. Had they been taught early (as upper middle-class children often are taught) a "second language" like Spanish or French, they could have regarded it simply as another public language. In my case, such bilingualism could not have been so quickly achieved. What I did not believe was that I could speak a single public language.

2 Without question, it would have pleased me to have heard my teachers address me in Spanish when I entered the classroom. I would have felt much less afraid. I would have imagined that my instructors were somehow "related" to me; I would indeed have heard their Spanish as my family's language. I would have trusted them and responded with ease. But I would have delayed—postponed for how long?—having to learn the language of public society. I would have evaded—and for how long?—learning the great lesson of school: that I had a public identity.

3 Fortunately, my teachers were unsentimental about their responsibility. What they understood was that I needed to speak public English. So their voices would search me out, asking me questions. Each time I heard them I'd look up in surprise to see a nun's face frowning at me. I'd mumble, not really meaning to answer. The nun would persist. "Richard, stand up. Don't look at the floor. Speak up. Speak to the entire class, not just to me!" But I couldn't believe English could be my language to use. (In part, I did not want to believe it.) I continued to mumble. I resisted the teacher's demands. (Did I somehow suspect that once I learned this public language my family life would be changed?) Silent, waiting for the bell to sound, I remained dazed, diffident, afraid.

4 Because I wrongly imagined that English was intrinsically a public language and Spanish was intrinsically private, I easily noted the difference between classroom language and the language of home. At school, words were directed to a general audience of listeners. ("Boys and girls . . .") Words were meaningfully ordered. And the point was not self-expression alone, but to make oneself understood by many others. The teacher quizzed: "Boys and girls, why do we use that word in this sentence? Could we think of a better word to use there? Would the sentence change its meaning if the words were differently arranged? Isn't there a better way of saying much the same thing?" (I couldn't say. I wouldn't try to say.)

5 Three months passed. Five. A half year. Unsmiling, ever watchful, my teachers noted my silence. They began to connect my behavior with the slow progress my brother and sisters were making. Until, one Saturday morning, three nuns arrived at the house to talk to our parents. Stiffly they sat on the blue living-room sofa. From the doorway of another room, spying on the visitors, I noted the incongruity, the clash of two worlds, the faces and voices of school intruding upon the familiar setting of home. I overheard one voice gently wondering, "Do your children speak only Spanish at home, Mrs. Rodriguez?" While another voice added, "That Richard especially seems so timid and shy."

6 *That Rich-heard!*

7 With great tact, the visitors continued, "Is it possible for you and your husband to encourage your children to practice their English when they are home?" Of course my parents complied. What would they not do for their children's well-being? And how could they question the Church's authority which those women represented? In an instant they agreed to give up the language (the sounds) which had revealed and accentuated our family's closeness. The moment after the visitors left, the change was observed. "*Ahora,* speak to us only *en inglés,*" my father and mother told us.

8 At first, it seemed a kind of game. After dinner each night, the family gathered together to practice "our" English. It was still then *inglés,* a language foreign to us, so we felt drawn to it as strangers. Laughing, we would try to define words we could not pronounce. We played with strange English sounds, often over-anglicizing our pronunciations. And we filled the smiling gaps of our sentences with familiar Spanish sounds. But that was cheating, somebody shouted, and everyone laughed.

9 In school, meanwhile, like my brother and sisters, I was required to attend a daily tutoring session. I needed a full year of this special work. I also needed my teachers to keep my attention

from straying in class by calling out, *"Rich-heard!"*—their English voices slowly loosening the ties to my other name, with its three notes, *Ri-car-do.* Most of all, I needed to hear my mother and father speak to me in a moment of seriousness in "broken"—suddenly heartbreaking—English. This scene was inevitable. One Saturday morning I entered the kitchen where my parents were talking, but I did not realize that they were talking in Spanish until, the moment they saw me, their voices changed and they began speaking English. The gringo sounds they uttered startled me. Pushed me away. In that moment of trivial misunderstanding and profound insight, I felt my throat twisted by unsounded grief. I simply turned and left the room. But I had no place to escape to where I could grieve in Spanish. My brother and sisters were speaking English in another part of the house.

10 Again and again in the days following, as I grew increasingly angry, I was obliged to hear my mother and father encouraging me: "Speak to us *en inglés.*" Only then did I determine to learn classroom English. Thus, sometime afterward it happened: one day in school, I raised my hand to volunteer an answer to a question. I spoke out in a loud voice and I did not think it remarkable when the entire class understood. That day I moved very far from being the disadvantaged child I had been only days earlier. Taken hold at last was the belief, the calming assurance, that I *belonged* in public.

11 Shortly after, I stopped hearing the high, troubling sounds of *los gringos.* A more and more confident speaker of English, I didn't listen to how strangers sounded when they talked to me. With so many English-speaking people around me, I no longer heard American accents. Conversations quickened. Listening to persons whose voices sounded eccentrically pitched, I might note their sounds for a few seconds, but then I'd concentrate on what they were saying. Now when I heard someone's tone of voice—angry or questioning or sarcastic or happy or sad—I didn't distinguish it from the words it expressed. Sound and word were thus tightly wedded. At the end of each day I was often bemused, and always relieved, to realize how "soundless," though crowded with words, my day in public had been. An eight-year-old boy, I finally came to accept what had been technically true since my birth: I was an American citizen.

12 But diminished by then was the special feeling of closeness at home. Gone was the desperate, urgent, intense feeling of being at home among those with whom I felt intimate. Our family remained a loving family, but one greatly changed. We were no longer so close, no longer bound tightly together by the knowledge of our separateness from *los gringos*. Neither my older brother nor my sisters rushed home after school any more. Nor did I. When I arrived home, often there would be neighborhood kids in the house. Or the house would be empty of sounds.

13 Following the dramatic Americanization of their children, even my parents grew more publicly confident—especially my mother. First she learned the names of all the people on the block. Then she decided we needed to have a telephone in our house. My father, for his part, continued to use the word gringo, but it was no longer charged with bitterness or distrust. Stripped of any emotional content, the word simply became a name for those Americans not of Hispanic descent. Hearing him, sometimes, I wasn't sure if he was pronouncing the Spanish word *gringo*, or saying gringo in English.

14 There was a new silence at home. As we children learned more and more English, we shared fewer and fewer words with our parents. Sentences needed to be spoken slowly when one of us addressed our mother or father. Often the parent wouldn't understand. The child would need to repeat himself. Still the parent misunderstood. The young voice, frustrated, would end up saying, "Never mind"—the subject was closed. Dinners would be noisy with the clinking of knives and forks against dishes. My mother would smile softly between her remarks; my father, at the other end of the table, would chew and chew his food while he stared over the heads of his children.

15 My mother! My father! After English became my primary language, I no longer knew what words to use in addressing my parents. The old Spanish words (those tender accents of sound) I had earlier used—*mamá* and *papá*—I couldn't use any more. They would have been all-too-painful reminders of how much had changed in my life. On the other hand, the words I heard neighborhood kids call their parents seemed equally unsatisfactory. "Mother" and "father," "ma," "papa," "pa," "dad," "pop" (how I hated the all-American sound of that last word)—all these I felt were unsuitable terms of address for *my* parents. As a result, I never used them at home. Whenever I'd speak to my parents, I would try to get their attention by looking at them. In public conversations, I'd refer to them as my "parents" or my "mother" and "father."

16 My mother and father, for their part, responded differently, as their children spoke to them less. My mother grew restless, seemed troubled and anxious at the scarceness of words exchanged in the house. She would question me about my day when I came home from school. She smiled at my small talk. She pried at the edges of

my sentences to get me to say something more. ("What . . . ?") She'd join conversations she overheard, but her intrusions often stopped her children's talking. By contrast, my father seemed to grow reconciled to the new quiet. Though his English somewhat improved, he tended more and more to retire into silence. At dinner he spoke very little. One night his children and even his wife helplessly giggled at his garbled English pronunciation of the Catholic "Grace Before Meals." Thereafter he made his wife recite the prayer at the start of each meal, even on formal occasions when there were guests in the house.

17 Hers became the public voice of the family. On official business it was she, not my father, who would usually talk to strangers on the phone or in stores. We children grew so accustomed to his silence that years later we would routinely refer to his "shyness." (My mother often tried to explain: both of his parents died when he was eight. He was raised by an uncle who treated him as little more than a menial servant. He was never encouraged to speak. He grew up alone—a man of few words.) But I realized my father was not shy whenever I'd watch him speaking Spanish with relatives. Using Spanish, he was quickly effusive. Especially when talking with other men, his voice would spark, flicker, flare alive with varied sounds. In Spanish he expressed ideas and feelings he rarely revealed when speaking English. With firm Spanish sounds he conveyed a confidence and authority that English would never allow him.

18 The silence at home, however, was not simply the result of fewer words passing between parents and children. More profound for me was the silence created by my inattention to sounds. At about the time I no longer bothered to listen with care to the sounds of English in public, I grew careless about listening to the sounds made by the family when they spoke. Most of the time I would hear someone speaking at home and didn't distinguish his sounds from the words people uttered in public. I didn't even pay much attention to my parents' accented and ungrammatical speech—at least not at home. Only when I was with them in public would I become alert to their accents. But even then their sounds caused me less and less concern. For I was growing increasingly confident of my own public identity.

19 I would have been happier about my public success had I not recalled, sometimes, what it had been like earlier, when my family conveyed its intimacy through a set of conveniently private sounds. Sometimes in public, hearing a stranger, I'd hark back to my lost past. A Mexican farm worker approached me one day downtown. He wanted directions to some place. "*Hijito* . . . ," he said. And his voice stirred old longings. Another time I was standing beside my mother in the visiting room of a Carmelite convent, before the dense screen which rendered the nuns shadowy figures. I heard several of them speaking Spanish in their busy, singsong, overlapping voices, assuring my mother that, yes, yes, we were remembered, all our family was remembered, in their prayers. Those voices echoed faraway family sounds. Another day a dark-faced old woman touched my shoulder lightly to steady herself as she boarded a bus. She murmured something to me I couldn't quite comprehend. Her Spanish voice came near, like the face of a never-before-seen relative in the instant before I was kissed. That voice, like so many of the Spanish voices I'd hear in public, recalled the golden age of my childhood.

20 Bilingual educators say today that children lose a degree of "individuality" by becoming assimilated into public society. (Bilingual schooling is a program popularized in the seventies, that decade when middle-class "ethnics" began to resist the process of assimilation—the "American melting pot.") But the bilingualists oversimplify when they scorn the value and necessity of assimilation. They do not seem to realize that a person is individualized in two ways. So they do not realize that, while one suffers a diminished sense of *private* individuality by being assimilated into public society, such assimilation makes possible the achievement of *public* individuality.

21 Simplistically again, the bilingualists insist that a student should be reminded of his difference from others in mass society, of his "heritage." But they equate mere separateness with individuality. The fact is that only in private—with intimates—is separateness from the crowd a prerequisite for individuality; an intimate "tells" me that I am unique, unlike all others, apart from the crowd. In public, by contrast, full individuality is achieved, paradoxically, by those who are able to consider themselves members of the crowd. Thus it happened for me. Only when I was able to think of myself as an American, no longer an alien in gringo society, could I seek the rights and opportunities necessary for full public individuality. The social and political advantages I enjoy as a man began on the day I came to believe that my name is indeed *Rich-heard Road-ree-guess.* It is true that my public society today is often impersonal; in fact, my public society is usually mass society. But despite the anonymity of the crowd, and despite the fact that the individuality I achieve in public is often tenuous—because it depends on my being one in a crowd—I celebrate the day I acquired my new name. Those middle-class ethnics who scorn

assimilation seem to me filled with decadent self-pity, obsessed by the burden of public life. Dangerously, they romanticize public separateness and trivialize the dilemma of those who are truly socially disadvantaged.

22 If I rehearse here the changes in my private life after my Americanization, it is finally to emphasize a public gain. The loss implies the gain. The house I returned to each afternoon was quiet. Intimate sounds no longer greeted me at the door. Inside there were other noises. The telephone rang. Neighborhood kids ran past the door of the bedroom where I was reading my schoolbooks—covered with brown shopping-bag paper. Once I learned the public language, it would never again be easy for me to hear intimate family voices. More and more of my day was spent hearing words, not sounds. But that may only be a way of saying that on the day I raised my hand in class and spoke loudly to an entire roomful of faces, my childhood started to end.

Topics for Reading, Writing, and Discussion

RESPONDING

1 What changes did Rodriguez notice in his parents after the family began speaking only English at home? What is his response to those changes?

2 Explain the loss that Rodriguez experiences at having to give up his family language. Pay special attention to his analysis in paragraph 22. Have you had any similar experiences of comforting, familiar patterns you have had to discard in order to become part of a group or organization? Explain your response to such experiences.

EVALUATING

3 What incident started Rodriguez on the path to learning English as a language that he could call his own? Did he see this incident as primarily negative or primarily positive? Give specific examples to back up your evaluation.

4 Why does Rodriguez believe that he had to give up Spanish entirely (both in his home and outside his home) in order to become part of "public" society in the United States? Do you agree with this evaluation? Explain.

COMPARING

5 What does Rodriguez mean in paragraph 1 when he speaks of a private language and a public language? What distinctions does he see between the two, and how does he see these distinctions as significant to him?

6 Does your family have a "private language"? For example, do you use shorthand expressions or made-up words that only family members understand? Think about and analyze what is different in the way you express yourself with close relatives—and the way they express themselves with you—and the way any of you express yourselves to "outsiders."

ARGUING

7 According to Rodriguez's mother, why was his father shy? How did Rodriguez's evaluation of his father's shyness differ from the mother's interpretation? Which view do you find more convincing? Explain.

8 The United States is one of few nations where most educated people become fluent in only one language. Argue for or against the following proposition: More emphasis should be placed on the teaching of foreign languages, beginning in the elementary school.

TOPICS FOR LONGER PAPERS: PART TWO

1 Compare the experiences of the children described in "The Teacher Called Me Stupid, Mommy!" to the experiences of the students taught by Jacques d'Amboise. Write a paper proposing new methods of teacher education that will encourage the kind of classroom teaching style you believe would be the most beneficial to the largest number of students. (The style you favor may be different from those represented by either of these articles.)

2 In the selection from *A Memoir of a Bilingual Childhood,* Richard Rodriguez raises the question of the education of minorities in this country. In "Girlhood Among Ghosts," Maxine Hong Kingston addresses similar issues. Consider carefully the views represented by these two writers and then explain your own views on whether ethnic heritage and language should be valued and preserved or rejected and replaced by education that emphasizes primarily mainstream American culture.

3 Choose one controversial issue in education today. (Try reading the "Education" sections of popular magazines like *Time* and *Newsweek* if you have trouble identifying such issues.) Do research on this issue and then decide where you stand on the controversy. Write a paper explaining your findings.

4 Compare Patricia Keegan's "Playing Favorites" (pages 184–189) with Brent Collins's "Students' Indifference Erodes the Public Schools" (pages 181–183). Both writers criticize aspects of the current situation in American education. Are their criticisms connected in any way? Do any of their criticisms conflict? Explain the relationship you see between the two readings.

5 Most of the writers in this section suggest that there are serious problems with the American education system. Do your own experiences support or refute this view? Do you see the problems defined by these writers as significant to your own life (and the lives of those close to you)? Or do you see other issues as more pressing? Or do you see the present system as much more positive than do these writers? Explain.

TOPICS REQUIRING RESEARCH: PART TWO

(For Research Strategies and Skills, Consult Appendixes D and E)

1 With permission, observe a classroom (perhaps one of your own classes). Then write a paper explaining your observations about the interactions of male and female students and their teachers.

2 In "Playing Favorites" (pages 184–189), Patricia Keegan focuses on the differences between the learning styles of boys and girls. She also discusses the different treatment accorded boys and girls by their teachers. She does not, however, mention cultural differences. Read three articles on learning issues related to cultural differences and write an essay explaining your discoveries.

3 Read a biography of a famous athlete and compare his or her experiences with learning about the power of the body with the experiences Jacques d'Amboise describes (pages 190–194).

4 Interview a teacher you admire and respect. Ask him or her to describe examples of the most effective way to learn. Write an essay explaining and commenting on the interview.

5 Using the *Education Index* in your library, find an article on emotional abuse in the classroom. Compare the information in that article to the information you found in "The Teacher Called Me Stupid, Mommy!"

6 Interview someone whose first language is not English to discover his or her views about and experience with bilingual education. Write an essay describing the interview and your response to what you learned from the interview.

PART THREE

TELEVISION AND THE MOVIES

PLAY IT YET AGAIN, LUCY

RICHARD ZOGLIN

"Play It Yet Again, Lucy" first appeared in the December 2, 1991, issue of *Time.*

Predicting Questions

As you read, keep in mind the following questions, derived from this selection's title:

1 Who is the "Lucy" Zoglin mentions?
2 What is Lucy playing?
3 Why is it significant that she is playing it "yet again"?

Vocabulary Alert

As you read, watch for the following words: "cliché," "reprised" (paragraph 2); "infatuated," "virtually" (paragraph 3); "stellar," "homages" (paragraph 4); "nostalgia" (paragraph 6); "repository," "memorabilia" (paragraph 7); "pandering," "curatorial," "seminal" (paragraph 8); "insatiable" (paragraph 10); "melodramatic," "simplistic" (paragraph 11); "neuroses" (paragraph 12).

If you are unfamiliar with these words, try to determine their meaning from context clues. Which unfamiliar words do you need to look up in a dictionary? (In other words, which have meanings that cannot be determined from context yet are essential to understanding the meaning of the sentence or paragraph?)

---

1 Sooner or later, we always seem to wind up back in the candy factory. You remember the scene: Lucy and Ethel go to work on a candy-wrapping assembly line. A conveyor belt feeds them chocolates at a ridiculously fast clip. They try desperately to keep up, frantically stuffing the candy into their blouses, hats and mouths before the supervisor returns. A comedy classic.

2 And now a comedy cliché. Nearly 40 years after the scene was first aired—on Sept. 15, 1952, as the opening episode of *I Love Lucy*'s second season—it may be the most frequently repeated bit of film in television history. One recent sighting came in October, on the NBC special *Funny Women of Television*. It got a vigorous workout during all those TV tributes to Lucille Ball following her death in April 1989. It is one of two episodes reprised in full on a laser disc released by the Criterion Collection to commemorate the show's 40th anniversary. And, of course, on any given day it is probably being shown on some local station somewhere, part of the endlessly renewable cycle of *I Love Lucy* reruns.

3 Has a popular art form ever been so infatuated with its past? Increasingly, it seems that we are not viewing television so much as perpetually re-viewing it. A network show that becomes a hit is only starting its TV life cycle. The next step is a big syndication deal, then years and years of reruns on local stations and cable. Virtually every TV anniversary, star's death or Emmy Awards show provides an excuse to trot out another edition of Scenes We Like to See Over and Over Again: Ralph Kramden bickering with Alice, Elvis gyrating on *Ed Sullivan*, Lou Grant meeting Mary Richards for the first time ("I hate spunk!").

4 Even network prime time is falling under the spell of the past. Last February, CBS drew stellar ratings for a two-hour special celebrating *The Ed Sullivan Show*, and did nearly as well with tributes to *All in the Family* and *The Mary Tyler Moore Show*. Last weekend the network launched another classic-TV binge, with homages to *M*A*S*H* and *The Bob Newhart Show*, along with a second compilation of *Sullivan* clips. In June, to much fanfare, the network introduced a new sitcom from Norman Lear. The show, *Sunday Dinner*, was soundly beaten in the ratings by the program that followed it—20-year-old reruns of Lear's *All in the Family*.

5 TV's recycling process has been pushed to peak capacity by a profusion of cable channels searching for low-cost programming to fill their schedules. Nick at Nite woos baby boomers each evening with campy sitcoms like *The Donna Reed Show* and *Get Smart*. The Family Channel has cornered the market in old westerns (*Wagon Train, The Virginian*), while the Arts & Entertainment Network, originally conceived as a haven for fine-arts programming, now runs oldies like *The Avengers* and *Mrs. Columbo*. Ted Turner's cable operation may attract a lot of attention with MGM movie

blockbusters and environmental specials, but its most dependable ratings grabber is that unglamorous, uncolorized war-horse, *The Andy Griffith Show.*

6 Newer cable outlets are being forced to scrounge ever deeper in the vaults for fresh oldies. Comedy Central, the all-comedy cable network, has resurrected *C.P.O. Sharkey,* a dog from the mid-'70s starring Don Rickles. Nostalgia Television, a six-year-old network aimed at the "mature" audience, has unearthed such forgotten chestnuts as *Date with the Angels,* a short-lived '50s sitcom starring Betty White, and *The Dennis O'Keefe Show,* a one-season wonder from 1959–60.

7 The godfather of TV's back-to-the-past movement is the Museum of Television and Radio, a 15-year-old repository of memorabilia founded by former CBS chairman William S. Paley. At its elegant new quarters in midtown Manhattan, visitors can wander in and out of four screening rooms, browse through a computerized card catalog listing some 45,000 items, and repair to one of 96 TV and radio consoles to enjoy anything from President Kennedy's Inaugural Address to Don DeFore's inaugural appearance as Thorny on *The Adventures of Ozzie and Harriet.*

8 The museum's aggressive president, Robert Batscha, insists that his institution is not pandering to nostalgia but preserving an important social and cultural record. Sure enough, the museum has rounded up hundreds of kinescopes and tapes from TV's past that might otherwise have been lost. Its curatorial work, moreover, has sparked a revival of interest in such seminal TV figures as Jackie Gleason and Ernie Kovacs.

9 Rummaging through the museum's collection is rewarding on both levels—nostalgic and scholarly. A Woody Allen TV special from 1969, for example, provides a rare glimpse of Allen in his transitional phase from stand-up comic to film innovator. One segment is a brilliantly realized silent-movie short, with Allen as the Chaplinesque hero and a young Candice Bergen as his co-star. But the show's most startling revelation is a guest appearance by the Rev. Billy Graham, who joins Allen for a lighthearted but essentially serious discussion of God, morality and premarital sex. It is fascinating simply because it could never happen on a TV entertainment show today.

10 The vogue for vintage TV can be at least partly attributed to the baby-boom audience, which grew up on TV and has a seemingly insatiable appetite for revisiting the media icons of youth. But it may also reflect a rejection, by audiences of all ages, of the creative exhaustion and tired formulas of most current TV fare. Television of the past was, to be blunt, not only different but very often better.

11 An old drama series like *The Fugitive* (with David Janssen as Dr. Richard Kimble, on the run after being wrongly convicted of murder) looks hopelessly unfashionable today, with its melodramatic narration, simplistic characters and stubborn avoidance of social relevance (no date rapists to be found). It does offer, however, something rarely seen in current TV drama: dark, intense morality tales, pitting one man's instinct for survival against his instinct for doing good.

12 Not every recycled show holds up so well. Some fondly remembered oldies, like *The Many Loves of Dobie Gillis,* seem dated, and neither time nor camp tastes have improved *Mister Ed.* But even middling sitcoms like *The Patty Duke Show* are more effortlessly engaging than most of the nervous joke machines that pass for comedies today. Good ones like *The Dick Van Dyke Show* remind us that the trivial plot lines of old domestic comedies were often a mask for shrewd satire of suburban neuroses. The best ones, like *I Love Lucy,* which invented the vocabulary for the modern sitcom, have the formal perfection and infinite repeatability of great pop music.

13 Yes, even that darned candy factory.

Topics for Reading, Writing, and Discussion

RESPONDING

1 Write a paragraph describing your own response to any of the "rerun" television programs Zoglin mentions.

2 Do you enjoy watching reruns of the same episode of a program over and over again? Explain why or why not.

EVALUATING

3 Evaluate Zoglin's selection of programs to illustrate the points he makes. Does he omit any of your favorite reruns? If so, explain why you think they are worthy of mention.

4 Evaluate Zoglin's statement in paragraph 3 that currently "we are not viewing television so much as perpetually re-viewing it." Do you agree that reruns attract more attention than current programs? Keep track of your own television viewing for several days and then explain whether or not you conform to the pattern Zoglin describes.

COMPARING

5 Summarize several comparisons Zoglin makes between current television programs and older programs that are now in reruns.

6 Compare your own favorite rerun to your favorite current program.

After discussing their similarities and differences, explain which you would choose if you could only watch one.

ARGUING

7 Argue for or against Zoglin's contention that "Television of the past was, to be blunt, not only different but very often better." What criteria does he use to make this judgment?

8 Argue for or against the following proposition: Modern television directors and actors could learn a lot from watching reruns.

THE TROUBLE WITH TELEVISION

ROBERT MacNEIL

Robert MacNeil, author of two books related to the media, describes his career as a journalist in his most recent work, *The Right Place at the Right Time* (1982). His first book, *The People Machine: The Influence of Television on American Politics* (1968), criticizes what he sees as the growing trend of the networks to present news as entertainment rather than as information. In 1984, MacNeil, who is himself the co-anchor of the PBS *MacNeil/Lehrer Newshour,* delivered a speech to the President's Leadership Forum at the State University of New York warning of the dangers television brings to our society. The following selection, which first appeared in *Reader's Digest* in 1985, is a revised version of that speech.

Predicting Questions

As you read, keep in mind the following questions, derived from this selection's title:

1 What does the word "trouble" mean, as it is used in the article?

2 What does MacNeil see as the main problems caused by or related to television?

3 Does he offer any solutions to these problems?

Vocabulary Alert

As you read, watch for the following words: "august" (paragraph 6); "coherence" (paragraph 8); "anachronism" (paragraph 9); "functionally" (paragraph 10); "inalienable" (paragraph 11).

If you are unfamiliar with these words, try to determine their meaning from context clues. Which unfamiliar words do you need to look up in a dictionary? (In other words, which have meanings that cannot be determined from context yet are essential to understanding the meaning of the sentence or paragraph?)

---

1 It is difficult to escape the influence of television. If you fit the statistical averages, by the age of 20 you will have been exposed to at least 20,000 hours of television. You can add 10,000 hours for each decade you have lived after the age of 20. The only things Americans do more than watch television are work and sleep.

2 Calculate for a moment what could be done with even a part of those hours. Five thousand hours, I am told, are what a typical college undergraduate spends working on a bachelor's degree. In 10,000 hours you could have learned enough to become an astronomer or engineer. You could have learned several languages fluently. If it appealed to you, you could be reading Homer in the original Greek or Dostoyevsky in Russian. If it didn't, you could have walked around the world and written a book about it.

3 The trouble with television is that it discourages concentration. Almost anything interesting and rewarding in life requires some constructive, consistently applied effort. The dullest, the least gifted of us can achieve things that seem miraculous to those who never concentrate on anything. But television encourages us to apply no effort. It sells us instant gratification. It diverts us only to divert, to make the time pass without pain.

4 Television's variety becomes a narcotic, not a stimulus. Its serial, kaleidoscopic exposures force us to follow its lead. The viewer is on a perpetual guided tour: 30 minutes at the museum, 30 at the cathedral, 30 for a drink, then back on the bus to the next attraction—except on television, typically, the spans allotted are on the order of minutes or seconds, and the chosen delights are more often car crashes and people killing one another. In short, a lot of television usurps one of the most precious of all human gifts, the ability to focus your attention yourself, rather than just passively surrender it.

5 Capturing your attention—and holding it—is the prime motive of most television programming and enhances its role as a profitable advertising vehicle. Programmers live in constant fear of losing anyone's attention—anyone's. The surest way to avoid doing so is to keep everything brief, not to strain the attention of anyone but instead to provide constant stimulation through variety, novelty, action and movement. Quite simply, television operates on the appeal to the short attention span.

6 It is simply the easiest way out. But it has come to be regarded as a given, as inherent in the medium itself; as an imperative, as though General Sarnoff, or one of the other august pioneers of video, had bequeathed to us tablets of stone commanding that nothing in television shall ever require more than a few moments' concentration.

7 In its place that is fine. Who can quarrel with a medium that so brilliantly packages escapist entertainment as a mass-marketing tool? But I see its values now pervading this nation and its life. It has become fashionable to think that, like fast food, fast ideas are the way to get to a fast-moving, impatient public.

8 In the case of news, this practice, in my view, results in inefficient communication. I question how much of television's nightly news effort is really absorbable and understandable. Much of it is what has been aptly described as "machine-gunning with scraps." I think the technique fights coherence. I think it tends to make things ultimately boring and dismissible (unless they are accompanied by horrifying pictures) because almost anything is boring and dismissible if you know almost nothing about it.

9 I believe that TV's appeal to the short attention span is not only inefficient communication but decivilizing as well. Consider the casual assumptions that television tends to cultivate: that complexity must be avoided, that visual stimulation is a substitute for thought, that verbal precision is an anachronism. It may be old-fashioned, but I was taught that thought is words, arranged in grammatically precise ways.

10 There is a crisis of literacy in this country. One study estimates that some 30 million adult Americans are "functionally illiterate" and cannot read or write well enough to answer a want ad or understand the instructions on a medicine bottle.

11 Literacy may not be an inalienable human right, but it is one that the highly literate Founding Fathers might not have found unreasonable or even unattainable. We are not only not attaining it as a nation, statistically speaking, but we are falling further and further short of attaining it. And, while I would not be so simplistic as to suggest that television is the cause, I believe it contributes and is an influence.

12 Everything about this nation—the structure of the society, its forms of family organization, its economy, its place in the world—has become more complex, not less. Yet its dominating communications instrument, its principal form of national linkage, is one that sells neat resolutions to human problems that usually have no neat resolutions. It is all symbolized in my mind by the hugely successful art form that television has made central to the

culture, the 30-second commercial: the tiny drama of the earnest housewife who finds happiness in choosing the right toothpaste.

13 When before in human history has so much humanity collectively surrendered so much of its leisure to one toy, one mass diversion? When before has virtually an entire nation surrendered itself wholesale to a medium for selling?

14 Some years ago Yale University law professor Charles L. Black, Jr., wrote: " . . . forced feeding on trivial fare is not itself a trivial matter." I think this society is being force-fed with trivial fare, and I fear that the effects on our habits of mind, our language, our tolerance for effort, and our appetite for complexity are only dimly perceived. If I am wrong, we will have done no harm to look at the issue skeptically and critically, to consider how we should be resisting it. I hope you will join with me in doing so.

Topics for Reading, Writing, and Discussion

RESPONDING

1 Describe your initial reaction to MacNeil's description of the number of hours the average person watches television. Were you surprised? Horrified? Disbelieving? Explain.

2 In paragraph 12, MacNeil says, "Everything about this nation—the structure of the society, its forms of family organization, its economy, its place in the world—has become more complex, not less." What is your response to that idea? Give examples from your own life and observations that demonstrate circumstances that have become more or less complex during the past ten years.

EVALUATING

3 Briefly state the main idea of MacNeil's essay; use no more than three sentences. Then summarize three points MacNeil makes to support his main idea. Consider, for example, the point developed in paragraphs 4–6, the point developed in paragraphs 7–9, and the point developed in paragraphs 9–11.

4 Evaluate the supporting points you summarized for question 3. Which point do you believe most effectively demonstrates MacNeil's main idea? Which point is least effective? Explain.

COMPARING

5 Explain the analogy (comparison) MacNeil uses in paragraph 4. What point is he making with this comparison? What contrasts does he note? How does he use those contrasts to emphasize his point?

6 MacNeil compares television to a narcotic, to a kaleidoscope, and to a "perpetual guided tour." Develop your own comparison to explain how you see one particular type of television program. Use this formula to develop a list of possibilities:

Soaps are like ______ .
Situation comedies are like ______ .
Made-for-TV-movies are like ______ .

ARGUING

7 How does MacNeil use statistics to present his arguments? Where does he quote an authority to support his argument? How effective do you find these strategies? Explain.

8 Whether or not you agree with MacNeil, how would you argue against his contention in paragraph 14 that "this society is being force-fed with trivial fare"?

"REEL" VS. REAL VIOLENCE

JOHN RUSSO

John Russo is a writer, producer, and director. Among his recent films is *Heartstopper,* which stars Moon Unit Zappa. In the following selection, which first appeared in *Newsweek* magazine (February 19, 1990), Russo analyzes the relationship he sees between violence on screen and violence in real life.

Predicting Questions

As you read, keep in mind the following questions, derived from this selection's title:

1 How does Russo define "reel" violence?
2 How does he define "real" violence?
3 What does he see as the relationship between these two kinds of violence?

Vocabulary Alert

As you read, watch for the following words: "cautionary," "nefarious," "mayhem" (paragraph 6); "psychopathic," "vicarious" (paragraph 7); "pragmatic" (paragraph 8); "gratuitously" (paragraph 13).

If you are unfamiliar with these words, try to determine their meaning from context clues. Which unfamiliar words do you need to look up in a dictionary? (In other words, which have meanings that cannot be determined from context yet are essential to understanding the meaning of the sentence or paragraph?)

1 One day I switched on the evening news just in time to see a Pennsylvania politician waving around a .357 magnum, warning reporters to back off so they wouldn't get hurt, then sticking the gun in his mouth and . . .

2 Mercifully, the station I was watching didn't show him pulling the trigger, but I learned later that another Pittsburgh station showed the whole suicide unedited. What I saw was enough to make me ill. My stomach was in a knot, and I couldn't get the incident out of my mind. I still can't, even though three years have gone by.

3 I have a special reason for wondering and worrying about blood and violence on TV and movie screens. I write, produce and direct horror movies. I coauthored "Night of the Living Dead," the so-called "granddaddy of the splatter flicks." And since then I've made a string of movies depicting murder and mayhem.

4 I can watch these kinds of movies when they've been made by other people, and I can even help create the bloody effects in my own movies without getting a knot in my stomach. Yet I still retain my capacity to be shocked, horrified and saddened when something like this happens in real life.

5 So there must be a difference between real violence and "reel" violence. And if I didn't feel that this is true, I'd stop making the kinds of movies that I make. What are those differences?

6 My movies are scary and unsettling, but they are also cautionary tales. They might show witches at work, doing horrible things or carrying out nefarious schemes, but in doing so they convey a warning against superstition and the dementia it can spawn. They might show people under extreme duress, set upon by human or inhuman creatures, but in doing so they teach people how duress can be handled and blind, ignorant fear can be confronted and conquered. My purpose hasn't been to glorify or encourage murder and mayhem, but to give horror fans the vicarious chills and thrills that they crave.

7 The most powerful and, consequently, financially successful horror movies—"Night of the Living Dead," "The Texas Chainsaw Massacre," "Halloween" and "Friday The 13th"—feature a small cast in a confined situation that is made terrifying by the presence of a monster/madman/murderer. Usually the victims are young, beautiful women. Often the murders are filmed from the point of view of the murderer. For all these reasons, we filmmakers have been accused of hating women and portraying them as objects to be punished for being sexually desirable. Horror fans have been accused of identifying with the psychopathic killers portrayed in these movies and deriving vicarious enjoyment from watching the killers act out the fans' dark fantasies.

8 But there are two simple, pragmatic reasons why the victims are often filmed from the point of view of the killer. First, it's an effective technique for not revealing who the killer is, thus preserving an aura of suspense. Second, it affords dramatically explicit angles for showing the victim's terror—and the horror of what the killer is doing.

9 These films *are* horrifying because they reflect—but do not create—a frightful trend in our society. Murders, assaults and rapes are being committed with more frequency and with increasing brutality. Serial killers and mass murderers are constantly making headlines. Most of these killers are men, often sexually warped men, and they most often kill women. So we filmmakers have stuck to the facts in our portrayal of them. That's why our movies are so scary. Too many of our fellow citizens are turning into monsters, and contemporary horror movies have seized upon this fear and personified it. So now we have Jason, Michael and Freddy instead of Dracula and Frankenstein. Our old-time movie monsters used to be creatures of fantasy. But today, unfortunately, they are extensions of reality.

10 Recently, at a horror convention in Albany, I was autographing videocassettes of a show I had hosted, entitled "Witches, Vampires & Zombies," and a young man asked me if the tape showed actual human sacrifices. He was disappointed when I informed him that the ceremonies on the tape were fictional depictions. He was looking for "snuff movies"—the kind that actually show people dying.

11 Unfortunately, tapes showing real death are widely available nowadays. A video of the Pennsylvania politician blowing his brains out went on sale just a few weeks after the incident was broadcast. But I don't think that the people who are morbidly fixated on this sort of thing are the same people who are in love with the horror-movie genre.

12 I'm afraid that the young man I met in Albany has a serious personality disorder. And I don't think he's really a horror fan. He didn't buy my tape, but he would have bought it if the human sacrifices had been real. "Reel" violence didn't interest him. He didn't care about the niceties of theme, plot or character development. He just wanted to see people die.

13 I haven't seen any snuff movies for sale at the horror conventions I've attended. True horror fans aren't interested. They don't go to the movies just to see artificial blood and gore, either. The films that gratuitously deliver those kinds of effects usually are box-office flops. The hit horror films have a lot more to offer. While scaring us and entertaining us, they teach us how to deal with our deepest fears, dreads and anxieties.

14 But modern horror movies aren't to blame for these fears, dreads and anxieties. They didn't create our real-life Jasons, Michaels and Freddys any more than the gangster movies of the 1920s and 1930s created Al Capone and Dutch Schultz. If the movies reflect, with disturbing accuracy, the psychic terrain of the world we live in, then it's up to us to change that world and make it a safer place.

Topics for Reading, Writing, and Discussion

RESPONDING

1 What is your own response to horror films? Explain your reasons for enjoying or not enjoying "financially successful horror movies" such as those listed in paragraph 7.

2 Russo begins his essay with a report of something he saw on television. Try writing a brief essay using this introductory strategy. Use opening sentences following this pattern:

One day I switched on [name of program] just in time to see __________ . My immediate response was __________ .The more I thought about what I had seen, the more I became convinced that __________ .

(*Note:* You need not write about television violence. You might be responding to something you saw on a soap, a situation comedy, or a talk show.)

EVALUATING

3 What purpose is served by paragraphs 1–4? What do you learn about the writer? (Consider his style: his choice of words and his tone, for example.) What do you learn about his subject?

4 What is the point of the anecdote Russo tells about the young man at the horror convention who is looking for "snuff movies"? Do you agree with his interpretation of this encounter? Explain.

COMPARING

5 Which paragraph first directly focuses on the comparison implied by the title of the article? How does that paragraph suggest the author's purpose for exploring the comparison?

6 In paragraph 9, Russo briefly compares modern horror film monsters to classic monsters like Dracula and Frankenstein. Extend and develop this comparison, showing what you consider to be significant differences and similarities. Concentrate on one modern horror film and one classic horror film.

ARGUING

7 In paragraph 7, Russo discusses reasons filmmakers have been accused of portraying women as objects. Summarize these reasons. How does he refute these accusations? How would you argue in support of or against Russo's refutations?

8 Do you agree that horror movies "teach people how duress can be handled and blind, ignorant fear can be confronted and conquered"? Use specific examples from movies or television programs you have seen to refute or support Russo's contention.

THE EFFECTS OF TELEVISION ON FAMILY LIFE

MARIE WINN

Born in Czechoslovakia in 1937, Marie Winn has published more than a dozen books, many of them aimed at an audience of children. In addition, she has written two books addressing the pitfalls of growing up in late-twentieth-century America, *Children Without Childhood* (1983) and *The Plug-In Drug: Television, Children, and the Family* (1977; revised edition 1985). The selection that follows comes from the latest edition of *The Plug-In Drug;* in it Winn analyzes the effects she believes television viewing has on family relationships.

Predicting Questions

As you read, keep in mind the following questions, derived from this selection's title:

1. What does Winn identify as the effects of television on family life?
2. Does she see these effects as entirely positive, entirely negative, or a mixture of negative and positive?
3. Does she suggest action to be taken regarding the effects she observes?

Vocabulary Alert

As you read, watch for the following words: "equivocal" (paragraph 1); "skirmish" (paragraph 6); "regimented" (paragraph 7); "spontaneous" (paragraph 9); "mediating" (paragraph 10).

If you are unfamiliar with these words, try to determine their meaning from context clues. Which unfamiliar words do you need to look up in a dictionary? (In other words, which have meanings that cannot be determined from context yet are essential to understanding the meaning of the sentence or paragraph?)

---

1 Television's contribution to family life has been an equivocal one. For while it has, indeed, kept the members of the family from dispersing, it has not served to bring them *together.* By its domination of the time families spend together, it destroys the special quality that distinguishes one family from another, a quality that depends to a great extent on what a family *does,* what special rituals, games, recurrent jokes, familiar songs, and shared activities it accumulates.

2 "Like the sorcerer of old," writes Urie Bronfenbrenner, "the television set casts its magic spell, freezing speech and action, turning the living into silent statues so long as the enchantment lasts. The primary danger of the television screen lies not so much in the behavior it produces—although there is danger there—as in the behavior it prevents: the talks, the games, the family festivities and arguments through which much of the child's learning takes place and through which his character is formed. Turning on the television set can turn off the process that transforms children into people."[1]

3 Yet parents have accepted a television-dominated family life so completely that they cannot see how the medium is involved in whatever problems they might be having. A first-grade teacher reports:

4 "I have one child in the group who's an only child. I wanted to

[1] Urie Bronfenbrenner, "Who Cares for America's Children?" Address presented at the Conference of the National Association for the Education of Young Children, 1970.

find out more about her family life because this little girl was quite isolated from the group, didn't make friends, so I talked to her mother. Well, they don't have time to do anything in the evening, the mother said. The parents come home after picking up the child at the babysitter's. Then the mother fixes dinner while the child watches TV. Then they have dinner and the child goes to bed. I said to this mother, 'Well, couldn't she help you fix dinner? That would be a nice time for the two of you to talk,' and the mother said, 'Oh, but I'd hate to have her miss "Zoom." It's such a good program!' "

5 Even when families make efforts to control television, too often its very presence counterbalances the positive features of family life. A writer and mother of two boys aged 3 and 7 described her family's television schedule in *The New York Times:*

> 6 We were in the midst of a full-scale war. Every day was a new battle and every program was a major skirmish. We agreed it was a bad scene all around and were ready to enter diplomatic negotiations. . . . In principle we have agreed on 2 1/2 hours of TV a day, "Sesame Street," "Electric Company" (with dinner gobbled up in between) and two half-hour shows between 7 and 8:30 which enables the grown-ups to eat in peace and prevents the two boys from destroying one another. Their pre-bedtime choice is dreadful, because, as Josh recently admitted, "There's nothing much on I really like." So . . . it's "What's My Line" or "To Tell the Truth." . . . Clearly there is a need for first-rate children's shows at this time . . .[2]

7 Consider the "family life" described here: Presumably the father comes home from work during the "Sesame Street"–"Electric Company" stint. The children are either watching television, gobbling their dinner, or both. While the parents eat their dinner in peaceful privacy, the children watch another hour of television. Then there is only a half-hour left before bedtime, just enough time for baths, getting pajamas on, brushing teeth, and so on. The children's evening is regimented with an almost military precision. They watch their favorite programs, and when there is "nothing much on I really like," they watch whatever else is on—because *watching* is the important thing. Their mother does not see anything amiss with watching programs just for the sake of watching; she only wishes there were some first-rate children's shows on at those times.

[2] Eleanor Dienstag, "What Will the Kids Talk About? Proust?" *The New York Times*, December 24, 1972.

8 Without conjuring up memories of the Victorian era with family games and long, leisurely meals, and large families, the question arises: isn't there a better family life available than this dismal, mechanized arrangement of children watching television for however long is allowed them, evening after evening?

9 Of course, families today still do *special* things together at times: go camping in the summer, go to the zoo on a nice Sunday, take various trips and expeditions. But their *ordinary* daily life together is diminished—that sitting around at the dinner table, that spontaneous taking up of an activity, those little games invented by children on the spur of the moment when there is nothing else to do, the scribbling, the chatting, and even the quarreling, all the things that form the fabric of a family, that define a childhood. Instead, the children have their regular schedule of television programs and bedtime, and the parents have their peaceful dinner together.

10 The author of the article in the *Times* notes that "keeping a family sane means mediating between the needs of both children and adults."[3] But surely the needs of adults are being better met than the needs of the children, who are effectively shunted away and rendered untroublesome, while their parents enjoy a life as undemanding as that of any childless couple. In reality, it is those very demands that young children make upon a family that lead to growth, and it is the way parents accede to those demands that builds the relationships upon which the future of the family depends. If the family does not accumulate its backlog of shared experiences, shared *everyday* experiences that occur and recur and change and develop, then it is not likely to survive as anything other than a caretaking institution.

Topics for Reading, Writing, and Discussion

RESPONDING

1 Do you believe most modern families miss out on activities and relationships because they watch too much television? Explain.

2 Explain the alternatives to current viewing patterns Winn suggests. Do you find these alternatives appealing? Realistic? Positive? Negative? Explain.

[3] Ibid.

EVALUATING

3 Who does Winn see as primarily to blame for the negative effects she believes television has on family life? Do you agree with her assessment? What other individuals, organizations, or forces within society might also share the blame? Explain.

4 How has television affected your family life? Construct from memory several typical days (perhaps one weekday, one weekend day, and one holiday) and evaluate your family's viewing patterns on those days. Do your observations support or refute Winn's view of the effects of television viewing on family life?

COMPARING

5 In paragraph 9, Winn compares special events in family life with ordinary events in family life. Make lists of what you consider special events in your life and ordinary (yet pleasurable) events. Compare and contrast the significance of such events. In the conclusion of your comparison, consider how important daily rituals and special rituals (holiday customs, for example) are in keeping life "whole."

6 Compare your television viewing patterns today with your viewing patterns at some earlier time in your life (five or ten years ago, perhaps). Have your patterns changed? In what ways? What significance do you see in the changes (or lack of changes)?

ARGUING

7 In paragraphs 2, 4, and 6, Winn quotes other people commenting on the effects of television on the family. Summarize each quotation and explain how Winn uses each to advance her argument.

8 After you have considered how Winn uses quotations in her argument, plan an argument of your own responding to a quotation you take from *her* essay. Use this pattern:

In her essay "The Effects of Television on Family Life," Marie Winn says:

> XXXXXXXXXXXXXXXXXXXXXXXXXXXXXXXXXXXXXXX
> XXXXXXXXXXXXXXXXXXXXXXXXXXXXXXXXXXXXXXX
> XXXXXXXXXXXXXXXXXXXXXXXXXXXXXXXXXXXXXXX
> XXXX.

(*Note:* If you are quoting more than three typed lines—as shown in the model above—you set off and indent the quotation. Because the quotation is set off and indented, it need not be enclosed in quotation marks.)

After citing the quotation, go on to develop your argument regarding the point Winn makes in the quotation.

WHAT'S LEFT AFTER VIOLENCE AND ADVERTISING?

MAURINE DOERKEN

Maurine Doerken writes on issues concerning the media and education. In this selection, taken from *Classroom Combat: Teaching and Television* (1983), Doerken argues that television has other negative qualities besides the omnipresent violence and incessant advertising often cited by those concerned with the effects of television on children.

Predicting Questions

As you read, keep in mind the following questions, derived from this selection's title:

1 What is Doerken's attitude toward violence and advertising on television?
2 What other aspects of television concern her?
3 What problems does she see with these aspects?

Vocabulary Alert

As you read, watch for the following words: "rubric" (paragraph 1); "escapist" (paragraph 2); "lull," "diverting" (paragraph 3); "preliterate" (paragraph 4); "spectrum" (paragraph 5); "virtually" (paragraph 7); "implicitly," "recurring," "inversion" (paragraph 8); "socioeconomic," "ramifications" (paragraph 11); "aspiration" (paragraph 12); "incidental," "deferred" (paragraph 14).

If you are unfamiliar with these words, try to determine their meaning from context clues. Which unfamiliar words do you need to look up in a dictionary? (In other words, which have meanings that cannot be determined from context yet are essential to understanding the meaning of the sentence or paragraph?)

ATTITUDES TOWARD ENTERTAINMENT

1 If the average person on the street were stopped and asked what the three most frequent offerings on American television are (excluding commercials), he would probably answer action/adventure, situation comedy, and musical/variety talk

shows. This same person then most likely would turn around and classify these all under the rubric "entertainment."

2 But Shakespearean plays and grand opera are also "entertainment," yet they are hardly the same kind as is usually offered on our TV screens. This is a problem we Americans face when discussing television programming, . . . because we have grown so accustomed to think of TV material as general entertainment when it is, in fact, light fare of a very specific kind. The vast majority of TV offerings in this country have been and continue to be fantasy/escapist entertainment, *not* the entertainment we get from Othello or Beethoven. Some entertainment, to be sure, can be very engaging and very moving without being escapist, but those who organize TV material in America usually give the broad name "entertainment" to what is only a narrow section of the whole. This is not *always* the case, but generally it is.

3 Consequently, over the past thirty years, viewers have been exposed with great consistency to fantasy/escapist entertainment and a narrowing of tastes to fit "the average," not entertainment of a more serious, thought-provoking kind or one based predominantly on real life. So when we discuss the impact of television on young people, we are talking about the impact of three decades of fantasy/escapist fare. Even during the mid-fifties, light entertainment constituted approximately seventy-five percent of total TV time, and a brief glance at *TV Guide* today hardly reveals much of a change. Escapist entertainment still dominates the screen. In this sense, TV material has become what one broadcast historian calls a strategy word, for it minimizes the importance of what is presented.[1] Rather, entertainment is there to lull our critical faculties by sending us into the domain of low-involvement learning. It has no meaning, essentially, other than diverting and filling time between commercials.

4 This brings to mind several questions. With such a heavy diet of fantasy material, where are viewers, especially children and adolescents, to receive a comparable amount of reality presentations? Is it better to get a solid footing in reality or fantasy? Or at least an equal grounding in both? These questions are particularly relevant to preliterate youngsters who cannot read to counterbalance what they see and hear, for they are even more susceptible to informal television influence.

5 The effect of this fantasy/escapist entertainment has to be

[1] Erik Barnouw, *The Sponsor: Notes on a Modern Potentate*, Oxford University Press, New York, 1978, pp. 100–102.

different in character and kind than if we had had three decades of plays and dramas from renowned writers; a spectrum of musical offerings; fewer commercials; or more quality programming geared specifically toward children. This is self-evident. TV has been promoted as a window to the world, and in many cases, this has been true. But, in many other ways, it most certainly has not been so, due to the fantasy material which has dominated the screen. One need only look at American TV entertainment over the past three decades to see what a distorted view has been presented as life.

THE SEXES AND RACIAL GROUPS

6 As far as men, women, and various racial groups are concerned, television in this country has generally shown the following picture:

1. The most powerful group is the white American male. He usually is young, middle class, and unmarried—and is likely to be involved in violence.
2. Women make up a smaller proportion of all TV characters, regardless of ethnic background. They usually appear in a sexual context or in romantic roles. Two out of three are married or engaged, though this is now changing.
3. Women participate less in violence but are victimized more, and if a woman engages in aggression, she is not as likely to succeed as a man.
4. Women are also cast more frequently in domestic/comedic roles.
5. Married women are less likely to be victims of aggression. Housewives are not portrayed as villains as much as single women or those who are employed.[2]

7 It was not until 1968 that the first black series was offered over the TV airwaves. A young child growing up with TV during the fifties might have thought that blacks and other minorities did not exist. Not only were many people and races virtually ignored at TV's inception, but when they did appear, they often were presented as unfavorable stereotypes (i.e., Indians as bloodthirsty drunks or Chinese as cooks, servants, and laundry owners). For nearly three decades, television has concentrated on showing the twenty- to fifty-year-olds, thereby ignoring the very young and the elderly. There has been a constant push in the informal learning

[2] Liebert et al., *The Early Window*, pp. 18–19.

domain to telescope all age groups into a young adult market, focusing intently on the NOW.

THEMES AND FORMAT OF PROGRAMS

8 Not only has our escapist TV entertainment centered on specific races and ages, implicitly denying the existence of many other people and life styles, but recurring themes and ideas emerge as well. As indicated previously, violence has been a staple on the American TV screen, but even though it has occurred with mind-boggling regularity as "true-to-life action drama," it still follows the same pattern of unreality. Street crime, for example, has not been as important in the world of TV as it is in real life. Murder and assault have accounted for about fifty percent of all TV crime, yet this is not true of life on the outside. As one can see [in Table 1], almost a complete inversion has taken place.

TABLE 1: COMPARISON OF TELEVISION CRIMES AND REAL-LIFE CRIMES[3]

Frequency Ranking of FBI Crime Index from 1970	Frequency Ranking of TV Crimes from 1972
1. Burglary	1. Murder
2. Larceny	2. Assault
3. Auto Theft	3. Robbery
4. Robbery	4. Auto Theft
5. Assault	5. Burglary
6. Rape	6. Larceny
7. Murder	7. Rape

9 Generally, crime on American TV has:

1 overrepresented violent crimes directed against individuals; real-life crime is usually nonviolent and directed at property;

2 underrepresented blacks, young people, and lower-class individuals involved in crime;

3 reinforced the moral that crime does not pay; the main intent is to reassure society that right will prevail; in the real world, however, this obviously is not so, for crime often pays quite well;

[3] Chart from Joseph R. Dominick, "Crime and Law Enforcement on Prime-Time Television," *Public Opinion Quarterly*, 1973, Vol. 37, pp. 245–246.

4 concentrated on "the hunt" as being all-important rather than the legal processes involved after apprehension;

5 underrepresented nonwhites as murder victims;

6 underrepresented violent crimes between family members; and

7 made crime motives appear simple and easily understood; in real life, this often is not the case at all.[4]

10 Quite clearly, this picture has little to do with reality, even though it has been presented as "true" life. Yet, how much misinformation is being assimilated incidentally by children who watch a moderate to heavy amount? How much do they accept at face value? A very false image of the world could be in the making, which might be difficult to untangle later on.

TV EMPLOYMENT

11 Aside from these misrepresentations of various groups and crime in our society, another important aspect of television distortion concerns employment. Not surprisingly, the most frequent form of TV work is law enforcement. Nearly one-third of the American TV labor force at one time or another has been concerned with the pursuit of law and order. In reality, however, only about one percent of the population is so involved. . . . Jobs associated with entertainment rank second in the world of TV, which is hardly true to life either. Professional workers have been overrepresented, and there has always been that push for a higher socioeconomic status—informal messages consistent with the consuming world of TV. A corresponding underrepresentation of worker roles has been evident, though this is changing. As a source of incidental learning for young people about jobs and work, television provides a very slanted view of what is considered important, which could have serious ramifications in children's attitudes regarding employment later on.

12 A case in point: When a group of children was questioned about work, they overwhelmingly chose *power* as the most important factor to consider when thinking about employment. Money, prestige, and travel came next; helping others was last. The interesting point here is that these results held for both rich and poor children; urban and rural; male and female; dull and bright.[5]

[4] Same as above, p. 249.
[5] Melvin DeFleur, "Occupational Roles as Portrayed on Television," *Public Opinion Quarterly*, 1964, Vol. 28, p. 68.

Television's influence was pervasive in all areas of society. The fantasy/escapist material had been successful in changing their attitudes and aspirations toward a career.

13 Is this a form of programmed discontent? Does television teach unhappiness about work in general by presenting a false picture of the way life really *is?* If a child consistently sees powerful or dangerous jobs cast in glamorous settings, what kinds of ideas will he form about what he wants to be? His informal learning from television may be a source of disappointment and conflict when he finally starts to work, for it is not easy to become rich and powerful. In effect, such portrayals take the child away from the ordinary, which is a very real part of living, a part which needs to be met and dealt with often. How might all this influence his evaluation of work or his choice of job opportunities after leaving high school or college?

14 These instances of misrepresentation are but a few examples of how television escapist fare has twisted and turned images of life. All this may be obvious to the adult viewer, but how the past thirty years have affected children growing up under TV's powerful, informal gaze is another matter entirely. We are talking about analyzing human reactions and emotions in the area of incidental, deferred learning, which certainly is not an easy task. Yet, the impact of all this may be profound and go much deeper than many of us suspect.

Topics for Reading, Writing, and Discussion

RESPONDING

1. What television programs did you watch regularly as a child? Do you feel the criticisms leveled by Doerken could be fairly applied to most (or all) of those programs? Explain.
2. Doerken claims that most television programs are essentially escapist. What does she mean by this? What is your response to her claim?

EVALUATING

3. Reread paragraphs 6 and 7. Then consider the programs you watch on television. Would you make the same evaluations as Doerken concerning the way those programs depict the sexes and various racial groups? Explain.
4. Consider one program on television that focuses on a particular occupation. Evaluate how realistically you think that program presents this occupation.

COMPARING

5 Compare a television program you watch that you consider fantasy with one you watch that you consider realistic. Explain the differences and discuss your reasons for watching both programs.

6 Doerken implies that children and adults view television very differently. Do you agree? Compare your view of adult responses to your view of children's responses to the same kinds of programs. Explain the significance you see in the differences you describe.

ARGUING

7 How does Doerken use Table 1 to support her argument about the role of crime on television? Do you find this data convincing evidence? Explain.

8 Argue for or against the following proposition: Young children should watch television programs and films that give them a careful balance of reality and fantasy rather than programs and films that emphasize fantasy.

TOMOKO ON HER TELEVISION CAREER

TOMOKO, INTERVIEWED BY DAVID PLATH

In this selection, Tomoko, a television producer who lives in the southern Japanese city of Osaka with her son and husband, explains in her own voice her experiences as a woman from a traditional culture seeking a career in a modern field.

David Plath, who interviewed Tomoko, did graduate work in Japan and later returned to pursue studies in anthropology and Asian culture through observation and an extensive series of interviews. "Tomoko on Her Television Career" comes from Plath's *Long Engagements: Maturity in Modern Japan,* published in 1980 by Stanford University Press.

Predicting Questions

As you read, keep in mind the following questions, derived from this selection's title:

1 What was the career that Tomoko pursued?

2 What difficulties did she face?

3 What do her observations suggest about the culture in which she lives?

Vocabulary Alert

As you read, watch for the following words: "celibatarian" (paragraph 1); "feudalistic" (paragraph 8); "dodderer" (paragraph 10); "authoritarianism" (paragraph 13); "closed shop" (paragraph 16); "adamantly" (paragraph 21); "flunky job" (paragraph 32).

If you are unfamiliar with these words, try to determine their meaning from context clues. Which unfamiliar words do you need to look up in a dictionary? (In other words, which have meanings that cannot be determined from context yet are essential to understanding the meaning of the sentence or paragraph?)

---

1 I knew I had to have a career. In high school I became a celibatarian. I was not going to marry; I would dedicate myself to my profession. Then I began to think about what I would lose by going through life as an old maid. When I was even younger than that, I had wanted to become a concert pianist. I had been taking lessons ever since primary school. When it came time for high school, I asked people if I should go to a music academy. After all, you have to have the talent. I wasn't sure I did. The piano teacher said, well, as a music student your horizons would become very narrow, that after all I had taken up the piano as a hobby originally. So I dropped the idea of a career in it, and went to an academic high school.

2 After that I began to think about a career in the mass media—in publishing, newspapers, radio, it didn't much matter. I really knew little or nothing about how the media function, had only a few foggy notions. What I'm saying is that my ambitions were not well focused then, but I knew that as a celibatarian I was going to have to earn my own living.

3 My Education Papa had been warning me not to pin any hopes on becoming a pianist. He wanted me to concentrate on getting into a good university. So in high school I quit taking lessons and used the time instead to study for exams. I didn't touch the keyboard very often. Dad and I even argued over whether to lock it up. The first time around, I failed the exams magnificently. So I had to cram for them for another year, and that time got accepted into Osaka National University.

4 That was one of the most important watersheds in my life. It gave me the confidence that I can accomplish what I'm determined to do. Remember that in those days in a national university there might be three or four women to a hundred men. And it wasn't exactly easy for us to find jobs, either, after graduation. In the late

'50s, good jobs still were scarce. Of forty-five women in my graduating class, only ten of us found work, and the other nine were hired as schoolteachers. Hundreds of people applied to the network that year. When they picked me, I felt as if I had won a lottery.

5 The network has a training institute in Tokyo now, and new employees go there first. But when I joined the Osaka studio, TV was still a new idea. There were not many hours of broadcasting, and relatively few people had sets. You just trailed after an experienced producer and learned by imitating him.

6 I've changed since I first began working, and the change has its good and bad sides. In my student days I had been uncritical. I thought my professors were brilliant. I majored in German and took little else, nothing broadening, just narrow specialty courses. But my kind of work is broad ranging and I find myself asking, "What makes society tick?" and "Is an enemy obstructing our way of life?"

7 Most men seem to be going in the opposite direction. Maybe it's just that work and family are too heavy a burden for them, but whatever the reason they tend to withdraw, it seems to me. Possibly I'm too harsh on those who do that, but I get to feeling pity for them. And when a man is in a crunch, his wife not only fails to comfort him, she pokes him in the posterior. "Why aren't you being promoted faster?" Wives have got to become more independent.

8 People had told me that the private networks are more liberal than the public one. But along about the fourth year here, I began to be aware of what a feudalistic place ours is. They don't do a thing to help a woman develop her abilities. Some programs are utterly routine; on others you can take your time, spend money freely, do it the way you want it done. The men angle to be assigned to the good programs. And though I'm itching to take a shot at one, in more than a dozen years in the studio I've never once been given the chance. Women are stuck with the ordinary little daily programs, the ones the men don't want. And the promotions somehow come your way just a little more slowly.

9 Not that we stiff-upper-lip it all the time. I am no great admirer of the women in the studio, but it's a fact that they are better at their work than most of the men are. So when I see a man promoted early, even though he has just been mumbling around and not paying any attention to the world outside, I get sore. We complain, but there are so few of us we can be ignored. The administrators are transferred in and out so often that we can't get results by

complaining. Three years and there's a complete turnover in the station administrative staff. No continuity.

10 I've avoided taking administrative positions though they might give me more influence over policy than I have as a producer. As an administrator, you never know where you might be transferred next. You're a tool. You have to change your personality, and the tensions mount. All the men seem eager to go that route. But soon they look so awfully haggard and worn. Administrative work is sheer mental agony. You have no time to learn anything new. You die soon after you retire, or end up as another old dodderer.

11 Only about 10 percent of the professional staff are female now. There were more in the past, but they quit for various reasons and were replaced by men. The Fukuoka station is the worst: not even one woman on their staff any more on the broadcast side. Like it or not, the men there have to handle the Tea-and-flowers programs.

12 If I could start over again, I would take it from high school. I might not have been able to pass the exams for the college of science, but it may have been a mistake to have gone to the college of literature as I did. I wonder if I've gone into the wrong line of work? What I'm doing now probably could be done by just about anyone. Maybe I should have become a doctor or a judge.

13 Not that my work is uninteresting, but I find myself in something of a dilemma. I've begun to have doubts about the network. Lately I've begun to wonder whether the very existence of such vast organizations is contrary to the well-being of society, because of the authoritarianism (or whatever you want to call it) built into the very structure of such an institution. And yet here I am working in such a place. I'd been with the network for ten years before I began to think about it all.

14 Nothing would be solved by my quitting and going elsewhere. And the pay is not the point. I honestly did not expect a white-collar professional to be so hedged in by restrictions, but there is an invisible framework that you can't budge. For example, broadcasters are not to comment on the behavior of members of the Imperial Household. Senior men in the studio take that for granted, and if you try to insert anything about the Imperial Household into a program script, they clamp down on you without thinking. The three great taboos are the Emperor, the new religions, and sex. And for sure the network will not offer air time to a leftist or to anybody they think would have the nerve to denounce the very existence of the network itself.

15 When I'm putting together a program, if I think they might clamp down on me, I make a pitch at the planning conference and try for their approval. But I'm often left with the feeling that the

people I pick for my programs are just barely acceptable. The network's rule is to not air anybody who is known to be strongly biased in any direction, which is why you end up with nothing but dullards. What I'm saying is that I'm beginning to reconsider the role of the networks in society. The union pays attention only to the positive side of the role: the cultural and informational functions. That's no threat.

16 Ours is a closed shop; we're obligated to join the union. I took no interest in it when I first joined the network. The union itself was feeble then, though it has gained a little strength since. But in this line of work, you don't ordinarily think of yourself as a laborer, so most people are smugly indifferent to the union. Nobody wants to run for office, not even the men. I suspect that it's because as an officer you have to do battle with the establishment, and most men don't like to do that.

17 I was shop vice-chairperson for one term. Part of the reason why I agreed to do it was that I knew rather little about the union and wanted to learn, and part of the reason is that I apparently don't have the high professional pride the others have. While they're working they gripe and gripe. Then the minute an administrator turns up, they button lip. I hoped I could help make the atmosphere more open, that we wouldn't be so afraid to stand up for our point of view as workers. Well, I tried. . . .

18 If they ever fired me, I would go right out and get another job. I'd prefer one in the media, though in Japan it is just about impossible to find a position with any large organization once you are in midcareer. So it might mean I would have to free-lance. For the present, however, I'm doing my work for the studio peacefully and don't really want to leave it, for better or worse. I know I could get along as a free-lance commentator on women's affairs; offers come in frequently. Though I'm not certain I'd be really good at it. . . .

19 My life has gone along pretty much as I had hoped. I'm the stubborn kind: when a roadblock looms up in front of me, I blast my way through it. Not that adults didn't try to change my mind, when I was younger. When I was taking exams for the university, they said I should consider a woman's college instead. When I wanted to get married, both my parents were absolutely dead set against it. Dad warned me that the man I wanted to marry was the same age as me, that we were both in college, and it's a mistake to marry a man until you know for sure how he'll turn out. It's best to be five years younger than your husband, he said. Because when a woman marries a man her age she starts looking older sooner, and eventually he'll leave her.

20 Ours is far and away a better marriage than my parents'. But then, they were pressured into marrying each other. I don't regard that as marriage in the true sense of the word. That's where the fault lies, for Mom and Dad did not have a very happy relationship. I used to blame them for it, but over the years I've come to find a little sympathy for them. Otherwise, I suspect I would never have been willing to get married myself.

21 But from high school onward, I warned them that I had no intention of going into an arranged marriage. Mom was adamantly opposed to the idea of marrying for love, absolutely against it until the day she died. She had a fantastic sense of family pride. For that reason her death was a blessing—she died of cancer at forty-two. She'd have exploded if I had so much as ever hinted that I was fond of any particular man.

22 And she was uncompromising about ideas of liberation. She could very well accept the idea of a woman wanting a career. But as for marriage, she told me, if I would not agree to an arranged marriage, then I would have to stay single.

23 Your first year in college, suddenly you have much more freedom than you did in high school, and we hung around with boys pretty often. That made my mother furious. Called me a slut. If I would quit seeing boys, she said, I could trust her to find me a good man. But I told her that no matter how hard she searched, if he didn't appeal to me I would never marry him, so why not forget the whole thing. At times like that she would—how should I put it—become *very* worked up. "There you go, playing around the opposite sex just like your father!" she'd bellow. We'd battle. And it would leave me feeling victimized.

24 After all, I had been attending coed schools from the beginning. I was only being friendly with boys in the usual ways. But Mom could not understand that, our idea of friendship. We often sent letters to each other, and when Mom found out about it, she would get all emotional.

25 My first impressions of my husband were not exactly favorable, at that. Takeo seemed, oh, call it fragile, womanish. I had this feeling of Hmmmm—so there are men like this in the world, too? By fragile I mean delicate and slender, willowy, weak-looking. Not masculine. This is not the type for me, I said to myself.

26 We were in the same German class in college. Takeo was a science major. Now he's a research chemist for a pharmaceutical company. Little by little, I began to see his good points. He was kind to everybody, not blunt the way I am. I admired the way he had of always doing the right thing. He was nothing like my brothers, who are hard-boiled types. It occurred to me that he and I could help each other, that we might get along very well indeed.

And I found that I was intrigued by a man who would be continuing his studies even after he left college.

27 We were married two years after graduation. By then I was working, of course, but Takeo was still in graduate school. Most of our friends also married somebody they met in college, and in many of the couples both parties have careers. Among them, our dual-career marriage is nothing out of the ordinary. . . .

28 And he still surprises me. The network has a male-female talk show, and one night the topic was sex discrimination at retirement age. The two of us were watching. I got peeved because it was such a cheap imitation of a broadcast, but he was guffawing and getting a kick out of it. As far as I was concerned, they were not really facing up to the discrimination issue, they had turned it into a question of women's abilities. Somebody had stacked the panel, and the men were getting away with heaping scorn on women in biological terms. It made my blood boil, but Takeo said, "So what, it's a fun show." He believes that men and women are unquestionably different. Intellectually he can accept the idea that it is a result of different life experiences, but he can't accept it emotionally. Men must protect women, in his view. . . .

29 I do have friends among male colleagues at the station. I see eye to eye with a couple of them and enjoy talking to them. I like the way one of them thinks—he has such a fresh point of view on so many topics. And he's one of those rare individuals who doesn't brownnose the bosses. He's a good drinker, and I enjoy drinking with him when we're out on trips to gather material for a program. We've taken care not be become involved with each other—though of course the gossips in the studio say we are. I expect they're jealous. I see nothing wrong with that kind of friendship; a man and a woman can be good friends without its having to be an affair. I know that there are young women in the lab where Takeo works, and that they work on projects together. That doesn't upset me. But I've learned not to say anything about my friendships to him. He can't accept the idea.

30 In a sense, my husband is my best friend. We're trying to sustain a mutual understanding. Others tell me he is a very simpatico guy. And there is no question that I owe him a great deal. Without him I would not be able to have both a family and a career.

31 I would not protest if he accepted a position elsewhere, but it doesn't seem likely to happen. He isn't interested in the idea. If he did, however, I would not just give up my career to move with him. I believe that we could continue as a married couple even though we were living apart, but he detests the very thought of it. "What kind of life would that be?" he says. I sure don't go for the idea either. Sometimes I wonder if I'm not acting too much as if I don't

need my family. He's even been going out and buying his breakfast on his way to work. . . .

32 Ours was the first generation that came of age under postwar democracy, and many of us women wanted to work. The present generation seems to be moving backwards, with fewer and fewer women pursuing careers. My husband says that if a woman must work, then she needs a special skill so that she doesn't end up just pouring tea for the men. If it's a flunky job that anybody could do, then she is better off staying home and taking care of her family. Most men seem to feel that it's all right for a woman to work if she has talent, but that if it's only for the money it's a loss of face for her husband. Japanese are peculiar that way, not wanting to admit that they're doing anything for the money.

Topics for Reading, Writing, and Discussion

RESPONDING

1 As you read, did you find Tomoko's experiences very different or did they seem similar to what you have read or heard about American women who work in similar jobs?

2 Tomoko explains a number of personal relationships (with her father, her mother, her husband, and a male colleague). Summarize her description of one of these relationships and explain your response to that relationship. For example, do you think the relationship has helped or hindered her as a professional woman?

EVALUATING

3 Read paragraphs 16 and 17 and then summarize Tomoko's experience with the union to which she belongs. Evaluate her description of her experiences and explain her attitude toward the union.

4 In paragraphs 13–15, Tomoko explains limitations imposed by the networks on television programming. How do the limitations she explains compare to your understanding of limitations imposed (or not imposed) on television producers in the United States? Evaluate the pros and cons of such limitations.

COMPARING

5 Explain the comparison Tomoko makes in the final sentence of paragraph 4. Consider the rest of the selection as you explain why she felt as if she had won a lottery.

6 What are the differences Tomoko sees between the jobs of men and women in the Japanese television industry? What do you see as significant about these differences? For example, what might these differences suggest about Japanese culture?

ARGUING

7 What are the complaints Tomoko makes about being a woman in the field of television in Japan? Consider the evidence she gives to support her complaints and explain why you do or do not find those complaints well founded.

8 Read the description of the talk show in paragraph 28. Then write a description of an American talk show and argue for or against the following premise: [Name of talk show] addresses topics that distort the relationship between men and women.

TOPICS FOR LONGER PAPERS: PART THREE

1 Both Robert MacNeil ("The Trouble with Television") and Marie Winn ("The Effects of Television on Family Life") see television as a negative influence on our society. Compare, contrast, and evaluate MacNeil's and Winn's ideas.

2 Several selections in Part III present a negative view of television. Brainstorm to gather a list of possible positive aspects of television. Then write a paper explaining those positive aspects.

3 Compare observations about Japanese television as reported by Tomoko in her interview with David Plath with observations in other selections about American television. Comment on the significance you see in the similarities and differences you discover.

4 Imagine a conversation among John Russo, Robert MacNeil, Marie Winn, and Maurine Doerken. What issues do you think they might agree on? What issues to you think would cause significant differences? Write the dialogue you think might take place.

TOPICS REQUIRING RESEARCH: PART THREE

(For Research Strategies and Skills, Consult Appendixes D and E)

1 Watch three different nightly news programs, including at least one network broadcast and one local broadcast. Do your observations

support or challenge Robert MacNeil's description of "television's nightly news effort" (paragraph 8)?

2 Read a review of a television program, and then watch several episodes of the program. Summarize the reviewer's main idea and key supporting points. Explain why you agree or disagree with the reviewer. (*Note:* Reviews of television programs may be found in such publications as *TV Guide* as well as in many newspapers.)

3 Read a short story that incorporates elements of horror (for example, a short story by Edgar Allan Poe such as "The Tell-Tale Heart" or "Fall of the House of Usher"). What do you see as significant differences between horror that one reads and horror that one sees on a movie screen or on television?

4 Write a survey of at least ten questions concerning the impact of television on family life. Find at least ten people who will respond to the survey and then write a report explaining the results.

5 In "What's Left After Violence and Advertising?" (page 240, paragraph 7), Maurine Doerken claims that television "ignores the very young and the elderly." Watch several television programs for the next two weeks and then write a paper using specific examples from your viewing to argue for or against Doerken's point.

6 Do some research on careers for women in American television. Compare your findings with the picture Tomoko (pages 244–251) gives of careers for women in Japanese television. How are the problems faced and rewards gained similar or different?

P A R T F O U R

WORKING

FROM BLUE-COLLAR JOURNAL

JOHN COLEMAN

John Coleman earned degrees in sociology from the University of Toronto and University of Chicago and then taught at Carnegie Institute of Technology and Massachusetts Institute of Technology before becoming president of Haverford College. During a sabbatical leave from Haverford, he spent a year working in various blue-collar jobs. This selection includes excerpts from his description of the time he spent as a kitchen worker at a famous Boston restaurant and as a trash collector.

Predicting Questions

As you read, keep in mind the following questions, derived from this selection's title:

1 What is significant about blue-collar work?
2 How does blue-collar work differ from other work?
3 Why did Coleman keep a journal about blue-collar work?

Vocabulary Alert

As you read, watch for the following words: "Quaker," "marsupials" (paragraph 10); "maneuvers" (paragraph 24).

If you are unfamiliar with these words, try to determine their meaning from context clues. Which unfamiliar words do you need to look up in a dictionary? (In other words, which have meanings that cannot be determined from context yet are essential to understanding the meaning of the sentence or paragraph?)

MONDAY, MARCH 26

1 Cold rain after the warmth of Sunday. Spring has pulled back to wait for a while. Few people seemed to want to eat, even Oyster

House food. Not many customers, not much excitement, not much work.

2 This was a half day for me. Because I'd be getting my own dinner on the hot plate back in my room, I slipped over to the Faneuil Hall markets about 2:00 to get a piece of meat and some vegetables. My uniform worked wonders this time. At the three counters where I stopped, I got warm greetings and questions about how business was at the Oyster House. Had I been in my Haverford clothes, I'd have received the polite "May-I-help-you" treatment that I get at the Wayne Farmers' Market near home every Saturday morning at 7:00. But today the butcher and the vegetable men gave me the "Here's-one-of-us" treatment. It felt good.

3 I didn't pay any less for what I bought. But I did get told at one counter, "No, you don't want that one," and had a better squash placed in my hand. That's almost the same as paying less.

TUESDAY, MARCH 27

4 One of the waitresses I find hard to take asked me at one point today, "Are you the boy who cuts the lemons?"

5 "I'm the man who does," I replied.

6 "Well, there are none cut." There wasn't a hint that she heard my point.

7 Dana, who has cooked here for twelve years or so, heard that exchange.

8 "It's no use, Jack," he said when she was gone. "If she doesn't know now, she never will." There was a trace of a smile on his face, but it was a sad look all the same.

9 In that moment, I learned the full thrust of those billboard ads of a few years ago that said, "BOY. Drop out of school and that's what they'll call you the rest of your life." I had read those ads before with a certain feeling of pride; education matters, they said, and that gave a lift to my field. Today I saw them saying something else. They were untrue in part; it turns out that you'll get called "boy" if you do work that others don't respect even if you have a Ph.D. It isn't education that counts, but the job in which you land. And the ads spoke too of a sad resignation about the world. They assumed that some people just won't learn respect for others, so you should adapt yourself to them. Don't try to change them. Get the right job and they won't call *you* boy any more. They'll save it for the next man.

10 It isn't just people like this one waitress who learn slowly, if at all. Haverford College has prided itself on being a caring, considerate community in the Quaker tradition for many long years. Yet when I came there I soon learned that the cleaning

women in the dormitories were called "wombats" by all the students. No one seemed to know where the name came from or what connection, if any, it had with the dictionary definition. *The American College Dictionary* says a wombat is "any of three species of burrowing marsupials of Australia . . . somewhat resembling ground hogs." The name was just one of Haverford's unexamined ways of doing things.

11 It didn't take much persuasion to get the name dropped. Today there are few students who remember it at all. But I imagine the cleaning women remember it well.

12 Certainly I won't forget being called a boy today.

WEDNESDAY, MARCH 28

13 A day off once again.

14 I went into a restaurant downtown, the first time since I started work as a sandwich man. My curiosity won out. I ordered a club sandwich just to see how well it held together. It was noon, and I knew the man or woman in the kitchen must be having a rough time at that hour, but I ordered it just the same.

15 The sandwich looked fine, and its ingredients were fresh. I sent my compliments to the sandwich man, but I think the waitress thought I was nuts.

16 The place where I really wanted to eat was the Oyster House. I wanted to sit down at one of the tables and have someone—one of the many waitresses I like—bring me the menu. I wanted to order that stuffed fillet of sole, after some oysters at the bar. And I wanted the salad on the side, complete with cherry tomato and cucumber slice, and blue cheese dressing on top. I know some of the inside secrets of the place. I know, for example, that yesterday a customer got a thumbtack in his corn chowder (he was very nice about it). But I know too that the sanitation is generally good and that the people who work here care. I just wanted to see the whole meal come together as a production, fashioned by people whom I knew.

17 I'll eat there someday as a customer. And nothing that happens will escape my eye.

SUNDAY, APRIL 1

18 It was hard, steady work all day long.

19 The rhythm of each day and even of each week is familiar enough that it should be getting boring by now. It doesn't seem that way yet. There is enough variety in the flow of orders and of people too that I seldom feel I have been through all this before. Cleaning up the aluminum trays, where my supplies are kept, at

the end of each day is dull; I'd happily skip that if I could. But even in that there is a small element of suspense: the question each time is how far I can get with closing up for the night before the last waitress comes in with an order that requires getting the supplies out again.

20 I wonder how many loaves of bread and heads of lettuce I'd go through if I stuck at this job until retirement age.

FRIDAY, APRIL 6

21 We made the first stop. I had thought to bring gloves along with the work clothes in my gear, and I had them with me now. I was the only one who pulled gloves on. Each of us took a very large green or orange plastic barrel out of the back of the truck. Each barrel had a hole near the top to hold it by.

22 Steve took me into the first yard with him. "This is the way it's done," he said as he dumped the contents from three containers at the back door into his tub. Then in a flash he jumped into the barrel and trampled down what was there. "This way we can get more houses in one trip," he said as he jumped. In another flash he was out of the barrel, the load was on his back, and he was off for the house next door.

23 That was the training course.

24 He told me which houses to "pull." With three of us on the crew and only two sides to the street, Steve had some maneuvers to work out as to who pulled where. For the most part, he left Kenny on one side and me on the other, while he crossed back and forth to get the trash a few doors ahead of where we were. He also moved the truck.

25 I don't know just what I expected to find in the first householder's can on my route, but I know I took the lid off gingerly. It was full of garbage. Right on, I thought.

26 I couldn't quite bring myself to jump in and out of the barrel the way Steve had done. Instead, I pushed down hard with my gloved hand to make room for the next set of cans. With two houses pulled, the barrel was full. I lifted it up to my shoulder with a grunt (that seemed easier than swinging it around and onto my back) and headed for the truck. All kids—and many grown men—have an urge to throw at least one load of garbage into the waiting jaws of a sanitation truck and to pull the lever that sets the compacting unit to work. I threw my first load in with a feeling of fulfillment.

27 One thing about being a trashman is that, after your first load, you pretty well know the job. The only progress from then on comes in learning your route, developing your muscles, and picking

up speed. I could never have imagined how heavy some of those barrels could be. Most times I got three households' worth of trash into one load, since that was the best way to save time on the route. But sometimes the resulting weight was more than I could lift even to my waist, let alone shoulder high. I had to drag some of those loads down the driveway or across the lawn to the truck. The noise of the barrel being dragged on the road gave me away, of course. Steve smiled patiently at that, and Kenny pretended not to see. It sobered me too to note that, while they never once dragged a load, they both cursed the weight on their backs a couple of times. I knew then that there's no such thing as getting used to what we had to heave.

28 This work was a far cry from what I had watched the Haverford Township sanitation men do back home. They work hard and fast, and they probably pull a longer route than we do. But their work consists of lifting the householders' cartons or cans from the curb to the truck. They miss the extra miles of walking through yards, the hoisting of loads to the shoulder or back, and the extra physical contact with the trash as it goes from the cans into the barrel. The driver there stays in the truck; perhaps he is someone who has done his share of years on the dirty end of the truck. Here he pulls trash with his crew. Still, I now feel an affinity with the Haverford Township men that I hadn't quite felt before.

29 Steve was in charge at all times. He directed us where to go, kept tabs on us, and kept the truck moving ahead so that we never had far to walk once we got out loads from the backyards to the street. This has been his route for well over a year and he knows every house on the route well. (We are the only crew working this part of town. The other trucks from Liberty Refuse go to other towns in this county, and the part of Dryden lying across the county line is serviced by some other firm.) He had scared me with that talk early in the morning about keeping up with him. A look at his muscles and the way he moved told me I was in for a test. But, as the day went by, I saw I didn't have to be afraid of him. I was not as fast as he or Kenny, but he never once got on my back. He set an example instead.

30 Two mysteries about the job were cleared up for me on this first day. One was where we could have lunch. The answer to that one was that we didn't have any. We worked straight through until the route was done. Then we drove back to the yard, punched the clock, and went home to eat as we chose. I was glad my breakfast was big.

31 The other mystery was about taking care of bodily functions at work. Dryden is strictly residential. There are no gas stations on our route and no cafés. There are woods at the end of a few streets but they're spaced far apart. There didn't seem to be householders who were about to invite us into their homes. But happily we carried our own facilities with us. Next time I see a trashman jump into the open space where the garbage goes at the back of the truck and seem to stare at the curved metal wall in front of him, I'll know he's not looking for flaws. He's taking a leak.

32 It was after 3:30 when we pulled back into the yard. I knew I had done a day's work. Nothing I saw in the cans today took away from the joy of a big meal tonight, nor did I leave any scraps on my plate. I wasn't going to make extra work for the trashman tomorrow.

Topics for Reading, Writing, and Discussion

RESPONDING

1 Think of a job you have held and write several journal entries reflecting your experiences.

2 Imagine that you are one of the blue-collar employees with whom John Coleman worked. You have just read his published journal. Describe your response to that journal in a letter to Coleman.

EVALUATING

3 Briefly summarize Coleman's experience when he goes to the Faneuil Hall markets (open-air farmers' markets located near the Boston restaurant where he works). Why does he receive different treatment when he is wearing his Oyster House uniform than he would have at the market near his home where he would be wearing clothes typical of a college president?

4 When most professors get sabbatical leaves, they spend their time traveling or doing research or writing books and articles. Why would Coleman—a college president—instead choose to take a series of blue-collar jobs? Think about these questions by trying to imagine how Coleman might have responded to colleagues who were critical or skeptical of his decision to spend his year of leave doing blue-collar work.

COMPARING

5 Why is Coleman upset that one of the waitresses calls him "boy"? Compare these pairs of words: "boy/man" and "girl/woman." How would you feel if someone called you a "boy" or a "girl"? Would you be complimented? Insulted? As you explain your response, consider how you would define these words: girl, woman, boy, man.

6 What do you see as the main distinctions between blue-collar and white-collar work? What are the benefits and drawbacks of each of these kinds of work?

ARGUING

7 Argue for or against the following proposition: Blue-collar workers deserve just as much respect as do white-collar workers.
8 Argue for or against the following proposition: Blue-collar workers deserve to get pay equivalent to that of white-collar workers.

WHAT DID YOU DO IN THE WAR, GRANDMA?

ZOË TRACY HARDY

During World War II, Zoë Tracy Hardy was one of the millions of women who worked in jobs formerly held primarily by men. Like Hardy, many of these women worked in the defense plants that made weapons and other supplies for the war. Following the summer described in this essay, Hardy graduated from college and taught English in colleges in Arizona, Guam, and Colorado. This essay was first published in the April 1985 issue of *Ms.* magazine, forty years after the end of World War II.

Predicting Questions

As you read, keep in mind the following questions, derived from this selection's title:

1 What war does the title refer to?
2 What is the significance of the question?
3 What did the woman to whom the question is addressed do?

Vocabulary Alert

As you read, watch for the following words: "queasy," "Superfortresses" (paragraph 4); "unbridled" (paragraph 11); "dearth" (paragraph 14); "napalm," "incendiary" (paragraph 15); "scaffolding" (paragraph 16); "mediocre" (paragraph 17); "euphemisms" (paragraph 18); "disheveled," "spontaneous" (paragraph 25); "cosmic" (paragraph 38); "tentative" (paragraph 48); "precarious" (paragraph 61); "jeopardy" (paragraph 68).

If you are unfamiliar with these words, try to determine their meaning from context clues. Which unfamiliar words do you need to look up in a dictionary? (In other words, which have meanings that cannot be determined from context yet are essential to understanding the meaning of the sentence or paragraph?)

---

1 It was unseasonably cool that day in May, 1945, when I left my mother and father and kid brother in eastern Iowa and took the bus all the way to Omaha to help finish the war. I was 18, and had just completed my first year at the University of Iowa without distinction. The war in Europe had ended in April, the war against the Japanese still raged. I wanted to go where something *real* was being done to end this bitter war that had always been part of my adolescence.

2 I arrived in Omaha at midnight. The YWCA, where I promised my family I would get a room, was closed until 7 A.M., so I curled up in a cracked maroon leather chair in the crowded, smoky waiting room of the bus station.

3 In the morning I set off on foot for the YWCA, dragging a heavy suitcase and carrying my favorite hat trimmed in daisies in a large round hatbox. An hour of lugging and resting brought me to the Y, a great Victorian house of dark brick, where I paid two weeks in advance (most of my money) for board and a single room next to a bathroom that I would share with eight other girls. I surrendered my red and blue food-ration stamp books and my sugar coupons to the cook who would keep them as long as I stayed there.

4 I had eaten nothing but a wartime candy bar since breakfast at home the day before, but breakfast at the Y was already over. So, queasy and light-headed, I went back out into the cold spring day to find my job. I set out for the downtown office of the Glenn L. Martin Company. It was at their plant south of the city that thousands of workers, in around-the-clock shifts, built the famous B-29 bombers, the great Superfortresses, which the papers said would end the war.

5 I filled out an application and thought about the women welders and riveters and those who operated machine presses to help put the Superfortresses together. I grew shakier by the minute, more and more certain I was unqualified for any job here.

6 My interview was short. The personnel man was unconcerned about my total lack of skills. If I passed the physical, I could have a job in the Reproduction Department, where the blueprints were handled.

7 Upstairs in a gold-walled banquet room furnished with examination tables and hospital screens, a nurse sat me on a stool

to draw a blood sample from my arm. I watched my blood rolling slowly into the needle. The gold walls wilted in the distance, and I slumped forward in a dead faint.

8 A grandfatherly doctor waved ammonia under my nose, and said if I would go to a café down the street and eat the complete 50-cent breakfast, I had the job.

9 The first week in the Reproduction Department, I learned to cut and fold enormous blueprints as they rolled from a machine that looked like a giant washing machine wringer. Then I was moved to a tall, metal contraption with a lurid light glowing from its interior. An ammonia guzzler, it spewed out smelly copies of specifications so hot my finger-tips burned when I touched them. I called it the dragon, and when I filled it with ammonia, the fumes reminded me of gold walls dissolving before my eyes. I took all my breaks outdoors, even when it was raining.

10 My boss, Mr. Johnson,[1] was a sandy-haired man of about 40, who spoke pleasantly when he came around to say hello and to check our work. Elsie, his secretary, a cool redhead, seldom spoke to any of us and spent most of her time in the darkroom developing negatives and reproducing photographs.

11 One of my coworkers in Reproduction was Mildred, a tall dishwater blond with a horsey, intelligent face. She was the first woman I'd ever met with an earthy unbridled tongue.

12 When I first arrived, Mildred warned me always to knock on the darkroom door before going in because Mr. Johnson and Elsie did a lot of screwing in there. I didn't believe her, I thought we were supposed to knock to give Elsie time to protect her negatives from the sudden light. "Besides," I said, "there isn't room to lie down in there." Mildred laughed until tears squeezed from the corners of her eyes. "You poor kid," she said. "Don't you *know* you don't have to lie down?"

13 I was stunned. "But it's easier if you do," I protested, defensive about my sex education. My mother, somewhat ahead of her time, had always been explicit in her explanations, and I had read "Lecture 14," an idyllic description of lovemaking being passed around among freshman girls in every dormitory in the country.

14 "Sitting, standing, any quick way you can in time of war," Mildred winked wickedly. She was as virginal as I, but what she said reminded us of the steady dearth of any day-to-day presence of young men in our lives.

[1] All names but the author's have been changed.

15 We were convinced that the war would be over by autumn. We were stepping up the napalm and incendiary bombing of the Japanese islands, the British were now coming to our aid in the Pacific, and the Japanese Navy was being reduced to nothing in some of the most spectacular sea battles in history.

16 Sometimes, after lunch, I went into the assembly areas to see how the skeletons of the B-29s were growing from our blueprints. At first there were enormous stark ribs surrounded by scaffolding two and three stories high. A few days later there was aluminum flesh over the ribs and wings sprouting from stubs on the fuselage. Women in overalls and turbans, safety glasses, and steel-toed-shoes scrambled around the wings with riveting guns and welding torches, fitting fuel tanks in place. Instructions were shouted at them by hoarse, paunchy old men in hard hats. I cheered myself by thinking how we were pouring it on, a multitude of us together creating this great bird to end the war.

17 Away from the plant, however, optimism sometimes failed me. My room at the Y was bleak. I wrote letters to my unofficial fiancé and to other young men in the service who had been friends and classmates. Once in a while I attempted to study, thinking I would redeem my mediocre year at the university.

18 During those moments when I sensed real homesickness lying in wait, I would plan something to do with Betty and Celia, friends from high school, who had moved to Omaha "for the duration" and had jobs as secretaries for a large moving and storage company. Their small apartment was upstairs in an old frame house in Benson, a northwest suburb. Celia and Betty and I cooked, exchanged news from servicemen we all knew and talked about plans for the end of the war. Betty was engaged to her high school sweetheart, a soldier who had been wounded in Germany and who might be coming home soon. We guessed she would be the first one of us to be married, and we speculated, in the careful euphemisms of "well-brought-up girls," about her impending introduction to sex.

19 By the first of July, work and the pace of life had lost momentum. The war news seemed to repeat itself without advancing, as day after day battles were fought around jungly Pacific islands that all seemed identical and unreal.

20 At the plant, I was moved from the dragon to a desk job, a promotion of sorts. I sat on a high stool in a cubicle of pigeonholed cabinets and filed blueprints, specs, and deviations in the proper holes. While I was working, I saw no one and couldn't talk to anybody.

21 In mid-July Betty got married. Counsel from our elders was always to wait—wait until things settle down after the war. Harold, still recuperating from shrapnel wounds, asked Betty not to wait.

22 Celia and I attended the ceremony on a sizzling afternoon in a musty Presbyterian church. Harold was very serious, gaunt-faced and thin in his loose-hanging Army uniform. Betty, a fair-skinned, blue-eyed brunet in a white street dress, looked pale and solemn. After the short ceremony, they left the church in a borrowed car. Someone had given them enough gasoline stamps for a honeymoon trip to a far-off cabin on the shore of a piney Minnesota lake.

23 Celia and I speculated on Betty's introduction to lovemaking. I had "Lecture 14" in mind and hoped she would like lovemaking, especially way off in Minnesota, far from the sweltering city and the war. Celia thought it didn't matter much whether a girl liked it or not, as long as other important parts of marriage got off to a good start.

24 That weekend Celia and I took a walk in a park and watched a grandfather carefully pump a seesaw up and down for his small grandson. We saw a short, middle-aged sailor walking with a sad-faced young woman who towered over him. "A whore," Celia said. "Probably one of those from the Hotel Bianca." Celia had been in Omaha longer than I and knew more of its secrets.

25 I wanted, right then, to see someone young and male and healthy cross the grass under the trees, someone without wounds and without a cap, someone with thick disheveled hair that hadn't been militarily peeled down to the green skin on the back of his skull. Someone wearing tennis shorts to show strong, hair-matted legs, and a shirt with an open neck and short sleeves revealing smooth, hard muscles and tanned skin. Someone who would pull me out of this gloom with a wide spontaneous smile as he passed.

26 In the next few days, the tempo of the summer changed subtly. From friends stationed in the Pacific, I began to get letters free from rectangular holes where military censors had snipped out "sensitive" words. Our Navy was getting ready to surround the Japanese islands with a starvation blockade, and our B-29s had bombed the industrial heart of the country. We were dropping leaflets warning the Japanese people that we would incinerate hundreds of thousands of them by firebombing 11 of their major cities. Rumors rippled through the plant back in Omaha. The Japanese Empire would collapse in a matter of weeks, at most.

27 One Friday night, with Celia's help, I moved out of the Y to Celia's apartment in Benson. We moved by streetcar. Celia carried my towels and my full laundry bag in big rolls, one under each

arm, and wore my straw picture hat with the daisies, which bobbled wildly on top of her head. My hatbox was crammed with extra underwear and the war letters I was determined to save. When we climbed aboard the front end of the streetcar, I dropped the hatbox, spilled an armload of books down the aisle, and banged my suitcase into the knees of an elderly man who was trying to help me retrieve them.

28 We began to laugh, at everything, at nothing, and were still laughing when we hauled everything off the car and down one block to the apartment, the daisies all the while wheeling recklessly on Celia's head.

29 It was a good move. Summer nights were cooler near the country, and so quiet I could hear the crickets. The other upstairs apartment was occupied by Celia's older sister, Andrea, and her husband, Bob, who hadn't been drafted.

30 Late in July, an unusual thing happened at the plant. Mr. Johnson asked us to work double shifts for a few days. The situation was urgent, he said, and he wanted 100 percent cooperation from the Reproduction Department, even if it meant coming to work when we felt sick or postponing something that was personally important to us.

31 The next morning no one from the day shift was missing, and the place was full of people from the graveyard shift. Some of the time I worked in my cubicle counting out special blueprints and deviations. The rest of the time I helped the crews sweating over the blueprint machine cut out prints that contained odd lines and numbers that I had never seen before. Their shapes were different, too, and there was no place for them in the numbered pigeonholes of my cubicle. Some prints were small, about four inches square. Mildred said they were so cute she might tuck one in her shoe and smuggle it home as a souvenir even if it meant going to the federal pen if she got caught.

32 During those days I learned to nap on streetcars. I had to get up at 4:30, bolt down breakfast, and catch the first car to rumble out of the darkness at 5:15. The double shift wasn't over until 11:30, so I got home about one in the morning.

33 The frenzy at the plant ended as suddenly as it had begun. Dazed with fatigue, I slept through most of a weekend and hoped we had pushed ourselves to some limit that would lift us over the last hump of the war.

34 On Monday the familiar single shift was not quite the same. We didn't know what we had done, but an undercurrent of anticipation ran through the department because of those double shifts—and the news. The papers told of factories that were already gearing up

to turn out refrigerators, radios, and automobiles instead of bombs and planes.

35 In Reproduction, the pace began to slacken. Five hundred thirty-six B-29s, planes we had put together on the Nebraska prairie, had firebombed the principal islands of the Japanese Empire: Hokkaido, Honshu, Kyushu, Shikoku. We had reduced to ashes more than 15 square miles of the heart of Tokyo. The battered and burned Japanese were so near defeat that there couldn't be much left for us to do. With surprising enthusiasm, I began to plan for my return to college.

36 Going home on the streetcar the first Tuesday afternoon in August, I heard about a puzzling new weapon. Some excited people at the end of the car were jabbering about it, saying the Japanese would be forced to surrender in a matter of hours.

37 When I got home, Andrea, her round bespectacled face flushed, met me at the head of the stairs. "Oh, come and listen to the radio—it's a new bomb—it's almost over!"

38 I sat down in her living room and listened. There was news, then music, then expanded news. Over and over the newscaster reported that the United States had unlocked a secret of the universe and unleased a cosmic force—from splitting atoms of uranium—on the industrial seaport of Hiroshima. Most of the city had been leveled to the ground, and many of its inhabitants disintegrated to dust in an instant by a single bomb. "Our scientists have changed the history of the world," the newscaster said. He sounded as if he could not believe it himself.

39 We ate dinner from our laps and continued to listen as the news pounded on for an hour, then two, then three. I tried, at last, to *think* about it. In high school physics we had already learned that scientists were close to splitting an atom. We imagined that a cupful of the tremendous energy from such a phenomenon might run a car back and forth across the entire country dozens of times. I could visualize that. But I could not imagine how such energy put into a small bomb would cause the kind of destruction described on the radio.

40 About nine, I walked over to McCollum's grocery store to buy an evening paper. The headline said we had harnessed atomic power. I skimmed through a front page story. Science had ushered us into a strange new world, and President Truman had made two things clear: the bomb had created a monster that could wipe out civilization; and some protection against this monster would have to be found before its secret could be given to the world.

41 Back out in the dark street, I hesitated. For the first time I

could remember, I felt a rush of terror at being out in the night alone.

42 When I got back to the apartment, I made a pot of coffee and sat down at the kitchen table to read the rest of the paper. President Truman had said: "The force from which the sun draws its power has been loosed against those who brought war to the Far East. . . . If they do not now accept our terms they may expect a rain of ruin from the air the like of which has never been seen on this earth." New and more powerful bombs were now being developed.

43 I read everything, looking for some speculation from someone about how we were going to live in this new world. There was nothing. About midnight Andrea knocked on my open door to get my attention. She stood there a moment in her nightgown and curlers looking at me rather oddly. She asked if I was all right.

44 I said yes, just trying to soak it all in.

45 Gently she told me I had better go to bed and think about how soon the war would be over.

46 The next day Reproduction was nearly demolished by the spirit of celebration. The *Enola Gay,* the plane that had dropped the bomb, was one of ours. By Thursday morning the United States had dropped a second atomic bomb, an even bigger one, on an industrial city, Nagasaki, and the Russians had declared war on Japan.

47 At the end of the day, Mr. Johnson asked us to listen to the radio for announcements about when to return to work, then shook hands all around. "You've all done more than you know to help with the war," he said.

48 We said tentative good-byes. I went home and over to McCollum's for an evening paper. An Army Strategic Air Forces expert said that there was no comparison between the fire caused by the atomic bomb and that of a normal conflagration. And there were other stories about radiation, like X-rays, that might cripple and poison living things for hours, weeks, maybe years, until they died.

49 I went to bed late and had nightmares full of flames and strange dry gale winds. The next noon I got up, exhausted, and called Mildred. She said they were still saying not to report to work until further notice. "It's gonna bore our tails off," she moaned. "I don't know how long we can sit around here just playing hearts." I could hear girls laughing in the background.

50 "Mildred," I blurted anxiously, "do you think we should have done this thing?"

51 "Why not? Better us than somebody else, kid."

52 I reminded her that we knew the Japanese were finished weeks ago and asked her if it wasn't sort of like kicking a dead horse—brutally.

53 "Look," she said. "The war is really over even if the bigwigs haven't said so yet. What more do you want?"

54 The evening paper finally offered a glimmer of relief. One large headline said that serious questions about the morality of *Americans* using such a weapon were being raised by some civilians of note and some churchmen. I went to bed early and lay listening to the crickets and thinking about everyone coming home—unofficial fiancés, husbands, fathers, brothers—all filling the empty spaces between kids and women and old men, putting a balance in our lives we hadn't known in years.

55 Yet the bomb haunted me. I was still awake when the windowpanes lightened up at daybreak.

56 It was all over on August 14, 1945. Unconditional surrender.

57 For hours at a time, the bomb's importance receded in the excitement of that day. Streetcar bells clanged up and down the streets; we heard sirens, whistles, church bells. A newscaster described downtown Omaha as a free-for-all. Perfect strangers were hugging each other in the streets; some were dancing. Churches had thrown open their doors, and people were streaming in and out, offering prayers of thanksgiving. Taverns were giving away free drinks.

58 Andrew wanted us to have a little whiskey, even though we were under age, because there would never be another day like this as long as we lived. I hated the first taste of it, but as we chattered away, inventing wild, gratifying futures, I welcomed the muffler it wrapped around the ugliness of the bomb.

59 In the morning Mildred called to say our jobs were over and that we should report to the plant to turn in our badges and get final paychecks. She had just talked to Mr. Johnson, who told her that those funny blueprints we had made during double shift had something to do with the bomb.

60 "Well, honey," she said, "I don't understand atomic energy, but old jazzy Johnson said we had to work like that to get the *Enola Gay* and the *thing* to go together."

61 I held my breath, waiting for Mildred to say she was kidding, as usual. Ordinary 19- and 20-year-old girls were not, not in the United States of America, required to work night and day to help launch scientific monsters that would catapult us all into a precarious "strange new world"—forever. But I knew in my bones

that Mildred, forthright arrow-straight Mildred, was only telling me what I had already, unwillingly, guessed.

62 After a long silence she said, "Well, kid, give me your address in Iowa, and I'll send you a Christmas card for auld lang syne."

63 I wanted to cry as we exchanged addresses. I liked Mildred. I hated the gap that I now sensed would always be between me and people like her.

64 "It's been nice talking dirty to you all summer," she said.

65 "Thanks," I hung up, slipped down the stairs, and walked past the streetcar line out into the country.

66 The whole countryside was sundrenched, fragrant with sweet clover and newly mown alfalfa. I leaned against a fence post and tried to think.

67 The President had said we had unleashed the great secret of the universe in this way, to shorten the war and save American lives. Our commitment to defeat the Japanese was always clear to me. They had attacked us first. But we had already firebombed much of the Japanese Empire to char. That seemed decisive enough, and terrible enough.

68 If he had asked me whether I would work very hard to help bring this horror into being, knowing it would shorten the war but put the world into jeopardy for all time, how would I have answered?

69 I would have said, "No. With all due respect, Sir, how could such a thing make a just end to our just cause?"

70 But the question had never been asked of us. And I stood now, in the warm sun, gripping a splintery fence post, outraged by our final insignificance—all of us who had worked together in absolute trust to end the war.

71 An old cow stood near the fence switching her tail. I looked at her great, uncomprehending brown eyes and began to sob.

72 After a while I walked back to the apartment, mentally packing my suitcase and tying up my hatbox of war letters. I knew it was going to be very hard, from now on, for the whole world to take care of itself.

73 I wanted very much to go home.

Topics for Reading, Writing, and Discussion

RESPONDING

1 Hardy's thoughtful essay describes her changing responses to her job at the defense plant. Write a journal entry that describes your
55 changing responses to a job you have held (your topic might be a

job that you have done for pay; a chore you were assigned at home; a job for which you volunteered).

2 What is your response to Hardy's description of her relationship with the other workers? What, if anything, does she learn from them?

EVALUATING

3 What event (or series of events) causes Hardy to reevaluate her feelings about the war? Explain the process that she goes through as she changes her attitudes toward the war.

4 Evaluate Hardy's feelings about the introduction of atomic power into the world. Does she see only negative possibilities? Or does she also see positive aspects?

COMPARING

5 Hardy's essay was published forty years after the events she describes. Compare her fears, hopes, and concerns with the fears, hopes, and concerns you feel about military possibilities in the world today.

6 In the early part of the essay, Hardy describes her attitudes toward and beliefs about sex and marriage. How do her beliefs and attitudes compare with those of women her age today? What significance do you see in these differences?

ARGUING

7 At the end of the essay, Hardy says that if she had known she was participating in the creation of the atomic bomb, she would have refused to do the job. Write an argument defending or attacking her position.

8 Do you think workers should be informed of all the implications of their work? For instance, should they be informed that a drug they are working on might be used to induce abortion? Write an argument for or against fully informing workers on such matters.

A SHORT COURSE IN BUSINESS ETHICS

LESTER C. THUROW

Lester C. Thurow, dean of the Sloan School of Management at Massachusetts Institute of Technology, has written extensively about issues related to the world of business. In this selection, he expresses his concern about the role of business schools in encouraging ethical business behavior.

Predicting Questions

As you read, keep in mind the following questions, derived from this selection's title:

1 What are business ethics?
2 Why is a short course in business ethics needed?
3 What can be learned in a short course in business ethics?

Vocabulary Alert

As you read, watch for the following words: "barraged" (paragraph 1); "injunctions," "potential" (paragraph 4); "Aristotle" (paragraph 5); "arbitrary" (paragraph 7); "secular" (paragraph 9); "monetary" (paragraph 14); "premise" (paragraph 16).

If you are unfamiliar with these words, try to determine their meaning from context clues. Which unfamiliar words do you need to look up in a dictionary? (In other words, which have meanings that cannot be determined from context yet are essential to understanding the meaning of the sentence or paragraph?)

---

1 As dean of a leading business school, I am barraged with questions about what I am going to do to improve business ethics. The questions are usually accompanied by a strong undercurrent of accusation that business schools are responsible for the bad ethics of corporate America.

2 The best solution, the accusers suggest, would be to abolish business schools, but if that is impossible, the schools should at least take responsibility for the mess they have created and clean it up.

3 These assertions are unfair. Business students come to us from our society. If they haven't been taught ethics by their families, their clergy, their elementary and secondary schools, their liberal arts colleges or engineering schools, or the business firms where most of them have already worked prior to getting a business degree, there is very little we can do.

4 Injunctions to "be good" don't sway young men and women in their mid to late 20s. In the final analysis, what we produce is no worse than what we get. If some group of potential business people were more ethical than others, we would be glad to limit our admissions to the more virtuous, but I know of no such applicant pool.

5 Nor is this a new problem. Aristotle had some rather harsh things to say about the ethics of tradesmen more than 2,000 years ago. They were to be carefully excluded from what now would be called the "corridors of power." The financial scandals of the 1920s occurred before business schools were established, and West Germany is currently uncovering financial crookedness at Volkswagen without the benefit of having business schools. No business schools dot the Japanese landscape, but Japanese business ethics also seem on occasion to be something less than desirable.

6 While such defenses are more than sufficient if one is simply attempting to counter silly accusations, they are ultimately inadequate. The serious collective interest for improving business ethics merits more than a debating response from officials at schools of management.

7 The key to what must be done is found in the words "collective interest." Ethical questions arise because we live in communities that function according to rules and laws that promote the long-run interests of the community. Ethics is not arbitrary. It is functional, but it functions to allow a group of human beings to successfully live with each other.

8 A hermit can neither be ethical or unethical. He simply exists. Ethical dilemmas arise when a person's actions may contribute to the common good of the community but at the same time hurt his self-interest. Choosing to sacrifice one's appetites and self-interest is at the heart of ethical action.

9 The doctrine that one should sacrifice self-interest for the collective good, however, is a message that is seldom preached in America. In our secular religion, the importance of the individual greatly overshadows the importance of the community. The bumper sticker "The Man Who Dies With the Most Toys Wins" depicts the current state of American ethics.

10 If the only legitimate goal is maximizing personal income, then there are no ethical principles that must be obeyed. Individuals simply face a cost-benefit calculus where there is some probability of being punished if one is caught violating society's ethical principles. A person may obey the law because the costs of getting caught outweigh the benefits of getting away with it, but in doing so he or she is being clever or cautious, not ethical.

11 How can this country restore the belief that social goals and social responsibilities are so important that they override one's

personal gratification? Ethics will be restored when most individuals come to the realization that they play for a common team and are willing to sacrifice self-interest for the team. While such a message is regarded as self-evident in sports, it is seen as strangely wrong in economics and business. There only self-interest counts.

12 Those who do believe that the team sometimes merits priority over the individual have to preach that message at all levels of American society if our ethics are to be improved. Business schools are in a unique position to preach ethics in the field of economics.

13 To do this, business schools cannot simply add courses in ethics to the curriculum. We have to change what is taught in business classes.

14 Today's finance classes teach that the sole goal of business managers should be to maximize the net worth of shareholders. Managers follow this principle because doing so maximizes his or her personal net worth. If the only goals of firms and individuals are monetary, however, it is but a short jump to maximizing those monetary variables with means that are illegal or unethical. To create ethical business behavior, we must place higher value on goals other than personal or shareholder net worth.

15 Business law courses outline what is legal and imply that firms and individuals should go right up to the line between legality and illegality. Ethics does not consist of asking one's lawyer, "Is it legal?" The question, "Is it right?" is not the same as "Is it legal?" Yet most Americans act as if it were so.

16 Sacrificing self-interest for the common good is not going to be advocated by business schools or accepted by our students unless a majority of Americans also support the premise. In the end, business ethics is merely a reflection of American ethics.

Topics for Reading, Writing, and Discussion

RESPONDING

1 Summarize briefly the accusation described in paragraphs 1 and 2. What is Thurow's response to this accusation?

2 What changes does Thurow propose for business schools as a means of addressing business ethics? What is your response to these proposals?

EVALUATING

3 Evaluate Thurow's use of the hermit example to define the origin of ethics. How does he believe questions of ethics arise?

4 Thurow makes several suggestions for changing the ethical outlook of the business world. Evaluate these suggestions. What additional suggestions for improvement can you make?

COMPARING

5 What comparison does Thurow make between Japanese and German business practices and American business practices? What are some of the implications of this comparison?

6 Compare your own picture of ethics in the business world today with Thurow's image. Give examples to back up your ideas.

ARGUING

7 In paragraph 9, Thurow describes a bumper sticker that says, "The Man Who Dies With the Most Toys Wins." What does this bumper sticker mean? Do you agree with Thurow that the sticker's message "depicts the current state of American ethics"? Explain.

8 Why does Thurow believe that the entire curriculum in business schools needs to be changed rather than simply introducing courses in business ethics? Do you think these changes would make any difference in the behavior of students after they graduate and become part of the corporate world? Write an argument to defend your views.

DISINFORMATION ADVERTISING

ALICE WALKER

Alice Walker, an acclaimed writer, is the author of *The Color Purple;* her latest book, *Her Blue Body Everything We Know: Earthling Poems 1965–1990 Complete,*" was recently published by Harcourt Brace Jovanovich. After "Disinformation Advertising" appeared in the March/April 1991 issue of *Ms.*, both *New Woman* and Ford apologized. *New Woman* ran a statement acknowledging that the ad appeared without Walker's consent or knowledge while Ford agreed to make substantial donations to several of Walker's favorite activist organizations.

Predicting Questions

As you read, keep in mind the following questions, derived from this selection's title:

1 What is meant by "disinformation"?
2 How does "disinformation" relate to advertising?
3 What is Walker's attitude toward disinformation advertising?

Vocabulary Alert

As you read, watch for the following words: "logo," "emblazoned" (paragraph 2); "auspices" (paragraph 6); "touting," "complicit" (paragraph 7); "subtle," "percolate" (paragraph 8).

If you are unfamiliar with these words, try to determine their meaning from context clues. Which unfamiliar words do you need to look up in a dictionary? (In other words, which have meanings that cannot be determined from context yet are essential to understanding the meaning of the sentence or paragraph?)

---

1 One day a friend asked me whether I'd ever done an advertisement for Ford. The automobile manufacturer. "I don't even like Fords!" I said, laughing.

2 "Don't laugh," she said, handing me a clipping a friend of hers had sent her. Indeed, it was a full-page profile of me, complete with photograph, with the Ford logo emblazoned across the top. It had been torn from the pages of a popular women's magazine [*New Woman*]. Attached to it was a letter from a woman who asked:

3 "What does this ad mean? It appears as though Alice Walker was paid several thousand dollars to make a Ford promotion look good. . . . This means writers with her success and status will someday be on TV advertising diet Sprite or spaghetti sauce?"

4 I was stunned.

5 I had had nothing whatsoever to do with this ad, had never been asked permission to use my image or career to advance Ford's corporate cause, and furthermore have never, to this day, driven a Ford.

6 I immediately sent off a letter of protest to the magazine, and letters to my attorney and agent requesting they do something about this ad that misrepresented me, though not, ironically, in its content—which tended to praise my accomplishments—but in its presentation of my life and image under the auspices of a corporation to which I had not given permission and about which I know little. All I *do* know about Ford is that the truck, to me, has always symbolized perfectly the dominant white male American culture: blunt, boxy, powerful, and square.

7 When I first read the letter that asked whether I and other "successful" writers would soon be touting diet Sprite and spaghetti sauce I was annoyed by the writer's assumption that I was complicit in the creation of the ad. What have I ever done, I fumed, that would lead anyone to think I would sink so low as to endorse an automobile company! But then I remembered hearing a black man say on television that he would do a commercial for the

Ku Klux Klan for fifteen million dollars, the sum Michael Jackson had apparently been paid to endorse a soft drink. Even as I saw the words leave his mouth I couldn't believe it. How, in fact, *is* a reader to know that there are some writers and artists whose images and lives are not for sale to corporate giants?

8 May I suggest that if you, dear reader, should ever come across an ad that makes you wonder about the person being presented, do exactly what my friend's friend did: bring it to the attention of the person involved. *This is important.* Because I don't read magazines regularly there was no way of knowing about the Ford ad unless someone told me about it. It is true that you may actually find writers who do endorse Ford and other corporations, but my guess is that the writers that you assume would not do so, don't. Write to writers in care of their publishers, clip the offending article or ad, and send it along. I fear we are in for another long period of disinformation in the United States, and some of it will probably be extremely subtle. (For example, when I showed one friend the ad he couldn't see why I was so upset, since everything said in it was complimentary.) As women, people of color, and white activist men, we will have to keep our faith in each other strong. Question everything that seems strange or wrong to you concerning the mainstream presentation of your allies. It is better to annoy a writer by alerting her or him to erroneous "news" than to let it percolate unrefuted in the community, to the detriment of the writer and the community.

9 Nor am I saying that anyone has the time or energy to refute every lie or distortion that appears, but, perhaps from time to time we can, individually or collectively, communicate a general indication of where we stand.

Topics for Reading, Writing, and Discussion

RESPONDING

1 What is your response to advertising that features people whose professions are prestigious or glamorous? Do you find such advertising appealing and convincing?

2 Summarize Walker's response to discovering that she was featured in an advertisement for Ford.

EVALUATING

3 Explain the evaluation Walker makes of famous people who endorse commercial products. Do you agree with her evaluation?

4 Evaluate Walker's advice to the reader in paragraph 8. Do you agree with what she says? Explain how and why you do or do not follow her advice.

COMPARING

5 Compare Walker's attitude with the attitude of the man described in paragraph 7. What values are suggested by these two attitudes? Do you agree completely with one view or the other—or do you hold some other view? Explain.

6 Compare the view Walker says she had of Ford (paragraph 6) with the view the advertisement she describes was probably intended to convey.

ARGUING

7 Briefly summarize the argument Walker makes in her essay and explain whether you find this argument convincing.

8 Argue for or against the following proposition: People who work at professions that bring them fame and public acclaim should not endorse commercial products.

EVERY WOMAN WHO WRITES IS A SURVIVOR

SUSAN GRIFFIN

Susan Griffin is a feminist poet who teaches writing. The following selection comes from the transcript of a talk on the creative process that Griffin gave at Stanford University in 1973. This selection first appeared in print in "Women and the Creative Process: Lighting the Dark," in *Made from This Earth: An Anthology of Writings* (1982) by Susan Griffin.

Predicting Questions

As you read, keep in mind the following questions, derived from this selection's title:

1 Why is every woman who writes a survivor?
2 How do these women survive?
3 What do these women write about?

Vocabulary Alert

As you read, watch for the following words: "attrition" (paragraph 1); "carcass," "cheque," "trivial" (paragraph 2).

If you are unfamiliar with these words, try to determine their meaning from context clues. Which unfamiliar words do you need to look up in a dictionary? (In other words, which have meanings that cannot be determined from context yet are essential to understanding the meaning of the sentence or paragraph?)

---

1 There is another struggle that goes on in the life of a woman writer which was pointed out by Tillie Olsen in her extremely important essay 'Silences in Literature'. It's about the silences in the life of writers, ones that are unnatural interruptions. Very few women who have achieved great work in writing have been mothers, and she points this out in that essay. Those who have been mothers have been in an economic class allowing them to have constant help with their children. This is changing now, there are a lot of women who are mothers and are writing, but it's a process of attrition. I want to read you something about that, rather than speaking about it. And after I read this, let me talk a little bit about the form of it, which is to me also interesting. And I hope it is to you.

2 This is the story of the day in the life of a woman trying to be a writer and her child got sick. And in the midst of writing this story someone called her on the telephone. And of course, despite her original hostile reaction to the ring of the telephone, she got interested in the conversation which was about teaching writing in a woman's prison, for no pay of course, and she would have done it if it weren't for the babysitting and the lack of money for a plane fare, and then she hung up the phone and looked at her typewriter, and for an instant swore her original sentence was not there. But after a while she found it. Then she began again, but in the midst of the second sentence, a man telephoned wanting to speak to the woman she shares the house with who was not available to speak on the telephone and by the time she got back to her typewriter she began to worry about her sick daughter downstairs. And why hadn't the agency for babysitters called back and why hadn't the department for health called back because she was looking for a day sitter and a night sitter, one so she could teach the next day and one so she could read her poetry. And she was hoping that the people who had asked her to read poetry would pay for the babysitter since the next evening after that would be a meeting of teachers whom she wanted to meet and she could not afford two nights of babysitters let alone one, actually. This was the second day her child was sick and the second day she tried to write (she had been trying to be a writer for years) but she failed entirely the first day because of going to the market to buy Vitamin C and to the toy store to buy cut outs and crayons, and making soup from the chicken carcass that had been picked nearly clean to make sandwiches for lunch, and watering the plants, sending in the mortgage cheque and other cheques to cover that cheque to the bank, and feeling tired, wishing she had a job, talking on the telephone, and putting out newspaper and glue and scissors on the kitchen table for her tired, bored child and squinting her eyes at the clock waiting for *Sesame Street* to begin again. Suddenly, after she went upstairs to her bedroom with a book having given up writing as impossible, it was time to cook dinner. But she woke up on the second day with the day before as a lesson in her mind. Then an old friend called who had come to town who she was eager to see and she said, 'Yes, I'm home with a sick child', and they spent the morning talking. She was writing poetry and teaching she said. He had written four books he said. Her daughter showed him her red and blue and orange coloured pictures. She wished he didn't have to leave so early she thought but she didn't say, and went back to pick up tissue paper off the floor and fix lunch for her and her child and begin telephoning for babysitters because she knew she had to teach the next day. And the truth was, if she did not have a sick child to care for, she was not sure she could write anyway because the kitchen was still there needing cleaning, the garden there needing weeding and watering, the living room needing curtains, the couch needing pillows, a stack of mail needing answers (for instance, if she didn't call the woman who had lived in her house the month before about the phone bill soon, she would lose a lot of money). And besides, she had nothing to write. She had had fine thoughts for writing the night before but in the morning they took on a sickly complexion. And anyway, she had begun to think her life trivial and so it was, and she was tired writing the same words, or different words about the same situation, the situation or situations being that she was tired, tired of trying to write, tired of poverty or almost poverty or fear of poverty, tired of the kitchen being dirty, tired of having no lover. She was amazed that she had gotten herself dressed, actually, with thoughts like these, and caught herself saying maybe I should take a trip when she realized she had just come back from a trip and had wanted to be home so much she came back early. And even in the writing of this she thought I have written all this before and went downstairs to find her daughter had still not eaten a peanut butter sandwich and she wondered to herself what keeps that child alive?

Topics for Reading, Writing, and Discussion

RESPONDING

1 What is your response to the description of the woman given in the second paragraph? Who do you think she is? Explain.

2 If you were a friend of the woman described in the second paragraph, what advice would you give her about balancing her work (writing) with the rest of her life? Write a letter to her explaining your advice.

EVALUATING

3 Why does Griffin mention Tillie Olsen in the opening paragraph? Why is it significant that Olsen talks about silences in the lives of women who write?

4 What is the main idea of this excerpt? Is the main idea stated anywhere? How did you figure out what the main idea was? Write a brief statement of the main idea and then write a brief evaluation explaining which details or examples led you to focus on the main idea you have described.

COMPARING

5 Read the second paragraph and try separating it into two lists. In one list, write in chronological order the details that relate to the woman's writing. In the other list, write in chronological order the details that relate to other aspects of the woman's life. What do you discover about the way the details in the second list affect the details in the first list?

6 Try writing a paragraph patterned on the second long paragraph that describes a day when you found yourself with too much to do and too little time. Notice that Griffin uses the word "and" many times. Usually writers avoid repeating a word like "and," but Griffin makes the choice to emphasize the pace of her day.

ARGUING

7 Given the details in this excerpt, would you define the woman described in the second paragraph as a survivor? Write an argument for or against using this term to describe her.

8 Write an argument for or against the following proposition: It is more difficult for women to pursue nearly any profession than it is for men to pursue the same profession.

THE PALMERS

SHIVA NAIPAUL

Shiva Naipaul was born and educated in Trinidad and then won a postgraduate scholarship to Oxford University. He wrote extensively, particularly on problems of the Third World, up to his death in 1985. The following excerpt comes from his book *North of South: An African Journey* (1979). To gather information for this book, Naipaul traveled extensively in Africa; he met and interviewed the Palmers in Kenya.

Predicting Questions

As you read, keep in mind the following questions, derived from this selection's title:

1 Who are the Palmers?
2 Why are they significant?
3 What is the author's attitude toward the Palmers?

Vocabulary Alert

As you read, watch for the following words: "visceral" (paragraph 1); "replete," "tenaciously," "tarmac" (paragraph 3); "Kilimanjaro" (paragraph 4); "Alsatian," "hygienic" (paragraph 5); "pilfering" (paragraph 9); "fawning" (paragraph 19); "atrocious," "paternalism" (paragraph 31).

If you are unfamiliar with these words, try to determine their meaning from context clues. Which unfamiliar words do you need to look up in a dictionary? (In other words, which have meanings that cannot be determined from context yet are essential to understanding the meaning of the sentence or paragraph?)

---

1 The ridges of the Kikuyu country stretched away on all sides, wave upon wave sweeping toward the horizon. Where the land was cut away to accommodate the passage of the road, its red heart was startlingly exposed to view. Looking at that bloody redness one sensed not only the richness of the land but—more disturbingly—its visceral appeal. It seemed to symbolize the Kikuyu's fierce attachment to it, the unity of soil and tribe. In *Facing Mount Kenya* (first published in 1938), Kenyatta[1] expressed

[1] Jomo Kenyatta, the first president of Kenya. He served from 1963 until his death in 1978 [Ed.].

his tribe's attitude toward the land they considered peculiarly theirs. "The Gikuyu," he wrote, "consider the earth as the 'mother' of the tribe. It is the soil that feeds the child through lifetime; and again after death it is the soil that nurses the spirits of the dead for eternity. Thus the earth is the most sacred thing above all that dwell in or on it . . . an everlasting oath is to swear by the earth." Those oaths were to surface, in a more murderous form, during the Mau Mau insurrection.

2 The road, which to begin with had been wide enough for two cars, narrowed to a single lane. We left behind the forest reserve through which we had been traveling and entered the coffee belt, the leaves of the neatly staked-out shrubs glistening in the soupy sunlight. "Kenya is lucky," my companion said, gesturing at the plantations on either side of us. "The Brazilian crop has been hit by frost this year."

3 We passed through a straggling township replete with the usual beer parlors and "ration" shops and unsightly hoardings advertising detergents, refrigerators, and vacuum cleaners. The air was noisy with jukebox music. A roadside market was in progress. Long strips of colorfully dyed cloth were spread out on the ground. Young boys danced out in front of the car flourishing fruit and vegetables. Beyond the township was typical *shamba* country: small plots planted with corn; foraging goats and cows and pigs and chickens. This, even in colonial days, had been a "native" area, and it clung tenaciously to its traditional character. The coffee plantations reappeared. A veil of pearly mist obscured the more distant reaches of the open, undulating landscape. Its "English" character was emphasized by the scattered condensations of color created by stands of trees set amid the acres of coffee. The tarmac ended. Clouds of red dust billowed in our wake. We were climbing now, and after a time, the coffee country gave way to tea country. The tea gardens, emerald green, even-topped, forming an unbroken wave of cultivation, were like a scaly sheath thrown over the land.

4 It was almost noon when we reached the Palmers' farm. Mrs. Palmer, jovial and red-faced, her hair bunched in a scarf, greeted us amiably. It was cool enough for a sweater. The day was autumnal. Gray clouds hid the sun, and there was a vapor of blue mist in the shallow valleys. A chill, clammy wind blew. The Palmers' house—a modest-sized brick bungalow—was finely situated on a rising piece of ground. We stood for a while on the well-kept lawn surrounding it, admiring the extensive views. "In good weather," our hostess said, "you can see Kilimanjaro." We gazed in the direction she indicated, paying the invisible mountain ritual homage. Then we went inside.

5 A fire was going in the brick fireplace; an Alsatian was stretched out on the rug in front of it. Two high-backed armchairs with chintz coverings were drawn up in front of the fireplace. Ancestral photographs lined the walls. A piano, piled with papers, occupied a corner. Next to it was a large, brass-studded chest. Agricultural journals, old copies of *The Times,* and some back numbers of the *Illustrated London News* were distributed in neat piles on a low table in the center of the room. A complete set of *Chambers' Encyclopedia* filled a small bookshelf. I noticed no other books apart from those. The wooden floor gleamed. There was not a speck of dust to be seen. It was a forbiddingly hygienic room. I felt that nothing new had happened here for a long time—just endless dusting, cleaning, preserving.

6 "I hear it's been a lovely summer in England," Mrs. Palmer said. "We've been reading all about it." She nodded at the pile of newspapers. "Now here you are on the Equator—and sitting in front of a fire. It must seem strange."

7 She rang a bell. A barefooted "boy" appeared. She ordered him to bring ice and glasses. "And Simon . . ." Simon, who had started to leave, paused but did not turn around. Mrs. Palmer smiled. ". . . when you put the ice in the glasses, do please remember to use the tongs and not your fingers. That's what the tongs are *for.* Now off you go."

8 Simon disappeared into the kitchen.

9 Mrs. Palmer was still smiling when she turned to face us. "Simon seems to have a block about using those tongs. I can't understand it. I've told him so many times. Still, Simon has one great virtue. He hasn't been *spoiled.* Not as yet, anyway. I'm keeping my fingers crossed. It's amazing how quickly they do get spoiled, though. There used to be an old saying in this country: put a native in shoes and that's the end of him. Nowadays, of course, they've all got shoes and we aren't even allowed to call them natives." Mrs. Palmer sighed, staring out the window toward invisible Kilimanjaro. Taking a key from the pocket of her dress, she unlocked the liquor cabinet. "I'm sorry to seem so jailerlike," she said, "but pilfering, I'm afraid, is a big problem. I have to keep everything under lock and key. They take the oddest things sometimes, things they can't possibly have any use for. The other day my shower cap disappeared." She peered at the ranks of bottles. "I close my eyes to the sugar and flour they take from the larder—but I *do* draw the line at our precious Scotch. Simon is still fairly trustworthy. But you can never be sure. Leaving bottles of Scotch hanging about the place is more than a temptation. It's an invitation. And once they get a taste for alcohol, that's the end."

10 "Worse even than putting them into shoes," my companion said.

11 "Much worse," Mrs. Palmer replied, not catching the irony. "In the old days people used to say that to give a native alcohol was like putting a loaded gun in the hands of a child. In my opinion that's still true. But . . ." She sighed again.

12 She extracted bottles of whiskey, gin, and sherry.

13 Simon came in carrying a bowl of ice in one hand and three glasses in the other.

14 "Simon . . . Simon . . ." Mrs. Palmer wagged her head.

15 Simon looked at her expressionlessly.

16 "Why didn't you use the tray, Simon?" Mrs. Palmer relieved him of his burdens. "You can carry several things at once on a tray. That's what a tray is *for.*"

17 My eyes strayed to Simon's bare, uncorrupted feet.

18 "You see what I mean," Mrs. Palmer said when Simon had left the room. "The tray is another of his peculiar blocks." She poured generous measures of whiskey into our glasses.

19 The Alsatian sprang up, barking loudly: Mr. Palmer had arrived. He came in chattering apologies for his late arrival. He was dressed in khaki—short-sleeved khaki shirt tucked into short khaki trousers, matching knee-high socks and thick-soled brown shoes; a lean, wiry man of medium height, probably in his midfifties. He fondled and pummeled the fawning dog.

20 "Awfully sorry about the weather," he said. "Wish we could have put on a better show for you. On a fine day you can see Kili."

21 The tea gardens—the Palmers had about three hundred acres under tea—began not many yards beyond the lawn surrounding the house. The day's work was drawing to a close, and the pluckers, bent under leaf-filled nets slung from their shoulders, were filing down the aisles between the rows of bushes, slowly making their way to the weighing shed. The afternoon had become colder and gloomier. Thickening mists obscured the summits of neighboring ridges. The wind was cutting. Smoke rose from a group of huts clustered together on the shallow slope of a nearby depression. A moorland bleakness overhung the scene. The pluckers—men, women, and children—crept like an army of subdued ghosts through the premature twilight, the sharp odor of the raw leaf they carried tanging the chill air. A muted murmur of conversation rose among them as they waited for the product of their day's labor to be weighed. All were equipped with shining aprons, reaching from neck to knee, made of vinyl.

22 "I supply the aprons myself," Mr. Palmer said. "They are very appreciative. It reduces the wear and tear on their clothing."

23 "They like the bright colors," Mrs. Palmer said. "They are very fond of bright colors."

24 The estate employed roughly two hundred people. Most of them had been brought in from outside the district—or had migrated of their own accord in search of work. The local people were not particularly interested in agricultural labor of the type offered by the Palmers. Nairobi, less than a hundred miles away, was a powerful magnet.

25 "The local people have been spoiled," Mrs. Palmer said. "Many actually prefer to be beggars and prostitutes in Nairobi than to earn an honest living from the soil. They consider it to be beneath their dignity." She pursed her lips.

26 The pluckers smiled and saluted as they shuffled past with their loads. Mrs. Palmer's scarf snapped like a flag as she surveyed the beasts of burden who marched past her. They could, with luck, earn up to a pound a day.

27 "I know it sounds appallingly little by English standards," Mr. Palmer said. "But by *their* standards it's a good wage. *They* don't complain. *They* are grateful that they can actually work and earn something. It's only certain left-wing journalists looking for a sensational story who come here and weep crocodile tears on their behalf."

28 Mr. Palmer stooped, picked up a tea leaf from the ground, and stared at it critically.

29 "These people," he went on, "are simple, hardworking folk. They're not spoiled . . ."

30 "Not as yet," Mrs. Palmer put in grimly. Her scarf fluttered and snapped.

31 "Their needs are basic," Mr. Palmer said. "They want to have food in their bellies, to be warm, to have a roof over their heads. *I* supply those basic needs. Many of them, you know, prefer to work for us whites than to work for their own people. Their own people often treat them like slaves. They don't pay them properly, they offer no medical facilities, they house them in atrocious conditions. Paternalism like mine has something to be said for it, don't you think?" He grinned at me.

32 He beckoned over a boy of about ten. "Have a look at this *toto.*" He squeezed the boy's arms and legs, lifted up his shirt and exhibited the well-fleshed diaphragm. "Six months ago Sammy was skeletal, covered with sores, had a bad cough. He's all right now, though. Aren't you, Sammy?" He chucked the boy under the chin.

The boy, not knowing what was happening to him, gazed at us with wild, frightened eyes. His mother watched from a distance, obviously pleased to see her son the focus of her master's attention.

33 "In the old days we used to have an estate shop," Mrs. Palmer said. "That way you made sure they got reasonably fed. Now they spend their money how and where they like." She laughed grimly. "Maize meal isn't good enough for them these days. They want rice."

34 "Rice is more nutritious than maize meal," Mr. Palmer said.

35 "But more expensive."

36 "It's their money."

37 Mrs. Palmer sighed. We returned to the house for lunch.

Topics for Reading, Writing, and Discussion

RESPONDING

1. This excerpt focuses on the Palmers and their observations. Imagine that you are in Simon's place. Write a journal entry describing his response to his work and to the foreign journalists' visit.
2. Read the sections that describe the Palmers' house. How do these descriptions reflect the Palmers' personalities and their lives? As a response, try writing one or two paragraphs describing a room or a house that reflects the personality of the person who lives there.

EVALUATING

3. Several times the Palmers refer to Kenyans who are "spoiled." What do they mean by that word? Evaluate their reasons for wanting to employ people who are not "spoiled."
4. Evaluate the attitude of Naipaul and his companion toward the Palmers. Analyze specific words and phrases that indicate their feelings and responses to what they see and hear at the Palmers' plantation.

COMPARING

5. Compare the role Mrs. Palmer plays in the household and the work she does to the role played by Mr. Palmer and the work he does. What significance do you see in the difference you've noted?
6. What is the purpose of the first two paragraphs of this selection? How does the attitude of the black Kenyans toward the land compare to the Palmers' attitude toward their tea plantation? How does

Naipaul use this comparison to develop the main idea of this excerpt?

ARGUING

7 According to Mrs. Palmer, why do many of the natives not want to work on the tea plantation? What other reasons can you think of that might encourage these people to seek other circumstances in the large cities? How would you argue against the points made by Mrs. Palmer?

8 The Palmers argue that they really treat help quite well and that these people should be grateful for the opportunity being given them. Imagine that you are a worker who has chosen to leave the plantation and you are arguing against what the Palmers are saying.

TOPICS FOR LONGER PAPERS: PART IV

1 Compare John Coleman's and Zoë Tracy Hardy's experiences as blue-collar workers. Which experience seems more positive? Why would you define it that way?

2 Two selections in this section concern women at work. Do you see any similarities in the issues raised by these selections? What differences do you see in the lives and work of the women on whom these selections focus?

3 What comparisons can you see between the way the Palmers think of and treat their workers and the experiences of John Coleman as a blue-collar worker? What significance do you see in these comparisons?

4 Lester C. Thurow, Zoë Tracy Hardy, and Alice Walker address ethical concerns related to the world of work. After reading these essays, consider what you believe to be the most important ethical issue facing workers today. Think about your own experiences at work as well as the experiences of those you know or have heard about.

5 After reading several of the selections in this section, design an ideal work situation. What would you consider most important? Think about such issues as the significance of the product or service your work provides; the relationship between managers and workers; the physical set-up of the work situation; the relationship of the work to the rest of one's life; the financial rewards; the chance to grow and learn at work; the amount of pressure and competition at work.

TOPICS REQUIRING RESEARCH: PART IV

(For Research Strategies and Skills, Consult Appendixes D and E)

1. Read more of John Coleman's journal and write an evaluation of one chapter or section of the book that was not included in the excerpt printed in this text (pages 254–259).
2. Interview a person who has done both blue-collar and white-collar work to determine that person's attitude toward and satisfaction with each kind of work. Write an essay explaining what you discovered.
3. During World War II, a woman who worked in war plants was called "Rosie the Riveter." In a history text, or some other source, read about women who did such work. Compare what you have learned with the description of the work given by Zoë Tracy Hardy (pages 260–269).
4. During World War II, women entered the work force by the thousands. What happened to these women after the war ended? In a history text or other source, discover the after-effects of this massive shift in the work force and then write an essay describing your findings.
5. What experiences have you had working as part of a team? Do you prefer such work to working as an individual? Conduct a survey of at least twenty people to discover their reasons for preferring to work as a member of a team or as an individual. Write an essay explaining what you learn from the results of the survey.
6. After reading "The Palmers," read some background information on Kenya to explain how Europeans came to be landholders there. How does knowing this historical background affect your response to the Palmers and their beliefs and actions?

APPENDIX A

REVISION GUIDELINES AND PROOFREADING/EDITING GUIDELINES

THE REVISION GUIDELINES AND Proofreading/Editing Guidelines serve as summaries of the points you may consider while you work to improve each draft of a paper. Remember that revision and proofreading/editing are two separate processes (although sometimes they overlap).

REVISION Revision means literally "re-seeing." As you revise, you see your subject, your organization, your word choice, your sentence structure, your choice of examples (to name a few considerations) with new eyes. It's a mistake to think of revision as something that takes place only after you have a nearly complete draft. Revision takes place constantly during any writing project.

For example, you may initially choose one aspect of a topic to discuss and then—as you mull the idea over—you may decide to work on another aspect instead. In this case, revision would have taken place before you ever committed words to paper. In the guidelines that follow, then, the items are intended as suggestions. You may not use all of them with any given paper, and you certainly should not look at the items as part of a checklist, steps to be noted and crossed off once you have done them. In fact, you may return to some of these steps many times during one writing project.

PROOFREADING AND EDITING In contrast to the process of revision, proofreading and editing take place mainly near the completion of a paper. Although many people automatically correct misspellings, typographical errors, or problems with punctuation whenever they notice them, you should focus especially carefully on proofreading and editing as you work with your next-to-final draft and your final copy. While you may not need to use all the guidelines for every paper, every point should be considered during that last step before you submit your work to its audience.

Revision Guidelines

1 Is the topic sufficiently narrow, yet broad enough to permit full treatment, given the length of the paper and the time you have to write?
2 Do you let the reader know early in the paper through a clear thesis statement(s) what topic you'll be addressing?
3 Does your thesis statement tell the reader what you'll be saying about the topic rather than simply announcing it?
4 Have you gathered plenty of information to develop your topic and support your ideas?
5 Have you used several discovery/invention strategies to explore your topic? (See pages 11–16, 141–143). Do you need to try more brainstorming, freewriting, listing, and so forth, to define your topic more clearly?
6 Have you taken clear notes so that you can look at the information rather than simply tossing it around in your head?
7 Have you organized the information—perhaps by using piles of notecards or by making a preliminary outline?
8 Have you thought about an organizational strategy for writing—a way to present your ideas logically on paper?
9 Have you considered the interests, abilities, beliefs, and opinions of your audience?
10 Does your planning/writing address those interests, abilities, beliefs, and opinions?
11 Do you have a clear, lively opening paragraph that gets the readers' attention?
12 Does each paragraph within the paper develop one main point or idea?
13 Does each paragraph have enough reasons, details, and examples to support its main idea?
14 Are there clear transitions so that the reader understands the relationship among paragraphs and among sentences within paragraphs?
15 Do you have a concluding paragraph or paragraphs that do more than summarize what the paper says?
16 Does the conclusion follow logically from what goes before?
17 Have you been careful to reason logically and to avoid fallacies?

18 Have you been careful to appeal to emotions only in a fair and not in a manipulative way?

19 Have you varied sentence structure to avoid a paper that sounds either choppy or monotonous?

20 Have you chosen words that are precise and accurate, considering both connotation and denotation?

Proofreading/Editing Guidelines

1. Have you followed format guidelines given by your instructor? For instance, you may be asked to follow these standard rules:
   A. Type or write clearly on white paper using dark blue or black ink.
   B. If assignment is typed, use double spacing.
   C. Left-hand margin is usually one and one half inches; right, bottom, and top margins are one inch.
   D. Page numbers are placed in the upper righthand corner of each page, beginning with page 2. The first page is *not numbered.*
   E. If a title page is required, center the title of paper in the middle of the page. Your name, the name of the course, the instructor's name, and the date go in the lower right corner.
   F. If a title page is not required, put your name and the date in the upper right corner of the first page.
   G. Whether or not a title page is required, the title is given on the first page, centered on the top line. Double space between the title and text of paper.
   H. Title is not underlined or put in quotation marks.
   I. Title is correctly capitalized.
   J. Title is a carefully selected phrase suggesting the main topic.
2. Have you written effective sentences?
   A. Each sentence should express a complete thought. (See pages 300–305.)
   B. No sentence should fuse two complete thoughts or splice two complete thoughts with a comma. (See pages 305–312.)
   C. Modifying phrases or clauses should relate clearly to the word or words they describe. (See pages 328–332.)
   D. Sentence structure should be varied to avoid confusing or boring the reader.
3. Have you checked for mechanical and grammatical correctness?
   A. Every word should be spelled correctly. (See pages 358–363.)
   B. Subjects and verbs should agree. (See pages 312–318.)

C. Pronouns should have clear antecedents and agree with their antecedents. (See pages 318–324.)
D. Verb tense should switch only to indicate a time change. (See pages 324–328.)
E. Commas, colons, semicolons, and other marks of punctuation should be correctly used. (See pages 337–343 and 343–349.)
F. Possessives should be formed correctly, using apostrophes (except for possessive pronouns like *his, hers, theirs,* and *yours*). (See pages 346–347.)
G. No apostrophes should be used in simple plurals. (See pages 347–349.)
H. If you have used quotations or paraphrases, they should be formatted correctly and you should document them correctly, giving credit to your source. (See pages 333–337.)
I. Typographical errors should be corrected. If there are more than three typos on a page, recopy that page before submitting the paper.

APPENDIX B

GUIDE TO EDITING*

WRITERS' IDEAS ARE, OF COURSE, the essential ingredients that make a piece of writing meaningful and effective. And, as the first four sections of this book suggest, the ways writers organize ideas, evaluate their audience, and choose their words are also important. But no matter how brilliant the ideas, how sensible the organization, how accurate the evaluation of audience, or how powerful the choice of words, no writer can communicate effectively without strong proofreading and editing skills. Although most people do some editing throughout the writing process, almost automatically correcting a spelling or typographical error, the major proofreading and editing tasks are undertaken when a piece of writing has already been thoroughly developed and revised.

(*Note:* For the distinction between revision strategies and proofreading/editing strategies, see the guidelines on pages 290 and 291.)

Strong editing skills make your writing clear, and in addition, they send a message that you value what you have written and that you care about what your audience thinks about that piece of writing. Developing accurate editing skills might be equated with knowing how to present yourself at a job interview. Of course you expect that the interviewer will be most interested in your skills, your knowledge, your education, and your experience. Yet if you attend the interview dressed in ripped jeans, a stained T-shirt, and untied tennis shoes, your appearance will create such a negative impression and will be so distracting to the interviewer that you may never have a chance to demonstrate your strong qualifications. So it is with editing skills. If your writing is filled with grammatical and mechanical errors, your readers may not be able to see past those annoying distractions to get to your ideas.

This appendix reviews the main principles that professional editors

* On pages 363–382, you will find suggested responses to all of the exercises, except those called "Editing in Context." These suggested responses allow you to do the exercises in this section on your own and then to compare your editing changes with those made by a professional writer and editor.

use as they proofread manuscripts. These principles appear in nearly every English handbook you have ever seen, beginning in grade school, so what you'll read here constitutes a focused review session. The rules for effective editing are not difficult, but they do require concentration and attention. The reward for expending the effort required to learn these principles will be confidence in the impact of your writing on its readers.

This guide begins with a short preface that reviews the structure of the English sentence. Understanding the sentence is essential as you work to develop proofreading and editing skills. The preface is followed by twelve Editor's Focus sections, each reviewing a different editing issue. Each of the twelve sections has four parts: an evaluation exercise that asks you to proofread and shows whether you can already identify the particular error being addressed; an explanation of the error and of ways to correct it; an editing exercise to allow you to practice identification and correction of the error; and a cumulative exercise that asks you to identify and correct not only the error addressed by the section you have just completed but also the errors addressed by previous sections.

While these explanations and exercises are helpful in alerting you to grammatical and mechanical issues and in demonstrating proofreading skills, the best way to become an expert editor is to work with your own writing. As you become more aware of these editing strategies, it is essential to concentrate on applying them to the writing you do not only for English classes but also for other classes, for work, for community involvement, and so on. Remember that although most readers do not return papers, proposals, reports, or letters with grammatical and mechanical errors marked in red ink, those errors nevertheless are often noticed and judged harshly.

Even if you have a computer program that helps to check spelling, grammar, and style, you need to understand the principles and rules involved in order to make sensible editing responses to the program's queries. Excellent editing does not require years of advanced study, but it does require commitment and a determination to take control of your own writing rather than depending on other people (or machines) to notice and correct your errors. This guide helps you to make that commitment and thus enables you to be in control.

Understanding the Structure of the Sentence

To become a proficient editor, you need to understand the basic structure of the English sentence: The sentence has two parts, the subject and the predicate. The *subject* indicates who or what is acting, being acted upon, or being described. The *predicate* indicates what the subject is doing, indicates what is being done to the subject, or describes the subject.

Here are some examples of typical sentences. In each sentence, the subject is underlined and the predicate is not underlined. The subject and predicate are separated by a slash (/).

SUBJECT PREDICATE
Lafayette, a French General, / visited the United States in 1925.

(The subject is acting; the predicate indicates the action.)

SUBJECT PREDICATE
An alligator / was presented to Lafayette as a gift.

(The subject is acted upon; the predicate indicates the action.)

SUBJECT PREDICATE
This alligator / was nine feet long and had a row of sharp teeth.

(The subject is described by the predicate.)

(*Note:* Although the subject is first and the predicate last in many sentences, there are exceptions. Consider the following examples.)

PRED. SUBJECT PREDICATE
Do / most historians / know about this strange incident?

(In a question, the predicate—or part of the predicate—sometimes comes before the subject.)

PREDICATE SUBJECT
There are / few written reports of this alligator.

(In sentences that begin with "there is" or "there are," the subject follows that expression. "There is" or "there are" describe the subject and serve as the predicate of the sentence.)

The core of the subject is the simple subject. The core of the predicate is the verb. To understand these parts of the sentence and to learn to edit sentences effectively, you must learn to identify nouns and pronouns used as simple subjects. You must also learn to identify verbs.

Identifying Nouns

Nouns are words that name persons, places, objects, or concepts.

Examples: woman, Elizabeth Blackwell, country, South Africa, camera, love.

EXERCISE 1

Directions Circle the nouns in the following paragraph.

(1) Awoman, Patience Lovell Wright, was the first American to become a professional sculptor. (2) Wright took her models

from life and made statues of many important people in British and American society. (3) Praised for their beauty and grace, these statues were much admired. (4) Unfortunately, only one of her works has survived, the statue of William Pitt, the Elder, which she completed in 1799. (5) This statue can now be seen in Westminster Abbey.

Nouns can be used as simple subjects. The *simple subject* of the sentence is the person, place, object, or concept that acts, is acted upon, or is described.

EXAMPLES:

SUBJECT
Her love grew every day.

(The love has done the acting; it has grown.)

SUBJECT
Where has the judge gone?

(The judge has acted; he or she has gone someplace.)

(*Note:* In this sentence, the subject comes in the middle of the verb phrase. To find the subject in a question, turn the question into a statement: "The judge has gone where."

SUBJECT
The car is being repaired.

(The car is being acted upon.)

SUBJECT SUBJECT
The car and the motorcycle are being repaired.

(The car and the motorcycle are being acted upon.)

(*Note:* In this sentence, two nouns connected by "and" make up the subject. This is called a compound subject.)

SUBJECT
There are six Cadillacs in the garage.

(The Cadillacs are being described.)

EXERCISE 2

Directions Underline the simple subjects in the following sentences.

(1) Cocoa and chocolate are favorite desserts in Europe and the United States. (2) The United States, England, Germany, the Netherlands, and France now import four-fifths of the world's chocolate. (3) Where did chocolate originally come from? (4) Five

hundred years ago, this confection was totally unknown in Europe. (5) This fact may seem amazing. (6) Hernando Cortez explored Mexico in the early sixteenth century. (7) The Aztecs drank a dark frothy beverage called *chocolatl.* (8) The beans that were used to make the drink were regarded as a gift from the gods. (9) Today, chocolate lovers can understand why the Aztecs considered this delightful sweet to be a divine gift. (10) Wealthy people can even buy a sculpture of themselves for several hundred dollars made by an exclusive candy shop in New York City.

Identifying Pronouns

Pronouns are words that take the place of nouns. Common pronouns are *I, me, my, mine, we, us, our, ours, you, your, yours, he, his, him, she, her, hers, it, its, they, their, theirs, them, this, that, which, who, whom.* In addition, words like *anyone, everyone, some,* and *any* can be used as pronouns. Like nouns, pronouns may be used as the simple subject of a sentence.

EXERCISE 3

Directions In the following sentences circle the pronouns that are used as simple subjects of sentences. Then underline the nouns that are used as simple subjects.

(1) Every summer, many people head for the beach. (2) They lie in the sun, thinking a tan will look great. (3) However, scientists call sun bathing a hazardous activity. (4) It carries great risks, including premature aging, eye damage, and immune system damage. (5) These are not the greatest threats, however. (6) Medical experts agree that ultraviolet rays from the sun are the chief cause of skin cancer.

Identifying Main Verbs

Main verbs are words that show action or express a state of being.

Examples of action verbs: run, breathe, think, exist, jump, fall
Examples of being verbs: am, are, is, was, were, be, been

EXERCISE 4

Directions In the following sentences, write "A" over the action verbs and "B" over the being verbs.

(1) The cheetah is the world's fastest mammal. (2) Both its speed and its rate of acceleration are amazing. (3) It runs at a maximum speed of sixty to sixty-three miles per hour. (4) In addition, the cheetah accelerates from a standing start to a speed of forty-five miles per hour in two seconds. (5) After about three hundred yards, however, the exhausted cheetah stops suddenly. (6) The chase is over.

Identifying Auxiliary Verbs

Some verbs are used in combination with other verbs. These verbs are called "auxiliary" or "helping" verbs because they help to complete the meaning of the main verb by forming a verb phrase.

Examples of verbs that can be used as auxiliaries:

be	have	do	can	may	will
am	has	does	could	might	shall
are	had	did	should		
was		done	would		
were		doing			
been					
being					

Examples of verbs used in sentences:

ACTION VERB
A group of scholars studied two hundred of Grimm's fairy tales.

HELPING VERB ACTION (MAIN) VERB
They had decided to look at male and female characters.

BEING VERB
There are sixteen wicked stepmothers and only three wicked fathers or stepfathers.

HELPING VERB ACTION (MAIN) VERB BEING VERB
Do you think there are any male witches?

ACTION VERB
In the two hundred tales, the Grimm brothers created twenty-three

ACTION VERB
evil female witches, but they only described two evil male witches.

EXERCISE 5

Directions In the following sentences, write "A" over the action verbs, "B" over the being verbs, and "H" over the helping verbs

(1) The *Fanny Farmer Cookbook* is now quite famous. (2) In 1896, however, Little, Brown Publishing Company refused the manuscript. (3) Finally, Farmer raised the money and paid the publishing costs herself. (4) Over the years, her book has sold millions of copies. (5) It is now known throughout the world and has been translated into more than thirty different languages.

Regular and Irregular Verbs

Most English verbs show changes in time (tense) by using the same patterns. (See page 325 for futher explanation of tense.)

Present	Past	Past Participle
work	worked	(have, has, had) worked
walk	walked	(have, has, had) walked
describe	described	(have, has, had) described

As you can see, the past and past participle of all regular verbs end in "ed."

However, many English verbs are irregular, and you must memorize the past and past participle forms. Here are some commonly used irregular verbs:

Present	Past	Past Participle
become	became	become
begin	began	begun
bring	brought	brought
burst	burst	burst
come	came	come
do	did	done
drink	drank	drunk
eat	ate	eaten
give	gave	given
lay (put)	laid	laid
lie (recline)	lay	lain

Present	Past	Past Participle
make	made	made
run	ran	run
say	said	said
set (place)	set	set
sit (be seated)	sat	sat
speak	spoke	spoken
swim	swam	swum
take	took	taken
teach	taught	taught
throw	threw	thrown
write	wrote	written

EXERCISE 6

Directions: In the following sentences, write the correct form of the irregular verb indicated in the parentheses that follow the sentence.

1 After he ______________ his first book, Jarvis Norton was filled with regret. (write, *past*)

2 The man who had ______________ him to write was included as a minor character. (teach, *past participle*)

3 Norton ______________ the character a different name than his teacher's. (give, *past*)

4 Nevertheless, a friend commented to the author, "I ______________ you've put our old friend in your book." (see, *present*)

5 Unfortunately, the book shows the sad truth: In his old age, the teacher ______________ an alcoholic. (become, *past*)

EDITOR'S FOCUS 1

AVOIDING SENTENCE FRAGMENTS

Proofreading Evaluation Exercise 1A

Directions To evaluate your skill at identifying and correcting sentence fragments, read the following paragraph and identify any sentence fragments. Then rewrite the paragraph, correcting the fragments.

(1) A war now rages between the defenders of animal rights and the scientists who support using animal subjects for medical experiments. (2) Some animal rights activists who belong to an organization known as People for the Ethical Treatment of Animals (PETA). (3) These activists claim that medical experimenters are as cruel as Nazis. (4) During World War II. (5) As most people know, doctors in concentration camps carried out incredibly painful experiments on the human inmates. (6) The public must decide whether or not to accept the comparison made by PETA members. (7) And then what action to take concerning this stunning accusation. (8) Of course, we must consider also the beliefs of medical doctors concerning animal research. (9) According to a survey of the American Medical Association, conducted in 1988. (10) Ninety-seven percent of doctors support it.

Editing Strategy: Identification and Correction of Sentence Fragments

A *fragment* is a group of words that is not a sentence, but is punctuated as if it were.

In formal, written English avoid fragments.

Examples of Fragments

FRAG.

NO: She returned to school. Because she needed new work skills. She decided to start classes immediately.

EXPLANATION "Because she needed new work skills" is not a sentence. It depends either on the sentence before it or on the sentence after it to complete its meaning.

Where should it go logically? Should it go with "She returned to school"? Or should it go with "She decided to start classes immediately"? Either connection makes sense. As the writer, you must decide and tell your audience.

YES: She returned to school because she needed new work skills. She decided to start classes immediately.

She returned to school. Because she needed new work skills, she decided to start classes immediately.

Identifying Fragments

A fragment cannot stand alone for one of these four reasons:

1 There is no subject.

Example: Needed (VERB) a steady, reliable income.

2 There is no verb.

Example: The young widow (SUBJECT) with two small children.

3 There is neither a subject nor a verb.
Example: With two small, dependent children.

4 The fragment has a subject and a verb, but begins with or contains a word like "because," "that," "who," or "when" that makes it dependent on another sentence for its meaning.

Example: ***Because*** she needed to earn at least $20,000 per year.
Example: The young widow, **who** needed to earn at least $20,000 per year.

It's often easy to pick out a fragment when it appears in an isolated list like this:

1 Because she needed new work skills.

2 She returned to school.

Many people see right away that number 1 is a fragment while number 2 is a complete sentence. It's more difficult, however, to notice fragments in context. If you think you have difficulty identifying sentence fragments, try reading one or two of your paragraphs backward (read the last sentence, then the next-to-the last, and so forth). Often fragments become more obvious when you use this strategy.

Revision Strategies

After identifying a fragment, the next step is to choose the most effective revision strategy. *Remember that the strategy you choose must create a complete sentence that has a verb and subject and that does not depend on another sentence to complete its meaning.* Consider the following possibilities:

1 Combine the fragment with the sentence that precedes it.

EXAMPLE:

NO: In the nineteenth century, British lawyers tied official papers together with thin red ribbon. Which they called red tape. (FRAG.)

YES: In the nineteenth century, British lawyers tied official papers together with thin red ribbon, which they called red tape.

2 Combine the fragment with the sentence that follows it.

EXAMPLE:

NO: Like many legal processes today. (FRAG.) Court proceedings were extremely complicated in Victorian England.

YES: Like many legal processes today, court proceedings were extremely complicated in Victorian England.

3 Provide a subject to create a complete sentence.

EXAMPLE:

NO: Lawyers often purposely dragged cases out for years. Making money while their clients lived in poverty. (FRAG.)

YES: Lawyers often purposely dragged cases out for years. They made money while their clients lived in poverty.

4 Provide a verb to create a complete sentence.

NO: Novelist Charles Dickens, one of the first to use the expression "red tape" to mean "legal complications." (FRAG.)

YES: Novelist Charles Dickens was one of the first to use the expression "red tape" to mean "legal complications."

(*Note:* When you are using any of these strategies to revise a fragment, remember that you may have to add words or change the form of words for the sentence to make sense. Notice, for instance, in strategy 3 that the word "making" becomes "made.")

Proofreading Evaluation Exercise 1B: Identifying and Correcting Fragments

Directions Read each of the following groups of words carefully. When you find a group of words that is a fragment, rewrite it as a complete sentence. If necessary, when you rewrite, you may use words from the sentences preceding or following the fragment or you may add words of your own.

1 Many people fear failure.

2 Which they define as loss of self-esteem, of money, or of social status.

3 If you are one of these people, help is available.

4 Experts such as psychiatrists, medical doctors, and even financial advisers.

5 Certain basic strategies are recommended to help you cope with feelings of failure.

6 First, experts suggest eliminating the word "failure" from your vocabulary.

7 Replacing it with "setback," "glitch," or even "challenge."

8 Next, you should stop blaming and berating yourself.

9 Because other people are likely to accept as true the image you have of yourself.

10 You should make every effort to be financially prepared for unexpected difficulties.

11 Money buys time.

12 Which may well give you the opportunity to evaluate your situation carefully and, therefore, to act intelligently.

13 Finally, caring friends and relatives who can be your most essential resource during difficult times.

14 If you remember these strategies, you'll be able to face nearly any obstacle life can offer.

Proofreading Evaluation Exercise 1C: Editing in Context

Directions Read the following paragraph and correct any errors you find. You will be looking for sentence fragments as you read.

(1) Today we know that physical problems need not keep a person from achieving great deeds. (2) In addition, individuals from the past who set great examples. (3) Beethoven, partly deaf at age thirty-two and totally deaf at forty-six. (4) Yet he wrote his greatest music during his later years. (5) Regarded by

many as France's greatest actress, Sarah Bernhardt was lamed by a knee injury in 1905. (6) Continuing to act for nearly ten years after complications of that knee injury forced the amputation of her leg in 1914. (7) Joseph Pulitzer is another outstanding example. (8) Although he went blind at age forty. (9) He continued various activities as a journalist, publisher, and congressman. (10) Leaving a large endowment to fund the Pulitzer Prizes.

EDITOR'S FOCUS 2

AVOIDING FUSED SENTENCES AND COMMA SPLICES

Proofreading Evaluation Exercise 2A

Directions To evaluate your editing skill, read the following paragraph and identify any fused sentences or comma splices. Then rewrite the paragraph, correcting the errors you found.

(1) When Hannah Snell's husband left her and their daughter in 1744, the deserted wife set out to find him. (2) First Hannah disguised herself in her brother's clothes, then she left London and headed for Coventry. (3) She found no trace of her husband instead she found a new life. (4) Using her brother's name, Hannah Snell enlisted in General Guise's regiment of the British Army she called herself James Gray. (5) After being punished unjustly, Hannah deserted from the army. (6) She fled to Portsmouth and, continuing to pose as her brother, enlisted as a marine. (7) Hannah, who was thought to be a young boy because of her clean-shaven face and small size, was admired by the other marines for her mending and cooking skills. (8) In combat, however, she fought fiercely she received six wounds in a battle against the French in India one of the wounds was in

her lower body. (9) Fearing that treatment of that wound would lead to discovery of her true sex, she cut open the wound and removed the musket ball herself. (10) Finally, Hannah met a man who knew her husband's fate. (11) He told Hannah that her husband had been arrested for murder then he was executed. (12) Hannah's quest was over when the ship next docked in England she revealed that she was a woman. (13) She immediately received a marriage proposal from a shipmate who admired her. (14) Hannah refused, she valued her freedom highly. (15) For the rest of her life, she was successful as an actress who most often played male roles.

Editing Strategy: Identification and Correction of Fused Sentences and Comma Splices

In formal, written English, closely associated ideas may appear in the same sentence only if connecting words or proper punctuation shows the relationships among these ideas.

Do not write *fused sentences* (sometimes called *run-on sentences*). Fused sentences cram together two or more separate ideas with no punctuation or connecting words.

Do not write *comma splices.* Comma splices connect two separate ideas with only a comma.

Examples of a Fused Sentence and a Comma Splice

FUSED SENTENCE

NO: She returned to school because she needed new work skills she decided to start classes immediately.

COMMA SPLICE

NO: She returned to school because she needed new work skills, she decided to start school immediately.

WHY Both fused sentences and comma splices may confuse readers. You need to let them know where one idea begins and the next ends.

YES: She returned to school because she needed new work skills. She decided to start classes immediately.

Or

She returned to school. Because she needed new work skills, she decided to start classes immediately.

YES: She returned to school because she needed new work skills, and she decided to start classes immediately.

YES: She returned to school because she needed new work skills; she decided to start classes immediately.

Identifying Fused Sentences and Comma Splices

Watch for two or more complete thoughts that are joined either without punctuation or with just a comma. Fused sentences and comma splices are often found in the following circumstances:

1 When two very short sentences are closely related:

EXAMPLES:

COMMA SPLICE
Spring rain falls, then flowers bloom.

FUSED SENTENCE
Spring rain falls then flowers bloom.

2 When the second sentence provides reasons, examples, explanations, or additional details related to the first sentence:

EXAMPLES:

During his term as president, Franklin Roosevelt supported many programs designed to help the economy, [COMMA SPLICE] many consider the Tennessee Valley Authority (TVA) the most important of these programs.

During his term as president, Franklin Roosevelt supported many programs designed to help the economy [FUSED SENTENCE] many consider the Tennessee Valley Authority (TVA) the most important of these programs.

3 When the second sentence begins with a pronoun that refers to a noun in the previous sentence.

EXAMPLES:

Eleanor Roosevelt was an extremely controversial first lady, [COMMA SPLICE] she was both praised as a heroine to the downtrodden and criticized as an interfering do-gooder.

Eleanor Roosevelt was an extremely controversial first lady [FUSED SENTENCE] she was both praised as a heroine to the downtrodden and criticized as an interfering do-gooder.

4 When the two sentences are joined by a conjunctive adverb (a word like *however, nevertheless, meanwhile, then, instead, therefore*) or by a transitional expression (a word or phrase like *for example, also, in comparison, finally, in conclusion, consequently*).

EXAMPLES:

COMMA SPLICE
Franklin Roosevelt was elected to a fourth term in office, however, he died before he could complete that term.

Eleanor Roosevelt supported her husband's work while he was in
FUSED SENTENCE
office after his death she continued to work for human rights causes on her own.

It's often easy to pick out a comma splice when it appears in an isolated list like this:

1 In 1929 the stock market crashed, the Great Depression followed in the 1930s.
2 Thousands of people were out of work many lived in cardboard boxes or on the streets.

Many people see right away that number 1 is a common splice and number 2 is a fused sentence. It is more difficult, however, to notice comma splices and fused sentences in context.

If you think you have difficulty identifying fused sentences, try reading your writing aloud. You will almost always drop your voice at the point where a fused sentence should be divided.

(*Note:* People also drop their voices at other places—for example, at places that require commas. Nevertheless, if you drop your voice and see *no mark of punctuation,* look carefully to see whether a fused sentence exists or whether some other mark of punctuation is needed.)

If you think you have difficulty identifying comma splices, try this strategy. When you see a sentence that has a comma and you think you might have written a comma splice, cover all the words to the right side of the comma and then ask, "Do the remaining words form a complete sentence?" If the answer is "No," then there is no comma splice. If the answer is "Yes," repeat the process, this time covering all the words to the left side of the comma. If the answer is "No," then there is no comma splice. If the answer is "Yes," check to see whether the first word is a coordinating conjunction (a word like *and, or, but, nor, so*). If the first word is a coordinating conjunction, then there is no comma splice. If that first word is not a coordinating conjunction, however, and if the groups of words on both sides of the comma can stand alone as complete sentences, then there is a comma splice.

This "cover" test is cumbersome and time consuming. Of course, you will not do this with every sentence for the rest of your writing life. As you become skilled in identifying comma splices, you will automatically run the cover test in your mind as you read through whatever you are proofreading and editing.

Revision Strategies

After identifying a fused sentence or a comma splice, the next step is to choose the most effective revision strategy. Consider the following possibilities:

1 Make the two parts of the fused sentence or comma splice separate sentences.

EXAMPLE:

NO: During his term as president, Franklin Roosevelt supported many programs designed to help the economy, [COMMA SPLICE] many consider the Tennessee Valley Authority (TVA) the most important of these programs.

YES: During his term as president, Franklin Roosevelt supported many programs designed to help the economy. Many consider the Tennessee Valley Authority (TVA) the most important of these programs.

2 Add a *conjunction* (a connecting word) that shows the relationship between the two complete thoughts. (Conjunctions include the following words: *and, but, or, nor, so.*) Use a comma before a conjunction that connects two complete thoughts.

EXAMPLE:

NO: Eleanor Roosevelt supported her husband's work while he was in office [FUSED SENTENCE] after his death she continued to work for human rights causes on her own.

YES: Eleanor Roosevelt supported her husband's work while he was in office, **and** after his death she continued to work for human rights causes on her own.

3 Use a semicolon to connect two very closely related thoughts.

EXAMPLE:

NO: Spring rain falls [FUSED SENTENCE] then flowers bloom.

YES: Spring rain falls; then flowers bloom.

4 Use a semicolon before a conjunctive adverb or transitional word or phrase to join two complete thoughts.

EXAMPLE:

COMMA SPLICE

NO: Franklin Roosevelt was elected to a fourth term in office, however, he died before he could complete that term.

YES: Franklin Roosevelt was elected to a fourth term in office; however, he died before he could complete that term.

5 Make one part of the comma splice or fused sentences into a group of words that depends on the rest of the sentence to complete its meaning.

EXAMPLE:

COMMA SPLICE

NO: In 1929 the stock market crashed, the Great Depression followed in the 1930s.

YES: **After** the stock market crashed in 1929, the Great Depression followed in the 1930s.

Proofreading Evaluation Exercise 2B: Identifying and Correcting Fused Sentences and Comma Splices

Directions Read each of the following groups of words carefully. When you find a group of words that is a fused sentence or a comma splice, revise it.

1. A dog may be a man's best friend, a man may be a dog's best friend.
2. The Earl of Bridgewater, who lived in Paris in the 1820s, kept twelve dogs as house pets.
3. Each night, he ordered his finest dining table set with elegant china in addition a red silk napkin was provided for each guest.
4. The guests were his twelve pet dogs each sat in a chair while a servant tied the silk napkin around its neck.
5. According to those who observed the strange dinner parties, the dogs behaved perfectly.
6. They usually ate carefully from their plates, they seemed like perfect ladies and gentlemen.
7. Sometimes, however, one dog would become greedy and steal from another's plate, perhaps another would snarl at one of the waiters.

8 The next evening, the offender was not allowed to attend the dinner party, however, he or she was still served at a table and still wore the red silk napkin.

9 Following the dinner parties, Lord Bridgewater invited his dogs to ride in his carriage through the streets of Paris.

10 To be sure their feet didn't get dirty, he provided boots for his pets.

11 The boots were made of the finest leather each dog had a different pair for each day of the year.

12 Lord Bridgewater lined up the boots in the hall, then he used them to count the passing days of the year.

Proofreading Evaluation Exercise 2C: Editing in Context

Directions Read the following paragraph and correct any errors you find. You will be looking for sentence fragments, comma splices, and fused sentences as you read.

(1) People often complain about the lack of public transportation in the United States. (2) Which forces nearly everyone to own an automobile. (3) Experts dream about a future where American cities would be joined by transportation networks, then we could move easily from place to place even without owning a car. (4) What we forget is that this ideal situation once existed at the turn of the century streetcars and trolleys linked major cities to even the smallest towns. (5) Trolley lines were used by salesmen who brought their goods to rural homes, farmers, on the other hand, used the public transportation to deliver their fresh produce to the cities. (6) In the early 1900s, it was possible to ride the trolley from Boston to New York City for the amazing price of four dollars! (7) Although frequent changes of line were required. (8) One streetcar route covered a distance of over one thousand miles, it went from Freeport, Illinois, to Utica, New York. (9) The

fastest modern trains rarely go over sixty miles an hour it's hard to believe that the standard operating speed of the intercity streetcar lines was eighty miles an hour. (10) Amazing as it may be, the cars that ran between Cedar Rapids and Iowa City, Iowa, even reached top speeds of 110 miles per hour.

EDITOR'S FOCUS 3

CHECKING SUBJECT-VERB AGREEMENT

Proofreading Evaluation Exercise 3A

Directions To evaluate your editing skill, read the following paragraph and identify any problems with subject-verb agreement. Then rewrite the paragraph so that all verbs agree with their subjects.

(1) Children in the current decade watches more television than ever before. (2) The young child and the teenager is equally affected by television programming. (3) A recent study by the Council on Children, Media, and Merchandising shows amazing statistics. (4) During an average ten months' time, 3,832 advertisements for sugared cereal appears on weekend daytime television. (5) During the same time period there is 1,627 commercials for candy and chewing gum. (6) On the other hand, advertisements for meat or poultry appear only twice. (7) Vegetables and cheese is each advertised once. (8) Every concerned parent and teacher in this country know that children or the average teen is swayed by the constant bombarding of such advertising. (9) Experts agree that the worst part of such advertising are the long-term effects on young people's eating habits. (10) An adult's diet and nutrition are profoundly affected by what the individual learns during the early years of life.

Editing Strategy: Identification and Correction of Problems with Subject-Verb Agreement

> Verbs must agree with their subjects.
>
> When a sentence has a singular subject (a subject that is only one object, place, concept, or person), it must also have a singular verb.
>
> When a sentence has a plural subject (a subject that is more than one object, place, concept, or person), it must also have a plural verb form.

Examples of Singular Subject with Singular Verb

Singular Subjects	Singular Verbs
Time	heals
A doctor	examines
Ice	cools
Africa	changes

Examples of Plural Subjects with Plural Verbs

Plural Subjects	Plural Verbs
Times	change
Doctors	examine
Icebergs	melt
Nations	grow

These are very simple examples. Most native speakers of English would automatically select the verb forms in the lists above to go with the corresponding subjects. There are, however, more complicated sentence structures that sometimes cause problems for the editor who is checking for subject-verb agreement. Consider the following examples.

Identifying Problems with Subject-Verb Agreement

PROBLEM *Words come between the subject and the verb.*

EXAMPLES:

SUBJECT VERB
NO: The box of pens are on the table.

SUBJECT VERB
YES: The box of pens is on the table.

SUBJECT VERB
NO: One of the most serious questions concern the environment.

SUBJECT VERB
YES: One of the most serious questions concerns the environment.

Editing Strategy

Identify the subject and the verb. Then block out the words that come between them. (At first you may want to block the words physically with the corner of an index card or with your fingers. Later, you'll do the blocking in your mind.)

PROBLEM *The word order in the sentence is inverted.*

EXAMPLES:

VERB SUBJECT
NO: Has the threats finally stopped?

VERB SUBJECT
YES: Have the threats finally stopped?

VERB SUBJECT
NO: There is many good reasons.

VERB SUBJECT
YES: There are many good reasons.

Editing Strategy

Turn the sentence around so that it reads in standard order, with the subject coming before the verb:

The threats have finally stopped.
Many good reasons are there.

Although the sentence may sound awkward, the subject and verb should be easily identified. This process makes checking subject-verb agreement simple.

PROBLEM *The subject is an indefinite pronoun (a word like* any-one, each, every, everybody, everything, nobody, no one, nothing, someone*).*

EXAMPLES:

SUBJECT VERB
NO: Everybody say something different.

YES: Everybody says something different.

Editing Strategy

Remember that even though indefinite pronouns like those listed above may seem to refer to a plural concept, they take singular verbs.

Exceptions to this rule are the indefinite pronouns some, all, more, *and* most. *These pronouns may take a plural verb.*

PROBLEM *The subject of the sentence is a collective noun (a word that names a group of people, animals, or objects: for example,* class, committee, club, flock, audience).

EXAMPLES:

SUBJECT VERB
YES: The committee has announced the results of its vote.

SUBJECT VERB
YES: The committee spend from two weeks a year to two months a year taking their vacations.

Editing Strategy

Remember that the context of the sentence determines whether a collective noun takes a singular or a plural verb. In the first example, the committee acted as one unit when announcing its vote; therefore, the verb is singular. In the second example, each committee member acts separately by going on vacation for a different length of time; there are several vacations taken. Therefore, the verb is plural.

PROBLEM *There are two or more singular subjects joined by* and.

EXAMPLES:

SUBJECT SUBJECT VERB
NO: Both Alice and her sister attends meetings regularly.

SUBJECT SUBJECT VERB
YES: Both Alice and her sister attend meetings regularly.

Editing Strategy

Remember that when two or more singular subjects are joined by the word and, *those subjects are, in effect, added together. Because they are added together, the singular subjects become plural and must have a plural verb.*

PROBLEM *There are two or more subjects joined by words like* or, nor, either . . . or, neither . . . nor.

EXAMPLES:

SUBJECT SUBJECT VERB
NO: Either John or the waiters takes care of the order.

SUBJECT SUBJECT VERB
YES: Either John or the waiters take care of the order.

SUBJECT SUBJECT VERB
NO: Either the waiters or John take care of the order.

SUBJECT SUBJECT VERB
YES: Either the waiters or John takes care of the order.

Editing Strategy

Remember that when subjects are separated by words like or, nor, either . . . or, neither . . . nor, *the verb agrees with the part of the subject nearest to it. If the part of the subject nearest the verb is singular, the verb will be singular. If the part of the subject nearest the verb is plural, the verb will be plural.*

To make editing sentences like these easy, block out the first part of the subject and read only the part of the subject nearest the verb. At first you may want to physically block out the first part of the subject. Later, you will automatically do the blocking out in your mind.

Proofreading Evaluation Exercise 3B: Identifying and Correcting Problems with Subject-Verb Agreement

Directions Read each sentence carefully. When you find a subject and verb that do not agree, correct that error.

1 Fifty years ago, the average family in the United States were supported by one breadwinner.

2 Today, nearly 27.7 million American households has two breadwinners.

3 What is the causes and effects of this dramatic change?

4 Either increased expenses or the women's movement motivate many of the wives who now work outside the home.

5 There's many employed women who continue to shoulder the primary responsibility for household tasks.

6 In two-income families, the man typically has a larger voice in major household decisions than do the woman.

7 For instance, wives often move to other cities to help their husbands' careers.

8 Few men, however, in the same situation moves to help their wives' careers.

9 A wife, on the average, earn only 62 percent as much as her husband when each work full-time.

10 The family with two employed parents often takes their vacations separately.

11 Often neither the husband nor the wife find enough time for leisure pursuits.

12 Nevertheless, women are growing more confident of their knowledge and abilities, and men are learning to share family responsibility and power.

Proofreading Evaluation Exercise 3C: Editing in Context

Directions Read the following paragraph and correct any errors you find. You will be looking for sentence fragments, comma splices, fused sentences, and problems with subject-verb agreement as you read.

(1) Each new season of films bring several horror titles to the screen. (2) Although today's technology allows for highly realistic special effects and frighteningly lifelike monsters. (3) Most horror movie fans have a special place in their hearts for King Kong, the original menacing jungle monster. (4) King Kong was the creation of movie producer Merian Cooper, he had read of the "Komodo dragons," ten-foot-long lizards that lived on an exotic South Pacific island. (5) Out of this inspiration came the idea of a giant, prehistoric ape. (6) Discovered in a remote jungle and then transported to civilization. (7) Cooper wrote a proposal for the film, scenery, characters, and plot incidents were all included. (8) At first, neither Hollywood film companies nor any private investor were interested in the proposal. (9) They thought the project was impossible. (10) Fortunately for generations of horror film fans, there was one man and one special technique that could make Cooper's dream come true. (11) Willis O'Brien, a specialist in stop motion

animation, a technique that made lifeless objects seem to move on their own. (12) O'Brien took over the project, creating what appeared to be a giant ape from a two-foot-tall replica.

EDITOR'S FOCUS 4

CHECKING PRONOUN REFERENCE AND AGREEMENT

Proofreading Evaluation Exercise 4A

Directions To evaluate your editing skill, read the following paragraph and identify any problems with pronoun reference or pronoun agreement. Then rewrite the paragraph, correcting any errors you found.

(1) In 1987, monkeys made their place in the news. (2) John Schneider, an A.S.P.C.A. animal-care technician got a call from a frantic security guard while he was on duty at Kennedy International Airport. (3) He reported that monkeys were loose among the passengers disembarking from one plane. (4) Needless to say, they were causing a riot. (5) Schneider eventually captured the monkey he had identified as the leader and put her back in the cage. (6) The other monkeys followed, and Schneider reported his success to the guard. (7) This, of course, calmed the agitated passengers. (8) Everyone can agree that they would not want rioting monkeys to interrupt an air flight. (9) Also in 1987, a monkey on a Soviet space flight made headlines. (10) A good Soviet space trainer makes certain their animals are well suited for their journeys. (11) This one, however, must have made some error. (12) During a satellite flight, one monkey, Yerosha, got his left arm free. (13) It then tinkered with everything within his reach. (14) The committee to investigate this disruption said in their report that the

monkey lived up to his name. (15) In Russian, it means "troublemaker."

Editing Strategy: Identification and Correction of Problems with Pronoun Reference and Agreement

Pronouns are words that can be used in place of nouns. Examples: *I, me, my, mine, we, us, our, ours, you, your, yours, he, his, him, she, her, hers, it, its, they, their, theirs, them, this, that, which, who, whom.*

Pronouns must refer clearly to one specific *antecedent* (the noun or nouns that the pronoun replaces).

Pronouns must agree with their antecedents in number. When a pronoun has a singular antecedent (an antecedent that is only one object, place, concept, or person), the pronoun must also be singular.

When a pronoun has a plural antecedent (an antecedent that is more than one object, place, concept, or person), the pronoun must also be plural.

Pronouns must agree with their antecedents in person. First-person pronouns must refer to the person speaking (*I, me, my, mine, we, us, our, ours*). Second-person pronouns must refer to the person being addressed (*you, your, yours*). Third-person pronouns must refer to the person being described (*he, she, it, him, her, hers, its, they, them, their, theirs*).

Examples of Pronoun Reference Problems

NO: The director [ANTECEDENT?] told the producer [ANTECEDENT?] he [PRONOUN] was concerned about his [PRONOUN] latest endeavor.

WHY: The reader cannot tell whether "he" and "his" refer to the director or to the producer. Either reading would make sense. The writer must make the reference clear.

YES: The director [ANTECEDENT] said to the producer, "I [PRONOUN] am concerned about my [PRONOUN] latest endeavor."

YES: The director [ANTECEDENT] said to the producer [ANTECEDENT], "I [PRONOUN] am concerned about your [PRONOUN] latest endeavor."

YES: The director spoke to the producer, expressing concern about the producer's latest endeavor.

(Uses no pronouns)

YES: The director, James Colt, spoke to the producer, Antonio Casselli. Colt expressed concern about Casselli's latest endeavor.

(Uses no pronouns)

ANTECEDENT PRONOUN PRONOUN
YES: The director, who was concerned about his latest endeavor, spoke to the producer.

REVISION STRATEGY *If you have particular problems with making pronoun references clear, try using a highlighter to mark each pronoun in your draft. Then check to make certain there is no question about what noun the pronoun replaces. If the reference is not clear, try some of the strategies demonstrated in the examples above. For instance:*

- Use direct conversation.
- Rewrite the sentence so that the pronouns can be replaced with nouns.
- Rewrite the sentence so that the pronouns closely follow the nouns to which they refer.

NO: In 1908 and again in 1947, objects struck the earth with enough force to destroy a whole city. Fortunately, these objects fell in isolated regions of Siberia. This (PRONOUN) does not particularly worry scientists.

EXPLANATION The reader cannot tell whether "this" refers to the objects striking the earth with force or to the fact that they fell in Siberia. The writer must make the intention clear.

YES: In 1908 and again in 1947, objects struck the earth with enough force to destroy a whole city. Fortunately, these objects fell in isolated regions of Siberia. Such objects do not particularly worry scientists.

YES: In 1908 and again in 1947, objects struck the earth with enough force to destroy a whole city. Fortunately, these objects fell in isolated regions of Siberia. The location does not particularly worry scientists.

YES: Scientists are not particularly worried about the objects that struck the earth in 1908 and again in 1947 with enough force to destroy a whole city. Fortunately, they fell in isolated regions of Siberia.

REVISION STRATEGY *Watch carefully for words like* it, that, which, *and* this. *Often the antecedent for such words is not clear. To focus the meaning precisely, try rephrasing the sentence that precedes the troublesome pronoun. Another effective strategy is to replace the pronoun with a word or phrase that will make the reference clear.*

Examples of Pronoun Agreement Problems

ANTECEDENT PRONOUN
NO: A good father takes an interest in their children.

EXPLANATION The noun "father" is singular; therefore, the pronoun referring to this noun must also be singular.

ANTECEDENT PRONOUN
YES: A good father takes an interest in his children.

REVISION STRATEGY *Highlight or circle pronouns and then check to be certain they agree in number with the noun or nouns to which they refer. To correct any errors, you may change the form of either the noun or the pronoun. Sometimes, it is easiest and most graceful to change the form of the noun.*

ANTECEDENT PRONOUN
NO: Either the doctors or the father left their notes behind.

EXPLANATION When antecedents are joined by *or, nor, either . . . or, neither . . . nor,* the pronoun should agree with the antecedent closest to it.

ANTECEDENT PRONOUN
YES: Either the doctors or the father left his notes behind.

ANTECEDENT PRONOUN
YES: Either the father or the doctors left their notes behind.

REVISION STRATEGY *Because the plural pronoun usually sounds more sensible in a sentence like the one above, it's a good idea to put the plural antecedent nearest the pronoun so that a plural pronoun may correctly be used.*

ANTECEDENT PRONOUN
NO: A United States senator has an obligation to his constituents.

EXPLANATION The word "senator" can refer to either a man or a woman; therefore, it is inaccurate to use the masculine pronoun.

ANTECEDENT PRONOUNS
YES: A United States senator has an obligation to his or her constituents.

ANTECEDENT PRONOUN
YES: United States senators have obligations to their constituents.

REVISION STRATEGY *Many major publishing companies, corporations, academic institutions, and government agencies request or require that writers use nonsexist language. Usually the most graceful way to use such inclusive language is to change a singular noun to a plural or to recast the sentence entirely. For example, consider this correctly written sentence:*

A new senator often finds that he or she has unexpected duties.

This sentence would be smoother (and also correct) in the following two forms:

New senators often find that they have unexpected duties.

Unexpected duties often await the new senator.

ANTECEDENT PRONOUN
NO: Many students owe your success to the encouragement of one very special teacher.

EXPLANATION The word "students" is third person (person described). The pronoun "your" is second person (person addressed). Mixing the two makes the sentence confusing to the reader.

ANTECEDENT PRONOUN
YES: Many students owe their success to the encouragement of one very special teacher.

REVISION STRATEGY *Highlight or circle pronouns and then make sure they agree in person with the noun to which they refer. Remember that "you" (second person) is seldom used in formal writing. Many professors also prefer that students avoid the first person, "I," in formal writing.*

Proofreading Evaluation Exercise 4B: Identifying and Correcting Problems with Pronoun Reference and Pronoun Agreement

Directions Read each sentence carefully. When you find a pronoun reference problem or a pronoun agreement problem, correct that error.

1 Although the physician is a respected member of the scientific community, they are not responsible for many medical discoveries.

2 Leonardo Da Vinci, an artist who had great scientific curiosity, dissected cadavers and made accurate anatomical drawings. This gave medical doctors their first precise pictures of the cavities of the brain.

3 Every modern doctor knows that he is indebted to Anton van Leeuwenhoek, the Dutch merchant who discovered bacteria, protozoa, and spermatozoa.

4 Either several youthful party-goers or William Clarke, a young chemistry student, deserves their place in medical history.

5 Clarke observed friends of his sniffing ether at a party, and he then used the gas for a dental operation.

6 Louis Pasteur, a French chemist, discovered how to pasteurize milk and also created a vaccine for anthrax and rabies. For this, many people owe him our lives.

7 Acupuncture, a respected medical procedure in China, was discovered by the emperor Shen Nung in 2700 B.C. He studied herbs and made a carefully annotated list of those he found most effective.

8 A professor of mathematics and physics, Wilhelm Roentgen, discovered X rays during an investigation of cathode rays. He called it "X" rays because no one then knew the source that caused them.

9 Dutch physicist Heike Omnes surprised his mentor with the unexpected discovery of cryogenics, the quick freezing of blood plasma. He then went on to explain to him the possible applications of this technique to the treatment of Parkinson's disease.

10 Marie Curie and her husband, Pierre, identified the elements polonium and radium. These led to the development of radiotherapy and other valuable medical techniques.

Proofreading Evaluation Exercise 4C: Editing in Context

Directions Read the following paragraph and correct any errors you find. As you read, you will be looking for sentence fragments, for comma splices and fused sentences, and for problems with subject-verb agreement, with pronoun reference, or with pronoun agreement.

(1) Ruth Benedict and Margaret Mead both made profound contributions to her field of expertise, anthropology. (2)

Benedict, one of the earliest anthropologists to suggest that each society produces its own unique personality. (3) Mead researched and wrote extensively on child rearing, her study of adolescence in Samoa challenged Western concepts. (4) Each woman wrote a book that have become classics. (5) In *Patterns of Culture,* Benedict claimed that every society identifies a narrow range of personality traits and cultural ideals. (6) That are to be admired and developed. (7) The results of this process is not surprising. (8) A group personality emerges, and every member of the group share the most significant ways of thinking and behaving. (9) Both Mead and Benedict have been accused of stereotyping, but she has contributed new approaches and innovative ways of thinking. (10) This makes their work well worth studying today.

EDITOR'S FOCUS 5

CHECKING VERB TENSE AGREEMENT

Proofreading Evaluation Exercise 5A

Directions Before you read the information on verb tense agreement, do the following exercise. It is designed to help you evaluate your skill at identifying and correcting problems with verb tense agreement.

As you read the following paragraph, note any problems with verb tense agreement. Then rewrite the paragraph, so that verb tenses agree.

(1) Do you ever wonder why your favorite television program no longer broadcasts? (2) Why do some shows continue on the air for many years while other go off after only a few weeks? (3) The answer was simple: numbers! (4) Sponsors will pay for most shows, and of course they want to reach a large audience. (5) They did not want to pay for shows that are not popular.

Editing Strategy: Identification and Correction of Verb Tense Shifts

> Verbs show tense (time). In any piece of writing, all verbs should be in the same tense unless you intend to show a change in time.

UNDERSTANDING TENSE The following chart shows examples of several verbs written in six tenses possible in the English language. Note that some verbs change dramatically as they switch from one tense to another while other verbs require only minor changes for tense change.

Past tense (a completed action)	I went	He studied	They gave
Present tense (an action currently happening)	I go	He studies	They give
Future tense (an action that has not yet happened)	I will go	He will study	They will give
Past Perfect tense (an action that was completed before another action took place)	I had gone	He had studied	They had given
Present Perfect (an action begun in the past and continuing in the present)	I have gone	He has studied	They have given
Future Perfect (an action that will be completed before some specific time)	I shall have gone	He will have studied	They will have given

Identification Practice

In the following sentences, circle the verbs. Then identify the tense of each verb.

1 Today, surgeons know a great deal about organ transplants.

2 In 1835, however, a pioneering British army doctor performed a successful corneal transplant.

3 He had noticed his pet antelope's diminishing sight.

4 He transplanted the cornea of a newly killed antelope to his pet.
5 Colleagues laughed when he proclaimed, "Now my antelope will see again!"
6 The army doctor had predicted correctly.
7 His antelope's vision returned.
8 Modern science has gained much knowledge from such early experiments.
9 By the year 1999, scientists will have developed even more transplant techniques.
10 Thousands of people benefit from such surgery.

> Do not switch tense unless you have a reason to do so. For example, if you begin writing in the present tense, do not shift to past unless you mean to discuss something that has happened earlier.

Examples of Verb Tense Use

PRESENT PRESENT PAST
NO: I go into the room, look around, and then dropped my shoes.

(Shift from present to past is illogical.)

PAST PAST PAST
YES: I went into the room, looked around, and then dropped my shoes.

(All verbs are in past tense.)

PRESENT PRESENT PRESENT
YES: I go into the room, look around, and then drop my shoes.

(All verbs are in present tense.)

PRESENT PRESENT PRESENT
YES: Today I go into the room, look around, and remember that
PAST
yesterday I dropped my shoes.

(Time change is intended here, so switch from present to past is logical.)

Identifying Verb Tense Shifts

1 Make certain you understand the different tenses in English. (See page 325.)
2 Remember that you only change tense to indicate change of time.
3 If you have trouble with tense shifts, go through your drafts and high-

light each verb with a marker. Then move from one verb to the next. When you see a shift in tense, mark it with a question mark.

REVISION STRATEGY

1 After following the three steps above, return to tense shifts you have marked.
2 Read the sentences containing the verbs that do not agree.
3 If you intended to indicate a shift in time, continue with your reading.
4 If you did not intend to indicate a change, edit to make the incorrect verb form consistent with those in the rest of the essay.

(*Note:* When you are writing about a film, a television program, or a work of literature, use present tense even though the action of the film, program, or work has been completed.)

EXAMPLE:
Born on the Fourth of July **takes** place during the 1950s, 1960s, and 1970s. The hero **grows** up in a small town, **volunteers** for the marines, and **fights** in Vietnam. Most of the action of the film **takes** place after he **is** wounded and **returns** to the United States.
(All verbs are in present tense; this usage is called historic present.)

Proofreading Evaluation Exercise 5B: Identifying and Correcting Verb Tense Shifts

Directions Read each of the following sentences carefully. When you find a shift in tense that is not logical, revise so that the sentence reads correctly.

1 How do sponsors find out how many people watch a program?
2 They hire experts who did the counting for them.
3 These experts will not call everyone in the country; instead they have carefully contacted a sample of the population.
4 Studying the sample population gives clues about what the whole population watches.
5 The researchers want their sample to be big enough to be accurate, but they did not want to spend money contacting an overly large sample population.

Proofreading Evaluation Exercise 5C: Editing in Context

Directions Read the following paragraph and correct any errors you find. As you read, you will be looking for sentence fragments, for comma splices and fused sentences, and for problems with subject-verb agreement, with pronoun reference, with pronoun agreement, or with verb tense shifts.

> (1) One of the most famous audience-counting companies, A.C. Neilsen. (2) During each new television season, Neilsen uses a sample of twelve hundred households that represented the 70 million households in the United States. (3) Neilsen does not always use the same households, every year they add some new ones while other households were dropped. (4) What counts in the end is numbers. (5) Neilsen does not measure the enthusiasm of the viewer; all that matters is what they are watching. (6) For example, if ten million people watches a show simply because they are too lazy to turn off the set following the World Series, that program gets a higher rating than a show with 5 million deeply devoted fans. (7) Sometimes, however, a show with initially low ratings are saved by viewer protests. (8) The original *Star Trek* had provided the most famous example. (9) When its ratings fell below the cutoff point. (10) The network announced plans to drop the program. (11) Within a few weeks, thousands of viewers sent protests to the network and sponsors, the show was quickly brought back. (12) So when your favorite program is about to be canceled, you know what to do, write a letter and send it airmail!

EDITOR'S FOCUS 6

CHECKING FOR MISPLACED AND DANGLING MODIFIERS

Proofreading Evaluation Exercise 6A

Directions Before you read the information on misplaced and dangling modifiers, do the following exercise. It is designed to help you evaluate your skill at identifying and correcting misplaced and dangling modifiers (descriptive words or phrases that are incorrectly placed in the sentence).

As you read the following paragraph, note any problems with misplaced or dangling modifiers. Then rewrite the paragraph so that those problems are eliminated.

> (1) To start an organic garden, farmers only will need to understand a few simple processes. (2) Keeping a compost heap throughout the winter, rich soil for spring planting will be the gardener's reward. (3) Insects that eat garden pests will be an easily accessible help to rural organic farmers when ordered by mail. (4) Such insects will play an important role because they will allow the organic farmer to eliminate the use of pesticides. (5) Gathering the harvest in the fall, all the time and effort spent on the garden will seem worthwhile.

Editing Strategy: Identification and Correction of Misplaced and Dangling Modifiers

> A modifier is a word or group of words that describes some place, person, object, action, or idea.
>
> To make the meaning clear, a modifier should be placed near the word or phrase it modifies.

Examples of Misplaced Modifiers

NO: The CEO drove to her office where she uses costly, state-of-the-art computers **in a rusting, battered van.**

YES: The CEO drove **in a rusting, battered van** to her office where she uses costly, state-of-the-art computers.

(The CEO does not use costly, state-of-the-art computers in a rusting, battered van as the "no" example implies. The revision properly places the modifying words near "drove," which is the word they describe.)

NO: **Waiting for a late bus,** the deserted streets made Tom nervous.

YES: **Waiting for a late bus,** Tom was made nervous by the deserted streets.

BETTER: As Tom waited for a late bus, the deserted streets made him nervous.

(The deserted streets were not waiting for a late bus as the "no" example implies. The "yes" revision correctly places the descriptive phrase near "Tom." The "better" example shows that sometimes a revision changes the form of the modifier.)

NO: **At age three,** Mozart's father recognized his son's talent.

YES: Mozart's father recognized his son's talent when the boy was three.

(Mozart's father was not three years old when he recognized his son's talent as the "no" example implies. Note that the "yes" example changes the form of the modifying phrase, "at age three," so that the sentence will read smoothly.)

Identifying Misplaced and Dangling Modifiers

Note the examples of misplaced and dangling modifiers given above.

Develop the habit of watching for modifying words and groups of words and of noting whether they are placed close to the words or groups of words they describe.

Pay particular attention to groups of words that introduce a sentence, for example, groups of words like "To balance the budget," "While waiting at the bank," or "Having read the newspaper report." When you see introductory words like these, the word or words they describe should follow immediately:

To balance the budget, the president requested that Congress release the funds.

(It is the president who wants "to balance the budget"; therefore the words "the president" should immediately follow the introductory phrase.)

While waiting at the bank, Captain Johaness saw several suspicious individuals.

(It is Captain Johaness who was "waiting at the bank"; therefore, the words "Captain Johaness" should immediately follow the introductory phrase.)

Having read the newspaper report, the committee made its decision.

(It is the committee who "read the newspaper report"; therefore, the words "the committee" should immediately follow the introductory phrase.)

Revision Strategies

After identifying a misplaced or dangling modifier, the next step is to choose the most effective revision strategy. The following approaches are helpful.

1 If only one word is misplaced, simply move it to the correct location.

NO: He **even** didn't answer one question correctly.

YES: He didn't **even** answer one question correctly.

YES: He didn't answer **even** one question correctly.

(Note that the two revisions have slightly different meanings. Here the writer would have to decide whether *even* modified "answer" or "question.")

2 When a phrase is misplaced, sometimes you simply need to change its location.

NO: Most large textile mills in the nineteenth century, depended on immigrant workers, especially those with tight labor budgets.

YES: Most large textile mills in the nineteenth century, especially those with tight labor budgets, depended on immigrant workers.

3 When a phrase is misplaced, sometimes you need to revise, delete, or provide additional words.

NO: Commenting on the film, the reviewer's disgust was obvious.

YES: Commenting on the film, the reviewer showed her obvious disgust.

YES: When the reviewer commented on the film, her disgust was obvious.

YES: The reviewer's disgust was obvious when she commented on the film.

As you revise, remember to remain flexible and to correct misplaced or dangling modifiers in a way that will sound smooth and make sense in your paper. The strategies given here are only suggestions; there are many other ways to use modifiers correctly.

Proofreading Evaluation Exercise 6B: Identifying and Correcting Misplaced and Dangling Modifiers

Directions Read each of the following sentences carefully. When you find a misplaced or dangling modifier, rewrite the sentence correctly.

1 Dating from medieval times, Americans are sometimes astonished by European monarchies.

2 Some Europeans think monarchies should be abolished.

3 It's certainly true that the monarchy violates the egalitarian principles of democracy with its rituals, lavish ceremonies, and strict class structure.

4 Nevertheless, in this final quarter of the twentieth century, monarchies flourish in Western Europe.

5 Unlike fairy tale kings and queens, hard work and difficult lives are the lot of today's royals.

Proofreading Evaluation Exercise 6C: Editing in Context

Directions Read the following paragraph and correct any errors you find. As you read, you will be looking for sentence fragments, for comma splices and fused sentences, and for problems with subject-verb agreement, with pronoun reference, with pronoun agreement, with verb tense shifts, or with misplaced and dangling modifiers.

(1) A respected public opinion poll covering several European monarchies show that nearly 80 percent of the citizens are proroyalist. (2) The typical European monarch exerts their influence in matters of style as well as government and commerce. (3) For example, Princess Diana whose clothes and hair cuts are widely imitated. (4) Yet Diana also works hard at such difficult social tasks as changing public opinion on AIDS patients, she even visits with such patients, shaking hands with them and hugging children with AIDS. (5) In Spain, when the citizens overthrew a fascist dictatorship. (6) Showing strong leadership ability, a parliamentary democracy was established by King Juan Carlos. (7) Queen Beatrix of Holland followed her mother to the throne she has been known as the monarch who demystified royalty. (8) She won the respect of her people when she takes—and passed—the entrance exam to be admitted to university rather than claiming simply her "divine right." (9) Denmark, too, has a remarkable queen who has many gifts and talents. (10) She paints professionally, designs silverware, and has translated works of literature from French into Danish she is so popular that many political experts believe she would be chosen as president if she ran for that office.

EDITOR'S FOCUS 7

USING QUOTATION MARKS CORRECTLY

Proofreading Evaluation Exercise 7A

Directions Before you read the information on using quotation marks, do the following exercise. It is designed to help you evaluate your skill at using quotation marks and accompanying marks of punctuation.

As you read the following paragraph, note any problems with the use of quotation marks or the marks of punctuation that accompany quotation marks. Then rewrite the paragraph so that those problems are eliminated.

(1) The United States celebrated its two-hundredth birthday with a "far out" celebration. (2) "Newsweek" magazine described this celebration in an article titled "Happy Birthday, America". (3) Even the words "lavish" and "spectacular" are too mild to describe the elaborate fireworks displays, the gigantic parades, and the impressive pageants that were held throughout the nation. (4) It was a time for looking at the "bright" side of the American experience. (5) "The hallmark of the American adventure." said President Ford at the dedication of the Smithsonian's new Air and Space museum. "Has been a willingness—even an eagerness to reach for the unknown.

Editing Strategy: Understanding and Identifying the Correct Use of Quotation Marks

Quotation marks should be used in the following situations:

1 To enclose direct quotations taken from something that someone else has written

2 To enclose an individual's spoken words

3 To enclose titles of newspaper, magazine, and journal articles; titles of poems, short stories, television and radio programs, songs, and chapters or sections of books (*Note:* Titles of books, films, and plays and names of magazines, journals, and newspapers are underlined or put in italics.)

4 To discuss a word as a word (*Example:* "Amorous" comes from the Latin word for "love.")

Using Quotation Marks Correctly

1 When a quotation is introduced by a phrase like "As Dr. Smith notes," "Paul Garcia contends," or "Annie Dillard says," a comma should follow the introductory phrase.

Example: Margaret Mather observes, "I was always slightly apart from my family."

2 When a quotation is followed by a phrase like those described above, a comma separates the quotation and the explanatory phrase.

Example: "I was always slightly apart from my family," observes Margaret Mather.

(*Note:* If the quotation is a question, separate the quotation and the explanatory phrase with a question mark and no comma.)

Example: "Why was I always on my own?" Mather asks.

3 When a quotation is combined with the writer's own words, sometimes a comma is called for and sometimes no punctuation is required.

Example: Novelist Amanda Ellis notes that "inspiration comes slowest during the dark winter months."

(No comma needed)

Example: Amanda Ellis dreads, like so many of us, "the dark winter months."

(Comma needed)

4 When a quoted sentence is divided by explanatory words, commas set off those words.

Example: "I find inspiration comes slowest," notes novelist Amanda Ellis, "during the dark winter months."

5 Place periods and commas inside quotation marks.

Example: President Kennedy said, "Ask not what your country can do for you, but what you can do for your country."

(Exception: When you give parenthetical documentation following a quotation, the quotation marks come before the parentheses and the period follows the parentheses. (See Appendix E: Documenting Sources, pages 410–427.)

Example: Walter K. Mathis notes that "the gross national product has changed markedly in the past decade" (75).

6 Place colons and semicolons outside quotation marks.

Example: Jennifer stated flatly, "I will never marry Paul"; six months later they were husband and wife.

7 Place question marks and exclamation marks inside the quotation marks unless the whole sentence is a question or an exclamation.

Example: Professor Johnson asked, "When will we face the truth about environmental pollution?"

Example: Did Professor Johnson say, "Twenty years from now there may not be any clear trout streams in Vermont"?

Example: Did Professor Johnson ask, "When will we face the truth about environmental pollution"?

(*Note:* When both the quotation and the sentence containing the quotation are questions, use only one question mark and place it outside the quotation marks.)

8 Use single quotation marks to enclose a quotation within a quotation.

Example: According to anthropologist Janice Ackroyd, "Early Amazon women almost certainly used phrases like 'God, our mother' and 'Praise be to her' in their worship ceremonies."

9 Do not use quotation marks to excuse slang in formal writing.

EXAMPLE:

NO: Many people believe that those who survive heart attacks usually lead "laid back" lives.

YES: Many people believe that those who survive heart attacks usually lead calm, unstressful lives.

10 Do not use quotation marks to indicate irony or humor.

EXAMPLE:

NO: She was constantly making "witty" remarks.

YES: She was constantly making remarks that only she found witty.

Proofreading Evaluation Exercise 7B: Using Quotation Marks Correctly

Directions Read each of the following sentences carefully. When you find quotation marks that are missing or misused, make appropriate revisions. Watch also for marks of punctuation that accompany quotation marks and make sure they are used correctly. Correct any errors you find.

1 In "Daily Lives," a section of the textbook "Nation of Nations," the authors note that "Europeans acquired their first knowledge of sugar" from their conquests in "the Mediterranean, North Africa, and Spain."

2 In the Middle Ages, commoners never tasted sugar, and even royalty asked plaintively, "When is the next shipment due?"

3 "Europeans classified sugar as a spice" notes historian James West Davidson.

4 The cooks in castle kitchens tried to outdo each other by creating baked sugar sculptures that were very delicate and, taking their name from the word "subtle," were called subtleties.

5 Davidson states that the, "pattern of consumption started to change as Europeans turned to African slave labor to grow sugar for them;" sugar suddenly became cheaper.

6 Was it the drop in price that made "sugar essential to the poorest Europeans?"

7 Whatever the reason, "Sugar became the status symbol of the eighteenth-century middle-class." (Davidson, 56)

8 After using molasses for years, the English working class probably thought tea with sugar was "far-out."

9 Today, some experts, including those in the "Surgeon General's Office," believe sugar to be a major threat to our health.

10 To many of us "sweet-tooths", that's very "sour" news!

Proofreading Evaluation Exercise 7C: Editing in Context

Directions Read the following paragraph and correct any errors you find. As you read, you will be looking for sentence fragments, for comma splices and fused sentences, and for problems with subject-verb agreement, with pronoun reference, with pronoun agreement, with verb tense shifts, or with misplaced and dangling modifiers. You will also be watching for the correct use of quotation marks.

(1) Many people think of comic books as uniquely American. (2) They think they are only familiar to American readers. (3) In fact, although comics were invented in the United States, they are far more popular abroad, they are especially appealing to European and Japanese readers. (4) Because many adults as well as children were comic fans in such countries as Italy and France. (5) There is highly organized and very active comic fan clubs in those countries. (6) When choosing a comic book, the superhero does not particularly interest the European reader. (7) Instead, according to popular culture experts Murray Suid and Ron Harris in their book "Made in America," they prefer "exotic adventures, detectives, spies, westerns and science-fiction".

EDITOR'S FOCUS 8

USING COMMAS CORRECTLY

Proofreading Evaluation Exercise 8A

Directions Before you read the information on using commas, do the following exercise, which is designed to help you evaluate your skill at using commas.

As you read the following paragraph, note any problems with the use of commas. Then rewrite the paragraph so that those problems are eliminated.

(1) If there were one person who developed the alphabet that person would probably be the greatest inventor in human history. (2) Books, newspapers magazines and journals would be very different without the alphabet. (3) Writing would be possible without the alphabet but it would not be as accessible and precise. (4) Early peoples such as the Egyptians and the Babylonians wrote without an alphabet. (5) They used a form,

of writing, known as a logographic system. (6) In this system each symbol represents a word. (7) Chinese, a difficult complex language, is the most well-known modern, logographic writing system. (8) A third writing system is the syllabic which is used by the Japanese. (9) This system uses symbols, that represent syllables. (10) The three systems exist in countries that seem similar in many other ways. (11) For example in one corner of the world we find three neighboring countries, China, Japan, and Korea, each using different writing systems. (12) Chinese use the logographic, Japanese the syllabic and Koreans the alphabetic.

Editing Strategy: Understanding and Identifying the Correct Use of Commas

Commas give readers valuable clues concerning the writer's meaning, yet they are the mark of punctuation that is most commonly misused in English.

To use commas correctly, you need to learn two categories of rules:

1. Rules relating to places that commas *should* be used.
2. Rules relating to places that commas *should not* be used.

The following guidelines do not give every rule concerning comma use, but they cover approximately 95 percent of situations where commas should and should not be used.

Use Commas in the Following Places

1. After an introductory word or group of words

   EXAMPLES:

   After the long speech, the candidates were bored.

   When they returned to their rooms, they were shocked.

   Nevertheless, they all took naps.

2. Before a conjunction (a word like "and," "but," "so") that joins to-

gether two groups of words, each of which expresses a complete thought

Example: The candidates met at their headquarters, and they began to plan their strategy.

3 Between items in a series

Example: Wit, wisdom, and warmth were their watchwords.

4 Between adjectives that equally describe a noun or pronoun (use a comma between adjectives only when you could logically substitute the word "and" for the comma.)

EXAMPLE:

YES: The long, difficult campaign was nearly over.

(Because you can say: The long and difficult campaign was nearly over.)

NO: The three, wisest candidates were elected.

(Because you cannot say: The three and wisest candidates were elected.)

5 To set off nonessential elements (words or groups of words that are not absolutely necessary to the meaning of the sentence)

EXAMPLES:

The newly elected mayor chose an inexpensive gown, which was admired by many people.

The new city hall, which is located two blocks from the old building, cost the tax payers $6 million.

One room was filled with files containing old birth records, dating from 1800 to 1910.

Catherine Porter, the mayor's assistant, explained that the records were being transferred to microfilm.

6 To set off transitional expressions

EXAMPLES:

The mayor, therefore, was not held responsible for the use of the files.

She expects in the future, however, to monitor such decisions closely.

The former mayor, by the way, was unavailable for comment.

7 To set off nouns used to directly address a person or group

EXAMPLES:

Fellow citizens, consider the opportunities that lie before us.

Your work with the campaign, Aaron, helped us greatly.

8 To set off the words "yes" and "no"; mild exclamations; short questions

EXAMPLES:

Yes, this administration expects to balance the budget.

Oh, I find that hard to believe!

All candidates promise lower taxes, don't they?

9 After words that lead to a direct quotation; after a direct quotation that is followed by a description of who said the words

EXAMPLES:

"My administration will be different," she promised.

She firmly stated, "I mean no new taxes!"

10 With titles, dates, numbers, and addresses

EXAMPLES:

Arline M. Dupras, Ed.D.

Ernest Gostomiz, Jr.

John Leopold, M.D., addressed the convention.

On March 1, 1990, she was installed in office.
He was born on Wednesday, August 6, 1941.

We own 10,000 shares of stock worth $1,000.
They own 1,000 shares of stock worth $10,000.

Her first school was located in Highgate, England.
Please send the transcripts to 266 Barnstable Road, Winslow, Maine 04078.

Do Not Use Commas in the Following Places

1 Between parts of a sentence joined with a conjunction when each part does not, by itself, express a complete thought

EXAMPLES:

NO: The city council, and the mayor disagreed.
YES: The city council and the mayor disagreed.

NO: The citizens still don't realize that their city is in economic crisis, and that they are facing huge budget cuts.

YES: The citizens still don't realize that their city is in economic crisis and that they are facing huge budget cuts.

2 To separate the subject from the verb or the verb from the direct or indirect object

EXAMPLES:

NO: The former campaign manager, walked away from the conflict.

YES: The former campaign manager walked away from the conflict.

NO: He did not see, the many rewards that awaited him.

YES: He did not see the many rewards that awaited him.

3 Before the first or after the final item in a series

EXAMPLES:

NO: Services to be affected by the budget cuts include, schools, fire department, and police department.

YES: Services to be affected by the budget cuts include schools, fire department, and police department.

NO: The schools, fire department, and police department, will all lose staff members.

YES: The schools, fire department, and police department will all lose staff members.

4 To set off essential elements (words or phrases that are necessary to the meaning of the sentence)

EXAMPLE:

NO: Citizens, who cast their votes for Ms. Bennet, are now having second thoughts.

YES: Citizens who cast their votes for Ms. Bennet are now having second thoughts.

5 Before a parenthesis or after "such as" or "like"

EXAMPLES:

NO: The mayor, (who graduated from City High School) was shocked.

YES: The mayor (who graduated from City High School) was shocked.

NO: Many cities, such as, Miami and Chicago, are investigating a voucher system of public education.

YES: Many cities, such as Miami and Chicago, are investigating a voucher system of public education.

Proofreading Evaluation Exercise 8B: Using Commas Correctly

Directions Read each of the following sentences carefully. When you find commas that are missing or misused, make appropriate revisions.

1 Over 100 million Americans including two-thirds of all adults now wear glasses.

2 Nearly another 10 million, regularly use contact lenses.

3 Of course we all should be grateful for the invention of glasses.

4 Corrective lenses rank among the most significant, useful discoveries of all time, such as, printing, paper electricity and atomic power.

5 Remember, however, that eyeglasses were not commonly worn anywhere in the world until, about, 450 years ago.

6 It's hard to imagine life without the possibility of glasses isn't it?

7 In ancient times, many, aging scholars had to give up reading, but those who were wealthy could pay others to read for them.

8 Lenses existed in ancient Rome but they were used only for burning.

9 Medical reporter James Sayed Ph.D. says "Early Anglo-Saxons advised persons with poor vision to comb their heads, eat little meat, and drink wormwood before meals."

10 Fourth-century Italians, (who studied the stars carefully) believed that a person, who looked directly at a falling star, would go blind.

Proofreading Evaluation Exercise 8C: Editing in Context

Directions Read the following paragraph and correct any errors you find. As you read, you will be looking for sentence fragments, for comma splices and fused sentences, and for problems with subject-verb agreement, with pronoun reference, with pronoun agreement, with verb tense shifts, or with misplaced and dangling modifiers. You will also be watching for the correct use of quotation marks and commas.

(1) Roger Bacon an Englishman was the first to suggest using lenses to read. (2) He described a lens, that could be held near a

book to magnify the printing, the reader would then be able to see more clearly. (3) Searching for the exact discovery date of eyeglasses, an interesting fact came to light. (4) A tombstone in Florence Italy which describes the person who is buried there as the "inventor of spectacles". (5) He died in 1317, but when Marco Polo returns from the Orient during the 1270s, he claimed to have found an old, Chinese, scholar reading with glasses. (6) Unfortunately, he was unable to communicate with him because of the language barrier. (7) Because the average European, who lived during the Middle Ages, could not read, they were not very impressed or concerned with the discovery of glasses. (8) Also, all early lenses were convex, they could only be used to improve farsighted vision and could not help nearsighted people. (9) By the eighteenth century, however concave lenses could be manufactured. (10) In addition, middle-class people were learning to read, and so valued their eyesight more than ever.

EDITOR'S FOCUS 9

USING COLONS, SEMICOLONS, AND APOSTROPHES CORRECTLY

Proofreading Evaluation Exercise 9A

Directions Before you read the information on using colons, semicolons, and apostrophes, do the following exercise, which is designed to help you evaluate your skill at using these marks of punctuation.

As you read the following paragraph, note any problems with the use of colons, semicolons, and apostrophes. Then rewrite the paragraph so that those problems are eliminated.

(1) Locks are used to guard many things, homes, cars, bicycles, desks, jewelry boxes, and even diaries. (2) A good lock is like love, it must not be forced. (3) With the proper use of the proper

key; a lock should open and close easily. (4) Law-abiding people admire a good lock, a thief regards it as a challenge. (5) Thieve's have no respect for other peoples' property, however, a good lock can sometimes teach them respect.

Editing Strategy: Understanding and Identifying the Correct Use of Colons, Semicolons, and Apostrophes

Colons are used mainly to call attention to the words that follow.

Semicolons are used mainly to separate short sentences or to separate various parts of sentences.

Apostrophes are used mainly to show ownership or to indicate where letters are omitted in a contraction.

Colons, semicolons, and apostrophes (like commas) are governed by two sets of rules: those that explain when these marks of punctuation *should* be used and those that explain when they *should not* be used.

Use Colons in the Following Places

1 Between two sentences when the second sentence explains or summarizes the first

Example: Last month, seventeen workers left their positions at Z-Cron Company: Like so many workers before them, they were worried about their company's safety record.

(*Note:* The sentence that follows the colon may begin with either a capital letter or a lowercase letter.)

2 After a complete sentence to lead into a list

Example: If you apply for the position, please send the following: a résumé, a transcript of your grades in college, two letters of recommendation.

3 After the greeting in a formal letter

Example: Dear Senator Johnson:

4 To indicate hours and minutes

Example: 6:45 A.M.

5 To indicate subtitles

Example: Tess of the D'Urbervilles: A Pure Woman

Do Not Use Colons in the Following Places

1 To indicate a list that follows a group of words that is not a complete sentence

EXAMPLE:

NO: The picnic consisted of: a loaf of bread, a bottle of wine, and a basket of fresh fruit.

("The picnic consisted of" is not a sentence, so no colon should come before the list.)

YES: The picnic consisted of a loaf of bread, a bottle of wine, and a basket of fresh fruit.

YES: The picnic consisted of the following items: a loaf of bread, a bottle of wine, and a basket of fresh fruit.

("The picnic consisted of the following items" is a complete sentence, so a colon follows it and comes before the list.)

2 To link a sentence with a group of words that is not a sentence

EXAMPLE:

NO: When the company audited the books: the treasurer left town.

YES: When the company audited the books, the treasurer left town.

Use Semicolons in the Following Places

1 Between two short sentences that are closely related

Example: Destruction is easy; construction is hard.

2 Between two complete thoughts that are joined with a transitional word or phrase

Example: The orchestra had begun playing; however, the audience was still talking.

3 Between items in a series when those items contain commas

Example: Dickens's most popular novels are *David Copperfield,* with its spirited Aunt Betsey Trotwood; *Great Expectations,* with its disappointed bride, Miss Havisham; and *Oliver Twist,* with its sad, haunted Nancy.

Do Not Use a Semicolon in the Following Places

1 To link a sentence with a group of words that is not a sentence

EXAMPLE:

NO: When you find a good novel; you look forward to the times when you are free to read it.

YES: When you find a good novel, you look forward to the times when you are free to read it.

2 To introduce a list

EXAMPLE:

NO: For a successful camping trip, bring the following supplies; a tent, food, water, matches, wood, and a first-aid kit.

YES: For a successful camping trip, bring the following supplies: a tent, food, water, matches, wood, and a first-aid kit.

Use Apostrophes in the Following Places

1 To indicate that a noun shows ownership

Example: This is John's book.

When a noun does not end in *s*—whether it is singular or plural—add *'s*.

Example: This is the children's book.

When a noun is singular and ends in *s*, add *'s*.

Example: This is Avis's book.

When a noun is plural and ends in *s*, add *only an apostrophe*.

Example: This is the Bachman sisters' book.

When two people own something jointly, add *'s* only to the final name. (If the final name is plural and ends in *s*, add *only an apostrophe*.)

Example: This is Anne and Joyce's book.

(Anne and Joyce are joint owners of the book.)

When two people own different things, add *'s* to both names. (If either name is plural and ends in *s*, add *only an apostrophe* to that name.)

Example: These are Anne's and her two sisters' books.

(Anne and her two sisters own different books.)

When a noun is compound, use 's with the last part of the word.

Example: This is her mother-in-law's book.

2 To show that an indefinite pronoun is possessive

Example: It is anyone's guess whether the rain will stop.

3 To mark letters left out of a contraction

Example: Don't you intend to enroll? ("Don't" stands for "do not": The apostrophe indicates that the "o" in "not" has been omitted.)

(*Note:* "It's" is the contraction that stands for "It is." [*Example:* It's fine with me if you want to leave.] "Its" is a possessive pronoun. [*Example:* The house had shed its new coat of paint.])

4 To make numbers plural and to discuss numbers, letters, words, and abbreviations

EXAMPLES:

Her grades were a string of perfect 100's.

The children waved banners marked with large A's.

I do not want to hear any if's or but's.

After the fight, the M.P.'s took the young soldier to his commanding officer.

Do Not Use Apostrophes in the Following Places

1 With nouns that are not possessive

EXAMPLE:

NO: Some students' are allowed to live off campus.

YES: Some students are allowed to live off campus.

2 With the possessive pronouns *hers, his, its, ours, yours, theirs,* and *whose*

EXAMPLE:

NO: The car had lost both it's hubcaps.

YES: The car had lost both its hubcaps.

3 With the present-tense form of a verb

EXAMPLE:

NO: He drive's as if he just got his license.

YES: He drives as if he just got his license.

Proofreading Evaluation Exercise 9B: Using Colons, Semicolons, and Apostrophes Correctly

Directions Read each of the following sentences carefully. When you find colons, semicolons, or apostrophes that are missing or misused, make appropriate revisions.

1 The progress of human history has seen a continual improvement of the ingenuity of two profession's; the locksmith and the burglar.

2 The battle of wits is not over, as the locksmith creates new locks, the burglar invents new ways to open them.

3 Most ancient peoples' lived in communities where homes were smali, friends, relatives, and neighbors were close by, and strangers were regarded with hostility, anger, and suspicion.

4 These people did not need locks, they lived simply and securely.

5 Early civilizations used locks to prevent unauthorized entry to sacred places, however, those locks were often ineffective.

6 An ancient Egyptians lock usually consisted of a vertical wooden bar fixed to his' doorpost; and a wooden crossbar or bolt.

7 To open such locks required the following steps; inserting a key through the hole in the bolt, levering the key upward, pushing the pins of the key through matching holes in the bolt, turning the bolt to release the bar from it's holder.

8 Early Greeks and Egyptians homes were different.

9 The typical Egyptian home had many exposed windows, however; the Greeks' homes faced protective courtyards.

10 In Egypt, thieve's movements could be controlled by locked doors.

Proofreading Evaluation Exercise 9C: Editing in Context

Directions Read the following paragraphs and correct any errors you find. As you read, you will be looking for sentence fragments, for comma splices and fused sentences, and for problems with subject-verb agreement, with pronoun reference, with pronoun agreement, with verb tense shifts, or with misplaced and dangling modifiers. You will also be watching for the correct use of quotation marks, commas, colons, semicolons, and apostrophes.

(1) Locks in the Middle Ages and Renaissance were more decorative, than useful. (2) For example, those that used

intricately designed key-ways and obstructions around the keyhole to foil potential lockpickers. (3) The main problem concerning the locks were that the camouflage worked too well, thieves could not pick the locks but owners often could not open them, either. (4) Henry VIII, the infamous English monarch always traveled with a massive heavy gold-plated lock. (5) King Henry who feared assassins always had a carpenter travel with him. (6) Each evening he orders him to screw the lock to his bedroom door. (7) The kings' precautions evidently paid off, his bedrooms remained secure and according to his court historian he died at the age of fifty-six from, "a surfeit of quinces".

(8) The history of the lock continues in the nineteenth century when British authorities offered a substantial cash prize to anyone who's ingenuity could invent a cheap unpickable lock. (9) In less than three days, Jeremiah Chubb submitted the winning design to an astonished government official that was inexpensive, efficient, and also beautiful. (10) An imprisoned locksmith and lockpicker was summoned, after ten weeks of extremely, intensive work, he admitted defeat Chubbs' lock was unpickable.

EDITOR'S FOCUS 10

USING THE ELLIPSIS, THE DASH, AND PARENTHESES CORRECTLY

(*Note:* In this Editor's Focus, quoted material from the following passage will be used in exercises and explanations.)

In the nineteenth century, dress reform for women attracted adherents with a variety of social agendas. Some feminists, like Elizabeth Miller, simply sought greater freedom of movement. And Elizabeth Cady Stanton, for example, commended bloomers to all busy wives and mothers "who wash and iron, bake and brew, carry water and fat babies upstairs and down, bring potatoes, apples, and pans of milk from the cellar, run our own errands, through mud or snow, shovel paths, and work in the garden." Other feminists went further, seeing dress reform as essential to establishing the equality of the sexes. Sarah Grimké contended that "so long as we submit to being dressed like dolls, we can never rise to the stations of duty and usefulness from which they desire to exclude us."

from J. W. Davidson et al., *Nation of Nations,* page 422.

Proofreading Evaluation Exercise 10A

Directions Before you read the information on using ellipses, the dash, and parentheses, do the following exercise, which is designed to help you evaluate your skill at using these marks of punctuation.

As you read the following paragraph, note any problems with the use of the ellipsis, the dash, and parentheses. Then rewrite the paragraph so that those problems are eliminated.

(1) Clothing styles for women—especially working women, have changed radically during the past hundred years, 1890–1990. (2) In *Nation of Nations,* the authors note that Elizabeth Cady Stanton a noted feminist "commended bloomers to all busy wives and mothers. . . ." (3) Stanton was primarily interested in making work easier for overburdened, usually lower-class, women. (4) Other feminists, for example, Sarah Grimké, saw "dress reform as essential to equality of the sexes."

> The ellipsis (a series of three dots) is used to indicate words omitted from a quotation.
>
> The dash and parentheses are both used to set off words or groups of words that are not essential to the meaning of the sentence.

Using the Ellipsis

1 Use the ellipsis to show that you have deleted words from material you are quoting.

Example: According to the authors of *Nation of Nations,* "Some feminists . . . simply sought greater freedom of movement. . . . Other feminists went further, seeing dress reform as essential to establishing the equality of the sexes."

2 If you omit words at the beginning of a quotation, you do not have to use an ellipsis.

EXAMPLE:

NO: According to the authors of *Nation of Nations,* many nineteenth-century reformers recommended changes in women's dress styles to allow ". . . greater freedom of movement."

YES: According to the authors of *Nation of Nations,* many nineteenth-century reformers recommended changes in women's dress styles to allow "greater freedom of movement."

3 If you stop quoting before the end of the sentence in the original, but your own sentence continues, use an ellipsis to show that you have omitted words.

Example: According to the authors of *Nation of Nations,* "Dress reform attracted adherents . . ." who came from many different parts of the political spectrum.

4 If you stop quoting before the end of the sentence in the original, and your own sentence does not continue, use an ellipsis, then a space and a period to indicate the end of your own sentence.

Example: During the nineteenth century, according to the authors of *Nation of Nations,* "Dress reform attracted adherents . . . ."

5 If you stop quoting before the end of the sentence in the original, and the quotation is followed by parenthetical documentation, use an ellipsis, then the closing quotation marks, then the parenthetical reference, and finally the sentence period.

Example: During the nineteenth century, according to the authors of *Nation of Nations,* "Dress reform attracted adherents . . ." (422).

Using the Dash

1 If you are typing or using a word processor, use two hyphens to form a dash (--). Do not put spaces before or after the dash.

Example: Some physicians– –often viewed as alarmists– –warned that tight corsets worn by pregnant women could cause birth defects in their babies.

2 Use dashes to set off material you want to emphasize.

Example: An amazing assortment of material– –from steel bands to thin wands of whale-bone– –was used to reduce the waistline of the nineteenth-century woman.

3 Use dashes to set off a group of explanatory words that contains commas.

Example: Serious medical problems– –broken ribs, collapsed lungs, and uterine disorders– –resulted from the use of tightly laced corsets.

4 Use a dash to prepare your reader for a list, a summary, or a marked change in thought or tone.

EXAMPLES:

The typical nineteenth-century middle-class woman went out to work in her garden burdened by layers of clothing– –corsets, corset covers, petticoats, slips, crinolines, and heavy outer skirts.

Elizabeth Cady Stanton had worked for many reform causes– –abolition, temperance, and women's suffrage.

Catherine's maid laced her mistress into a beautiful ball gown and stepped back to admire the young duchess– –but Catherine, unable to breathe, had fainted.

5 Do not use dashes unless there is a specific reason for doing so.

EXAMPLE:

NO: Sarah gasped– –she ran to get help– –she had no idea what was wrong with her mistress– –all she knew was that Lady Catherine lay in a crumpled heap on the floor.

YES: Sarah gasped; she ran to get help. She had no idea what was wrong with her mistress. All she knew was that Lady Catherine lay in a crumpled heap on the floor.

Using Parentheses

1 Use parentheses to enclose explanatory information, especially information that makes a minor digression from the topic.

Example: Popular women's magazines in the nineteenth century (like similar magazines today) promoted fancy fashions and opposed simple, inexpensive clothes.

2 Use parentheses to enclose letters or numbers that label items in a series.

Example: The following items were considered essential for the wardrobe of the upper-class nineteenth-century bride: (1) six petticoats of cotton, (2) three petticoats of silk, (3) two sets of crinolines, one in light color and one in dark, (4) three sets of corsets, (5) two waist-cinchers, and (6) four camisoles.

Proofreading Evaluation Exercise 10B: Using Ellipses, the Dash, and Parentheses Correctly

Directions Read each of the following sentences carefully. When you find ellipses, dashes, or parentheses that are missing or misused, make appropriate revisions.

(*Note:* The sentences in Proofreading Evaluation Exercises 10B and 10C refer to the following quotation.)

Slaves resorted to various means to enliven their drab diet. Wherever their masters permitted it, they tended their own vegetable gardens after work or raised chickens and other animals. Not only did this practice provide eggs and other items not included in the weekly rations, but it also enabled slaves to sell their surplus to the master or to town's people and use their earnings to buy small quantities of luxuries such as coffee, sugar, and tobacco.

from J. W. Davidson et al., *Nation of Nations,* page 476.

1 During the pre–Civil War years, slaves received food rations only once a week with no exceptions for illness or childbearing.

2 Rations predictable and boring varied little from plantation to plantation.

3 Each adult slave received the following items: 1 a peck of cornmeal, 2 three or four pounds of bacon or salt pork, and 3 some molasses for sweetening.

4 According to the authors of *Nation of Nations,* slaves often ". . . tended their own vegetable gardens after work. . . ." (476)

5 Gardening allowed slaves "to sell their surplus to the master or to town's people" and then use the money they received to buy other items.

Proofreading Evaluation Exercise 10C: Editing in Context

Directions Read the following paragraph and correct any errors you find. As you read, you will be looking for sentence fragments, for comma splices and fused sentences, and for problems with subject-verb agreement, with pronoun reference, with pronoun agreement, with verb tense shifts, or with misplaced and dangling modifiers. You will also be watching for the correct use of quotation marks, commas, colons, semicolons, apostrophes, the ellipsis, the dash, and parentheses.

(1) In addition to the basic supplies of cornmeal, salt pork, and molasses some master's added these foods; vegetables, fruits, or sweet potatoes. (2) Milk reserved for children when it was available was usually sour when delivered. (3) On rare occasions slaves were given small amounts of other items. (4) Like wheat flour, beef, lean meat, poultry, or eggs. (5) Although this monotonous diet provided the average adult slave with about 5,500 calories a day- -over 80 percent of their calories came from corn and pork. (6) Diet-related diseases for example pelagra and beriberi are often noted among the slave population. (7) According to the authors' of *Nation of Nations,* some slaves "raised chickens and other animals. . . ." (8) This practice allowed them to earn money "to buy coffee, sugar, and tobacco". (9) Although wealthy, the diets of slave owners were also often lacking in essential nutrients. (10) The master might eat a better cut of meat, but they usually ate few fresh fruits and vegetables. (11) On Christmas, a few slaveowners provided beef, mutton, roast pig- -coffee, wheat bread- -pies and other rare dishes. (12) Slaves were allowed few comforts or pleasures, the Christmas feasts were anxiously anticipated for the whole year.

EDITOR'S FOCUS 11

USING CAPITAL LETTERS CORRECTLY

Proofreading Evaluation Exercise 11A

Directions Before you read the information on capitalization, do the following exercise, which is designed to help you evaluate your skill at using capital letters. As you read the following paragraph, note any problems with the use of capitals. Then rewrite the paragraph so that those problems are eliminated.

(1) On april 10, 1849, a New York Native, Walter Hunt, m.d., was granted a patent for a device he called a Safety Pin. (2) Hunt was not destined to be called the inventor of the Safety Pin, however, since devices similar to it had been in use since the days of Ancient Greece. (3) Dr. Hunt is quoted as saying, "the safety pin should have made me rich!" (4) In spite of his protests, the Doctor never made a penny on his invention. (5) The story of his life was recently broadcast on pbs.

> Capital letters are used to indicate that a word or group of letters has some special significance.

Using Capital Letters

1 Use capital letters to begin nouns that name specific persons, places, or things (proper nouns). Do not use capital letters to begin other nouns (common nouns).

EXAMPLES—PROPER NOUNS:	*EXAMPLES—COMMON NOUNS:*
Atlantic Ocean	the ocean
Romania	a country
Aunt Susan	her aunt
Biology 102	a science course
Internal Revenue Service	a federal agency

(*Note:* Months, days of the week, and holidays are considered proper nouns. Seasons and numbers of the days of the month are considered common nouns.)

EXAMPLES—CAPITALIZE:	*EXAMPLES—DO NOT CAPITALIZE:*
June	spring
Friday	the thirteenth
Thanksgiving	holiday

2 Use capital letters to begin words that come from proper nouns.

EXAMPLES:

China	Chinese
Queen Victoria	Victorian
Charles Dickens	Dickensian

(*Note:* Names of school subjects are capitalized only if they are the names of languages or if they are the names of specific courses.)

EXAMPLES—CAPITALIZE:	*EXAMPLES—DO NOT CAPITALIZE:*
French	geology
Topics in Western Thought	philosophy

3 Use a capital letter for the first word of a sentence.

Example: The governor vetoed the tax bill two weeks before the election.

4 Use capital letters for the first, last, and all major words in titles and subtitles of books, articles, films, songs, and other such works.

EXAMPLES:
Do the Right Thing
The Life of Martin Luther King: Eyes on the Prize
"A Rose for Emily"

5 Use capital letters to begin titles of people when those titles are used as part of the person's name. Do not use capitals to begin titles when they are used alone.

EXAMPLES:

The outstanding teacher award goes to Professor Kathleen Cain.

David's professor requires two research papers each semester.

6 Use a capital letter to begin the first word of a quoted sentence.

Example: Eleanor Roosevelt declared, "No one can make me feel inferior without my permission."

7 Use capital letters for abbreviations of corporations, government departments and agencies, and the call letters of radio and television stations.

Examples: RCA, IRS, NATO, WBZ

Proofreading Evaluation Exercise 11B: Using Capital Letters Correctly

Directions Read each of the following sentences carefully. When you find capital letters that are missing or misused, make appropriate revisions.

1 In 1896 on the Sixth of June, a carpenter, George Harbo, and a plumber, Frank Samuelson, left New York Harbor in an Eighteen-foot Rowboat.

2 Staunch members of the Republican Party, then often called the gop "for grand old party," harbo and Samuelson were cheered by members of a Republican Club from their hometown in New jersey.

3 Although the Spring weather brought rain, the pair rowed diligently for approximately eighteen hours Per Day.

4 On july 15, they were picked up in the Middle of the Atlantic Ocean by a Freighter.

5 When their water was replenished, they continued rowing and after Fifty-Six days at sea they landed on an island off the Coast of England.

6 Later, they published an article called "the Impossible Journey."

Proofreading Evaluation Exercise 11C: Editing in Context

Directions Read the following paragraph and correct any errors you find. As you read, you will be looking for sentence fragments, for comma splices and fused sentences, and for problems with subject-verb agreement, with pronoun reference, with pronoun agreement, with verb tense shifts, or with misplaced and dangling modifiers. You will also be watching for the correct use of quotation marks, commas, colons, semicolons, apostrophes, the ellipsis, the dash, parentheses, and capital letters.

(1) The frisbee, the brand name given to the plastic flying saucer so commonly seen on beaches and college campuses. (2) This intriguing device owes it's life to two things; pies and creatures from mar's. (3) The flying disc that gave the Frisbee it's name was a pie tin, only from the Frisbie Pie company of

bridgeport Connecticut. (4) The Pie Company was extremely successful in the 1920s a great many students from yale university bought and ate their pies. (5) One enterprising student soon found a way to use the empty plates, they gathered friends together and tossed the plates from one to another. (6) Instead of studying, the Spring of 1922 was filled with Yale Students learning the ultimate art of coaxing pie trays to fly through the air and do tricks. (7) During that famous spring, dedicated Frisbee artists will even convince the President of the University to try his hand at the sport. (8) Many years later in 1947, to be exact Walter Morrison a carpenter and part-time inventor from California. (9) He remembered seeing Yale students who, near his childhood neighborhood, was tossing the shiny disks. (10) Morrison took advantage of the new craze, that had taken the nation by storm, he developed and marketed the Frisbee. (11) 1947 was a year that saw reports of hundreds of flying saucer sightings. (12) Morrison told reporters "I've never seen a flying saucer, but I can make one"!

EDITOR'S FOCUS 12

SPELLING WORDS CORRECTLY

Proofreading Evaluation Exercise 12A

Directions Before you read the information on spelling words correctly, do the following exercise, which is designed to help you evaluate your skill at proofreading for and correcting spelling errors. As you read the following paragraph, note any misspellings and correct them.

(1) A favorit liesure pursuit for many people is attending the circus. (2) Everyone loves the elephants and the monkies, but the most popular act maybe the clowns. (3) In circus slang,

every clown is called a "Joey," a nickname that is suppose to come from Joseph Grimaldi. (4) Grimaldi was a clown who performed in London, where he acheived great popularity. (5) In the early 1800s, when Grimaldi apeared, Londoners would give him there full attention. (6) Although Grimaldi lived too a ripe old age, his frist perfomance was all most his last. (7) His parents, both circus stars, had their twenty-three month old son, Joey, play the roll of a monkey. (8) In one scene, Joey's father swung his sun around on a chane. (9) When the chane broke, the little boy sailled out into the crowd. (10) Fortunatly, he landed in the lap of a fat, old gentlman and so lived to become famous and give his name to generacions of future clows.

> Proofreading to check for misspellings is an essential part of the editing process.

Developing Good Spelling Skills

English spelling is not easy; it helps to remember how many words you now know and to recognize that you can spell the vast majority of those words correctly. Words that still trouble you can be learned, just as you have learned those that you already know. The following strategies will help you to develop proofreading and editing skills related to spelling.

1 Identify commonly used words that you misspell, make a list of them, and then use flashcards along with repetitive writing to set them correctly in your mind.

2 Identify spelling errors that you make with words that sound alike but are spelled differently. Learn the definitions of these words and work to remember them.

Be especially conscious of the following words:

their (indicates possession)

- *Their* car was stolen.

there (indicates place or can be part of an introductory expression)

- Go over *there.*
- *There* are two books.

they're (contraction for "they are")

- *They're* going to school.

3 Identify patterns in your spelling errors. These patterns may indicate that you need to learn a spelling rule. For example, if you have trouble adding suffixes (endings) to words that end in silent (unpronounced) "e," learn this rule: Drop the "e" when you add a suffix (an ending) that begins with a vowel:

word	+	*suffix*	=	*new word*
serve		ile		servile
page		ing		paging

Keep the "e" when you add a suffix that begins with a consonant:

word	+	*suffix*	=	*new word*
time		ly		timely
atone		ment		atonement

Like so many rules, this one has exceptions:

word	+	*suffix*	=	*new word*
argue		ment		argument
die		ing		dying
hoe		ing		hoeing
true		ly		truly

Many dictionaries include a section in the beginning that provides spelling rules. Consult such a dictionary if you see a pattern in your spelling errors and suspect that there might be a rule to help you.

4. Whenever you have to look up a word in a dictionary, try to use the same dictionary. Each time you look up a word, put a check next to it. When you have five check marks next to any word, add it to your list of words you are working to commit to memory.

5 Remember that many misspellings are caused by incorrect pronunciations. For instance, some people say "Feb*u*ary" instead of "Feb*ru*ary," so they leave out the "r." If you discover that you are misspelling a word because you are mispronouncing it, simply changing the way you say the word should eliminate the problem.

6 Try to find a memory device that will help you recall correct spellings of particularly troublesome words. For instance, one student had trouble with the word "separate" until her professor said, "Remember, there's 'a rat' in 'sep *a rat* e.' "

7 Remember that you will recall correct spelling more easily and successfully if you fix the word in your mind with as many senses as possible: Make flashcards (or a giant sign over your mirror) with troublesome words; spell the words aloud; write the words; print the words; type the words; close your eyes and try to "see" the words in your mind.

8 Use a spellchecker on a word processor. When the spellchecker stops, see if you can figure out the correct spelling before you ask the program to suggest a correction. Also, on notecards, keep a list of misspelled words that the spellchecker discovers. When the word is a repeat, just put a check on the card. When there are five checks, consider the word an emergency and work hard to learn to spell it.

(*Note:* Remember that a spellchecker cannot tell the difference between words that sound alike but are spelled differently. If you mean "there" but write "their," the spellchecker will not pick up your error. Also, if you write "I *was* two new books in the bookstore" (when you mean "I *saw*"), the spellchecker will take no note; it will only see that you have correctly spelled the word "was." Most spellcheckers do not yet understand the context in which words are used, so you have to check carefully to avoid the type of error just described.)

PROOFREADING STRATEGIES TO DISCOVER SPELLING AND TYPOGRAPHICAL ERRORS

1 *Provide a friend with a copy of your paper.* Have the friend read it aloud to you, including marks of punctuation. Listening to the words will slow you down and help you to concentrate. Next, swap roles. You read aloud while your friend follows on her or his copy. Sometimes this strategy brings to your attention an error that might have gone unnoticed.

2 *Read the paper backward.* This process focuses your attention on individual words. Note, however, that you'll also need to read the paper from beginning to end because when you read from end to beginning, you cannot find spelling errors or typographical errors that occur because of context. (For instance, you will not note that you used "their" instead of "there.")

3 *Use a ruler to follow each line.* This tactic helps to concentrate your attention and also slows your reading speed. You are less likely to skip words—or lines—when you use this process.

Proofreading Evaluation Exercise 12B: Spelling Correctly

Directions Read each of the following sentences carefully. When you find words that are misspelled, make appropriate revisions.

1 The grate tennor Enrico Caruso was in the midle of a performence in San Franciso on Apirl 17, 1906, when the famous earthquake ocurred.

2 As chimleys toppled and buildings crummbled, the terified singer took only one thing from the opra house—a pichur of President Theodore Roosevelt, personnelly autographed too Caruso.

3 Later, he tried to get on a trane with other members of the opera compangy, but the guards, who did not recognize him, tryed to seperate him from his freinds.

4 When Caruso showed his picture of the presidant, he was issed a bording pass and was then able to get too safty.

Proofreading Evaluation Exercise 12C: Editing in Context

Directions Read the following paragraph and correct any errors you find. As you read, you will be looking for sentence fragments, for comma splices and fused sentences, and for problems with subject-verb agreement, with pronoun reference, with pronoun agreement, with verb tense shifts, or with misplaced and dangling modifiers. You will also be watching for the correct use of quotation marks, commas, colons, semicolons, apostrophes, the ellipsis, the dash, parentheses, and/or capital letters and for misspelled words.

(1) Television comercials show people with insomnia the inability to fall asleep as comic figures. (2) These advertizements suggest that the problem could easily be cured if the sufferer would just take two pills he or she would be fine. (3) Throughout history; however, insomnia has been no laughing matter, and has troubled many famous people. (4) Catherine the Great for example demanded that her personnel maid brush her hair every evening as she reclyned in bed, she hoped to relax and fall asleep by useing this ritchual. (5) Another famous insomniac was Charles Dickens the

reknowned victorian novelist. (6) In order to fall asleep, his bed must be placed with its head pointing exactly due North. (7) Then while lying in bed he would measure the space at the sides with his arms. (8) Finding the exact center and staying there hoping these complex actions would allow him to fall asleep. (9) The Inventer Thomas Edison, who's most famous invention were light bulbs, claimed "I never had a full nights' sleep in my adult life." (10) Evidentally, Edison is able to survive on cat naps of thirty to forty minutes every five hours or so. (11) Like these famous Historical insomniacs, the modern sleepless person finds various ways to solve their problem. (12) For instance, hollywood author Jacqueline Susann edits her days' writting until she falls asleep.

Possible Responses to Selected Exercises in Appendix B: Guide to Editing

The following responses are provided so that you can see possible correct ways to rewrite the exercises in Appendix B. In some cases, there is more than one correct response. In these cases, not every correct response is provided. Instead, a single acceptable response is provided.

EXERCISE 1 *(pages 295–296)*

(1) A woman, Patience Lovell Wright, was the first American to become a professional sculptor. (2) Wright took her models from life and made statues of many important people in British and American society. (3) Praised for their beauty and grace, these statues were much admired. (4) Unfortunately, only one of her works has survived, the statue of William Pitt, the Elder, which she completed in 1799. (5) This statue can now be seen in Westminster Abbey.

EXERCISE 2 *(pages 296–297)*

(1) Cocoa and chocolate are favorite desserts in Europe and the United States. (2) The United States, England, Germany, the

Netherlands, and France now import four-fifths of the world's chocolate. (3) Where did chocolate originally come from? (4) Five hundred years ago, this confection was totally unknown in Europe. (5) This fact may seem amazing. (6) Hernando Cortez explored Mexico in the early sixteenth century. (7) The Aztecs drank a dark frothy beverage called *chocolatl.* (8) The beans that were used to make the drink were regarded as a gift from the gods. (9) Today, chocolate lovers can understand why the Aztecs considered this delightful sweet to be a divine gift. (10) Wealthy people can even buy a sculpture of themselves for several hundred dollars made by an exclusive candy shop in New York City.

EXERCISE 3 *(page 297)*

(1) Every summer, many people head for the beach. (2) They lie in the sun, thinking a tan will look great. (3) However, scientists call sun bathing a hazardous activity. (4) It carries great risks, including premature aging, eye damage, and immune system damage. (5) These are not the greatest threats, however. (6) Medical experts agree that ultraviolet rays from the sun are the chief cause of skin cancer.

EXERCISE 4 *(page 298)*

(1) The cheetah is[B] the world's fastest mammal. (2) Both its speed and its rate of acceleration are[B] amazing. (3) It runs[A] at a maximum speed of sixty to sixty-three miles per hour. (4) In addition, the cheetah accelerates[A] from a standing start to a speed of forty-five miles per hour in two seconds. (5) After about three hundred yards, however, the exhausted cheetah stops[A] suddenly. (6) The chase is[B] over.

EXERCISE 5 *(page 299)*

(1) The *Fanny Farmer Cookbook* is[B] now quite famous. (2) In 1896, however, Little, Brown Publishing Company refused[A] the

manuscript. (3) Finally, Farmer raised the money and paid the publishing costs herself. (4) Over the years, her book has sold millions of copies. (5) It is now known throughout the world and has been translated into more than thirty different languages.

EXERCISE 6 *(page 300)*

1 After he **wrote** his first book, Jarvis Norton was filled with regret.

2 The man who had **taught** him to write was included as a minor character.

3 Norton **gave** the character a different name than his teacher's.

4 Nevertheless, a friend commented to the author, "I **see** you've put our old friend in your book."

5 Unfortunately, the book shows the sad truth: In his old age, the teacher **became** an alcoholic.

EDITOR'S FOCUS 1

AVOIDING SENTENCE FRAGMENTS

Proofreading Evaluation Exercise 1A (pages 300–301)

A war now rages between the defenders of animal rights and the scientists who support using animal subjects for medical experiments. Some animal rights activists who belong to an organization known as People for the Ethical Treatment of Animals (PETA) claim that medical experimenters are as cruel as Nazis. During World War II, as most people know, doctors in concentration camps carried out incredibly painful experiments on the human inmates. The public must decide whether or not to accept the comparison made by PETA members and then what action to take concerning this stunning accusation. Of course, we must consider also the beliefs of medical doctors concerning animal research. According to a survey of the American Medical Association, conducted in 1988, 97 percent of doctors support it.

Proofreading Evaluation Exercise 1B: Identifying and Correcting Fragments (pages 303–304)

1 Many people fear failure.

(Not a fragment)

2 Which they define as loss of self-esteem, of money, or of social status.

(Fragment; combine with sentence 1: *Many people fear failure, which they define as a loss of self-esteem, of money, or of social status.*)

3 If you are one of these people, help is available.

(Not a fragment)

4 Experts such as psychiatrists, medical doctors, and even financial advisers.

(Fragment; combine with sentence 5: *Experts such as psychiatrists, medical doctors, and even financial advisers recommend certain basic strategies to help you cope with feelings of failure.*)

5 Certain basic strategies are recommended to help you cope with feelings of failure.

(Not a fragment, but has been combined with sentence 4)

6 First, experts suggest eliminating the word "failure" from your vocabulary.

(Not a fragment)

7 Replacing it with "setback," "glitch," or even "challenge."

(Fragment; combine with sentence 6: *First, experts suggest eliminating the word "failure" from your vocabulary and replacing it with "setback," "glitch," or even "challenge."*)

8 Next, you should stop blaming and berating yourself.

(Not a fragment)

9 Because other people are likely to accept as true the image you have of yourself.

(Fragment; combine with either sentence 8 or sentence 10: *Next, you should stop blaming and berating yourself because other people are likely to accept as true the image you have of yourself.* Or *Because other people are likely to accept as true the image you have of yourself, you should make every effort to be financially prepared for unexpected difficulties.*)

10 You should make every effort to be financially prepared for unexpected difficulties.

(Not a fragment; might be combined with sentence 9)

11 Money buys time.

(Not a fragment)

12 Which may well give you the opportunity to evaluate your situation carefully and, therefore, to act intelligently.

(Fragment; combine with sentence 11: *Money buys time, which may well give you the opportunity to evaluate your situation carefully and, therefore, to act intelligently.*)

13 Finally, caring friends and relatives who can be your most essential resource during difficult times.

(Fragment; *Finally, caring friends and relatives can be your most essential resource during difficult times.*)

14 If you remember these strategies, you'll be able to face nearly any obstacle life can offer.

(Not a fragment)

EDITOR'S FOCUS 2

AVOIDING FUSED SENTENCES AND COMMA SPLICES

Proofreading Evaluation Exercise 2A (pages 305–306)

When Hannah Snell's husband left her and their daughter in 1744, the deserted wife set out to find him. First Hannah disguised herself in her brother's clothes. Then she left London and headed for Coventry. She found no trace of her husband; instead she found a new life. Using her brother's name, Hannah Snell enlisted in General Guise's regiment of the British Army. She called herself James Gray. After being punished unjustly, Hannah deserted from the army. She fled to Portsmouth and, continuing to pose as her brother, enlisted as a marine. Hannah, who was thought to be a young boy because of her clean-shaven face and small size, was admired by the other marines for her mending and cooking skills. In combat, however, she fought fiercely. She received six wounds in a battle against the French in India. One of the wounds was in her lower body. Fearing that treatment of that wound would lead to discovery of her true sex, she cut open the wound and removed the musket ball herself. Finally, Hannah met a man who knew her husband's fate. He told Hannah that her husband had been arrested for murder; then he was executed. Hannah's quest was over. When the ship next docked in England, she revealed that she was a woman. She immediately received a marriage proposal from a shipmate who admired her. Hannah refused because she valued her freedom highly. For the rest of her life, she was successful as an actress who most often played male roles.

Proofreading Evaluation Exercise 2B: Identifying and Correcting Fused Sentences and Comma Splices (pages 310–311)

1 A dog may be a man's best friend**;** a man may be a dog's best friend.

2 The Earl of Bridgewater, who lived in Paris in the 1820s, kept twelve dogs as house pets.
(Correct)

3 Each night, he ordered his finest dining table set with elegant china. **I**n addition a red silk napkin was provided for each guest.

4 The guests were his twelve pet dogs**, and** each sat in a chair while a servant tied the silk napkin around its neck.

5 According to those who observed the strange dinner parties, the dogs behaved perfectly.
(Correct)

6 They usually ate carefully from their plates **like** perfect ladies and gentlemen.

7 Sometimes, however, one dog would become greedy and steal from another's plate, **or** perhaps another would snarl at one of the waiters.

8 The next evening, the offender was not allowed to attend the dinner party**;** however, he or she was still served at a table and still wore the red silk napkin.

9 Following the dinner parties, Lord Bridgewater invited his dogs to ride in his carriage through the streets of Paris.
(Correct)

10 To be sure their feet didn't get dirty, he provided boots for his pets.
(Correct)

11 The boots were made of the finest leather**, and** each dog had a different pair for each day of the year.

12 Lord Bridgewater lined up the boots in the hall**;** then he used them to count the passing days of the year.

EDITOR'S FOCUS 3

CHECKING SUBJECT-VERB AGREEMENT

Proofreading Evaluation Exercise 3A (page 312)

(1) Children in the current decade **watch** more television than ever before. (2) The young child and the teenager **are** equally affected by television programming. (3) A recent study by the Council on Children, Media, and Merchandising shows amazing statistics. (4) During an average ten months' time, 3,832 advertisements for sugared cereal **appear** on weekend daytime television. (5) During the same time period there **are** 1,627 commercials for candy and chewing gum. (6) On the other hand, advertisements for meat or poultry appear only twice. (7) Vegetables and cheese **are** each advertised once. (8) Every concerned parent and teacher in this country **knows** that

children or the average teen is swayed by the constant bombarding of such advertising. (9) Experts agree that the worst part of such advertising **is** the long-term effects on young people's eating habits. (10) An adult's diet and nutrition are profoundly affected by what the individual learns during the early years of life.

Proofreading Evaluation Exercise 3B: Identifying and Correcting Problems with Subject-Verb Agreement (pages 316–317)

1 Fifty years ago, the average family in the United States **was** supported by one breadwinner.

2 Today, nearly 27.7 million American households **have** two breadwinners.

3 What **are** the causes and effects of this dramatic change?

4 Either increased expenses or the women's movement **motivates** many of the wives who now work outside the home.

5 There **are** many employed women who continue to shoulder the primary responsibility for household tasks.

6 In two-income families, the man typically has a larger voice in major household decisions than **does** the woman.

7 For instance, wives often move to other cities to help their husbands' careers.
(Correct)

8 Few men, however, in the same situation **move** to help their wives' careers.

9 A wife, on the average, **earns** only 62 percent as much as her husband when each **works** full-time.

10 The family with two employed parents often takes their vacations separately.
(Correct)

11 Often neither the husband nor the wife **finds** enough time for leisure pursuits.

12 Nevertheless, women are growing more confident of their knowledge and abilities, and men are learning to share family responsibility and power.
(Correct)

EDITOR'S FOCUS 4

CHECKING PRONOUN REFERENCE AND AGREEMENT

Proofreading Evaluation Exercise 4A (pages 318–319)

(1) In 1987, monkeys made their place in the news. (2) **While on duty at Kennedy International Airport,** John Schneider, an A.S.P.C.A. animal-care technician, got a call from a frantic security guard. (3) **The guard** reported that monkeys were loose among the passengers disembarking from one plane. (4) Needless to say, **these animals** were causing a riot. (5) Schneider eventually captured the monkey he had identified as the leader and put her back in the cage. (6) The other monkeys followed and Schneider reported his success to the guard. (7) This **report,** of course, calmed the agitated passengers. (8) Everyone can agree that **he or she** would not want rioting monkeys to interrupt an air flight. (9) Also in 1987, a monkey on a Soviet space flight made headlines. (10) Good Soviet space trainer**s** make certain their animals are well suited for their journeys. (11) This **trainer,** however, must have made some error. (12) During a satellite flight, one monkey, Yerosha, got his left arm free. (13) **He** then tinkered with everything within his reach. (14) The committee to investigate this disruption said in **its** report that the monkey lived up to his name. (15) In Russian, it means "troublemaker."

Proofreading Evaluation Exercise 4B: Identifying and Correcting Problems with Pronoun Reference and Pronoun Agreement (pages 322–323)

1. Although **physicians are** respected members of the scientific community, they are not responsible for many medical discoveries.
2. Leonardo Da Vinci, an artist who had great scientific curiosity, dissected cadavers and made accurate anatomical drawings. **These drawings** gave medical doctors their first precise pictures of the cavities of the brain.
3. Every modern doctor knows that **he or she** is indebted to Anton van Leeuwenhoek, the Dutch merchant who discovered bacteria, protozoa, and spermatozoa.
4. Either several youthful party-goers or William Clarke, a young chemistry student, deserves **a** place in medical history.
5. Clarke observed friends of his sniffing ether at a party, and he then used the gas for a dental operation.
   (Correct)
6. Louis Pasteur, a French chemist, discovered how to pasteurize milk and also created a vaccine for anthrax and rabies. For this **vaccine,** many people owe him **their** lives.
7. Acupuncture, a respected medical procedure in China, was discovered by the emperor Shen Nung in 2700 B.C. He studied herbs and made a carefully annotated list of those he found most effective.
   (Correct)
8. A professor of mathematics and physics, Wilhelm Roentgen, discovered X rays during an investigation of cathode rays. He called **them** "X" rays because no one then knew the source that caused them.
9. Dutch physicist Heike Omnes surprised his mentor with the unexpected discovery of cryogenics, the quick freezing of blood

plasma. **Omnes** then went on to explain to him the possible applications of this technique to the treatment of Parkinson's disease.

10 Marie Curie and her husband, Pierre, identified the elements polonium and radium. These **discoveries** led to the development of radiotherapy and other valuable medical techniques.

EDITOR'S FOCUS 5

CHECKING VERB TENSE AGREEMENT

Proofreading Evaluation Exercise 5A (pages 324–325)

(1) Do you ever wonder why your favorite television program no longer broadcasts? (2) Why do some shows continue on the air for many years while others go off after only a few weeks? (3) The answer **is** simple: numbers! (4) Sponsors pay for most shows, and of course they want to reach a large audience. (5) They **do** not want to pay for shows that are not popular.

Proofreading Evaluation Exercise 5B: Identifying and Correcting Verb Tense Shifts (page 327)

1 How do sponsors find out how many people watch a program?
(Correct)

2 They hire experts who **do** the counting for them.

3 These experts **do** not call everyone in the country; instead they carefully **contact** a sample of the population.

4 Studying the sample population gives clues about what the whole population watches.
(Correct)

5 The researchers want their sample to be big enough to be accurate, but they **do** not want to spend money contacting an overly large sample population.

EDITOR'S FOCUS 6

CHECKING FOR MISPLACED AND DANGLING MODIFIERS

Proofreading Evaluation Exercise 6A (pages 328–329)

(1) To start an organic garden, farmers will need to understand **only** a few simple processes. (2) Keeping a compost heap throughout the winter, **gardeners will be rewarded with** rich soil for spring planting. (3) **When ordered by mail,** insects that eat garden pests will be an easily accessible help to rural organic farmers. (4) Such insects will play an important role because they will allow the organic farmer to eliminate the use of pesticides. (5) Gathering the harvest in the fall, **the farmer will find worthwhile** all the time and effort spent on the garden.

Proofreading Evaluation Exercise 6B: Identifying and Correcting Misplaced and Dangling Modifiers (pages 331–332)

1 Dating from medieval times, **European monarchies often astonish Americans.**

2 Some Europeans think monarchies should be abolished. (Correct)

3 It's certainly true that the monarchy **with its rituals, lavish ceremonies, and strict class structure** violates the egalitarian principles of democracy.

4 Nevertheless, in this final quarter of the twentieth century, monarchies flourish in Western Europe.
(Correct)

5 Unlike fairy tale kings and queens, **today's royals work hard and lead difficult lives.**

EDITOR'S FOCUS 7

USING QUOTATION MARKS CORRECTLY

Proofreading Evaluation Exercise 7A (page 333)

(1) The United States celebrated its two-hundredth birthday with a **magnificent** celebration. (2) **Newsweek** magazine described this celebration in an article titled "Happy Birthday, America**."** (3) Even the words "lavish" and "spectacular" are too mild to describe the elaborate fireworks displays, the gigantic parades, and the impressive pageants that were held throughout the nation. (4) It was a time for looking at the **bright** side of the American experience. (5) "The hallmark of the American adventure**,"** said President Ford at the dedication of the Smithsonian's new Air and Space museum, "**h**as been a willingness—even an eagerness to reach for the unknown.**"**

Proofreading Evaluation Exercise 7B: Using Quotation Marks Correctly (pages 335–336)

1 In "Daily Lives," a section of the textbook **Nation of Nations,** the authors note that "Europeans acquired their first knowledge of sugar" from their conquests in "the Mediterranean, North Africa, and Spain**."**

2 In the Middle Ages, commoners never tasted sugar, and even royalty asked plaintively, "When is the next shipment due**?"**

3 "Europeans classified sugar as a spice**,"** notes historian James West Davidson.

4 The cooks in castle kitchens tried to outdo each other by creating baked sugar sculptures that were very delicate and, taking their name from the word "subtle," were called subtleties.
(Correct)

5 Davidson states that the "pattern of consumption started to change as Europeans turned to African slave labor to grow sugar for them**";** sugar suddenly became cheaper.

6 Was it the drop in price that made "sugar essential to the poorest Europeans**"?**

7 Whatever the reason, "Sugar became the status symbol of the eighteenth-century middle-class" (Davidson, 56)**.**

8 After using molasses for years, the English working class probably thought tea with sugar was **wonderful.**

9 Today, some experts, including those in the Surgeon General's Office, believe sugar to be a major threat to our health**.**

10 To many of us sweet-tooths**,** that's very sour news!

EDITOR'S FOCUS 8

USING COMMAS CORRECTLY

Proofreading Evaluation Exercise 8A (pages 337–338)

(1) If there were one person who developed the alphabet, that person would probably be the greatest inventor in human history. (2) Books, newspapers, magazines, and journals would be very different without the alphabet. (3) Writing would be possible without the alphabet, but it would not be as accessible and precise. (4) Early peoples, such as the Egyptians and the Babylonians, wrote without an alphabet. (5) They used a form

of writing known as a logographic system. (6) In this system, each symbol represents a word. (7) Chinese, a difficult, complex language, is the most well-known modern, logographic writing system. (8) A third writing system is the syllabic, which is used by the Japanese. (9) This system uses symbols that represent syllables. (10) The three systems exist in countries that seem similar in many other ways. (11) For example, in one corner of the world we find three neighboring countries, China, Japan, and Korea, each using different writing systems. (12) Chinese use the logographic, Japanese the syllabic, and Koreans the alphabetic.

Proofreading Evaluation Exercise 8B: Using Commas Correctly (page 342)

1 Over 100 million Americans**,** including two-thirds of all adults**,** now wear glasses.

2 Nearly another 10 million regularly use contact lenses.

3 Of course**,** we all should be grateful for the invention of glasses.

4 Corrective lenses rank among the most significant, useful discoveries of all time, such as printing, paper**,** electricity**,** and atomic power.

5 Remember, however**,** that eyeglasses were not commonly worn anywhere in the world until about 450 years ago.

6 It's hard to imagine life without the possibility of glasses**,** isn't it?

7 In ancient times, many aging scholars had to give up reading, but those who were wealthy could pay others to read for them.

8 Lenses existed in ancient Rome**,** but they were used only for burning.

9 Medical reporter James Sayed**,** Ph.D.**,** says**,** "Early Anglo-Saxons advised persons with poor vision to comb their heads, eat little meat, and drink wormwood before meals."

10 Fourth-century Italians (who studied the stars carefully) believed that a person who looked directly at a falling star would go blind.

EDITOR'S FOCUS 9

USING COLONS, SEMICOLONS, AND APOSTROPHES CORRECTLY

Proofreading Evaluation Exercise 9A (pages 343–344)

(1) Locks are used to guard many things**:** homes, cars, bicycles, desks, jewelry boxes, and even diaries. (2) A good lock is like love**:** it must not be forced. (3) With the proper use of the proper key, a lock should open and close easily. (4) Law-abiding people admire a good lock**;** a thief regards it as a challenge. (5) **Thieves** have no respect for other **people's** property**;** however, a good lock can sometimes teach them respect.

Proofreading Evaluation Exercise 9B: Using Colons, Semicolons, and Apostrophes Correctly (page 348)

1 The progress of human history has seen a continual improvement of the ingenuity of two **professions:** the locksmith and the burglar.

2 The battle of wits is not over**;** as the locksmith creates new locks, the burglar invents new ways to open them.

3 Most ancient peoples lived in communities where homes were small**;** friends, relatives, and neighbors were close by**;** and strangers were regarded with hostility, anger, and suspicion.

4 These people did not need locks**;** they lived simply and securely.

5 Early civilizations used locks to prevent unauthorized entry to sacred places**;** however, those locks were often ineffective.

6 An ancient **Egyptian's** lock usually consisted of a vertical wooden bar fixed to his doorpost and a wooden crossbar or bolt.

7 To open such locks required the following steps**:** inserting a key through the hole in the bolt, levering the key upward, pushing the pins of the key through matching holes in the bolt, turning the bolt to release the bar from **its** holder.

8 Early Greeks' and Egyptians' homes were different.

9 The typical Egyptian home had many exposed windows**;** however**,** the Greeks' homes faced protective courtyards.

10 In Egypt, **thieves'** movements could be controlled by locked doors.

EDITOR'S FOCUS 10

USING THE ELLIPSIS, THE DASH, AND PARENTHESES CORRECTLY

Proofreading Evaluation Exercise 10A (page 350)

(1) Clothing styles for women—especially working women—have changed radically during the past hundred years **(**1890–1990**).** (2) In *Nation of Nations,* the authors note that Elizabeth Cady Stanton—a noted feminist—"commended bloomers to all busy wives and mothers. . . ." (3) Stanton was primarily interested in making work easier for overburdened, usually lower-class, women. (4) Other feminists **(**for example, Sarah Grimké**)** saw "dress reform as essential to **. . .** equality of the sexes."

Proofreading Evaluation Exercise 10B: Using Ellipses, the Dash, and Parentheses Correctly (pages 353–354)

1 During the pre–Civil War years, slaves received food rations only once a week—with no exceptions for illness or childbearing.

2 Rations**—**predictable and boring**—**varied little from plantation to plantation.

3 Each adult slave received the following items: **(**1**)** a peck of cornmeal, **(**2**)** three or four pounds of bacon or salt pork, and **(**3**)** some molasses for sweetening.

4 According to the authors of *Nation of Nations,* slaves often "tended their own vegetable gardens after work **. . .**" (476)**.**

5 Gardening allowed slaves "to sell their surplus to the master or to town's people . . ." and then use the money they received to buy other items.

EDITOR'S FOCUS 11

USING CAPITAL LETTERS CORRECTLY

Proofreading Evaluation Exercise 11A (page 355)

(1) On **A**pril 10, 1849, a New York **n**ative, Walter Hunt, **M.D.,** was granted a patent for a device he called a **s**afety **p**in. (2) Hunt was not destined to be called the inventor of the **s**afety **p**in, however, since devices similar to it had been in use since the days of **a**ncient Greece. (3) Dr. Hunt is quoted as saying, "**T**he safety pin should have made me rich!" (4) In spite of his protests, the **d**octor never made a penny on his invention. (5) The story of his life was recently broadcast on **PBS.**

Proofreading Evaluation Exercise 11B: Using Capital Letters Correctly (page 357)

1 In 1896 on the **s**ixth of June, a carpenter, George Harbo, and a plumber, Frank Samuelson, left New York Harbor in an **e**ighteen-foot **r**owboat.

2 Staunch members of the Republican **p**arty, then often called the **GOP** for "grand old party," **H**arbo and Samuelson were cheered by members of a Republican **c**lub from their hometown in New **J**ersey.

3 Although the **s**pring weather brought rain, the pair rowed diligently for approximately eighteen hours **p**er **d**ay.

4 On **J**uly 15, they were picked up in the **m**iddle of the Atlantic Ocean by a **f**reighter.

5 When their water was replenished, they continued rowing and after

fifty-**s**ix days at sea they landed on an island off the **c**oast of England.

6 Later, they published an article called "**T**he Impossible Journey."

EDITOR'S FOCUS 12

SPELLING WORDS CORRECTLY

Proofreading Evaluation Exercise 12A (pages 358–359)

(1) A **favorite leisure** pursuit for many people is attending the circus. (2) Everyone loves the elephants and the **monkeys,** but the most popular act **may be** the clowns. (3) In circus slang, every clown is called a "Joey," a nickname that is **supposed** to come from Joseph Grimaldi. (4) Grimaldi was a clown who performed in London, where he **achieved** great popularity. (5) In the early 1800s, when Grimaldi **appeared,** Londoners would give him **their** full attention. (6) Although Grimaldi lived **to** a ripe old age, his **first performance** was **almost** his last. (7) His parents, both circus stars, had their twenty-three-month-old son, Joey, play the **role** of a monkey. (8) In one scene, Joey's father swung his **son** around on a **chain.** (9) When the **chain** broke, the little boy **sailed** out into the crowd. (10) **Fortunately ,** he landed in the lap of a fat, old **gentleman** and so lived to become famous and give his name to **generations** of future **clowns.**

Proofreading Evaluation Exercise 12B: Spelling Correctly (page 362)

1 The **great tenor** Enrico Caruso was in the **middle** of a **performance** in San **Francisco** on **April** 17, 1906, when the famous earthquake **occurred.**

2 As **chimneys** toppled and buildings **crumbled,** the **terrified** singer took only one thing from the **opera** house—a **picture** of President Theodore Roosevelt, **personally** autographed **to** Caruso.

3 Later, he tried to get on a **train** with other members of the opera **company,** but the guards, who did not recognize him, **tried** to **separate** him from his **friends.**

4 When Caruso showed his picture of the **president,** he was **issued** a **boarding** pass and was then able to get **to safety.**

APPENDIX C

PREPARING FOR AND TAKING ESSAY EXAMS

ESSAY EXAMS PROVIDE A PRACTICAL opportunity for practicing the combination of reading, writing, and thinking discussed and demonstrated in this text. Doing well on an essay exam provides at least two rewards. One is obvious and immediate—a good grade. The other is less obvious yet long-lasting—the sense of having learned a subject well and of having developed the ability to communicate what you have learned.

(*Note:* For a sample of two well-written essay exams, see pages 99–102.)

As with any other writing experience, the preparation begins long before you actually put pen to paper. Consider the following guidelines.

GUIDELINES: PREPARING FOR AN ESSAY EXAM

1. Take careful notes in class, paying special attention to any terms, charts, or explanations the instructor writes on the board.
2. Review your notes after each class. Ask questions about anything you do not understand, either in class or during a visit to your instructor's office.
3. Read the class assignments before the day they are due and take notes.
4. Notice the relationship between the instructor's lectures and the reading. Ask questions about any connections that do not seem clear to you.
5. If the course includes discussion, come to class prepared to participate actively. Listen to what other stu-

dents say and take notes during discussions. Ask questions about comments that are not clear.

6 Pay careful attention to anything the instructor says in class about what will be on the exam or what form the exam will take.
7 Organize your material for studying by transferring lecture, discussion, and reading notes to notecards and noticing how these notes fit together.
8 Use these notes to predict questions.
9 Jot down notes in outline form to suggest how you would answer the questions you anticipated.
10 Consider forming a study group so that you can compare your anticipated questions and projected responses with those of other students.

Once you have prepared for the essay exam, the next step is to use your writing and thinking skills to communicate what you have learned. Consider the following guidelines.

GUIDELINES: WRITING THE ESSAY EXAM

1 Arrive at the exam a few minutes early so that you can find a seat in a location that will be as comfortable as possible for you.
2 Bring all the materials you need with you (pens, exam booklets, a watch, and any books your instructor allows you to use as part of the exam).
3 Read through the entire exam before you begin writing, noting the directions carefully. (If the instructor only requires you to answer two questions, don't waste time answering them all!)
4 Mark *structuring* words (words that tell you how to organize the essay), paying special attention to exam terminology. (See Guidelines: Exam Terminology, below.)
5 Note the amount of time allowed for writing and plan your answers accordingly. Note also the amount of credit given for each question. Obviously, questions

that are worth more points should, in general, be answered more fully and thus given more time.

6 As you read the exam questions, jot down any ideas that come immediately to mind.

7 Before you begin writing, use your jotted notes to formulate a brief outline including all the major points you must cover.

8 Make sure the points are arranged in an order that makes sense.

9 Begin your essay with a sentence that turns the question into an assertion (a thesis statement).

10 Develop each of the points in your outline.

11 Consult your outline frequently to make sure you stay on the topic.

12 Allow time to revise and proofread briefly. As you revise, reread the question to make certain you have provided all the information required. (For instance, if the question asks for three examples, make sure you did not stop at two!)

GUIDELINES: EXAM TERMINOLOGY

As you read directions for writing an essay exam and as you plan what you will write, be sure you understand the following terms:

Analyze: Examine closely, looking at the parts—or at one part—in relation to the whole.

Attack or defend: Take a stand and make an argument for or against a certain point.

Compare or contrast: Explain similarities or differences or both and explain their significance.

Critique: Consider a subject by showing its strong or weak points or both.

Define: Explain what something means or what something is.

Discuss: Explain, analyze, elaborate, possibly debate. (Caution: This is a vague term. Think carefully what direction you want to take.)

Elaborate: Develop a detailed explanation; provide extra support and details.

Enumerate: List facts or details in order, point by point.

Evaluate: Judge, discuss the pros and cons.

Examine: Provide an in-depth look at the topic. Show all sides and possibilities.

The process of writing exams does not end when you pass your bluebook to your instructor. The final phase of writing the essay exam is evaluation—your own as well as your instructor's. When you get your exam back, consider the following guidelines.

GUIDELINES: EVALUATING THE ESSAY EXAM

1. Whether you are satisfied or dissatisfied with your grade, look for comments that tell you what the instructor considered especially strong. Look for other strengths in addition to those the instructor has mentioned.
2. Whether you are satisfied or dissatisfied with your grade, look for comments that tell you what the instructor believed needed improvement.
3. Make certain you understand the instructor's suggestions for improvement so that you will be able to strengthen your essay exam writing skills in the future.
4. Look for weak places that the instructor might not have mentioned and think about how you will work to eliminate these weaknesses. (For instance, you might have spent too long discussing the first point and then found yourself rushed on the final two points.)
5. Note any comments the instructor has made—negative or positive—that you do not understand and make an appointment to discuss the exam with him or her during office hours.

APPENDIX D

GUIDE TO RESEARCH

THE WORD *RESEARCH* MAY BRING to mind images of scholars toiling late into the night or of scientists working with complex experiments. Of course, scholars and scientists do carry out research. On the other hand, research is not a mysterious process far removed from everyday life. Almost everyone has done research of one kind or another. For instance, someone planning to make a major purchase (like a CD player or a car) usually tries to get information from various sources to find out which brand and which model would make the best choice. A potential car buyer, for example, may question friends about the various brands of cars they own. The buyer may also read a magazine like *Consumer Reports* to see what experts have to say about the brands being considered. Finally, the buyer will almost certainly go to various automobile dealerships, carefully look over the cars, and test drive certain models. Then, based on all of this research, he or she will decide which car to buy.

In the example of the car, note that there are several different kinds of research. The prospective buyer *talks* to other people, *reads* the opinions of experts, and makes personal *observations* and *experiments* (takes test drives). Research, then, is not one simple process, but rather a series of interconnected steps and approaches.

When you are assigned a research paper in a college course, you go through the same steps you take to write any paper. In addition, you use some or all of the research processes described above. No two research projects are exactly alike, so you need to pay close attention to the instructions you are given. In planning and writing a research paper, it is particularly important to have the purpose of the paper clearly in mind. For instance, is your professor asking you to gather information from various sources and then to explain your subject using those sources? Or does the assignment ask you to go beyond explaining? Are you, for instance, being asked to investigate a controversial issue, then take a stand, and use your research to support and argue for that position?

The second kind of paper (requiring taking a position) is commonly assigned in many disciplines. The remainder of this appendix follows one student as she works through such an assignment.

Planning a Researched Argument

This case study suggests the process followed by one student, Elaine Harrad. Not every researched argument you write will require every step, but if you understand each decision Elaine faces and each choice she makes, you'll have a useful set of possibilities for developing your own strategy, tailor-made to fit your assignment.

FINDING A TOPIC Elaine's English Composition instructor asked class members to discover a campus issue about which they felt genuine concern. They were then to research the issue, develop a strong stand, and finally write an argument defending their view of the issue.

Journal Entries When Elaine first received the assignment, she wrote the following journal entry.

> It's not that I don't care about things, and it's not that I don't see things to worry about on campus. The parking lot next to the Student Union is too dark at night. Lines for signing up for classes—then not getting the classes. Food in the commuter cafeteria. Too much fried stuff. Not enough choice of salads. But I can't write an argument—what would I say, that there should be more salad ingredients? Too boring. That just sounds silly. But as a nutrition major, I think about the food stuff a lot. And I've read so many scary things about what we eat and how bad the American diet is. But maybe the parking lot would be easier to do. Help!

Elaine's instructor made this note in the margin of her journal:

> Sounds like you're really interested in the nutrition angle—maybe try a few days of observing and note-taking in the cafeteria?

Observation and Conversations Following this suggestion, Elaine spent several hours during the next week in the cafeteria, sampling different foods, sitting at different tables, and talking to people, both cafeteria workers and cafeteria customers. One of the students who worked in the cafeteria mentioned that the food service was going to try something new because a lot of students, like Elaine, were concerned about too much fat in their diets. The cafeteria manager had decided to make some desserts using an artificial sweetener so that students would have a choice of "diet" desserts or "nondiet."

As she left the cafeteria, Elaine kept thinking about this comment. She hadn't said anything to the cafeteria worker, but she thought this decision was rather strange. It didn't really address the problem of too much dietary fat. Also, Elaine kept thinking about a television program she had seen that said something about dangers of artificial sweeteners.

Listing Here's part of the journal entry Elaine wrote in response to her cafeteria observations:

> I keep wondering about the "diet" desserts. People will still be eating more or less empty calories. Also, what about this program on TV. I keep trying to remember—there were problems—
>
> Depression
> Vision problems
> Headaches
> Sleep problems
> Birth defects
>
> But how do I prove this? Also what's my point? That they shouldn't make the desserts? Should I write to the TV station? Help (again)!

Elaine's instructor was impressed with the list she made and also with the way she was asking herself questions. Instead of responding directly to the "help" request, the instructor wrote in the margin of the journal: "Good questions to raise when we work in groups today."

After getting her journal back and reading the instructor's comment, Elaine had plenty of material to discuss when she met with the other three students who were part of her writing group for this project.

Collaborative Brainstorming Members of the group collaborated on narrowing the topics for their arguments and on finding a clear central focus—a main idea. Here's a transcript of part of the discussion that was particularly helpful to Elaine:

Elaine So I don't know whether to write to the television station or what. I don't know whether I think the cafeteria should not make the desserts with artificial sweetener or not, but it's a definite concern for me.

Dom Would it make a difference what artificial sweetener—I think there's different ones—maybe you should talk to the person who directs the cafeteria and find out. Also you could ask about the whole nutritional thing—dietary fat, what you said—and the director would definitely be an expert to quote.

Kate I would say, "Go to the library." I mean, I agree with Dom, about talking to the director, but first you should read some stuff on artificial sweeteners so you'll sound like you know what you're talking about.

PATRICE But she *does* know what she's talking about. From her nutrition course stuff. At least she knows to have a question about artificial sweeteners. I'd say, the director first, find out if they really are going to do this "light cooking" and then if they are, the library.

DOM So, if they are, then you might be arguing, like, that the cafeteria should not use artificial sweeteners because . . .

ELAINE I don't know—maybe that—or maybe notifying people what's in the puddings and stuff—maybe something like "The commuter cafeteria should not use artificial sweeteners that may be harmful" or "that have some dangerous effects"—something like that.

EXERCISE 1 *Choose a topic of interest to you that could be a legitimate subject for argument. For instance:*

Drunk driving laws
Suicide hot lines
Physical contact sports for young children
Mandatory labeling for record albums
Medical experiments on live animals
Flag burning
Campus racism
Paid parental leave (for childbirth and childcare)

Using one or more of the strategies just described (writing journal entries, having conversations, making observations, listing, collaborative brainstorming), explore that topic to discover specific controversial questions related to the subject.

NARROWING THE TOPIC AND PROPOSING A TENTATIVE MAIN IDEA When Elaine left her writing group, she knew that she needed to focus her topic more clearly. She had two steps in mind, the interview and the exploratory trip to the library. First, she called the director of Commuter Food Services and asked for an appointment to talk to him about the new "diet" desserts she had heard about. The director, Paul Lessard, said he'd be glad to talk to her.

INTERVIEWING Elaine's English instructor had discussed strategies for interviews, so Elaine knew that she should arrive for the interview on time and that she should write down the questions she wanted to ask. She prepared the following list:

1. Is the cafeteria going to offer "diet" desserts?
2. If so, why did you make this decision?
3. What kind of sweeteners, if any, will be used in these desserts?

4 Are there any dangers to using these sweeteners?
5 Have you considered any alternatives?

When Elaine arrived at his office, Paul Lessard invited her to sit down. She asked him if she could tape record the interview, and although he was a bit reluctant at first, he agreed. Elaine also took brief notes to remind herself of the key points of the interview. The following transcript of part of the conversation demonstrates a very important interview technique—the ability to follow up on a comment, even if it takes you away from the set pattern of questions. Elaine had just asked Paul what sweetener they would be using.

PAUL We'll be using "Sweet 'n' Tastee."
ELAINE I think I've heard something about that—it's a brand name for aspartame, isn't it?
PAUL Yes, I think so. Why?
ELAINE That would be something I'd want to know if I were going to eat those desserts.
PAUL Why would you want to know that?
ELAINE Because some of those sweeteners have dangerous side effects.
PAUL Well, this sweetener is used very widely. It's considered very safe.
ELAINE Yes, but still, wouldn't you put out a sign to label what you use?
PAUL Well, we can't list ingredients on everything!
ELAINE No, but this may be different.
PAUL I don't see the need.

When Paul mentioned the name of the sweetener, Elaine recognized it as a brand name for aspartame, an artificial sweetener she had heard about. Because of her interest, Elaine did not simply jump right along on her list to her next question. Instead, she pursued the idea of labeling and only then did she go on to the next point on her list.

INCUBATION On the way back to her car, Elaine kept going over the interview in her mind. She thought about everything she already knew about artificial sweeteners and about what Paul had said, but she still wasn't sure what the main idea—the thesis—of her argument would be. She was beginning to feel frustrated, so she put her notes away for the night and put the problem of the argument in the back of her mind.

The next morning, as she drove to school, Elaine realized that her argument might focus on providing information to student consumers rather than banning the "diet" products entirely. If aspartame really was as safe as Paul claimed, she might not argue against its use. Instead, she might propose something like this tentative main idea:

> The new commuter cafeteria "diet" desserts should be labeled so that students know they will be eating the artificial sweetener aspartame as part of that delicious low-calorie chocolate mousse.

EXERCISE 2 *Plan and carry out an interview related to your chosen topic. Follow the same process Elaine used (make an appointment, make a list of questions, arrive on time, ask permission if you plan to tape record the interview).*

Write a journal entry describing the interview. Explain what you learned about your topic. In addition, discuss what you thought was most useful about the interview and what you would change if you could do the interview over again.

EXERCISE 3 *Considering the work you did to discover a subject and the information you gained from your interview, write a tentative main idea for your researched argument. Remember that a main idea includes both the subject and what you are going to say about that subject.*

LIBRARY RESEARCH As you explore a tentative main idea, you make your own observations and you may conduct interviews, take surveys, or carry out experiments. These are important research strategies. In addition, you usually need to read what experts have to say on your topic. Finding the most recent information often requires several visits to the library.

As you read, you want to find out whether you can support what you believe to be true. Sometimes you may find yourself changing your mind. When this happens, it's important to refocus your argument to fit your new way of thinking. Do not try to force the evidence to fit an argument you no longer believe is true. On the other hand, many times your trips to the library will provide you with just the support you need to develop your argument and make it convincing to your readers.

During orientation week, Elaine had taken a library tour. She now pulled out her information brochure from that tour to review the four essential resources to consider for any project requiring research: *books, periodicals, newspapers*, and *specialized encyclopedias*. She also remembered that the guide on the library tour had told them the one absolutely essential rule to remember when doing research was this:

> *When in doubt, ask a librarian!*

Books To find books, Elaine knew she would use the computerized card catalogue that lists and indicates the location of every book owned by the library. Some libraries still have the card catalogue in a file cabinet with many small drawers, but most are replacing these with computerized systems. Whether they are in a file cabinet or in a computer system, the listings are arranged alphabetically. Each book is listed under its title, its author, and its subject.

Elaine went to the library with a particular book in mind. Her nutrition professor had mentioned in class a book called *The Nature of Life.* He said this book had a useful chapter on aspartame and human genetics. In the card catalogue, Elaine found the listing for *The Nature of Life,* so she knew her library owned the book. She also found out that the authors of the book were John H. Postlethwait and Janet L. Hopson and that the book was published in 1989. She was pleased that the date was recent so that the research represented would be up to date.

As part of the listing, Elaine found this combination of letters and numbers:

QH
308.2
P67

Elaine knew from her library tour that the first letters (the QH) indicated the category of the book and that all books in that category would be on the same floor. She knew that her library had a chart that would tell her where to find the floor where the "Q" books were located. Then she followed the letters and numbers of the book's call number to find it on the shelf.

Example of Title Card from Card Catalogue

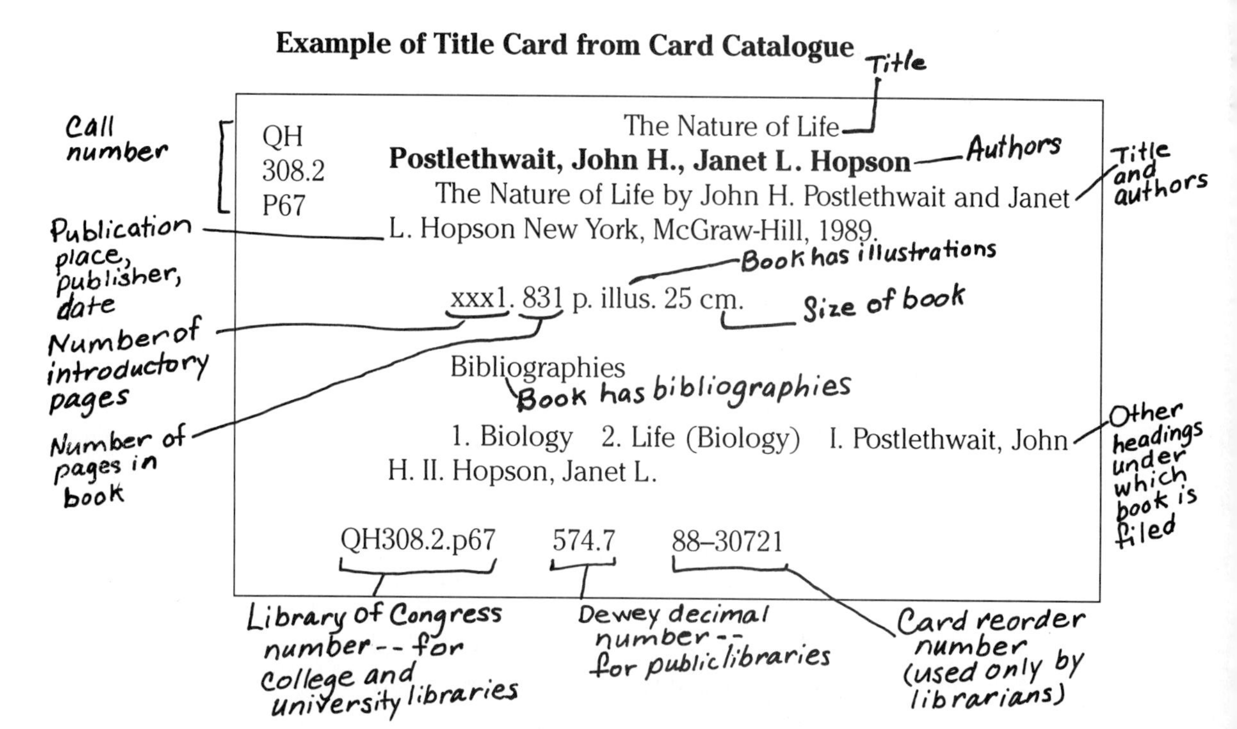

EXERCISE 4 *Go to the library and find a book that relates to your subject. If you do not find anything in the card catalogue under your specific subject, try a broader topic. For instance, you might not find a card for "campus racism," so try "racism" instead. If you still find nothing, ask the librarian to suggest possible subject areas.*

When you find the book, scan the table of contents and check the index to see whether it would be helpful to developing a researched argument on the main idea that is your focus. Write a journal entry explaining the process you went through to find the book and explaining why you do or do not think it would provide information relevant to your topic.

Periodicals Almost everyone knows that books can be found in libraries. However, when professors start saying things like, "Be sure to consult the periodicals" or "I want you to use appropriate journals," many students are baffled. *Periodicals* is a term meaning any publication that is issued on a regular basis (that is, any publication that appears "periodically"). For example, a magazine like *Time* or *Newsweek* is a periodical. In addition, every academic discipline has publications that are issued, for example, every month or four times a year. These periodicals are called *journals*.

Elaine had learned about periodicals on her library tour, but now she needed to know how to find periodicals related to her topic. She knew that some periodicals are bound into hard covers and kept on shelves while others are stored on microfilm or microfiche. What worried her was how she could ever find the time to look through hundreds of issues of various periodicals. Elaine asked a librarian whether magazine and journal articles would be listed in the card catalogue. The librarian told her they would not, but then she explained an extremely helpful shortcut.

Periodical indexes, the librarian told Elaine, allow readers to find what they are looking for without spending hours leafing through the pages of journals and magazines. One periodical index for commonly read magazines like *Time* is *The Reader's Guide to Periodical Literature.* But it's important to know that every academic discipline has its own index. For instance, there are *The Education Index, The Social Sciences Index, The Humanities Index,* and *The Business Index.* Some libraries hold these indexes in book form; others have them on discs that can be used with computer systems.

The company that prepares these indexes subscribes to all the important journals in the various academic disciplines. Then the company hires people to go through each issue of these journals and abstract the subjects, titles, authors, dates of the journal issue, and page numbers where the article can be found. The editors of the indexes take all this information and compile it, arranging the data alphabetically according to subject matter. They publish a new volume each year, as well as monthly or quarterly supplements to provide updated information.

Elaine asked the reference librarian which periodical index would list articles on issues of food and nutrition. The librarian recommended *The Social Sciences Index*, and Elaine looked in the most recent supplements under the heading "aspartame." When she didn't find anything of interest listed in the recent supplements, she moved to the most recent yearly, bound volume and found under "aspartame" several articles that sounded promising. Elaine wrote down all the information and then asked the librarian how to interpret it.

Example of Entry in Periodical Index

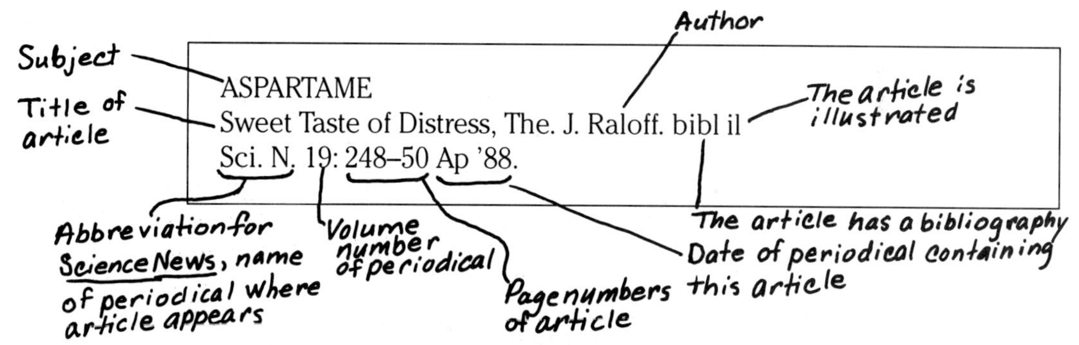

The librarian showed Elaine how to use the explanations in the front of each volume of the indexes. These explanations show how to interpret the listings in the index. Next, the librarian reminded Elaine that she had to check the library's "List of Periodical Holdings" to see whether that library had the magazines and journals she wanted to find.

The periodical indexes provide listings from every important journal in the field or discipline they cover. Not every library can subscribe to all those magazines. So it's important to check your library's "List of Periodical Holdings" to see whether they have the periodical you want *before* you go looking for it. The "List of Periodical Holdings" will also tell you when the library began subscribing, whether and when they stopped their subscription, and where the periodicals that the library does hold can be located (on shelves, on microfiche, or on microfilm, for example).

Elaine was able to find several articles in her library, including a particularly helpful short commentary in *Science News,* titled "The Sweet Taste of Distress." To read this article, which was stored on microfiche, Elaine asked a student assistant to show her how to run the microfiche machine. As she read, Elaine learned that the article described the findings of a psychiatrist, Ralph G. Walton, whose observations led him to connect depression, mood swings, and even seizures with use of aspartame.

Elaine also wanted to find some articles in journals that her library did not have. The librarian explained to Elaine how to get copies of articles—or to borrow books—through the *interlibrary loan system.* Most libraries belong to an interlibrary loan system. Understanding how to use these services provides you with options you might have thought were closed to you.

GUIDELINES: FINDING PERIODICAL ARTICLES

1. Go to the reference room of the library.
2. Ask the librarian which index(es) or on-line (computer-assisted) search strategies would be relevant to your topic.
3. Locate the periodical indexes.
4. Start with the most recent volume of the index(es) you are using.
5. Use the explanation in the beginning of the index to learn how to use it.
6. Look up your subject (subjects are listed in alphabetical order).
7. Write down any references that look as though they might be useful (remember to copy all the information: author, title of article, title of periodical, volume, date, and page numbers).
8. Repeat the process with other volumes or other indexes.
9. Check your library's "List of Periodical Holdings."
10. Locate those articles that are in periodicals to which your library subscribes.
11. Learn to use the microfilm and microfiche machines, if necessary, to read the articles you find.
12. Learn the process you would follow if you wanted to call an article from another library. (Ask a reference librarian or a library assistant.)

EXERCISE 5 *Using the topic you have chosen, go to the library and use the periodical indexes to find two articles that you think would be helpful. Consult the guidelines on this page. Write a journal entry explaining your process. Be sure to describe any problems or "detours" you took as you were looking for relevant information.*

EXERCISE 6 *Give a brief summary of the two articles you found for Exercise 5 and explain why you think they would or would not be helpful to developing your researched argument.*

Newspapers Elaine knew that newspapers could also provide information that might be relevant to her topic. The guide on her library tour had mentioned that the library had an index for *The New York Times.* This index lists all the articles that have appeared in *The New York Times,* arranging the articles in alphabetical order according to their subject. One volume of this index is published each year, and in addition, supplements are issued each month.

Like the periodical indexes, *The New York Times Index* has a guide in the beginning of each volume to explain how to understand the listings. Elaine studied the explanation carefully and then started looking for information.

As with the periodical indexes, she started with the most recent edition because she wanted the most up-to-date information on her topic. Starting with the most recent edition is the standard process. However, if you were researching a historical topic—for instance, the Kennedy assassination—you might start with the index that covered the year of the event (1963, in the case of the Kennedy assassination).

When Elaine looked in the 1989 volume of *The New York Times* under "aspartame," she found an article titled, "New Findings Back Use of Sweetener." Although the title suggested that the article might not support her theory concerning the potential danger of aspartame, Elaine decided to read it. She knew that it is essential to investigate all points of view on a topic. She hated facing the thought that the new evidence might make her change her main idea, but she wanted to be fair. In addition, she recognized that to write a strong argument, she had to understand any evidence opponents of her stand might use to refute her contention.

Because libraries hold *The New York Times* on microfilm (except for the most recent issues), Elaine knew she would have to use the microfilm reader. Before she went to the files where *The New York Times* microfilm was kept, she wrote down all the information she needed to find her article. She was especially careful to write down the year of the index volume she was using, checking the outside cover to get that information.

> (*Note:* The year of publication for indexed items appears *only* on the outside of *The New York Times Index* volumes. It does not appear as part of the inside listing. Be sure to check the cover of the volume and write down the year. You need this information to find the microfilm.)

When Elaine read the article, she discovered that scientists at the University of Illinois College of Medicine had run experiments leading them to believe that aspartame did not cause seizures in laboratory animals. Nevertheless, the article quoted an expert, Dave Hattan (chief of regulatory affairs for the Food and Drug Administration's Food Safety Center), who noted that other laboratories had found evidence to the contrary. Hattan also urged that tests be held on humans to "end the debate." This information helped Elaine to see the challenges that might logically be made to her main idea, but she also came up with some information (a quotation from an expert) to refute those challenges and to support her main idea.

GUIDELINES: FINDING INFORMATION IN *THE NEW YORK TIMES*

1. Go to the reference room of the library.
2. Locate *The New York Times Index.*
3. Begin with the most recent edition of the index (unless you are researching a historical topic).
4. Use the explanation in the beginning of the index to learn how to use it.
5. Look up your subject (subjects are listed in alphabetical order).
6. Write down any references that look as though they might be useful (remember to write down all relevant information: title of article, author, section, page, column in newspaper, and *especially* the date, *including the year,* which is found *only* on the outside of the index).
7. Repeat the process with other volumes of the index.
8. Find the storage location for *The New York Times* microfilms.
9. Use the microfilm reader to read the articles and decide on their usefulness.
10. Be aware that some microfilm readers allow you to make copies (ask a librarian or library assistant how the copying function works).

EXERCISE 7 *Using the topic you have chosen, go to the library and use* The New York Times Index *to locate an article that you think would be relevant. Consult the guidelines on this page. Use the microfilm reader to discover what information you might use. Write a journal entry explaining your process. Be sure to note any problems you encountered and discuss how you solved those problems. Briefly sum-*

marize the article you found and explain why you think it would or would not be useful for writing an argument on the topic you chose.

Specialized Encyclopedias The final source Elaine consulted at the library was a specialized encyclopedia. Like most people, Elaine had used general encyclopedias, like the *Encyclopaedia Britannica,* many times. Before she went on the library tour, however, she was not aware of the many specialized encyclopedias that deal with very specific topics and subject fields. A few of the specialized encyclopedias that Elaine found most interesting were these:

Encyclopedia of Artificial Intelligence
Encyclopedia of Feminism
Encyclopedia of Mental Health
Encyclopedic Handbook of Alcoholism
Foods and Nutrition Encyclopedia

There are hundreds of other specialized encyclopedias; these titles provide only a brief sample of the many topics they cover.

Because she wanted to find a definition for "aspartame," Elaine looked in the card catalogue under "nutrition" to find the call number of the *Foods and Nutrition Encyclopedia.* The call number had the letter "R" written above it, so Elaine knew that she had to go to the reference room. In fact, all the specialized encyclopedias are in the reference room, and like all books in the reference room, they do not circulate. You have to use them at the library.

Elaine found the *Foods and Nutrition Encyclopedia* easily. She knew that subjects were listed alphabetically, and when she found "aspartame" she was very pleased to discover much more than a definition. She found a description of the research that had been done on the safety of aspartame (through 1987). In addition, she wrote down this quotation: "In the United States, a label statement is required to alert parents of children with the metabolic disease phenylketonuria of the presence of phenylalanine (present in aspartame), which must be restricted in their diets." Elaine was gratified to find this precedent for labeling foods that contain aspartame.

GUIDELINES: USING SPECIALIZED ENCYCLOPEDIAS

1 Ask your librarian if there is a list of your library's specialized encyclopedias (if possible, keep a copy for ready reference).

2 Use the card catalogue to find encyclopedias relevant to the field you are investigating.
3 Write down the name of the encyclopedia as well as the call number.
4 Locate the encyclopedia (remember that it will be in the reference room).
5 Look up your subject by following alphabetical order.

EXERCISE 8 *Using the topic you have chosen, locate a specialized encyclopedia relevant to your subject. Look up a term related to your subject that you want to define or to know more about. Write a journal entry summarizing the information you found in the specialized encyclopedia. Explain how you might use this information in developing an argument on your topic.*

TAKING AND ORGANIZING NOTES Once Elaine had completed her library research, she looked over the information she had gathered. She had the tapes from the interview with Paul Lessard as well as some notes she had made while they were talking. In addition, Elaine had checked several books out of the library. She had also photocopied articles from journals and newspapers as well as significant sections from the *Foods and Nutrition Encyclopedia* (because journals, newspapers, and reference books cannot be taken out of the library). When she made the photocopies, she was careful to write all the information about the source right on the photocopy (author; title of article; title of journal, newspaper, or encyclopedia; volumes; dates; and pages). She wrote this information because she knew she would need it later for her Works Cited list and also for giving credit for any quotations within her paper. (See Appendix E: Documenting Sources.)

Now that she had all this raw material, she needed to take more specific notes. She listened to the interview tape and wrote down relevant quotations, making sure to be totally accurate. Next, she read parts of the books (she used the tables of contents and the books' indexes to help her find relevant sections). Elaine made careful notes. Sometimes she summarized in her own words; sometimes she wrote down direct quotations.

Finally, Elaine read the photocopied articles and sections from the encyclopedia. Because she owned the photocopies, she could underline particularly useful parts and also make notes to herself in the margins. Then she transferred some of the information she had underlined onto notecards. Sometimes she summarized and sometimes she quoted directly. Here are three sample notecards. Notice that Elaine made a Works Cited card so that she did not have to recopy all the information each time she quoted from or summarized a source.

Raloff	Works Cited
	Raloff, John. "The Sweet Taste of Distress." Science News. 19 April 1988: 248–250.

Raloff	Paraphrase and quotation
	Ralph G. Walton—psychiatrist, Jamestown, NY, General Hospital—found evidence "that aspartame can cause a marked rise in certain brain chemicals involved in mood and behavior."
	Page 248

Raloff	Paraphrase
	Walton thinks high intake aspartame brings on seizures! manic symptoms in some of his patients.
	Page 248

After Elaine took all the notes she believed were important, she sorted through the notecards and began putting them in categories. She tried different arrangements, but finally ended up with this organization:

- One pile of cards described the situation (using aspartame in cafeteria desserts with no warning label) and defined terms.

- One pile of cards explained problems with aspartame.
- One pile of cards offered evidence defending aspartame.

Sorting the cards this way helped Elaine to see several different possibilities for organizing her argument effectively. After considering several options, she decided to open by explaining the problem and making her proposal:

> Desserts made with aspartame should carry warning labels.

Next she decided to offer evidence supporting her claim. Then she would acknowledge evidence defending aspartame, and she would respond to that evidence. Finally, she would write a conclusion emphasizing how important she believed the labeling to be.

EXERCISE 9 *Using the sources that you discovered in Exercises 2, 4, 5, 6, 7, and 8, take notes on notecards and organize them in several different ways that would be useful for writing a researched argument on your topic. Write a journal entry describing the options you developed for organizing your information.*

Evaluating Audience

Before she began to write, Elaine thought about her readers. She was writing this paper for her English class, so the professor was certainly part of the audience. She also hoped to get the argument published in the school newspaper, so the college community—particularly commuters—must also be considered. Finally, she wanted to convince Paul Lessard that her proposal made sense. He was the person, after all, who could actually make changes based on the evidence she provided. Elaine knew that she should consider the interests, the biases, and the knowledge of her readers. She believed that her English professor and the college community as a whole would have only general knowledge of aspartame. Paul Lessard knew a great deal more about aspartame, but to address all her readers, Elaine would have to define this artificial sweetener as well as explain the research that had been carried on regarding aspartame.

Elaine believed that her professor and the college community as a whole would have some interest in the safety of their food, but they probably would not have strong feelings one way or another about labeling food made with aspartame. Paul Lessard had some interest in the subject of labeling, but he showed resistance to Elaine's proposal. He was not hostile, but he was reluctant, and Elaine knew she would have to work hard to convince him of the validity of her argument.

Like Elaine, you will often find that you have a complex audience rather than one that can be defined as having one specific level of expertise or one common set of biases. Evaluating your audience carefully helps you decide exactly what you must include in your argument to appeal to the largest possible number of readers.

EXERCISE 10 *Consider your topic and the main idea of your researched argument on that topic. Then think of three different audiences for whom you might write that argument. For example, if you were writing on college entrance exams, you might have as your audience prospective college professors, college students, and the students' parents. After determining three possible audiences, write a journal entry describing their differences by considering the following questions.*

1. *What level of knowledge would they have regarding your topic? What would you have to explain to them or define for them?*
2. *What are their values? What do they consider important in life? (For example, are they more concerned with money than with safety—or vice versa?) How might their values relate to your topic?*
3. *What are their interests? How might their interests relate to your topic?*
4. *What are their biases concerning your topic? Will they be friendly or hostile readers?*

Establishing Voice

By the time Elaine finished her research, she was convinced that the cafeteria should label the desserts that contained aspartame. In addition, she felt somewhat annoyed that Paul Lessard—a trained dietician—had been resistant to her suggestion and had brushed off her questions by making the blanket statement that aspartame was very safe. She knew, however, that she wouldn't convince him—or many of her other readers—of the need for labeling if she took an angry, crusading approach. She also tried hard to think about Paul's point of view. Labeling would require extra work and cost extra money; no wonder he resisted her initial suggestion. Elaine recognized that she needed to stand back and take an objective view so that she could write in a calm, firm voice that would show the careful research that supported her conviction.

EXERCISE 11 *Using the audience analysis you made in Exercise 10, write a journal entry explaining the voice you would use to write your researched argument for each group of readers. If you would* *change your voice, explain why. If you would not, explain why you think that voice would be appropriate to all three audiences.*

Writing a Researched Argument

After you have done research, taken and organized notes, evaluated audience, and established the voice you will use, you are ready to write the first draft of your argument. To do this, follow the process you have developed through experimenting with the suggestions for writing given in the first four sections of this text.

ORGANIZING Plan the general structure you will use before you start writing. You might simply use the piles of notecards—as Elaine did—or you might jot down a brief, informal outline.

WRITING THE INTRODUCTION The introduction should make both the subject of your argument and your stand on the subject clear. In addition, important terms are often defined in the introduction.

(*Note:* Some writers like to compose the body of their argument first and then return to the introduction. When you are writing a draft, you can begin wherever you find most convenient.)

WRITING THE BODY

- Following your organizational plan, you introduce evidence to support your argument.
- In addition, you consider opposing points of view and explain why your argument still holds true. Sometimes you refute the opposing points; sometimes you simply acknowledge them but show that they do not outweigh the evidence you have offered.
- As you write, you work hard to avoid the problems with logical or emotional appeals described on pages 128–139.

USING DIRECT QUOTATIONS AND PARAPHRASES When you use direct quotations, paraphrases, or facts that are taken from sources other than your own common knowledge, be sure to consider the following points:

1 Using a *quotation* means using the exact words someone else has written or spoken. Using a *paraphrase* means taking someone else's words, changing them very little, and then using the slightly changed words in your paper.

When you use a quotation or a paraphrase, you must always acknowledge your source. Failing to do so is *plagiarism*, which is intellectual dishonesty. Many instructors fail a paper that is guilty of plagiarism. (Consult Appendix E, pages 410–427, for examples of how to set up, punctuate, and acknowledge direct quotations and paraphrases.)

2 When you quote or paraphrase, do not simply drop the words into the paper without letting your reader know both the source and the relationship between the quotation or paraphrase you are making and your topic.

For example, consider the difference in these two paragraphs, the first taken from Elaine's draft and the second from the final copy.

Draft: Quotations Not Clearly Integrated

> "Aspartame can cause a marked rise in certain brain chemicals involved in mood and behavior" (Walton 248). High intake of aspartame triggered seizures and manic symptoms in several patients. This theory is backed up by the research of other scientists. Aspartame can bring on "associated with depression, sleep disorders, vision loss and seizures" (Wurtman 22).

Final Copy: Quotations Clearly Integrated

> In an article in *Science News,* John Raloff notes that Ralph G. Walton, a psychiatrist at Jamestown, N.Y., General Hospital, has found evidence "that aspartame can cause a marked rise in certain brain chemicals involved in mood and behavior" (248). Walton believes that high intake of aspartame triggered seizures and manic symptoms in several of his patients. Walton's theory is backed up by the research of other scientists. For example, Richard Wurtman, an endocrinologist at M.I.T., has done animal studies that "have linked aspartame to changes in the brain associated with depression, sleep disorders, vision loss and seizures" (22).

Commentary In the final copy, the first quotation is introduced with the name of the person being quoted and an explanation of his qualifications. This is one way of introducing a quotation.

To introduce the second quotation, the name of the person being quoted and his qualifications are added. In addition, the structure of the sentence has been changed so that Elaine's words and the quoted words work together to form a logical sentence.

When you use quotations, keep the guidelines below in mind.

GUIDELINES: USING QUOTATIONS

1 Introduce or follow the quotation with your own explanatory words so that it fits smoothly with what you are writing. For instance:

As anthropologist Janis Hayes notes, ". . ."
". . . ." argues Paul Goodman in his highly praised book, *Treatise.*

2 Make sure your words and the words of the person you are quoting fit together logically.

NO: Janis Hayes's argument makes sense for some people "professions that require higher education."
YES: Janis Hayes's argument makes sense for some people whose work will "require higher education."

3 Use Appendix E (pages 410–427) to learn how to give credit to your source.
4 Use Appendix E (pages 410–427) to learn how to write a Works Cited list acknowledging your sources.

WRITING THE CONCLUSION As with any essay, article, or report, the conclusion should follow logically from the details, reasons, and examples that have been provided to support your main idea. In a researched argument, the conclusion often does one of the following:

- Sums up the evidence presented, closing with the strongest piece of evidence
- Makes specific proposals for instituting a reform or taking a recommended course of action
- Makes a plea for considering a point of view that had previously been ignored or rejected without fair or full evaluation
- Urges a new definition—or a broader or narrower definition—for a controversial term

Revising

Revising an argument requires all the steps for revising any piece of writing. (See, for example, Section 1, pages 24–30, Section 4, pages 147–150, and Appendix A, pages 289–291.) As you revise an argument, pay careful attention to the special aspects of argument that have been introduced in this appendix. Ask yourself—or your peer editor or writing group—the following questions:

1. Do I make clear the subject and point of view (thesis) of my argument?
2. Do I show that I have evaluated my audience accurately?
3. Have I responded to that evaluation by establishing a convincing voice and by providing information my readers need to know?
4. Have I presented enough evidence to make my argument convincing? Do I need more evidence? Should I eliminate evidence that is repetitive or weak?
5. Have I fully considered and addressed opposing views?
6. Have I avoided problems with logical or emotional appeals?
7. Does my conclusion follow logically from the evidence I've presented?
8. Have I proofread and edited accurately? (See Appendix A, pages 289–292.)

Elaine followed all these steps. She revised her argument twice, following suggestions from her English professor and from her writing group. In addition, she went back to the library to get additional information on tests run by the Food and Drug Administration. After writing, revising, and proofreading, Elaine submitted copies of the following final paper to her professor, to the campus newspaper, and to Paul Lessard.

EXERCISE 12 *As you read Elaine's essay, make annotations indicating what you see as strengths. In addition, note where you see weaknesses and explain any changes you would suggest for writing a revision.*

BITTER SWEET

Most humans crave sweets even though the front page is full of the dangers of being overweight, and the fashion magazines feature ultra-slim models. What we all wish for is a way to eat a butterscotch pudding or a chocolate eclair without adding empty calories to our diets. In an effort to fulfill that wish, the campus cafeteria has decided to provide a new line of "diet" desserts made with the sweetener aspartame. Technically, aspartame is "not an artificial sweetener since it is composed of two amino acids, phenylalanine and aspartic acid, which are natural constituents of proteins in such foods as milk, eggs, and meat" (*Foods and Nutrition Encyclopedia* 156). Nevertheless, since many experts have questioned the effects of aspartame on human beings, the cafeteria should clearly label any desserts containing this substance.

In an article in *Science News,* John Raloff notes that Ralph G. Walton, a psychiatrist at Jamestown, N.Y., General Hospital, has found evidence "that aspartame can cause a marked rise in certain brain chemicals involved in mood and behavior" (248). Walton believes that high intake of aspartame triggered seizures and manic symptoms in several of his patients. Walton's theory is backed up by the research of other scientists. For example, Richard Wurtman, an endocrinologist at M.I.T., has done animal studies that "have linked aspartame to changes in the brain associated with depression, sleep disorders, vision loss and seizures" (22). Wurtman also believes that medical doctors should be aware that these side effects could develop in their human patients. Since many experts believe that people can experience negative effects from eating foods or drinking beverages with aspartame, it seems only fair to notify those who eat at the cafeteria what foods contain that sweetener.

More important than the side effects described by Walton and Wurtman are the disastrous effects aspartame can have on people born with a rare genetic disease called phenylketonuria or PKU (Postlethwait and Hopson 260). People born with this disease "lack the enzyme to metabolize the amino acid phenylalanine" (Postlethwait and Hopson 261). Because of this lack, PKU sufferers cannot eat or drink products with phenylalanine, a major component of aspartame. If they do eat or drink phenylalanine, they can become mentally retarded. For this reason, the U.S. Food and Drug Administration has ordered that soft drinks with aspartame must have a warning label. Even though very few people have PKU disease, any who do should have the chance to know what they are eating. A warning label on the cafeteria "diet desserts" would give them this warning.

Campus Food Service Director Paul Lessard said in an interview that aspartame is widely used and considered very safe. His point is backed up by an article in *The New York Times* stating that Philip Jobe, chairman of the Department of Basic Sciences at the University of Illinois College of Medicine, questioned one of the tests of aspartame performed on rats who later suffered seizures. Jobe noted that the rats "were prone to seizures and were likely to suffer seizures anyway" ("New Findings" 30:6). However, another expert, Dave Hattan, chief of regulatory affairs for the Food and Drug Administration's Food Safety Center, said, "Other laboratories have models in which there appears to be an enhancement of seizure expression"

("New Findings" 30:6). Since there is still disagreement among experts, certainly it would be wise to let students, faculty, and staff know what they are eating when they reach for that low-calorie dessert.

Providing such labeling would cost the cafeteria extra time and money, but that could be paid for by charging a higher price for the new desserts. Since students pay separately for desserts anyway, this process should not cause any serious difficulty. We all have the right to make choices about our own health. Labels on food containing aspartame would insure that we make informed, knowledgeable decisions.

Works Cited

"Aspartame." *Foods and Nutrition Encyclopedia.* 1983.

Corey, Joseph. "Sweetest Game in Town." *U.S. News and World Report.* 22 July 1988: 22–24.

Lessard, Paul. Personal interview. October 13, 1989.

"New Findings Back Use of Sweetener." *New York Times.* 16 August 1987, I 30.

Postlethwait, John H., and Janet L. Hopson. *The Nature of Life.* New York: McGraw, 1989.

Raloff, John. "The Sweet Taste of Distress." *Science News.* 19 April 1988: 248–250.

EXERCISE 13 *After reading the description of Elaine's process, write a researched argument defending the main idea you developed on your topic. Use Elaine's paper as a model. Notice that she uses direct quotations from her research to support her argument. Note also that she documents her quotations and that she provides a Works Cited list. To help with documentation and with compiling your own Works Cited list, see Appendix E.*

APPENDIX E

DOCUMENTING SOURCES (MLA AND APA FORMATS)

MANY WRITERS LOOK AT DOCUMENTING sources as a formidable chore. In fact, giving credit to your research sources is really a remarkably mechanical task that simply requires attention to detail and the ability to follow an example. Although some experienced researchers do memorize a few basic documenting formats, most writers in the academic and professional worlds keep lists (such as those that follow) near at hand to guide them.

For those of you who may have learned to use footnotes or endnotes to acknowledge your sources, there is good news. Since 1986, the Modern Languages Association (MLA)—originator of the documentation style used by the humanities—has recommended a simplified format. Their format is now similar—but not identical—to the American Psychological Association (APA) style that is used by the social sciences. Because these two formats are among the most widely used by both academic and professional writers, sample entries are provided here.

CAUTION Because there are many styles of documentation besides MLA and APA, when you are writing a paper or proposal requiring research, whether in a class or at work, make sure to ask the person assigning the task what style you should use. Some professors have their own preferred formats, and many companies provide their employees with "style sheets" demonstrating the form they require.

MLA Documentation Within the Paper

Whenever you paraphrase or directly quote someone else, whether your source is an interview, a book, a magazine, or a newspaper, you must let your reader know that you are using your source's ideas. Here's how you do that, using MLA style.

Using and Documenting the Source: MLA Format

Original Source for the First Four Examples

Statistics are often used to demonstrate educational decay, but let's consider our literacy crisis through the perspective provided by another set of numbers. In 1890, 6.7 percent of America's fourteen- to seventeen-year-olds were attending high school; by 1978 that number had risen to 94.1 percent. In 1890, 3.5 percent of all seventeen-year-olds graduated from high school; by 1970 the number was 75.6 percent.

from Mike Rose, *Lives on the Boundary*, page 6.

1 *Using a brief quotation, mentioning the author's name:*

Mike Rose notes that statistics are frequently cited "to demonstrate educational decay" (6).

Because you give the author's name in the introduction to the quotation, you document it simply by giving the page number from which you took the quotation. Place the page number *after* the quotation marks, *within* parentheses, *before* the ending punctuation.

2 *Using a brief quotation without mentioning the author's name:*

We must remember that by 1978 the number of high school graduates "had risen to 94.1 percent" of young people in America, aged fourteen to seventeen (Rose 6).

Because you do not give the author's name, it must appear in parentheses along with the page number. Use only the author's last name. If there are two different authors with the same last name, use both first and last name—for example (Robert Browning 72) or (Elizabeth Barrett Browning 89). If you are quoting more than one source by the same author, use an abbreviated title (often the first word—other than "a," "an," or "the") to identify the work—for example (Rose, *Lives* 6).

3 *Using a paraphrase, summary, or statistic:*

Mike Rose urges us to think about the reported decay of education in this country by remembering that in 1890 only 6.7 percent of young people ages fourteen to seventeen were attending high school while by 1978, 94.1 percent attended (6).

Even though none of Rose's sentences or phrases is quoted directly, the writer uses this author's statistics and ideas. Therefore, credit must be given. Because Rose's name is mentioned, only the page number (in parentheses, before the final punctuation) is necessary. If the author's name were not mentioned, his last name would appear within the parentheses just before the page number (Rose 6).

4 *Using a longer quotation:*

Those who are concerned with the supposed decline in standard test scores should consider the following:

> Statistics are often used to demonstrate educational decay, but let's consider our literacy crisis through the perspective provided by another set of numbers. In 1890, 6.7 percent of America's fourteen- to seventeen-year-olds were attending high school; by 1978 that number had risen to 94.1 percent. In 1890, 3.5 percent of all seventeen-year-olds graduated from high school; by 1978 the number was 75.6 percent. (Rose 6)

When you quote more than four typed lines, indent the quotation ten spaces. Use the normal right margin. *Omit the quotation marks.* The final citation appears within parentheses *after the final mark of punctuation.* If the author's name is not given in the introduction to the quotation, it must be included in the citation. If the author's name is given, provide only the page number.

5 *Using a quotation from an unsigned source (for instance, an unsigned newspaper article):*

Original Source

Saudi Arabia said yesterday it will pump an extra 2 million barrels of oil daily if its OPEC partners refuse to increase production to meet global shortages caused by the Iraqi invasion of Kuwait.

from "Saudis ready to help cut oil shortage," *Boston Globe,* August 19, 1990, p. 10.

The *Boston Globe* noted that Saudi Arabia offered to "pump an extra 2 million barrels of oil daily" ("Saudis" 10).

Because the article has no author's byline, use an abbreviated title (often the first word other than "a," "an," or "the") and the page number in parentheses.

6 *Using a source written by two or more people:*

If the source is written by two or three people, use all authors' names. For instance, if your source is *Elements of Style* by William

Strunk and E. B. White, you would use the following citation formats.

The careful writer will make certain to "omit useless words" (Strunk and White 54).

or

Strunk and White advise the careful writer to "omit useless words" (54).

If the source is written by more than three people, use only the name of the first person listed, followed by et al. (*Note:* "et" is not an abbreviation; it is the Latin word for "and." Therefore, do not use a period after "et" but do use one after "al.," which is an abbreviation for the Latin *alia,* meaning "others.")

For instance, if your source is *Nation of Nations* by James West Davidson, William Gienapp, Christine Leigh Heyrman, Mark Lytle, and Michael Stoff, you would use the following citation formats:

Of course, we must remember that immigration "had been disrupted by the Napoleonic Wars in Europe" (Davidson et al. 251).

or

As Davidson et al. remind us, we must remember that immigration "had been disrupted by the Napoleonic Wars in Europe" (251).

Compiling a Works Cited List: MLA Format

If you are used to the old MLA footnote style of documentation, you may be wondering how your reader would use the brief, parenthetical citations just demonstrated to locate such information as the publisher, the place of publication, and the date of publication.

That information can easily be found in the Works Cited list, which appears at the end of the paper. (See the argument paper using sources, page 409, for an example of a Works Cited list.) Because the entries in the Works Cited list are arranged alphabetically, the reader can quickly find the full reference.

In the old MLA form, the paper ended with the bibliography (a list of all materials consulted or quoted). The Works Cited list is basically like a bibliography, but in it you include *only the works from which you quote, paraphrase, summarize, or abstract statistics.* In other words, only those sources that you have *already cited in parentheses* appear. You *do not* list every source you consulted.

The following sample entries show how to write Works Cited entries for the sources most commonly used in academic writing. If you are using a source not listed here, you will need to consult a more extensive handbook or style guide like *The McGraw-Hill Handbook*.

SAMPLE ENTRIES

1 *Book by one author:*

Rose, Mike. Lives on the Boundary. New York: Penguin, 1989.

- The name of the author comes first.
- The author's last name is first, then a comma, then the first name and middle initial (if any).
- Titles of books are underlined or in italics.
- The author's name, the title, and the place of publication are separated by periods.
- The place of publication, the publisher's name, and the date of publication follow the title.
- The place of publication is separated from the publisher's name with a colon.
- The date of publication is separated from the publisher's name with a comma.
- The second and subsequent lines of entries are indented five spaces.
- A period ends the entry.

2 *Book by two or three authors:*

Bunnin, Brad, and Peter Beren. Author Law and Strategies.
   Berkeley: Nolo, 1983.

(The first author's name appears in reversed order, but the second [and third, when there is one] appear in standard order.)

3 *Book by more than three authors:*

Davidson, James West, et al. Nation of Nations. New York:
   McGraw, 1990.

(Note that publishers' names are abbreviated. For instance, "McGraw" instead of "McGraw-Hill." Usually, you use only the first name listed as the abbreviation ["Holt" for "Holt, Rinehart, and Winston"; "Prentice" for "Prentice-Hall"].)

4 *Book with an editor:*

Sterba, Günther, ed. The Aquarium Encyclopedia. Cambridge:
   MIT P, 1983.

5 *Two or more books by the same author:*

Gardner, Howard. Frames of Mind: The Theory of Multiple Intelligences. New York: Basic Books, 1985.

___. The Mind's New Science: A History of the Cognitive Revolution. New York: Basic Books, 1983.

6 *Works in an anthology or collection:*

Bambara, Toni Cade. "What It Is I Think I'm Doing Anyhow." The Writer on Her Work. Ed. Janet Sternberg. New York: Norton, 1980.

Brontë, Charlotte. Jane Eyre: Authoritative Text, Backgrounds, Criticism. Ed. Richard J. Dunn. 2nd ed. New York: Norton, 1987.

(When there is more than one edition of a book, list the edition number and give the publication date of that edition.)

7 *Multivolume work:*

Graves, Robert. The Greek Myths. 2 vols. New York: Braziller, 1967. Vol. 2.

(The number of volumes should be cited *before the place of publication.* If you only cite one volume, write the number of that volume at the end of the entry as shown.)

8 *Article from a monthly or bimonthly magazine:*

Schell, Jonathan. "Our Fragile Earth." Discover Oct. 1989: 44–50.

(The name of the article appears in quotation marks, the name of the magazine is underlined or in italics, and the pages on which the article appears follow the date.)

9 *Article from a weekly or biweekly magazine:*

SIGNED ARTICLE:

Will, George F. "Jim Florio's Left Jab." Newsweek 16 July 1990: 68.

(The day of publication precedes the month.)

UNSIGNED ARTICLE:

"Do American Farmers Need New Handouts?" Newsweek 16 July 1990: 22.

(The title of this article ends with a question mark. The question mark stands as the final mark of punctuation for that part of the entry. Do not add a period before going on to list the name of the magazine.)

10 *Article from a professional journal that pages each issue separately (each new issue begins with page 1):*

Johns, Ann M. "The ESL Student and the Revision Process." Journal of Basic Writing 5.2 (1986): 70–80.

(The volume number, then the issue number, and finally the date of the issue [in parentheses] follow the name of the journal.)

11 *Article from a professional journal that pages issues continuously throughout the year (that is, issue one of 1990 might begin with page 1 and end with page 330; issue two, then, would begin with page 331, and so on):*

Bergmann, Harriet F. " 'Teaching Them to Read': A Fishing Expedition in The Handmaid's Tale." College English 51 (1989): 847–854.

(The words "Teaching Them to Read" appear within single quotations because the author uses quotation marks in her title. The Handmaid's Tale is underlined because it is the title of a book and the author of the article thus underlined it in her title. When you cite a title, follow the author's punctuation exactly.)

12 *Article in a newspaper:*

SIGNED:

Dumanoski, Dianne. "Higher Oil Imports Seen As Reagan Legacy." Boston Globe 19 Aug. 1990: 10.

UNSIGNED:

"Saudis ready to help cut oil shortage." Boston Globe 19 Aug. 1990: 10.

13 *Editorial:*

"Environmentalists on Safari." Editorial. Eagle-Tribune [Greenville, MN] 6 March 1989: 9.

(The place of publication is provided because the city or town is not part of the title of the newspaper like the *Boston Globe* or the *New York Times.*)

14 *Letter to the Editor:*

Loomis, Tristan. "Return to the Bad Old Days." Letter. Washington Post 21 March 1990: A68.

(The "A" that precedes the page number is the section number of the paper.)

15 *Article from an encyclopedia:*

SIGNED:

Camras, Marvin. "Acoustics." Funk and Wagnalls New Encyclopedia. 1986 ed.

(Often encyclopedia articles are signed at the end with initials. You have to look at the beginning of the first volume for instructions on finding the list giving the names of contributors to match the initials.)

UNSIGNED:

"Acheans." Funk and Wagnalls New Encyclopedia. 1986 ed.

16 *Interview:*

TELEPHONE:

Cranston, Carolyn. Telephone interview. 8 December 1989.

PERSONAL:

Baroody, John. Personal interview. 27 December 1989.

17 *Published letter:*

Frost, Robert. Letter to Louis Untermeyer. 11 Nov. 1915. The Letters of Robert Frost to Louis Untermeyer. Ed. Louis Untermeyer. New York: Holt. 1963.

18 *Unpublished letter:*

Cain, Rebecca. Letter to the author. 6 Aug. 1941.

19 *Government publications:*

United States Post Office Department. Bureau of Operations. Directory of Post Offices. Washington: GPO, 1987.

(If a government publication has no author given, use the government agency as the first item in the entry. If the agency has more than one part, separate the parts with periods. Use GPO as the abbreviation for Government Printing Office.)

20 *Lectures or speeches:*

Smeal, Eleanor. Speech. Rivier College. Nashua, NH. 12 October 1988.

Assembling the Works Cited List: MLA Format

When you have collected all the items for your Works Cited list, you arrange them alphabetically according to the first word in the entry. Here is how a selection of the examples listed above would look if they were arranged in a Works Cited list.

Works Cited

"Acheans." Funk and Wagnalls New Encyclopedia. 1986 ed.

Cranston, Carolyn. Telephone interview. 8 December 1989.

Davidson, James West, et al. Nation of Nations. New York: McGraw, 1990.

"Do American Farmers Need New Handouts?" Newsweek 16 July 1990: 22.

Gardner, Howard. Frames of Mind: The Theory of Multiple Intelligences. New York: Basic Books, 1985.

___. The Mind's New Science: A History of the Cognitive Revolution. New York: Basic Books, 1983.

Johns, Ann M. "The ESL Student and the Revision Process." Journal of Basic Writing 5.2 (1986): 70–80.

Rose, Mike. Lives on the Boundary. New York: Penguin, 1989.

Smeal, Eleanor. Speech. Rivier College. Nashua, NH. 12 October 1988.

GUIDELINES: WORKS CITED LIST—MLA

- Leave double spaces between entries and between the lines in each entry.
- Begin the first line of each entry at the margin; indent the second and subsequent lines five spaces.
- Arrange items in alphabetical order, according to the first item in the entry.

(In the case of the two books by Howard Gardner, the alphabetizing mechanism becomes the item following the author's name. Because "a," "an," and "the" are not considered for the purpose of alphabetizing, look at the words "Frames" and "Mind's." Since "F" comes before "M," the entry with the title that begins with the word "Frames" comes before the entry with the title that begins with the word "Mind's.")

APA Documentation Within the Paper

When you are using American Psychological Association (APA) format, the following examples provide models for you to use whenever you paraphrase or directly quote someone else, whether your source is an interview, a book, a magazine, or a newspaper. Notice that although APA format is similar to MLA, it is not exactly the same.

Using and Documenting the Source: APA Format

The original source for the first four examples below appears on page 411.

1 *Using a brief quotation, mentioning the author's name:*

Mike Rose (1989) notes that statistics are frequently cited "to demonstrate educational decay" (p. 6).

(When you mention the author's name, provide the date of publication in parentheses immediately after the name. Provide the page number at the end of the sentence within parentheses, before the final sentence punctuation, and with the abbreviation p. [for page] or pp. [for pages] before the number.)

2 *Using a brief quotation without mentioning the author's name:*

We must remember that by 1978 the number of high school graduates "had risen to 94.1 percent" of young people in America, aged fourteen to seventeen (Rose, 1989, p. 6).

(Because you do not mention the author's name, it must appear in parentheses along with the year and the page number *the first time you cite that author.* After the first citation, give only the author and the page. Use only the author's last name.

Exceptions: If there are two different authors with the same last name, use first and middle initials as well as last names. If you are quoting more than one source by the same author, written in the same year, call the first work [according to alphabetical order] "a," the second "b," and so forth. Then use those letters to identify the source [Rose, 1989a].)

3 *Using a paraphrase, summary, or statistic:*

Mike Rose (1989) urges us to think about the reported decay of education in this country by remembering that in 1890 only 6.7 percent of young people ages fourteen to seventeen were attending high school while by 1978, 94.1 percent attended.

When you paraphrase or summarize, APA format requires that you credit the author and provide the date for the first citation of that author. The page is not generally required, although you should check with instructors on this matter.

4 *Using a longer quotation:*

Those who are concerned with the supposed decline in standard test scores should consider the following:

> Statistics are often used to demonstrate educational decay, but let's consider our literacy crisis through the perspective provided by another set of numbers. In 1890, 6.7 percent of America's fourteen- to seventeen-year-olds were attending high school; by 1978 that number had risen to 94.1 percent. In 1890, 3.5 percent of all seventeen-year-olds graduated from high school; by 1978 the number was 75.6 percent. (Rose, 1989, p. 6)

When you quote more than forty words, indent the quotation five spaces. Use the normal right margin. *Omit the quotation marks.* The final citation appears within parentheses *after the final mark of punctuation.* If the author's name is not given in the introduction to the quotation, it must be included in the citation. If the author's name is given, provide only the page number. If the citation is the first one for that source do one of the following:

- When the author's name is mentioned, put the publication date in parentheses following the name.
- When the author's name is not mentioned, give the last name, the date, and the page number in parentheses at the end of the quotation, following the final mark of punctuation (Rose, 1989, p. 6).

5 *Using a quotation from an unsigned source (for instance, an unsigned newspaper article):*

ORIGINAL SOURCE: SEE MLA EXAMPLE, PAGE 412

The Boston Globe noted that Saudi Arabia offered to "pump an extra 2 million barrels of oil daily" ("Saudis," p. 10).

Because the article has no author's byline, use an abbreviated title (often the first word other than "a," "an," or "the") and the page number in parentheses.

The title of an article or essay appears in quotation marks. The title of a book is underlined or italicized.

6 *Using a source written by two or more people:*

If the source is written by two people, use both authors' names. For instance, if your source is *Elements of Style* by William Strunk and E. B. White, you would use the following citation formats.

The careful writer will make certain to "omit useless words" (Strunk & White, 1985, p. 54).

or

Strunk and White advise the careful writer to "omit useless words" (1985, p. 54).

Do not forget to include the date when writing the first reference to any source.

Note that APA allows the use of the ampersand (&) to connect the two authors' names in a parenthetical citation.

If a work has from three to five authors, use all the authors' last names in the first reference. In subsequent references, use only the last name of the first author followed by "et al."

If the source is written by more than five people, use only the name of the first person listed, followed by "et al." for all citations.

Compiling a References List: APA Format

Readers of papers using APA format find further information about sources cited in the text by consulting the References list that appears at the end of the paper. Just as with the Works Cited list for MLA format, the References list includes *only the works from which you quote, paraphrase, summarize, or abstract statistics.* In other words, only those sources that you have *already cited in parentheses* appear. You *do not* list every source you consulted.

The following sample entries show how to write References list entries for the sources most commonly used in academic writing. If you are using a source not listed here, you will need to consult a more extensive handbook or style guide.

SAMPLE ENTRIES

1 *Book by one author:*

Rose, M. (1989). Lives on the boundary. New York: Penguin.

APA format uses only the author's last name and first initial or first and middle initials. MLA uses both first and last names. APA places the date immediately following the author's name. MLA places the date at the end of the citation.

APA format capitalizes only the first word of titles and subtitles and proper nouns; MLA format capitalizes all words except "a," "an," and "the," and prepositions with three or fewer letters (for example, "on," "for," "of").

2 *Book by two or three authors:*

Bunnin, B., & Beren, P. (1983). Author law and strategies.
Berkeley: Nolo Press.

Each author's name appears in reversed order. Use an ampersand (&) to separate the final name.

3 *Book by more than three authors:*

Davidson, J. W., Gienapp, W., Heyrman, C. L., Lytle, M., &
Stoff, M. (1990). Nation of nations. New York: McGraw-Hill.

List last names and initials of all authors. Give all names and initials in reversed order.

4 *Book with an editor:*

Sterba, G. (Ed.). (1983). The aquarium encyclopedia. Cambridge: MIT Press.

For books with more than one editor, use (Eds.).

5 *Two books or more by the same author:*

Gardner, H. (1983). The mind's new science: A history of the cognitive revolution. New York: Basic Books.

___. (1985). Frames of mind: The theory of multiple intelligences. New York: Basic Books.

List works by the same author in chronological order according to the dates they were published.

6 *Works in an anthology or collection:*

Bambara, T. C. (1980). What it is I think I'm doing anyhow. In J. Sternburg (Ed.), The writer on her work (pp. 153–168). New York: Norton.

APA format does not enclose the title of an essay or article in quotation marks; MLA does require quotation marks.

Brontë, C. (1987). Jane Eyre: Authoritative text, backgrounds, criticism. R. J. Dunn (Ed.), 2nd ed. New York: Norton.

When there is more than one edition of a book, list the edition number and give the publication date of that edition.

7 *Multivolume work:*

Graves, R. (1967). The Greek myths. (Vols. 1–2). New York: Braziller Press.

The number of volumes should be cited *before the place of publication.*

8 *Article from a monthly or bimonthly magazine:*

Schell, J. (1989, October). Our fragile earth. Discover, pp. 44–50.

The name of the article appears without quotation marks, the name of the magazine is underlined or italicized, and the pages on which the article appears follow the name of the magazine, preceded by the abbreviation pp. for pages or p. for page.

9 *Article from a weekly or biweekly magazine:*

SIGNED ARTICLE:

Will, G. F. (1990, July 10). Jim Florio's left jab. Newsweek, p. 68.

The year of publication precedes the month and day.

UNSIGNED ARTICLE:

Do American farmers need new handouts? (1990, July 10).
Newsweek, p. 68.

The title of this article ends with a question mark. The question mark stands as the final mark of punctuation for that part of the entry. Do not add a period before going on to give the date.

10 *Article from a professional journal that pages each issue separately (each new issue begins with page 1):*

Johns, A. M. (1986). The ESL student and the revision process.
Journal of Basic Writing, 5(2), 70–80.

The volume number, underlined or italicized, then the issue number, in parentheses, follow the name of the journal. A comma is placed after the issue number, followed by the page numbers on which the article appears. Do not use the abbreviations p. or pp.

11 *Article from a professional journal that pages issues continuously throughout the year (that is, issue one of 1990 might begin with page 1 and end with page 330; issue two, then, would begin with page 331, and so on):*

Bergmann, H. F. (1989). "Teaching them to read": A fishing
expedition in The handmaid's tale. College English 51.
847–854.

The words "Teaching them to read" appear within quotations because the author uses quotation marks in her title. The handmaid's tale is italicized (or underlined) because it is the title of a book and the author of the article thus italicized it in her title. When you cite a title, follow the author's punctuation exactly.

The volume number follows the title of the magazine or journal and is underlined. A comma is placed after the volume number and the page numbers follow. Do not use the abbreviations pp. or p.

12 *Article in a newspaper:*

SIGNED:

Dumanoski, D. (1990, Aug. 19). Higher oil imports seen as Reagan legacy." Boston Globe, p. 10.

UNSIGNED:

Saudis ready to help cut oil shortage. (1990, Aug. 19). Boston Globe, p. 10.

13 *Editorial:*

Environmentalists on safari. (1989, March 6). (Editorial). Eagle-Tribune (Greenville, MN), p. 9.

The place of publication is provided because the city or town is not part of the title of the newspaper like the *Boston Globe* or the *New York Times.*

14 *Letter to the editor:*

Loomis, T. R. (1990, March 21). Return to the bad old days. (Letter to the editor). Washington Post, p. A68.

The "A" that precedes the page number is the section number of the paper.

15 *Article from an encyclopedia:*

SIGNED:

Camras, M. (1986). Acoustics. In N. H. Dickey (Ed.), Funk and Wagnalls New Encyclopedia.

Often encyclopedia articles are signed at the end with initials. You have to look at the beginning of the first volume for instructions on finding the list giving the names of contributors to match the initials.

UNSIGNED:

Acheans. (1986). In Funk and Wagnalls New Encyclopedia.

16 *Interview: Personal oral communications, such as interviews, are documented only within the paper or article for APA format. They do not appear in the References list.*

17 *Published letter:*

Frost, R. (1963). Letter to Louis Untermeyer. In L. Untermeyer (Ed.), The letters of Robert Frost to Louis Untermeyer (pp. 361–67). New York: Holt, Rinehart, and Winston.

18 *Unpublished letter: Like interviews, unpublished letters are considered personal communications and so are documented only within the paper or article. They are not included in the References list.*

19 *Government publications:*

United States Post Office Department Bureau of Operations (1987). Directory of Post Offices. Washington, D.C.: U.S. Government Printing Office.

If a government publication has no author given, use the government agency as the first item in the entry. If the agency has more than one part, do not separate the parts.

20 *Lectures or speeches:*

Smeal, E. (1988, October 12). Speech presented at Rivier College, Nashua, NH.

Assembling the References List: APA Format

When you have collected all the items for your References list, you arrange them alphabetically according to the first word in the entry. Here is how a selection of the examples listed above would look if they were arranged in a References list.

References

Acheans. (1986). In Funk and Wagnalls New Encyclopedia.

Davidson, J. W., Gienapp, W., Heyrman, C. L., Lytle, M., & Stoff, M. (1990). Nation of nations. New York: McGraw-Hill.

Gardner, H. (1983). The mind's new science: A history of the cognitive revolution. New York: Basic Books.

___. (1985). Frames of mind: The theory of multiple intelligences. New York: Basic Books.

Rose, M. (1989). Lives on the boundary. New York: Penguin.

Smeal, E. (1988, October 12). Speech presented at Rivier College, Nashua, NH.

GUIDELINES: REFERENCES LIST—APA

- Leave double spaces between entries and between the lines in each entry.
- Begin the first line of each entry at the margin; indent the second and subsequent lines three spaces.
- Arrange items in alphabetical order, according to the first item in the entry.

(In the case of the two books by Howard Gardner, the citations are arranged in chronological order according to the date of publication.)

ACKNOWLEDGMENTS

Portions of the following copyrighted works have been reprinted in this book:

DANIEL G. BATES AND FRED PLOG, *Cultural Anthropology.* Copyright © 1990 Daniel G. Bates and Fred Plog. Published by McGraw-Hill, Inc. Reprinted by permission of McGraw-Hill, Inc.

MICHAEL BLUMENTHAL, "A Courage Born of Broken Promises," *New York Times,* July 23, 1989. Copyright © 1989 by The New York Times Company. Reprinted by permission.

SARAH BRADY, "The Case Against Them," *Time,* January 29, 1990. Copyright 1990 The Time Inc. Magazine Company. Reprinted by permission.

SUZANNE BRITT, "That Lean and Hungry Look," *Newsweek,* 1978. Reprinted by permission of the author.

URIE BRONFENBRENNER, "Who Cares for America's Children?" Address presented at conference of National Association for The Education of Young Children, 1970. Reprinted by permission of the author.

LISA BROWN, "Why I Want to Have a Family," *Newsweek,* October 1984. Copyright 1984 Lisa Brown.

J. WARREN CASSIDY, "The Case for Firearms," *Time,* January 29, 1990. Copyright 1990, The Time Inc. Magazine Company. Reprinted by permission.

MARILYN HOLM CHRISTENSEN, "The Teacher Called Me Stupid, Mommy," *Redbook,* October 1989. Copyright 1989.

JOHN COLEMAN, *Blue-Collar Journal.* Copyright © 1975 by John R. Coleman. Reprinted by permission of Collier Associates.

BRENT COLLINS, "Student Indifference Erodes the Public Schools," *Utne Reader,* September/October 1990. Reprinted by permission of Lens Publishing Co., Inc., and the author.

JACQUES d'AMBOISE, "I Show a Child What Is Possible," *Parade Magazine,* August 6, 1989. Copyright © 1989. Reprinted by permission of *Parade* and the author.

JAMES WEST DAVIDSON ET AL., "Clothing and Fashion," from *Nation of Nations.* Copyright © 1990, James Davidson et al. Published by McGraw-Hill, Inc. Reprinted with permission by McGraw-Hill, Inc.

ELEANOR DIENSTAG, "What Will the Kids Talk About? Proust?" *New York Times,* December 24, 1972. Copyright © 1972 by The New York Times Company. Reprinted by permission.

MAURINE DOERKEN, "What's Left After Violence and Advertising?" from *Classroom Combat: Teaching and Television.* Copyright 1983. Reprinted by permission of Educational Technology Publications, Englewood Cliffs, New Jersey.

JOSEPH R. DOMINICK, "Crime and Law Enforcement on Prime Time Television," from *Public Opinion Quarterly,* 1973, volume 37. Reprinted by permission of University of Chicago Press.

ELLEN GOODMAN, excerpt from "Being a Secretary Can Be Hazardous to Your Health." Copyright © 1987, The Boston Globe Newspaper Co./Washington Post Writers Group. Reprinted by permission.

ELLEN GOODMAN, "A Driving Fear." Copyright © 1989, The Boston Globe Newspaper Co./Washington Post Writers Group. Reprinted by permission.

SUSAN GRIFFIN, "Every Woman Who Writes Is a Survivor," from *Made from This Earth: An Anthology of Writings.* Copyright © 1982 by Susan Griffin. Reprinted by permission of HarperCollins Publishers, Inc.

EDWARD T. HALL, *The Hidden Dimensions,* chapter 11. Copyright © 1966 by Edward T.

Hall. Published by Doubleday. Reprinted by permission of Doubleday, a division of Bantam Doubleday Dell Publishing Group, Inc.

ZOE TRACY HARDY, "What Did You Do in the War, Grandma?" *Ms.* Magazine, August 1985. Copyright 1985.

JOHN S. HOPPOCK, "The Costs of Drinking," *New York Times,* July 1, 1981. Copyright © 1981 by The New York Times Company. Reprinted by permission.

ROBERT JASTROW, *The Enchanted Loom.* Copyright © 1981 by Reader's Library, Inc. Reprinted by permission of Simon & Schuster.

SUZANNE BRITT JORDAN, *see* Suzanne Britt.

PATRICIA KEEGAN, "Playing Favorites," *New York Times,* August 6, 1989. Copyright © 1989 by The New York Times Company. Reprinted by permission.

JOHN KELLMAYER, "Students in Shock." Published by Trend Publications. Copyright © 1990 by Townsend Press. Reprinted by permission of John Kellmayer and John Langan.

JOMO KENYATTA, *Facing Mount Kenya.* Reprinted by permission of Martin Secker and Warburg, Ltd.

MARTIN LUTHER KING, JR., "I Have a Dream." Speech presented in Washington, D.C., August 28, 1963. Copyright 1963 by Martin Luther King, Jr., renewed 1991 by Coretta Scott King. Reprinted by permission of Joan Daves Agency.

MAXINE HONG KINGSTON, "Girlhood Among Ghosts," from *The Woman Warrior.* Copyright © 1975, 1976 by Maxine Hong Kingston. Reprinted by permission of Alfred A. Knopf, Inc.

ANN LANDERS, "What Do Children Owe Their Parents?" *Family Circle,* September 1, 1978. Copyright 1978.

LIEBERT ET AL., *The Early Window.* Reprinted by permission of Pergamon Press, Ltd.

CHRISTINE LUBINSKI, "Alcohol Warning Labels Are Long Overdue," *USA Today,* November 14, 1989. Copyright 1989, USA TODAY. Reprinted by permission.

CAMPBELL R. McCONNELL AND STANLEY L. BRUE, *Macroeconomics.* Copyright © 1990, Campbell R. McConnell and Stanley L. Brue. Published by McGraw-Hill, Inc. Reprinted by permission of McGraw-Hill, Inc.

JEANNIE McDONALD, "Get Real Men of Steel," *Newsweek,* March 25, 1991. Copyright 1991, Jeannie McDonald.

ROBERT MacNEIL, "The Trouble with Television," *Reader's Digest,* March 1985. Originally delivered as a speech, "Is Television Narrowing Our Minds?" at The President's Leadership Forum, SUNY, Purchase, NY, November 13, 1984. Reprinted with permission of Reader's Digest Association and the author.

JOHN McPHEE, *Oranges.* Copyright © 1966, 1967 by John McPhee. Reprinted by permission of Farrar, Straus & Giroux, Inc.

MARILYN MACHLOWITZ, "Never Get Sick in July," *Esquire,* July 4, 1978. Copyright 1978, Marilyn Machlowitz.

SHIVA NAIPAUL, "The Palmers" from *North of South: An African Journey.* Copyright © 1979 by Shiva Naipaul. Reprinted by permission of Simon & Schuster.

JOHN NAISBITT, "Needed: High Tech Skills," from *Megatrends.* Copyright © 1982 by John Naisbitt. Reprinted by permission of Warner Books/New York.

JO GOODWIN PARKER, "What Is Poverty?" from *America's Other Children: Public Schools Outside Suburbia.* Reprinted by permission of University of Oklahoma Press.

DAVID PLATH, "Tomoko on Her Television Career," from *Long Engagements: Maturity in Modern Japan.* Copyright © 1980 by the Board of Trustees of the Leland Stanford Junior University. Reprinted by permission of the publishers, Stanford University Press.

JOHN H. POSTLETHWAIT AND JANET HOPSON, excerpt from *The Nature of Life.* Copyright © 1989, John Postlethwait. Published by McGraw-Hill, Inc. Reprinted by permission of McGraw-Hill, Inc.

WILLIAM RASPBERRY, "Missing: The Influence of Black Men," July 18, 1989. Copyright © 1989, Washington Post Writers Group. Reprinted with permission.

RICHARD RODRIGUEZ, "Aria: A Memoir of a Bilingual Childhood." First appeared in *The American Scholar.* Copyright © 1980 by Richard Rodriguez. Reprinted by permission of Georges Borchardt, Inc., for the author.

MIKE ROSE, *Lives on The Boundary.* Copyright © 1989 by Mike Rose. Reprinted by permission of The Free Press, a division of Macmillan, Inc.

JOHN RUSSO, "Reel vs. Real Violence," from *Newsweek,* February 19, 1990. Copyright 1990, John Russo.

CLAIRE SAFRAN, "Hidden Lessons: Do Little Boys Get a Better Education Than Little Girls?" from *Parade,* 1983. Copyright © 1983, Claire Safran. Reprinted by permission of *Parade* and the author.

KIRKPATRICK SALE, "The Miracle of Technofix," from *Newsweek,* 1980. © Kirkpatrick Sale 1992. Reprinted by permission of *Newsweek* and the author.

DEBORAH TANNEN, *That's Not What I Meant! How Conversation Style Makes and Breaks Your Relations with Others.* Copyright 1986. Reprinted by permission of William Morrow & Company.

LESTER C. THUROW, "A Short Course in Business Ethics," from "Ethics Doesn't Start in Business School," *New York Times,* June 14, 1987. Copyright © 1987 by The New York Times Company. Reprinted by permission.

SHEILA TOBIAS, "Who's Afraid of Math, and Why?" from *Overcoming Math Anxiety.* Copyright 1978. Reprinted by permission of W. W. Norton & Co., Inc.

ALICE WALKER, "Disinformation Advertising," from *Ms.* Magazine, March/April 1991. Copyright 1991. Reprinted by permission of *Ms.* Magazine.

DAN WARRENSFORD, "Alcohol Warning Labels Aren't Needed," *USA TODAY,* November 14, 1989. Copyright 1989, USA TODAY. Reprinted by permission.

MARIE WINN, "The Effects of Television on Family Life," from *The Plug-In Drug.* Copyright © 1977, 1985 by Marie Winn Miller. Used by permission of Viking Penguin, a division of Penguin Books USA, Inc.

ROBERT YEAGER, "Violence in Sports," from *Seasons of Shame: The New Violence in Sports.* Copyright © 1980, Robert Yeager. Published by McGraw-Hill, Inc. Reprinted by permission of McGraw-Hill, Inc.

RICHARD ZOGLIN, "Play It Again, Lucy," from *Time,* December 2, 1991. Copyright 1991 The Time Inc. Magazine Company. Reprinted by permission.

INDEX